SAGE was founded in 1965 by Sara Miller McCune to support the dissemination of usable knowledge by publishing innovative and high-quality research and teaching content. Today, we publish over 900 journals, including those of more than 400 learned societies, more than 800 new books per year, and a growing range of library products including archives, data, case studies, reports, and video. SAGE remains majority-owned by our founder, and after Sara's lifetime will become owned by a charitable trust that secures our continued independence.

Los Angeles | London | New Delhi | Singapore | Washington DC | Melbourne

DEVELOPMENTALISM AS STRATEGY

DEVELOPMENTALISM AS STRATEGY

Interrogating Post-colonial Narratives on India's North East

SAGE STUDIES ON INDIA'S NORTH EAST

Edited by
RAKHEE BHATTACHARYA

Los Angeles | London | New Delhi
Singapore | Washington DC | Melbourne

Copyright © Rakhee Bhattacharya, 2019
Cover image © Govind Bhattacharjee, 2019

All rights reserved. No part of this book may be reproduced or utilized in any form or by any means, electronic or mechanical, including photocopying, recording or by any information storage or retrieval system, without permission in writing from the publisher.

First published in 2019 by

SAGE Publications India Pvt Ltd
B1/I-1 Mohan Cooperative Industrial Area
Mathura Road, New Delhi 110 044, India
www.sagepub.in

SAGE Publications Inc
2455 Teller Road
Thousand Oaks, California 91320, USA

SAGE Publications Ltd
1 Oliver's Yard, 55 City Road
London EC1Y 1SP, United Kingdom

SAGE Publications Asia-Pacific Pte Ltd
18 Cross Street #10-10/11/12
China Square Central
Singapore 048423

Published by Vivek Mehra for SAGE Publications India Pvt Ltd. Typeset in 10.5/13pt Bembo by Zaza Eunice, Hosur, Tamil Nadu, India.

Library of Congress Cataloging-in-Publication Data

Name: Bhattacharya, Rakhee, editor.
Title: Developmentalism as strategy: interrogating post-colonial narratives
  on India's north east/edited by Rakhee Bhattacharya.
Description: First Edition. | Thousand Oaks: SAGE Publications India Pvt
  Ltd, [2019] | Includes bibliographical references and index. |
Identifiers: LCCN 2019003148 (print) | LCCN 2019013001 (ebook) | ISBN
  9789353283209 (Web PDF) | ISBN 9789353283193 (E pub 2.0) | ISBN
  9789353283186 (hardback: alk. paper)
Subjects: LCSH: Economic development—India, Northeastern. |
  Postcolonialism—India, Northeastern.
Classification: LCC HC437.I4 (ebook) | LCC HC437.I4 D48 2019 (print) | DDC
  338.954/1—dc23
LC record available at https://lccn.loc.gov/2019003148

ISBN: 978-93-532-8318-6 (HB)

SAGE Team: Rajesh Dey, Sandhya Gola and Rajinder Kaur

Contents

List of Tables vii
Foreword by C. P. Chandrasekhar ix
Prologue xiii

Introduction 1

Part I: Between Subsistence and Surplus

Chapter 1	Traditional Economy, Sustainability and Subsistence: Understanding India's North East by *Tiplut Nongbri*	45
Chapter 2	The Post-colonial Market: India's North East by *Samir Kumar Das*	67

Part II: Developmental Impacts on People

Chapter 3	Developmentalism and Consequences: Displacement and Marginalization in India's North East by *Walter Fernandes*	91
Chapter 4	India's Developmentalism in Northeast Region and Its Consequences: Identity, Uncertainty and Migration by *Deepak K. Mishra*	117
Chapter 5	Development and Women Labour Market in India's North East: An Empirical Understanding by *Archana Sharma*	148

Part III: New Development at the Periphery

Chapter 6	Neoliberal Developmentalism: State Strategy in India's North East by *Rakhee Bhattacharya*	169
Chapter 7	The Politics of Corridors: 'Seamless Connectivity', Trans-regional Engagements and Narratives of Development by *Anita Sengupta*	192
Chapter 8	Development of India's North East: Cross-border Market, Trade and Sub-regional Cooperation by *Gurudas Das*	214
Chapter 9	Development through Trade: Re-examining India's Act East Policy and the Northeastern Region by *Thongkholal Haokip*	231

Part IV: Alternative from Below

Chapter 10	Environmental Security and Human Rights: Foundations for Real Development? by *Felix Padel*	253
Chapter 11	Conservation versus Peoples' Entitlements: Contestations in Kaziranga National Park by *Akhil Ranjan Dutta*	280
Chapter 12	International Financial Institutions in India's North East: Pattern and Impact on People and Environment by *Jiten Yumnam*	305

About the Editor and Contributors	328
Index	334

List of Tables

4.1	Usual Status Unemployment in States of North East India (15–59)	123
4.2	Usual Status Unemployment (15–59): Rural and Urban	123
4.3	Usual Status Unemployment in North East India by Age Groups	124
4.4	Unemployment Rate by Education among the Working Age Group and Young Population in States	125
4.5	Unemployment by Educational Attainment of the Working Age Group and Young Population in North East India	126
4.6	Migration Rate in (per 1,000 Persons) Northeastern States	132
4.7	Distribution (per 1,000 persons) of Internal Migrants by Migration Streams for States of North East India	133
4.8	Number of Out-migrants (per 1,000 Persons) in Northeastern States	134
4.9	Shares of Inter-district, Inter-state and International Out-migrants among Total Out-migrants in States of North East India (per 1,000 Population)	135
4.10	Reasons for Migration of Out-migrants (per 1,000 Individuals) in North East India	136
4.11	Background Characteristics of Economic Out-migrants in North East India (percentages)	137
5.1	Work Participation Rates (Principal Status [PS] + Subsidiary Status [SS]) by Sex and Sex Ratios: All India (Rural and Urban), between 1993–1994 and 2001–2012	157

5.2	Work Participation Rates (PS+SS) by Sex and Sex Ratios: Assam (Rural and Urban), from 1993–1994 to 2011–2012	158
5.3	Work Participation Rates (PS+SS) by Sex and Sex Ratios: Arunachal Pradesh (Rural and Urban), from 1993–1994 to 2011–2012	158
5.4	Work Participation Rates (PS+SS) by Sex and Sex Ratios: Manipur (Rural and Urban), from 1993–1994 to 2011–2012	159
5.5	Work Participation Rates (PS+SS) by Sex and Sex Ratios in Work Participation: Meghalaya (Rural and Urban), from 1993–1994 to 2011–2012	159
5.6	Work Participation Rates (PS+SS) by Sex and Sex Ratios in Work Participation: Nagaland (Rural and Urban), from 1993–1994 to 2011–2012	160
5.7	Work Participation Rates (PS+SS) by Sex and Sex Ratio in Work Participation: Mizoram (Rural and Urban), from 1993–1994 to 2011–2012	160
5.8	Work Participation Rates (PS+SS) by Sex and Sex Ratio in Work Participation: Sikkim (Rural and Urban), from 1993–1994 to 2011–2012	161
5.9	Work Participation Rates (PS+SS) by Sex and Sex Ratio in Work Participation: Tripura (Rural and Urban), from 1993–1994 to 2011–2012	161
8.1	Share of NER's Trade with the Neighbouring Countries (1998–1999 to 2012–2013)	215
8.2	Commodity Structure of NER's Border Trade (1998–1999 to 2012–2013)	216
8.3	Myanmar's Share of Exports to and Imports from the Neighbouring Countries (2016)	220
8.4	Myanmar's Trade with Its Bordering Countries (2016; US$ Million)	221

Foreword

The chapters in this book attempt to reconstruct the narrative that explains why India's 'North East' has, from colonial times and through the different regimes of accumulation that have characterized post-Independence India, remained in the periphery and at the margins of 'national' development. As control by national and local elites over the 'region', its resources and its development trajectory is increasingly contested, and efforts are on to muddy the waters socially and politically, this is an attempt to return to a history that, while specific, reflects larger processes of subordination to national and global regimes.

An inherent feature of capitalist development is its unevenness across geographical spaces. One reason for this is that markets are not benign and tend to favour development in centres and regions that are relatively more advanced. A few metropolitan centres and their immediate hinterlands progress, while the rest of the economy (global, national and regional) falls behind. This, however, is not the determining reason for the reproduction of unevenness and inequality across spaces. Rather, as analysts of capitalist accumulation and development theorists have for long recognized, development in the 'core', advanced regions occurs at the expense of the underdeveloped periphery, which, besides supplying the primary products needed for industrialization and serving as a ready market for goods, is an important source of surplus to finance accumulation at the metropolitan centre.

It hardly needs stating that spatial references such as the 'core' and 'periphery' are abstract and have little to do with actual geographical positions on a globe that discriminates only in terms of climate, soil and natural resources. In fact, seen in those terms, the tropical colonies that proved to be a part of the periphery were far richer than the temperate colonizing regions. Complex historical and socio-economic factors that cannot be detailed here ensured that capitalist development began and gathered momentum in England and other parts of Europe and then spread in very different forms to the colonies and the 'regions of recent settlement' such as North America and Australia. While in the latter the best features of capitalism took root, though after the destruction of local populations, in the former, capitalist development did not displace pre-existing pre-capitalist formations and features but was superimposed on them. In the event, capitalist development in the periphery of today was not merely characterized by gradualism and the worst forms of exploitation but also by the reproduction of backwardness. This, however, served the interests of accumulation on a world scale, leading to the conclusion that backwardness and retarded development in the periphery were the other pole required to sustain development at the centre.

This dependence of metropolitan accumulation on the exploitation of the periphery meant that much of the periphery has remained in that 'space' close to three centuries now. Breaking out of backwardness is not just difficult but, when it happens, is the result of fortuitous circumstances as some East Asian examples illustrate. Persisting backwardness is the fate of much of the periphery. This is because the exploitation that permits accumulation at the core results not just in the reproduction of backward social formations (even in reconstructed forms) but also in the destruction of the environment, the plunder of natural resources and the stunting of local accumulation. This is not the fate of just the periphery at a world scale but also within peripheral formations that have their own stunted forms of capitalist development.

It is a perspective of this kind, elaborately laid out in the introduction, that the chapters in this book bring to bear on an understanding of India's 'North East'. Reduced to a periphery, despite being rich in resources and endowed with a well-evolved culture, the administratively compartmentalized region is the target of integration into a centre–periphery complex, a site for the reproduction of economic backwardness and the subject of varying forms of patronage under different systems of 'nationally' determined accumulation.

The chapters together are comprehensive in their scope, covering terrain stretching from the specific, culturally embedded, economy of the North East and the distortion of this by so-called 'modern' and market-friendly policies to the outcomes in terms of displacement, deprivation and cultural alienation and to the alternatives to be pursued as part of a more inclusive and equitable development strategy. They highlight the social engineering being resorted to in an attempt to 'integrate' the region with the 'mainstream', which under neoliberalism has meant tying it in the kind of 'open' cross-border relations favoured by corporate capital. In the process, the 'North East' is internationalized and its geography rhetorically re-imagined as the 'gateway' rather than as the 'periphery', even while in developmental terms the states of the region, which flaunt new infrastructural facilities, remain marginalized.

The issues are complex and the solutions hard to find and implement. But the chapters in this book are bound to influence the debate on the direction that all concerned need to take to allow the 'region' to find its own trajectory to an economically secure and sustainable future.

C. P. Chandrasekhar
Professor, Centre for Economic Studies and Planning
Jawaharlal Nehru University, New Delhi

Prologue

The book critically comprehends the conventional approaches to development and the role of the post-colonial developmental State in India. It reviews the consequences in one of India's most contentious regions, the North East. Due to its unique historical geography, the North East has been systematically marginalized and subsequently has become an 'exception' to India's economic nationalism. The book examines how the various dominant narratives of India's economic nationalism created an internal core–periphery structure and largely acted as a strategy within the North East in the context of resource appropriation and national security, producing new arrangements of knowledge, power and practices. The strategy started to change with India's neoliberal approach in the 1990s, and currently with the ongoing emphasis on 'market revivalism and expansionism, the developmental State of India is making' an ideational change towards achieving a competitive and integrated economy, where 'geographic marginality' of the North East is transforming with the semantics of 'natural gateway', 'engine of dynamism' and 'whirlwind of modernity'. Having a methodology primarily evolving from the 'margin' and with an interdisciplinary approach, the book attempts to break stereotypical narratives and looks for an alternative by means of rationality and objective knowledge about this region. The book is structured with a long introduction to spell out the trajectory of development in the post-colonial period, while the chapters are the narrations of the discourses of such development in India's North East. The cover page with two distinct images also describes the core theme of the book. Both the images spell out the existing connectivity infrastructure of the North East, which is one of the major determinants of the State's strategy on development and security in the North East. The top image is the 9.15-km-long Dhola-Sadiya Bridge on River Lohit, which was opened in 2017 to connect upper Assam and eastern Arunachal Pradesh, a region bordering China. The bottom image is an old bridge in the Anjaw district of Arunachal Pradesh, ensuring local connectivity and everyday lives across its hard and inhospitable hilly terrains.

The book has become possible with the immense support of all the eminent and distinguished scholars who have contributed with their diverse and insightful perspectives to achieve its goal. I am deeply thankful to all of them for their excellent cooperation. The idea of the book was initiated at the Special Centre for the Study of North East India, Jawaharlal Nehru University, New Delhi, after a series of discussion with faculty members on the necessity to bring out a critical series on the study of the North East; this series can benefit students and researchers to clear many of the existing elusive ideas on the region. The present book is an endeavour to understand economic development as the vantage ground to elucidate many such ideas on the North East. My sincere thanks therefore goes to all my colleagues. I am ever grateful to my son Gaurav, who always takes out time from his busy schedule to edit my drafts. I am thankful to my PhD scholar Devpriya Sarkar who helped me in arranging the bibliography of each chapter in the last hour. Last but not least, I express my sincere thanks and gratitude to the SAGE team for their kind consent and cooperation to publish this book. The weaknesses of the book would have been far greater without the kind of support from all of them.

Rakhee Bhattacharya

Introduction

Rakhee Bhattacharya

STATE AND DEVELOPMENT

Classical political economy laid down the premises for 'progressive modernity' and the emergence of developmentalist ideology. The fundamental was to create a new idea that is 'necessarily good and desirable in an era of progress' (Wallerstein 1992a, 1992b). This can be traced back to the eighteenth-century Enlightenment era with its assertion of the need for conscious rational reform of a society with sovereignty, where even the nation-state was reckoned to be 'free to direct and control developmentalist ideology'. The centrality of such liberalism and notion of progress of a nation became the 'ideological universe of capitalism' which acted upon wealth accumulation and circulation (Grosfoguel 2000, 347–74). While studying its consequence with historical data since 1820, the economic historian Angus Maddison found a rapid and rising gap between Western Europe and rest of the world (1995). By the next century, between the 1920s and 1930s, such liberal capitalist institutions and States became unstable and experienced the Great Depression and thus were rejected by many (Blyth 2002, 4). A variety of 'reflectionary and redistributive economic ideas like Keynesianism was developed', which later served as the ideological basis of the post-war 'embedded liberal' order as apprehended by Karl Ponanyi (see Berman 1998), who postulated the role of State control in market manipulation. As argued by Murphy and Augelli, in the 1940s and 1950s, the era of decolonization and post-World War II, the role of the League of Nations gradually became important in promoting the idea of development through the 'new system of international organisations' (1993). By 1944, the Bretton Woods Institutions based in the USA reprised this developmentalist ideology with a blueprint on economic modernization, industrialization and trade liberalization. This was based on Eurocentric assumptions and a neoclassical approach to hold back the State and essentialize market relations across national boundaries. Such a development trajectory, as argued by Escobar, was an exemplification by the World Bank as an institution and emerged in the context of a complex historical conjuncture. The growing importance of the USA in the capitalist world economy created new dynamics in the periphery and decolonized Asian, African and Latin American nations. 'Ground was prepared for the institution of development as a strategy to remake the colonial world and restructure the relation between colonies and metropoles' (1995, 20–71). Escobar has termed this as an 'invention of development' and 'emergence of new strategy' and presented as a historically singular experience and the creation of a 'domain of thought and action'. He found an interrelationship of three axes that define development: the form of knowledge that refers to it and evolves into theories and concepts, the system of power that regulates its practices and the forms of subjectivity fostered by this discourse within the recognizable domains of the developed or underdeveloped (1995, 10–24).

The triumph of the American institutional liberalism reached its zenith by the 1960s with W. W. Rostow's *schema* of development, where he proposed a five-stage process of growth from traditional to modern society, from stationary, to preconditions for take-off, take-off, drive to maturity, and high mass-consumption society. This came in the context of the appalling adversities across the world and was contested and critiqued by the Latin American *dependentista* school, which eventually became an 'important intervention to transform the imaginary of intellectual debates on developmentalist ideology in many parts of the world' (Grosfoguel 2000, 347–74). Thus, for example, Rostow's universalized 'notion of time and space' was analysed by the leading proponent of the *dependentista* school, Andre Gunder Frank, who introduced the concept of 'underdevelopment' as a positional state within Rostow's stages of growth. His binary of 'advanced modern societies' and 'backward traditional societies' can also be interpreted through Frank's suggested binary of metropoles of development, controlling piedmonts of sub-nodes in relative underdevelopment (1966, 21), where nodes begin in the metropolitan core and 'chain' outwards into the periphery, ending in the rural villages or resource-rich areas. The dynamics of this model was economic exploitation (Kelly 2008, 319–32). While analysing 'underdeveloped nations', the structuralist school eventually resisted the proposed 'stages of development' as exploitative and unequal within a defined core–periphery binary. W. Arthur Lewis's concept of dual economy in 1954 also explains development as the progressive encroachment of the modern upon the traditional and subsistence system of the peripheral areas, which was in need of active State policies to protect and develop their own national economies. Thus, as pointed out by Kohli, 'the search for development among late-late-industrialisers of Asia, Africa and Latin America intensified mainly after the Second World War, where numerous activist States emerged as sovereign' (Kohli 2004, 1). By the 1960s, these decolonized and late developer nation-states moved towards economic nationalism, and this school of thought emphasized the importance of State-led developmentalist ideology (Kelly and Kaplan 2001). The solution for 'dependency' was therefore to delink from the capitalist world system and organize a socialist society insulated from the influence and control of 'metropolitan capitalism' (Grosfoguel 2000, 347–74). As economic nationalism became the linchpin of decolonized developmental nation-states post-1945, indigenous industrialization and import substitution policy became their central counter-paradigms. The generic ideas of protectionism, welfarism and self-reliance in these nation-states including India became conspicuous in the twentieth century, having a strong root in their respective freedom struggles, nationalist movements and acute post-colonial economic crises. As the imagination of a nationalist-developmentalist State was posited and rose to dominance in this group of nations as the denial of the Eurocentric ideology of market capitalism, it became an articulation of the State economic project during the Cold War period, weighing nationalist industrialization in all the 'peripheries of the world economy', the origin of which was in the classic dependency's theoretical structure (Kelly 2008), and by the end of the twentieth century, such State-led development efforts have become successful at least in some parts of the global periphery (Kohli 2004, 1).

Having adopted this approach, post-colonial India articulated an economic policy in support of nationalist industrialization with import substitution. A State-led development planning model was introduced in 1951 in an extra-Constitutional framework called the Planning Commission. As argued by Prabhat Patnaik, it came into effect not just in India but in many other countries that were newly liberated from colonialism. It aimed to bring the country's natural resources back under national control and the production pattern was to be altered from what had been dictated by the colonial division of labour. The benefits of all these measures were to accrue to the people at large, by ensuring that wealth and income inequalities were in check (Patnaik 2015). This was in the line with Soviet's socialist welfare economic planning with active and purposive interventionist measures to 'govern the market' with a newly formed bureaucratic and technocratic structure. It laid down the rationale, mechanism and strategy to address the challenges of economic impoverishment, abject poverty, hunger and food shortage in post-colonial India, which were inherited from 'deindustrialization and drain of wealth' by the colonial capitalists. Planning ideology therefore was seen as a 'necessary legacy of the anti-colonial struggle in India'. It structuralized State industry, capital formation, import substitution, protectionism and the creation of metropolitan cores within the nation-state boundary, and such a State-led economy produced mixed results in India.

The planning institution, though a reflection of economic nationalism, welfarism and egalitarianism, was also a channel for 'modern India's political economy'. Therefore, like other nations, it was 'committed to national capitalist development through the formation of a local industrial bourgeoisie' (Grosfoguel 2000). The widespread belief that growth could be planned, which occupied an 'exalted position', meant that over time, planning ceased to be an affair of the socialist Left, and even many advance European nations sought long-term planning for economic growth. Planning became a useful economic instrument, linked to policy and the State across many parts of the world (Escobar 1995, 86). By the 1970s, the planning institution in India began to be largely authoritarian in terms of its decision-making process with the functional and technical capabilities of powerful governmental technology and apparatus. It manipulated and legitimized capital and capitalist class through a 'nexus of educated planning bureaucracy, political class and indigenous capitalists' (Bardhan 1984; Chatterjee 1997). As the planning institution directly lobbied and favoured India's 'dominant class' and its core regions, a clear dichotomy was observed between its theory and practice, and the planning model became a subject of debate (Chakravarty 1987). Through political interventions, authoritarianism and a network of power, the practice of planning reiterated the constructs of peripheral, marginal and underdeveloped spaces in the domain of national development and generated a 'local industrial bourgeoisie' which spoke of an 'internal core-periphery structure' (Misra 1980) and 'modern-tradition binary' (Sanyal 2007) across the vast geographical spaces of India. The planning ideology thus was increasingly marked by a sense of inevitability about this nature of economic change and political interventions.

STATE AND THE DEVELOPMENT PLANNING AT THE 'MARGIN'

As the nationalist-developmentalist State produced new 'cores' and 'modernities' in post-colonial India with planned industrialization, the status of several colonial 'peripheries' was reiterated. India's North East is one such space which was systematically pushed back at the 'margin' of post-colonial State activities and re-imagined as 'backward' due to its unique historical geography, and it became an 'exception' to India's idea of economic nationalism. Being a constructed geography of the colonial capitalist State, the North East was a 'resource frontier' and 'subject of periphery' for some economic purposes. The colonials made 'large scale penetration, subversion and violence on its traditional systems and rich resources' (Rothbard 2004) through 'primitive accumulation' and 'siphoning capitalism' (Bagchi 2010) by introducing a series of Constitutional arrangements of laws and Acts, which began with the Assam Waste Land Grant Rules in 1838. With the increasing power of colonial capitalists, like in other parts of the world, a sign of 'peripheral formation' began here with the transformative characteristics of agrarian capitalism, dominant foreign capital and merchandise trade in the newly created (tea) plantation economy (Amin 1976, 332). Such transformation, as argued by Samir Amin elsewhere, tends to incorporate a social formation represented by 'peripheral capitalism' with its existing historical origin, social structure and above all the dynamics of the accumulation of capital. As against 'central capitalism', which tends to gradually dissolve pre-capitalist modes, in peripheral social formations where the dominance of the capitalist mode of production is seen in some sectors, and is based on the external market, most of the pre-capitalist modes, particularly in the agrarian sector, remain preserved. This is the incomplete process of the development of capitalism as far as the forces and relations of production are concerned, and it is this which produces the structural features of so-called 'peripheral capitalism' with sectoral productivity differentials and 'disarticulation' of the economy (see Rosenberg 1981). In the space of North East, where such 'peripheral formation' began with 'colonial mode of production' and with newly created enclave economies in the (tea) plantation sector, like the tea industry in the plan areas, they were carefully protected by the colonial State with a set of policies. This in turn created a binary of hills and plains within the North East. Thus, the policies of exclusion and distinction, such as the Bengal Frontier Regulation Act, commonly known as the Inner Line Regulation Act in 1873, Non-regulated, Excluded Areas and Tracts and North East Frontier Track, were introduced to create sectoral differentials in production between the traditional and modern systems. Referring to Escobar, space is one of the most essential features of economic development with an implicit expression of core and periphery, and the social production of such spaces implicit in these terms is bound with production of differences and subjectivities. This 'colonization of reality' (within the North East) seeks to account for 'how certain representation became dominant and shaped indelibly the ways in which reality was imagined and acted upon' (1995, 5–9). Thus, with cautious and convenient colonial State interventions in this 'periphery', which were purposive towards primitive accumulation, resource extraction and trade surplus, it kept away the traditional cultural economies of many 'non-state' highland areas as 'uncolonized' (Nigam 2009) and 'ungoverned' (Scott 2009). However, though the capitalistic reorganization in the post-colonial period changed the order of domination from the colonial to the national State, it moved sequentially to reassert the logic of marketable surplus and resource access and accumulation. With such historical continuity, the structural metaphor of core-periphery had a linear sequentiality, and the nationalistic 'capitalist mode of production' could result in the North East (Assam) as the largest producer of tea in the country, and at the same time this national periphery became a major supplier of raw materials such as oil, gas and coal for India's industrialization. Thus, as hydrocarbon was the principal component of industrial landscape of post-colonial India, the 'colonial hinterland' North East was seen as the surplus reservoir of such a resource (Misra 1980), and the share of capital for such extraction activities in the North East came from outside and other states by the Indian big bourgeoisie (Goswami 1981; Misra 1980, 1357–64). So with the changes in semantic constellations, the capitalist developmentalist ideology for the northeastern periphery remained unbroken in post-colonial India. The North East was re-imagined as 'underdeveloped', and in this 'national road to transition', the emergence of such spatially differentiated transitions once again largely remained a State construct. This nationalistic mode of accumulation along with the role of different institutional and Constitutional actors and its own historical and geographical specificities created new narratives of the North East as a 'margin' and 'hinterland' and proved legacies as central to understand both the possibilities and limitations of transition from the colonial to the post-colonial era.

On the other hand, the colonial construct of long political boundaries of the North East gave a set of neighbourhood and complex external orientations and forced the post-colonial State to re-map it as a 'borderland'. With sensitive neighbours such as the Tibetan part of China, East Pakistan and Burma, the North East became a new subject of geopolitics in post-colonial India. The abiding logic of national security and subsequent militarization of the space became ardent in the post-border war with China in 1962. Gaining 'strategic significance', the North East was further imagined as an 'exception' to India's idea of economic nationalism and Statehood. This new imaginative geography with geopolitical content has accordingly shaped the approach and meaning of development within the North East for many decades to come. As a first step, the imperative of national security made an almost complete halt and reversal on connectivity infrastructure creation from the colonial State, which claimed about 6,920 km of road construction in this space, mostly in the plain areas, along with railways and waterways for various economic, trade and also military activities. The securitist State of India had closed many such colonial and even pre-colonial routes and created an alternative narrative for the North East as a 'landlocked' and 'isolated' space. With the renewed territorial formation in 1947 due to the Radcliffe Line, the Sylhet Province was demarcated from Assam and became a province of East Pakistan, and subsequently, several routes of the North East through Sylhet were closed with many of its economic activities sealed. This new long border made the North East a 'prisoner of geography'. It was imagined as a frontier, a borderland and a periphery, which were interchangeably used by the securitist-developmentalist State of India, and therefore remained largely at the margin of post-colonial State economic affairs.

Inducting the argument of Escobar (1995, 9), a development trajectory in the spaces of 'margin' creates an extremely efficient apparatus for producing knowledge about, and the exercise of power to create, a narrative of 'dependency'. In case of the North East, with various such newly created apparatuses in the post-1947 period, the nationalist State could produce new arrangements of knowledge, power and new practices within the North East. In the beginning, one such new arrangement was protectionism, which was grossly different from India's generic approach to protectionism, to shield country's newly formed domestic industrialization from foreign investment and build its national economy under the import substitution policy. On the contrary, in case of the North East, for example, a unique State protectionism was imagined for its hill and tribal areas and towards its indigenous systems and practices through the Constitutional arrangements of Sixth Schedule and Article 371A. This was to protect and safeguard their traditional systems, economies and laws. These State policies 'protected and preserved' traditional practices and systems with a policy of 'non-interference' and apparently to retain their 'own cultural traits and habits and leaving them to develop along their own lines without any compulsion from outside' (Khosla 2014, 58–59). This strategy of protectionism had created a lyre of governance called autonomous district councils and regional councils in these newly demarcated Sixth Schedule areas and began to operate with various respective village heads. Such councils were given financial power and also power to assess and collect land revenue, impose taxes, control over moneylending and trading with non-tribal communities. As this

Constitutional arrangement was also to introduce and then integrate such (ungoverned) areas with a modern State system of administration, while preserving the traditional autonomy of tribal people, there was a series of problems in the articulation of the existing customary laws within such 'legal positivism'. In reality, as argued by some scholars, this has ruptured various traditional systems, specially the land holding pattern, by transferring and legitimizing individual ownership, which, over time, has helped form the tribal elite class and created a disjunction between legal and social realities to proliferate into subsequent conflicts on issues of land, resource and identity (Fernandes 2005; Pereira 2005; Roy Burman 1989). Such coercive control and power, as pointed out by Kohli elsewhere, over a territory unfortunately cannot distinguish between public and private realms for a variety of historical reasons and results in a number of 'distorted states' with barely legitimate authority structures, personalistic leaders and bureaucracies of poor quality (Kohli 2004, 9). In the North East, as this new arrangement had undermined the role of the traditional village council, a time-tested local governance structure, there was a gradual degeneration and alienation of community land and resources, where the individual land-holding system penetrated through several manipulative mechanisms through village heads via a nexus within the public and private realms. So, though the protection of indigeneity, as argued by Postero elsewhere, can be considered as a site of ontological alternative to capitalism (Postero 2017), the protection of indigeneity in the North East by State mechanisms was not necessarily of this kind, as 'peripheral capitalism' continued with transition in the agrarian and land system along with other extractivisms.

This exceptional idea of 'preservation' also has propelled cosmetic and minimum intervention of development planning in the North East. Thus, against the vision of a national economic planning model, a sub-national economic model with an ad hoc and minimalist plan approach was in place for the 'tribal areas of North East' with an inappreciable number of schemes for their 'socio-economic uplift-ment'. The community development programme, multipurpose tribal blocks, tribal development block, development agencies, primitive tribal groups, integrated tribal development projects and the modified area development approach were some of them, which were granted with less than 1 per cent of total plan allocation. Such a State strategy thereupon created a fresh binary of 'backward' and 'advanced' areas within the country's emerging nationalist development landscape. As the Indian State clinically divided the 'advanced and core' areas with its support and the 'backward and peripheral' areas with its strategy, it also posed challenges of inequality and disparity. Such a State strategy for the North East as an 'exception' to India's idea of economic nationalism eventually proliferated some institutional channels and raised questions about its efficacy and success. To address these challenges, the State at the beginning of Fourth Five Year Plan adopted and enforced a redistribution mechanism through liberal plan assistance in such 'backward' areas under the Gadgil formula. The summary record of the 24th meeting of the National Development Council (NDC) in 1967 pointed out that, 'there was a general feeling that states such as Assam, Nagaland and Jammu and Kashmir would, in any way, have to receive special treatment' (see Bhattacharjee 2016, 17). Along with the Constitution of the Fifth Finance Commission in 1968, the Indian State recommended the devolution of funds through tax and grants to these states. The reports discussed huge disparity among 17 Indian states, with the richest state having a per capita income of ₹619, while the poorest ₹292 only. Concerns were raised for equalization among states with a redistribution policy. In 1969, development planning finally created an exceptional principle of the Special Category Status within India's asymmetric federal set-up for direct devolution of central funds mostly in terms of grants to the states of North East and Jammu and Kashmir which were 'characterized by certain common features and demanded special consideration'. By providing such status, the Indian State recognized this space as historically more disadvantaged than the others in terms of socio-economic and infrastructural development and difficult terrains. Article 275(1A) of the Constitution also recognized the need for such special assistance to the North East (Bhattacharjee 2016, 3). The Special Category Status was largely attributed to the geographical specificities of the North East, its international political borders and its population composition, which is mostly indigenous in nature. The planning mechanism eventually channelized liberal central funds to all the states of North East within the 90:10 formula ratio. Meanwhile, various up-rises from the hills of the North East and contestations against the hegemony of the nationalist State in general and Assam in particular culminated into various regional politics within the hill-plain binary, like the All Party Hill Leaders Conference in the early 1970s, which demanded a separate hill political entity. This eventually led to the North-Eastern Areas (Re-organisation) Act, 1971, to create smaller hill states within this geographical construct of the North East. These spatio-political entities on the basis of ethnicity within the territorial boundary of the North East created another gradation of geographical deadlocks and became part of the Special Category Status for 'special attention'. As estimated by Bhattacharjee, the central plan assistance for all Special category Status states has seen an increase from ₹682 crores in 1969–74 to ₹64,787 crores in 2007–10 (Bhattacharjee 2016, 30). Such a process of liberal fund transfer and 'patronage' (Chandra 2015) over the years had failed to achieve its goal and objective within a blurring, non-transparent and crony State apparatus, and the idea of the Special Category Status became a debated subject in the policy space. It has sharpened the State imaginary of 'backwardness' on the one hand, while creating a 'dependency syndrome' in the North East on the other hand. The idea is debated as a 'channel for corruption' and 'politics of care' (Bhattacharjee 2016; Das 2013) and remained another 'exception' to India's policy trend to imagine this periphery as an idler. Without having credible governance and accountability, the State was unable to deal with the rising issues of corruption, as was generally observed in other parts of India also (Mathur 2015; Witsoe 2012), and failed to 'discipline' the rise of the oligarchs through several nexus, while economic backwardness perpetuated in the North East. This exceptionality for the North East led to a general perception of being 'neglected' by the 'apathetic State', and fresh up-rises, contestations and movements were rooted to 'lack of economic development' in the North East, like the All Assam Students Union (AASU) movement during the late 1970s. The debates aroused to connect various internal conflicts with a general lack of development and also against the exploitative and extractive Indian State (Bhattacharya 2011; Misra 1980), and eventually some concrete economic projects like the Numaligarh oil refinery could be bargained while the Assam Accord was signed in 1985 and is currently a successful profit-seeking organization in the State.

The trajectory of development planning subsequently became more visible over time. To strengthen welfarism and redistribution in the tribal-hill areas, the Fifth Five Year Plan introduced the concept of Tribal Sub-Plan with marginally higher plan allocations, with about a 3 per cent share to address the rising poverty among many marginalized sections and provide basic social services of health and education. In the similar trajectory, development planning became even more proactive in the North East to address the issue of 'backwardness' through some institutional mechanism. The planning institution called the North Eastern Council (NEC) was established by the Act of Parliament in 1971 for 'northeastern region' (NER) of India. With this planning institution, the official document of Indian State redefined North East as a 'region', which conceptually can be seen as a geographical contiguity of hill and plain with a 'cohesive culture' and a certain homogeneity and 'common importance' (see Malgavkar and Ghiara 1975). A 'generalized spatial concept' (see Ackerman 1956) started to essentialize political and administrative boundaries (of the North East) for regional delimitation and formation of the State over time (see Turnock 1967). This reiterated the term 'North East' both as a fact of geography and as an act of administration. With such remarkable reorientation, regional development planning was envisioned in the North East for the first time in the post-colonial period, and the role of the developmental State henceforth shifted from 'non-interference' to a proactive approach. This was to create both economic and infrastructural planning in this 'region' with several inter-State transport and communication systems. Though this idea of regional development planning with a 'unified and coordinated regional plan' for the North East is another exception to India's planning model, but was significant in the next several decades. It gave voice to all the heads of the states in the North East in such a development process. Subsequently, for all five-year and annual plans, various development projects of inter-State nature in this 'region' were funded and monitored by the NEC, making this institution a dominant symbol in the regional planning model in post-colonial India. This significant shift and expansion of the planning strategy from an ad hoc and minimalist approach in the 1950s to a charitable approach of granting 90 per cent of financial assistance in the 1960s and then towards engaging with institutional planning in the 1970s could ameliorate State imagination of the North East. This idea of regional planning moved beyond the prism to understand the North

East as a strategic frontier and essentialized people's needs and access to economic activities and infrastructure for the first time in the post-colonial period. The NEC was assigned to build infrastructure within the North East, and its report claimed that it has created 9,800 km roads, 77 bridges and generated about 60 per cent of the region's hydroelectric power out of an installed capacity of 1,030 MW (Report 2015). It has also supported a large number of projects on various livelihood, health and education sectors to ensure benefits and building capacity for the people of the 'region'. Thus, the NEC, on the one hand, essentialized the need for economic development within the North East and, on the other hand, has acted as an instrument of integration with the rest of India in economic activities. However, with the changing trajectory of developmentalism in India, the role of development planning started to decline, and the NEC was also generally perceived as being 'cosmetic' and non-performing due to 'lethargic bureaucracy and corrupt practices', especially when other parts of India progressed economically in the post-1990s. A vicious circle of 'backwardness' and 'inaccessibility' largely continued to define this 'region' and created the ground for the State to see the role of NEC as inadequate, while more centralized and direct State intervention gradually started to change the narrative of 'underdevelopment' in the North East.

DEVELOPMENTALISM RE-IMAGINED AT THE 'MARGIN'

As the trajectory of India's developmentalism changed in the 1990s towards neoliberalism, the North East became a fresh subject of the developmental State and was re-imagined as a potential space for economic gains. In the Washington Consensus in 1989, the idea of economic nationalism of the 'underdeveloped' world was largely transformed through a metamorphosis towards global capitalism and trade revivalism, and the 'economic philosophy of planning and welfarism' became passé. The neoliberal growth and transnationalism made a significant structural shift in the ideology of developmentalism in the following decades. Around the same time in 1991, Krugman's idea of new economic geography also gained attention for achieving economic prosperity through the various ideas of agglomeration and integration of the economies in a contiguous geographical space (1991). These news ideas of economic expansionism across the borders have transformed the roles of States across the world for next 20 years. The State planning model and its idea of protectionism and close-bound economy started to shrink with progressively greater propensity for global economic interaction at various scales and dimensions. In India, this was done on the solid backstage of the substantive failure of earlier development planning model and with the devastating performances of the so-called 'Hindu growth rates', with around 2–3 per cent for decades together and therefore transformed to a strategy to move from national to international market system to bid global capital. Among policy changes that occurred in the 1990s, India aimed towards economic engagements with the neighbouring Eastern and Southeastern countries by essentializing various locational and geographical spaces, and in this context the North East was rediscovered by the developmental State as a significant space. 'Underdevelopment' and 'inaccessibility' of the space North East was thereafter recognized by the State apparatus as a hindrance to economic growth. 'Relatively inconspicuous and seemingly logical, the discovery was to provide the anchor to an important restructuring' of the development strategies and economic policies towards opening the border and engaging with neighbouring nations. As 'State interventionism became noticeable within the general model of economic liberalism', improving economic growth rates became a necessary route to development at this 'margin'. This structural shift in State policy towards the North East was initially to create a modus operandi for India to expand and engage more constructively with its Eastern and Southeastern neighbouring nations by using the geographical proximity of the North East (Bhattacharya 2017). As argued by Ji Mi (2006) elsewhere, in such a new strategy of cross-border engagement, the State is generally neither an opposing force of market nor a retreating force. The State rather is an actor to pursue and facilitate market-conforming liberalization to advance its developmental goals through policy reforms in various key economic sectors. The State in such a situation therefore retains its authority and recreates a new form of developmentalism through neoliberal markets (Ji Mi). This strategy was decisively demonstrated in the 1980s by East Asian developmentalism and its 'miracle' and the Chinese 'growth experience', where 'excessive State intervention' was seen as a facilitator of the market, and there was a broad consensus on the importance of 'hard' States that 'govern the markets' to gain more, especially through export industries (Naqvi 2015). This new role of the State, as argued by Ayşe Buğra, towards a neoliberal economy also has served the interests of 'politically privileged business people' with larger and unregulated accumulation of capital and faster commodification of land and labour (Buğra 2017). The re-imagination and reconstruction of the North East by the Indian State in the post-1990s with spatial advantages therefore also can be understood as a neoliberal agenda to access routes, resources, raw materials and accumulate capital.

With such alignment towards market forces, the developmental State of India re-strategized its policies and its much debated Look East Policy aimed towards a transnational market beyond the borders of the North East. Having locational specificities with five immediate neighbouring nations, Myanmar, Bangladesh, Nepal, Bhutan and China, and then the entire Southeast Asia, India's North East was re-imagined as an economically strategic space (Bhattacharya 2014). This spatio-economic significance enforced the developmental State once again to address the long-standing economic backwardness and infrastructural gap of the North East. For more intense penetration, State policy therefore started to invoke policies beyond regional planning. Thus, in 1995, a corporate financial institution called North Eastern Development Finance Corporation (NEDFi) was created for industrial development and capital formation in the North East. In the following year in 1996, a new policy called Non-Lapsable Central Pool of Resources (NLCPR) was introduced within the frame of exception. It proposed to earmark 10 per cent funds of all central ministries of India for investing on infrastructural development of the North East. This was subsequently followed by the first 'North East Industrial Policy' in 1997 to address the 'chronic industrial underdevelopment' in the region and attract the investment capital, create industrial surplus and enhance trade volume with neighbouring nations. On the other hand, India also invoked regional cooperation to turn post-colonial hostile neighbours towards an engaged relation. In this regard, some of the closed borders were made open after decades to 'formalize' economic interaction and border trade, like the Moreh-Tamu border route between Manipur and Myanmar and the Zokhawthar-Rhikhawdar border trade route between Mizoram and Myanmar in 1996. These changes were both significant and symbolic for the North East to change the narrative of 'isolation' towards an open economic policy. So as the geography of the North East became paramount for India's developmentalism in the post-1990s, the State started to create a set of policies suitable for its economy. The following decade became consequential for the 'region'. In 2001, a department for the Development of North East Region (DoNER) was created to make a paradigmatic shift in the role of the State from a securitist dogma to a developmentalist ideology. This department became a full-fledged ministry in 2004 and was the new architect to lay the tenets of development in the North East. The creation of the MDoNER was certainly another exception to India's existing ministerial structure, having a very specific purpose and role to develop a particular 'region' of India. By next 4 years, in 2008, the ministry drafted the *North Eastern Region Vision* 2020, where the need for economic growth at about an 8 per cent rate was highlighted to 'catch up' with the other states in India. This also created a new roadmap for the North East and its sectoral economic development and imagined North East once again as a connecting space for East and Southeast Asia. This new knowledge production through such an official document of India was transformative and ushered certain hopes for the 'region' to recover from economic 'backwardness' within the 'grammar of commerce' and set aside the 'logic of security' of the earlier decades. While the MDoNER was fractionally successful to generate new hope and consensus, it clearly reflected the State agenda of economic expansion and appropriation of resources of this space for national economic gains. As the developmental State became a direct actor to enforce a market in this 'strategically' located space, it largely subverted and tried to circumvent the role of the regional development planning institution NEC, which worked congruously and agreeably within the planning model to deliver in the 'region', while exercising a certain degree of autonomy and decentralization. With MDoNER as a centralized power centre, the autonomy of NEC was curved with substantive budget squeeze over time. As NEC eventually was merged within the structure of MDoNER, the idea is to turn it into 'a resource, research and innovative centre', and this is a clear gesture from the State to put an end to the role of decentralized development planning in the 'region'. Developmentalism in the North East, as observed by

Escobar elsewhere, became once again a top-down and centralized approach, which imagined people and their culture as abstract concepts and movements of statistical figures to evaluate economic growth as significant measures in the chart of progress (see Escobar 1995, 44). With such a clear strategy of State developmentalism, an engaged set of policies for the North East sans borders were further imagined. This was done by opening more border trade routes in the region in the 2000s with its immediate neighbouring areas to enhance local economy and livelihood while keeping the larger agenda for trade and exportable surplus of India. Thus, Nathu La was open for Indo-China trade through Sikkim, and Akhawra, Dawki and Sutarkandi were open for Indo-Bangladesh trade via land and river routes through Tripura, Meghalaya and Assam, respectively.

With this new trajectory, the space of the North East was increasingly perceived as a 'connecting corridor' for transnational economic affairs. This propelled the developmental State to become messianic in creating road infrastructure in the 'region'. In 2006, the Special Accelerated Road Development Programme for North East (SARDP-NE) was formulated by the State to create about 6,500 km of roads within the region to connect all 88 districts with two-lane roads and also to include the border areas of the North East. At the same time, some very important transnational highways were also conceptualized in collaboration with some global financial institutes such as the Asian Development Bank (ADB) and World Bank to connect the North East with the neighbouring nations through road infrastructure. This has snapped the post-colonial imagination of the North East as an 'isolated geography', and with such an ideational and strategic shift, India aimed to address the infrastructural 'durable disorder' of the North East and relocate it within 'mainland India'. This was to create a larger network of circulation and mobility of capital, goods and people. As argued by Buğra elsewhere, such unleashing of the new capitalist economy where State intervention is not only to put the market economy in place but also to achieve State objectives is a 'creative destruction' (Buğra 2017). Such State agenda can threaten various traditional livelihood activities and people's economic security, leading to serious land-resource conflicts between the State and its people. In most of the states in the North East, the poverty ratios already were much higher in the 2000s and the next decades. The NSSO unit data of 2011–2012 revealed that in some areas of the North East like the rural and hill areas of Manipur, poverty ratio was as high as 80 per cent (Bhattacharya and Bhattacharjee 2015). A large number of people lost their traditional livelihoods and were displaced and out-migrated (Hussain 2008; Ramesh 2016) due to various such State development projects through land acquisition, resource extraction and dam construction (Borah 2014). Such structural shifts, as pointed out by Buğra, may reflect on the deeper forces of geography, resources, ethnicity and a host of other cultural factors and can force one to reorient the relationship between the State and society over time (see Buğra 2017).

In recent times, more pronouncedly since 2014, the developmental State conveniently created a strategy and managed such dynamics within the 'existing historical variety of capitalism' and has heightened its policy focus on 'transformation' of the North East as the 'heart' of India. The method for such transformation was primarily by critiquing the earlier planning model, which was depicted as authoritative, 'top down' and non-performing within the rising asymmetry of the 'mainland and margin'. The role of the current State is reflected as a facilitator and mediator in the federal frame of 'cooperation', that is, with 'cooperative federalism'. With the replacement of the Planning Commission by the National Institute for Transforming India (NITI) Aayog, a policy think tank, in the Union Cabinet resolution of 2015, the approach of the developmental State towards peripheral spaces has further been transformed significantly. As the State embraced neoliberalism in the North East, it also started to partner with local social forces to create a channel for market forces and global financial captures. Here the developmental State is largely conditioned by the form of State organizations, State apparatuses and their nature of ties with dominant social interests. Through such 'embedded autonomy', as argued by Evans, the various actors of development, such as the State, its apparatus, private capital and social forces, work together for the execution of the assigned projects and for their outcomes (Evans 1989). This trajectory of development has become a new normal with an increasing eye for the influence over the resources of the North East, most clearly perhaps for oil, water and forest reserves, even in the hill areas, to increase exportable surplus.

FRONTIER BECOMES MAINLAND

When the Minister for MDoNER Mr Jitendra Singh stated the 'frontier becomes mainland' in his newspaper article on 16 March 2018, he clearly narrated the 'vision and development initiatives' of his government towards the 'integration of Northeast with rest of the country' (Singh 2018). The major constituent of this integration process indisputably is connectivity infrastructure and region formation, fundamentally different from earlier regimes. The formation of the proposed region is trans-spatial and broader in nature, where the space of North East needs to be seamlessly connected with its neighbouring areas. This has prioritized the route-mapping exercise of the developmental State of India with more intensity. For a fast and steady progress of the road infrastructure project, India's Ministry of Road Transports and Highways created a State corporate known as the National Highway and Infrastructure Development Corporation (NHIDC) Limited in 2014 with an estimated corpus of ₹1.01 lakhs crores to build a proposed 19,903-km stretch of road within the North East and across its international borders. Both global and corporate financial capital is in circulation for such a mammoth road construction project across the states of North East to transform the 'region' from its time-worn issue of inaccessibility and 'low density and poor-quality roads'. In the last 4 years, the North East has seen several new roadscapes and bridges over its hill and riverine terrains, notable among them is Asia's longest bridge which is 9.15 km. It is the Dhola-Sadiya bridge over River Lohit to connect the remotest and most cut-off Eastern Arunachal Pradesh, bordering China, with Assam. The central fund allocation has increased to ₹49,000 crores for the North East Road Sector Development Scheme (NERSDS) and the North East Special Infrastructure Development Scheme (NESIDS). Similarly, 15 new railway lines have been initiated in the North East to scale up the existing 2,600-km length, connecting only two state capitals of Assam and Tripura, which were primarily created by the colonial State. Also an allocation of ₹101,409 crores has been made for the revival of air connectivity and aviation infrastructure in the North East, which currently is seen as highly inadequate with only 11 airports. The nearest city Kolkata has so far been serving as the only hub for the region (Kashyap 2018a). The developmental State also has aimed to revive 'region's' inland waterway transportation network, which used to be a traditional mode of cheap and fast transportation in the North East with its two big Rivers Brahmaputra and Barak. This mode of connectivity had suffered immensely in post-colonial times. With the idea of reviving such traditional sustainable modes of transportation, the dredging and channel stabilization work were started by the State to create 20 new ports in these two river basins to enhance the connectivity across the transregional level to reduce freight movement costs and increase efficiency. Beyond physical connectivity, the State also has aimed at a comprehensive telecom plan with ₹5,336 crores to connect the 'region' digitally and make it a 'new energy centre' of the country. The only lifeline of post-colonial North East the 28-km stretch of a road corridor, called 'Chicken's Neck', passing through a small town of North Bengal, Siliguri, is expected to be replaced by such multiple connectivity networks and corridors, making it a 'natural gateway' to neighbouring nations, and it is expected to transform the stereotypes of the North East. In this long journey from invisibility to hyper-visibility of the North East, such spatial transformation has become the new marker of political and economic control and integration vis-à-vis contestation in the contemporary North East. As certain social realities are also coming into being in such new knowledge production, articulation of power of the 'visible and expressible' is becoming an 'inevitable and necessary' progressive route to development in the North East.

With connectivity, corridors and capitals as the buzzwords, a new normal is setting in the North East and the space now is at the interface of both geoeconomics and geopolitics. Reiterating the earlier construct of the North East with about 98 per cent of its international borders with Bangladesh, Bhutan, Myanmar and China, the report of the NITI Aayog claimed that the 'region' was a subject of geopolitics, and eluded all economic possibilities for a long period of time. About 95 per cent of India's total exports to these neighbouring countries have been taking place from regions other than the North East (2017). The centrality of trade in the development debate of the contemporary State is therefore logically imagining North East as a potential space. To expand trade partners, relation and volume towards East and Southeast Asia, the developmental State now aims to iron out various transit treaties (with Bangladesh in 2015) and create routes and transits at the trans-spatial level with physical infrastructure between the North East and its neighbouring countries. To achieve such larger agenda, the State necessarily needs to create means to 'consistently transform the society' with an intermediate role with other effective development programmes that can change the lives of people. Therefore, along with trade opportunities, the 'Three Year Action Agenda' report of the NITI Aayog also provided a roadmap for youth opportunities in the 'region'. Centrally sponsored schemes for the development of special industries including sericulture, floriculture, tea plantations, silk industry and the handicraft industry in the North East have been charted out for creating self-reliant local economies for the growing population, along with the idea to modernize the existing and new vocational and industrial training institutions for skill development in such industrial sectors. Thus, the State is negotiating and partnering with various such local spaces and voices. Interestingly, a noticeable threshold level of acceptance of such State agenda from various resisting forces is seen today in the North East, and many are gradually partnering with the State in the hope of having a new beginning and for empowerment and to prevent out-migration of the youth. State incentives for the local economy and livelihood are becoming acceptable for various groups of people in the North East, who were earlier the subjects of resistance and violence. Such groups are now partnering with the State and its changing political forces as they are either the victims of traditional customary systems or are trapped in economic 'underdevelopment'. Such 'constructive' engagements are aimed towards various development outcomes and largely to tie with societal interests for its transformation.

The development of such a market-friendly society and institutions in a democratic approach is the 'enhanced conditionality' of a neoliberal economy. The ideas of surplus economy, cash cropping and monetization of indigenous knowledge are gradually transforming the aspirations of people and tending towards 'mass consumption' and 'market society'. As there is a spree for local farmers, entrepreneurs and traders to move away from traditional practices towards various cash crops like tea and spices, it is creating space for connecting the local economy of the North East and its knowledge system to the larger global and neighbouring markets. Both political democracy and the market society are creating a space for such new partnering and cronyism, and the State is able to accumulate land and local resources by destroying the age-old hill–plain binary, displacing people, rupturing economic anthropology and threatening ecology and everyday life. Referring to a special report in the magazine *The Economist* published in 2012, entitled 'The rise of state capitalism: the emerging world's new model', the role of the developmental State and increasing global influences in the growth process in the 'emerging economies' (like the North East) and 'the invisible hand of the market is giving way to a visible and often authoritarian hand of the State' (see *The Economist* 2012). This new nexus of the developmental State through several governmental apparatuses, companies and social forces in the North East is also creating both crony capitalism for larger unregulated accumulation and ways for rentier and nouveau riche classes. This can therefore be seen as new euphemism and 'progressive extractivism' (Gudynas 2010) of State development model in the North East with (or without) pairing with redistribution (Postero 2017).

Interestingly, some of the complex external orientations of the North East began to change politically since the later part of the 2000s. With political transition towards democratization in some neighbouring nations of the 'region' like Bangladesh and Myanmar, a renewed agenda on regional economic cooperation has become important in India's 'Neighbourhood First Policy' and Act East Policy of 2014. This set of new policies has attempted to relocate North East as 'the heart' of it to 'augment national wealth'. The Act East Policy strategically relocated North East as the 'hub of trade' to enhance the 'national growth trajectory' and therefore also aims to create an industrial hub within the 'region' for exportable surplus. In this regard, the North Eastern Industrial and Investment Promotion Policy (NEIIP) of 2007 was revised in 2017 for next 10 years with a new set of incentives for the investors. As the State is increasingly aiming for an open economic policy for the 'region', various forums and instruments are being utilized at length for private investors. The summit 'Destination Assam' titled *Replicate Yunnan, Mekong Models to Make Northeast ASEAN-India Hub*, which was held in 2018, has been one such forum where an integrated development of infrastructure by enhancing transportation, urban planning, human capital, energy, agriculture, IT, tourism, health and education was discussed with many neighbouring participants to make North East an 'India-ASEAN hub' (Kashyap 2018b). Nineteen new power projects with 6 being commissioned, the State has prioritized energy trade through the 'region'. Such hegemonic policy transformations are the clear markers of the developmental State to imagine North East in a 'transnational theatre for commercial integration and neoliberal market expansion' (NITI Aayog 2017). With such market fundamentalism and its expansionism, the developmental State has made an ideational change towards an efficient, competitive and integrating economy, where 'geographic marginality' of the North East is being transformed with the semantic of an 'engine of dynamism'. Thus 'backward hinterlands and highlands' of the North East have become the 'whirlwind of modernity', and according to Minister Mr Jitendra Singh, the binary of 'hinterland' and 'mainland' is simply a blurring distinction in today's context (2018). The State is therefore ambitiously imagining various new geographies and enclaves within the states of the North East, for example, the 'State Capital Region' in Assam, comprising a large area with the spread of five adjoining districts of Assam as an ultra-urban space. The cities Shillong, Guwahati and Agartala are proposed to be among the 100 smart cities of India. All of these tend to create an urban capitalism in the 'region', adding to the demand for land for more construction and business sites.

As the developmental State necessarily coerces all its 'pet projects' to promote market, competition and capital, they may not always be best suited for the ecology of the North East and may not necessarily transform the society into a better one. Given the internal spatio-cultural dynamics of the North East, this developmental agenda, and its progressive encroachment upon its traditional systems, are likely to create complexities among the various ethnic groups and their idea of plurality. In the long run therefore as argued by Rao, such State projects may create another dimension of regional imbalance in the development strategy, while there would be a 'definite increase in the centre's control over states' control' (Rao 2015), and such a discursive strategy of the State may grant legitimacy to mesh with State and non-State fantasies of this space (see Gudynas 2010). The emergence of both market society and market economy within the North East may destroy and make extinct the traditional spaces and societies in the long run. Referring to Polanyi's argument on the unregulated market, unleashed forces of economic progress could be inimical to the survival of a society. Both its form and pace of progress therefore need to be politically determined on the basis of non-economic characters. The existence of the market is found in all kinds of societies in all historical periods without much problem, but what Polanyi analysed is the nineteenth-century market economy as a 'singular departure' from normal historical patterns where the economy remains *embedded* in society, subservient to the requirements of the norms that define the social order and assure its survival. It is only in the market society where the totality of economic activity is guided by market exchange and the economy constitutes an autonomous domain *disembedded* from society. Polanyi therefore invoked sustained regulatory interventions by the liberal State to protect such a society (see Nee 2000). The case of the North East also, to address such rising challenges of socially inefficient and regionally ineffective neoliberal market constructs, which are State induced, necessarily needs to be seen within an 'ideological category' and protected with regulations. Unfortunately, as argued by Buğra

> the State and society relations in the past could not provide any model that can be emulated in an attempt to change such present order. What must be acknowledged is the need for a serious assessment of both the pace and the direction of progress in light of the requirements of a viable and just society. It is possible to affirm that this is the main challenge facing critical approaches to economic development in our contemporary societies that increasingly appear to be neither viable nor just. (Buğra 2017)

In this context, given the sensitivity, complexity and social diversity of the space the North East, the canonical discipline of economics and its market forces as the prime State developmental agenda may tend to oversimplify the ground realities and can undermine the significance of the societal structure. Most importantly, it needs to be seen whether this space once again becomes a fresh subject of peripheral formation with such State economic affairs and becomes an exception to India's developmental trajectory by making the idea of the North East protuberant in the subsequent States' imaginations.

INSIGHTS FROM THE CONTRIBUTED CHAPTERS

In this milieu of developmental trajectories of the post-colonial period, the subsequent chapters of this book study the discourses by understanding and problematizing the State strategy vis-à-vis the 'hegemonic worldview of development', which, in the words of Escobar, 'increasingly permeates and transform the economic, social, and cultural fabrics' even with moderation at the local levels (Escobar 1995, 17–18). The North East being one of the most contentious peripheral spaces of India, most of the chapters of the book have carefully and critically examined the changing role of the developmental State in the postcolonial period to reflect on several sets of consequences in terms of marginalization, exclusion and exception, while some other chapters looked at the level of response and contestation to encounter such development trajectories, and there are chapters which have examined the scope and potentials of the North East in such an evolving role of the State. The North East is mostly (mis)understood from the vantage-grounds of conflicts and security, having political struggle at the core. Such a prism many a times overlooks the seven long decades of economic and developmental trajectories and their (mis)managements, which have also been deeply responsible for infuriating conflicts, while adding to the dichotomy and binary of the North East and the 'rest of India' within core–periphery and mainland–margin frames. Through both theoretical understanding and empirical discourse, the chapters of the book have tried to provide a discursive narrative for the North East and its challenges through the space of development and the domain of State strategies and then have attempted to explore an alternative from below by underscoring the traditional systems, people's rights and environmental conservation which are integral to the life and economy of the 'region'.

Chapter 1 has laid down a narrative of the traditional and cultural economy and its uniqueness within the North East. This detailed analysis provides a clear understanding of the 'self-reliant and self-sufficient' economic system of various communities that existed in the North East. By laying down such a narrative, the aim of the chapter is to demystify the North East and its traditional economy through an articulation of its indigenous knowledge in terms of traditional economy, resource sharing and its repository of ideas. This traditional economy and its institutions such as customary laws have an ingrained approach towards a sustainable economy and do not look beyond subsistence. The chapter has exhaustively laid down the landscape of various traditional livelihood practices that existed in this space during the pre-colonial and colonial periods, where economic activities in agriculture, manufacturing, trade and the collection of products from the forest were 'embedded' in their socio-cultural system. Interestingly a long chain of markets also existed along the foothills and mainly thrived on bartered goods. These 'practices not only point to the deep knowledge of indigenous people had of nature, drawn as it were from their close and intimate interaction with the natural world'. The subsequent socio-economic transformations, mostly due to State intervention, 'misunderstood and maligned' these livelihood strategies as 'primitive', 'uncivilized' and 'unscientific' and created the popular knowledge of an isolated entity of the North East during post-colonial times. The chapter then has engaged with a critical debate on how 'once self-sufficient and prosperous economy' became a subject of 'underdevelopment' in the post-colonial narratives, which were rooted to colonialism and its 'idea of progress through extracting the maximum from nature to maximize profit'. Unfortunately, structural transformation through subsequent State interventions and their narratives conveniently has ignored the principles of self-sufficiency and self-reliance that underline such traditional economies. The chapter therefore has provided a logical and rational 'cultural critique' of the developmental State and its strategies, where communities, people and their knowledge on sustainable economy were consciously marginalized for surplus appropriation.

In a subsequent interface of the State and society, Chapter 2 critically has brought out a set of questions on such transformations that started in this space through market regimes of State representations and their sustainability. Market, a closely intertwined concept in the development debate, is also a 'lived spaces of the communities'. Through the 'mediation of State' and its policies, the chapter shows how the North East has been unleashed with an 'unbridled development of market', especially in the current period to promote surplus value and integrate with global forces. It identifies this transformation with three moments. First is the moment of a 'market society', marked by the introduction of neoliberal State policies for the insertion of market culture into a region's traditional societies. This has sequentially led to the second moment, marking the 'arrival of an ethnically configured market' through various ethnic practices and subsequently contesting such State-induced market frames. Various traditional ethnic market systems in the North East are normally controlled by various local communities and are the defining spaces of their identities. Such ethnic markets also have resisting powers in terms of accepting or rejecting 'outside commodities' and many a times have exhibited such strength and have contested against State policies. This is connected to the third moment of 'moral economy' that the chapter has talked about to bring out the various incidents as well as the spirit of 'defending the traditional rights and customs' in times of such crises imposed by the State in the space of development. By critically bringing out the idea of an unbridled market within the meaning of development and the question of cultural politics around the frame of an ethnic social order in the North East, the chapter has contributed to theorizing the question of discursive transformation through such important 'moments' of changes that the North East is confronted with and has looked for an enunciation for an alternative.

As the North East is at the crossroads of traditional systems and market-driven developmentalism, the people are at the forefront with multiple challenges. The next three chapters therefore have brought out various consequences and implications of such moments of transformation in the spaces of development and on people's lives. The idea of development has not only created dualism and binary of traditional and modern spaces within this 'region' but also has generated major consequences in terms of people's rights, alienation, marginalization and opportunities.

Chapter 3 has shown how the corpus of 'sophisticated technology' of development since 1947 such as State laws, Acts, policies, planning and other institutional practices has helped create bodies of knowledge on State developmentalism and produced new subjects of impoverished and displaced people in the North East. The chapter has critically brought out the intricate relationship of the 'development paradigm' with land alienation and people's impoverishment, which goes back to the colonial Land Acquisition Act (LAA) 1894 and has continued for the next 119 years till it was enacted in 2013. The foundation of such legal changes brought in the concept of a new class system, a channel for tax collection and State capital formation. As the State started to acquire private property for 'public purpose' without the owner's consent, the concepts of common property resource and community land were largely disturbed. In the North East, such land acquisition began with Assam Land Rules 1938, which subsequently legitimized and facilitated immigration even in post-colonial times. The chapter has also articulated how various State developmental projects since 1947 such as water resources, refugee rehabilitation, environment protection, defence, transport infrastructure and industries have acquired massive amounts of land and displaced a large number of people, who eventually have lost their traditional land and livelihoods. Thus by paying close attention and supported by the empirical analysis to resource accumulation and its consequence on people's displacement and impoverishment, the chapter brings out the State's discursive construction of developmentalism within the North East and its new subjects of displaced and impoverished people. So the idea of economic modernity has largely intervened in various traditional systems and resources, and the paradox was seen between development and displacement of people. The chapter has therefore raised a genuine concern on their traditional rights over resources, which are being systematically targeted and grabbed due to the State's developmental strategies. In this context, the chapter has proposed an alternative by theorizing the idea of inclusive development in such a vulnerable space like the North East through a Gandhian philosophical alternative towards an 'equitable society'.

Chapter 4 in continuum has brought out another dimension of such paradox between State developmentalism and people's identity and migration, which have been the most contentious issues in this space and were reflected through a series of conflicts and contestations for a long period of time in the post-colonial period. Within a conceptual approach of 'ethnicized developmentalism', the chapter has carefully debated a connection of State developmental dynamics, labour market outcomes and the 'crisis of citizenship' within a 'prism of exceptionalism' in the North East. As the State with its cautious policies primarily aimed to consolidate governance infrastructure and mediate and legitimize the project towards capitalist transformation with institutional innovations at spatial scales, trans-border migration has been instrumental in this framework in a very complex and deep manner. The chapter has thrown an elaborate and analytical light on this discourse from the vantage ground of the labour market in the North East and has argued that there is a 'gross mismatch between its demand and supply'. It has contextualized the contour of migration particularly in agrarian transformation and 'direct interventions of the State' in it. With conscious State decisions on labour commodification and linking it to the 'reserve army of labour' within a typical capitalist frame, migrant labourers could easily be 'controlled' against an identity-based fragmented working class system within the North East for a very long period of time. In the process, the State was also able to set the webs of *othering* and made 'identity-based hierarchical citizenship a durable feature' in such an ethnicized space. Further, the neoliberal strategy has created another dynamics of (out-)migration of the educated youth and related dynamics of (in)security and *othering*. In this complex dynamics of State-sponsored migration towards engaging them in its capitalist developementalism, the labour class becomes the most victimized category. This critical narrative, based on sound empirical analysis, therefore raised concerns on the dire need and recognition of such issues and then proposed an alternative by ensuring basic economic rights of such 'migrant citizens', within and outside the North East.

Chapter 5 has also discussed the labour market in the North East in a sequence but with the emphasis on locating the position of women in the context of the changing economic landscape in the region through State intervention. The chapter has begun with an important debate on the benefits of development, which so far did not reach the majority of women, particularly women in the informal sector in India while there is a lack of detailed information on a peripheral region like the North East on the status of the woman labour market. It therefore has attempted to fill such an urgent gap and understand the position and vulnerability of various ethnic women communities in the North East in its emerging labour market through their workforce participation status. It has argued that, though the women are historically burdened asymmetrically with higher and more work among the indigenous ethnic communities, but in case of the enthicized North East, such 'asymmetric work participation' is not seen. To understand the changing role of women in the economy across the region deeply, the chapter structurally has moved away from the macro-understanding of the North East and has deconstructed it by taking the state as an individual unit to examine such a situation. On the basis of detailed empirical analysis, the chapter has argued that in the neoliberal period, the work participation pattern of women has made some visible changes within the North East, as more women are now in paid employment and are gradually moving away from traditional activities into 'better paid ones'. Thus, there has been a clear shift from traditional activities towards modern economic occupations, which are financially more rewarding. The State has been substantially able to penetrate such spaces by changing the production relations towards a capitalistic frame. This is increasingly taking away the distinctiveness of North East woman labour force as a category, who are identified with their unique skills in their traditional economic activities, and they are now seen more as a workforce category in modern economic affairs. In this changing scenario, the chapter therefore suggests that the region with regard to the woman labour policy need not necessarily be kept as an 'exception', and a more symmetrical relation all in terms of skill development, workforce participation, entrepreneurship and wage rate may help the region to break the imagery of the *other* in the woman labour market in the country.

In the context of such deep implications of State developmentalism on the people at the margin, the next four chapters have attempted to understand more critically the fundamentals of the State's neoliberal approach, which is forceful in transforming even the genesis of the space through market capitalism. The chapters have been broadly placed within the emerging and contemporary narrative of the State and in the debate of new regionalism, global capital and the political economy of regional development and have re-examined the position of the North East in such State-crafts.

Chapter 6 has critically brought out the spatial significance of the North East in this emerging State narrative and its moment of transformation. This has been done in a conceptual frame of (new) economic geography and its implications in market expansion policy at the transnational level. While creating such a frame, the chapter also has located the complexities of contemporary State patronage for new capital towards various renewed developmental activities and projects. This new capital is flowing in the region to create a mammoth infrastructure network for large-scale commercial trade and circulation of goods across the trans-border areas of India by making the space of the North East at the 'heart' and as a 'corridor'. The chapter has made a critical understanding of such State's approach towards 'internationalizing' the peripheral space of the North East for larger economic integration with the neighbouring nations. In this changing narrative, new social and economic dynamics are setting in the region, where some social groups are tending towards partnering with the State in search of economic alternatives and for 'better' livelihoods through surplus and cash economy, and this is necessarily creating a new nexus between the State and society within the North East. As this new reality may not be inclusionary in nature, the chapter therefore has raised concerns and has discussed about an endogenous economic agglomeration, by conceptualizing a 'tea-region' at the trans-regional level, where participant regions can ensure their share and rights more equally. Such endogenous approach may also provide a cultural affirmation in the face of such connected development and can make this contemporary moment of economic change relevant to the local communities *from below*. This search for an endogenous economic activity is an attempt to address the larger concern of the articulation of an alternative where connected developmental activity can also be experimented *from below* to encounter the ongoing embedded developmental regime in the North East and its neighbouring areas, which is largely facilitated by the strategy of State technology with market integration and by re-imagining the geography of the North East as a 'gateway'.

Chapter 7 in continuation has further elaborated such contemporary moments of transformation of the peripheral space like the North East in the larger context of an ongoing transport corridor network and 'seamless connectivity' projects in Asia. It has critically looked into the relation between connectivity and development in a historical-geographical narrative and further discussed the geopolitical compulsions of India to connect with East and Southeast Asia where its North East 'becomes the fulcrum of routes'. While critically laying down the conceptual details about the current 'politics of corridor', which is imagined as a solution for the underdeveloped and the conflict-prone space of the North East, the chapter has discussed various logistical visions of the Indian State for political, economic and social acceptance of such an idea of 'seamless connectivity'. Referring further to the various ongoing world-wide projects on economic corridors, it has argued that though they can enhance an efficient transport network within a geography through infrastructure, production centres, urban clusters, market integration and agglomeration and international gateways, it also 'entails a direct role for the authorities ruling in the spaces they cross, including city/village councils, regions and states'. Added to it, the chapter further has been apprehensive that various other international organizations in such cross-border activities also can produce 'new governing dynamics and management agencies' to create 'infrastructural logic' and 'infrastructural alliance'. The logic and strength of such an alliance is always measured by an increasing connectivity network and volume of flows, which is also seen to 'encounter over varying perceptions of political frontiers and frontiers of influence'. The chapter has unfurled an approach towards 'new lines of communication to the sub-regions of Asia' and its competing superpowers China and India. The approach, as argued in the chapter, 'holds the potential to reshape' the entire periphery, including India's North East, impacting its own emerging role in the Asian sub-region.

Chapter 8 on a different note has attempted to explore the potentials of this new approach in the debate of development and how useful this can be to reshape the peripheral space of the North East. It has identified objectively the specific areas of 'underdevelopment' in the 'peripheral geographical locations' and has argued that lack of connectivity and high transportation cost necessarily restrained economic growth, trade and transaction in the post-colonial times within the North East, especially with neighbouring nations, leaving aside 'mainland' India. Such an entry point of inquiry for economic underdevelopment has created the ground and logic for the chapter to imagine a pragmatic roadmap on the changing strategy of the developmental State towards engaging in cross-border trade and economic cooperation. These are seen as the inevitable apparatus for the alternative approach of geoeconomic affairs, which reflects the potential to transform the North East towards a better economic future. The chapter has studied empirically the potentials of opening the North East economy with three important neighbours—Bangladesh, Bhutan and Myanmar—where the cases of both complementarities and competitiveness in trade affairs have been found out to justify the State developmental agenda as the opportunity for the North East. As a fragmented market and high transport cost still restrain trade to move beyond the subsistence level, it tends to create a 'dyadic resource-trade linkage' in the North East. Therefore a 'triadic resource-industry-trade linkage' can look for surplus trade, which can now be achieved through sub-regional cooperation with the neighbouring nations. The chapter therefore has shown justification of such a new approach to make the borders of the North East gateways for trade and commerce, which in the long run can weaken the 'raison d'etre of ethnic militancy'. Articulation in the chapter makes way for global-local synergy by relocating the borders, which has been confronted with several perceptible disputes between the State and locals, where the former imagined locals as fringes living in the nation's borders and the latter considered the borders as militarized and guarded by others. This has led to a binary of the homeland-borderland, and conflict for a prolonged period, and has made border management in North East weak and ineffective, defeating the much larger and awaited development agenda.

Chapter 9 has laid down a critical alternative to understand 'development through trade' by relocating India's North East in its highly debated Act East Policy. The North East which was 'a meeting ground, a transit point and the southern trials of old trade routes' became a frontier region for various 'invading forces' and was experimented by various post-colonial State initiatives, development packages and political measures to 'reduce the frustration and schizophrenic alienation', which was created in the space. The chapter has argued that such State-led and bureaucracy-managed 'developmentalism' created unintended consequences in the region with inherent red-tape, economic stagnation and nexus of corruption. By the 1990s, India's open economic policy started to promote external trade with emphasis on immediate neighbours, and it directed its Look East Policy to connect with several East and Southeast Asian countries through the North East having cultural affinity with these neighbours. The State therefore shifted towards the strategy of cultural diplomacy for interdependent global and regional cooperation and explores the potential of geo-economics of the northeastern region as a 'gateway' and accordingly repositioned the space to 'prepare' for conducive trade, investment and entrepreneurial growth. Currently there has been another shift in the policy strategy, from cultural diplomacy to cultural economy with the renaming of 'Look East' to 'Act East' in 2014, and the North East once again is at the centre with its historical roots to these neighbours. While raising concerns about such policy shifts on the livelihood issues of individuals, the chapter has proposed long-term policy for sustainable development of the region by exploring comparative advantages in trade and giving stimulus in local partnership and entrepreneurship through a convergence of the State and market, which also needs to bring all elements of 'resistance' and 'rebellions' to a 'settlement' for sustainable peace at this periphery.

The next three chapters are the attempts to understand the contestation against the ongoing economic coercion of the State and market and explore an alternative from below by situating people's and environmental rights in such development discourses at the periphery.

Chapter 10 has made an elaborate exposition of the State developmental strategy with large-scale dam construction and extraction projects within the North East. The chapter has brought out probable long-term devastating impacts of such developmentalism on both communities and ecosystems, while 'benefiting the construction and power companies and the political-administrative-business elites'. It has also discussed the consequences of such 'economics of dams', which usually involves large-scale capital and eventually creates a crippling burden of debt, while curtailing policy choices. Such huge capital flow can also potentially create a parallel black economy, unmeasurable by definition, as bribes are widely understood to act as an incentive for State apparatus. In the next stage, the chapter also has brought out the possibilities of several natural disasters and loss of livelihoods of various communities who are at the fringes of such State economic activities. Such an economy therefore potentially can make extinct the 'sophistication of the ways of life' of the indigenous communities, which are time tested, sustainable and community based with an asset of ecological principles. Such simultaneous narrations in the chapter have provided a landscape of 'environmental, social, economic and political impacts of these projects' in the 'region' and have raised alarms against the damages posed by damming these groups' core culture, which tends to 'criminalize' indigenous ways of life and indigenous activism aimed at environmental protection. As the value of indigenous peoples' traditional culture is not something amenable to quantification and grossly contradicts the value systems of capitalism, it therefore tends to get completely overlooked and marginalized. The chapter therefore has ranked such developmentalism and its predominant symbol like dam construction as poor and unreliable indicators. It has attempted to throw light on an alternative which can ensure people's security of life, having basic amenities such as food, water and livelihood and, above all, respect for human rights and the security of 'healthy ecosystems to pass on to future generations' that is sustainable in nature.

In this larger issue of the developmental crisis at the 'margin', Chapter 11 has made a case study by bringing out one of the most current debates and dualisms of developmentalism within the approach of resource conservation and people's rights to entitlement by locating the world heritage space Kaziranga in Assam. With the changing agenda of various States from colonial to post-colonial times, the subjectivity of Kaziranga was shifted from a capitalist economy of plantation towards a 'conservation nationalism' to protect its incredible one-horned Rhinos and then to a neoliberal corporatization in contemporary times. With such changing perspectives, the space over time has become a site of conflicts, as these approaches largely overlooked the natural bondage of the forest, its animal and human habitats and therefore mostly remained State-centric and 'elitist in nature'. The chapter has provided a very fresh insight on the emerging dualism of developmentalism and environmentalism by invoking the third dimension of peoples' entitlements. Amidst a deep exposition of the ongoing friction of a corporate-driven economic development agenda against the elitist concerns of conservatism, the chapter has attempted to understand the genuine and desperate struggle of the indigenous people in and around Kaziranga, whose tradition, culture and livelihoods are closely connected to the resources of this place, which are increasingly under the threat of extinction. As Kaziranga currently is a testimony of such unresolved anxiety and struggle of the indigenous people against corporatized developmentalism and elitist conservatism, the chapter has uniquely placed the conflicts of three separate spaces—State apparatus, non-State intervention and societal contestation—which are constantly at conflict with each other, subsequently unfolding the larger issues concerning the 'faultiness in the political economy of conservation in Kaziranga'. By laying down such a complex theatre of developmentalism, which is apparently 'mutually incompatible', the chapter has proposed an alternative approach with a much deeper conceptual and policy rethinking of developmentalism. Thus, with an approach towards a green component of economic development, the chapter also has laid down an emancipation towards a participatory developmental arrangement between the State and community, which alone can create a balance in people's livelihoods and the State's ecological concerns in Kaziranga, the epicentre of current contention. Such an alternative can also be experimented in similar other contentious spaces in the North East.

The last chapter creates an important contrast by bringing out the debate of the global–local discord while articulating the power of visibility of international financial institutes in the development discourse of the North East in recent times. The 'aggressive pursuance of the Act East Policy' of the developmental State of India has created an evident discursive nature of capital towards a 're-signifying nature as resources' and its new strategies towards the expropriation and extraction of such resources. The chapter talks about the representation of corporatized capital as an agent of transformation of the North East, especially in infrastructure and connectivity areas, to make them catalysts for economic coercion and transnational trade surplus. The chapter has made a crux on the developmental apparatus of the State to allow financial institutions to work and be consistent with the neoliberal capitalist relation and agenda, which is to make the North East a strategic location towards cross-border regional cooperation for trade and investment. While establishing the logic of global capital to 'unlock the region' and connecting development to locally available resources, including hydropower, natural gas and renewable energy sources, the chapter has raised genuine concerns on the fate of local spaces and its people. The construction network of more than two hundred dams, for example, along with extensive oil exploration and mining projects and plantations of cash crops across the spaces of the North East without recognizing indigenous rights, practices and their ownership patterns are the sources of new anxiety here. The fear of another kind of marginalization is therefore evolving into several contestations for rightful participation within the North East. Similar concerns on its environmental impacts are growing in the 'region' amidst such 'infusion of financial capital', all of which, as the chapter has argued, may 'complicate the armed conflict situations pervading across North East' over the ongoing movement for self-determination. The chapter therefore ended with a note of apprehension that the corporatization process, which negates communities' rights and remains unaccountable through cronyism and nexus, can easily inflate the resentment of various communities within the peripheral space like the North East.

As various approaches to development so far have centralized economic prosperity and growth with their methodological foundations on reductionism, individualism and utilitarianism, there has been apprehension for a gross underestimation of the role and importance of societal aspects in such approaches, where 'the periphery has suffered greatly from economic instability' and was injured by the imposition of (neoliberal) developmentalism with the rejection of autonomous development strategies (Saad-Filho and Johnston 2005). With the market as a neutral space, rather than a socially created institute, the idea of accumulation, exchange and surplus has largely marginalized the concepts of sustenance and subsistence, which is the richness of any traditional society. Such a construct of developmentalism over time has created the fulcrums of binary, inequality, denial and exploitation. The alarming crisis is observed in the peripheral spaces where the market never plays a fair role and mostly remains the subject of State power and intervention. Thus, the crisis of developmentalism is proliferated in much deeper ways in such spaces than in 'mainland' areas. As this paradigm of developmentalism with economic coercion faces crises such as degrading ecology, decaying cultural diversity, denial of autonomy and disqualifying inclusion, all of these pose challenges for any kind of linear progress (Pieterse 2010), and peripheries and geographical outliers in this process continue to fall into newer traps of both State and market coercions. Thus, 'development is struggle' in various historical contexts and political circumstances, as it performs the role of representation for articulating and favouring a 'particular political and class interests and cultural preferences' and also some specific areas and regions. The central issue therefore becomes a relationship between knowledge and power. In this context, an alternative approach to development needs to grow by critiquing such mainstream development, which aims for growth and surplus and whose pillars are mostly coercion, appropriation and exploitation. A post-development approach thus attempts to seek for autonomy from external dependency within a power/knowledge regime and emphasizes on self-reliance at the local level, having a different approach from dependency thinking, which privileges the nation-state (Pieterse 2010). A pluralistic and a continuous democratization process in the approach of development can essentialize the participation at all levels within the defined spheres of agents, methods, objectives and values of development to encounter the 'ideological universe of capitalism' and resist the social and spatial peripheral formations.

REFERENCES

Ackerman, E. A. 1956. *Geography as a Fundamental Research Discipline*, 15. Research Paper No. 53. Chicago: University of Chicago, Department of Geography.

Amin, S. 1976. *Unequal Development: An Essay on the Social Formation of Peripheral Capitalism*. Delhi: Oxford University Press.

Bagchi, A. K. 2010. *Colonialism and Indian Economy*. New Delhi: Oxford University Press.

Bardhan, P. 1984. *The Political Economy of Development of India*. New Delhi: Oxford University Press.

Berman, S. 1998. *The Social Democratic Movement: Ideas and Politics in the Making of Interwar Europe*, 183–86. Cambridge: Harvard University Press.

Bhattacharjee, G. 2016. *Special Category States*. New Delhi: Oxford University Press.

Bhattacharya, R. 2011. *Development Disparities in Northeast India*. New Delhi: Cambridge University Press.

———. 2014. *Northeastern India and Its Neighbours: Negotiating Security and Development*. New Delhi: Routledge.

———. 2017. 'Insider or an Outsider: Where Is the Northeast in India's Act East Policy?' In *Mainstreaming the Northeast in India's Look and Act East Policy*, edited by A. Sarma and S. Choudhury. New Delhi: Springer.

Bhattacharya, R., and J. P. Bhattacharjee. 2015. 'Poverty and Inequality in India: Regional Disparities'. In *Regional Development and Public Policy Challenges in India*, edited by R. Bhattacharya, 19–72. New Delhi: Springer.

Blyth, M. 2002. *Great Transformations: Economic Ideas and Institutional Change in the Twentieth Century*. New York, NY: Cambridge University Press.

Borah, P. P. 2014. 'Development and Marginalisation: Sociological Study of Tribal Land Alienation in Assam'. *Asian Journal of Multidisciplinary Studies* 2(7): 78–84.

Buğra, A. 2017. 'Two Lives of Developmentalism: A Polanyian View from Turkey'. In *Development as a Battlefield*, edited by I. Bono and B. Hibou. Geneva, Boston: Graduate Institute Publications, Brill-Nijhoff.

Chakravarty, S. 1987. *Development Planning: The Indian Experience*. New Delhi: Oxford University Press.

Chandra, K. 2015. 'The New Indian State: The Relocation of Patronage in the Post-Liberalisation Economy'. *Economic and Political Weekly* 50(41): 46–58.

Chatterjee, P. 1997. 'Development Planning and the Indian State'. In *State, Development Planning and Liberalisation in India*, edited by T. Byres. New Delhi: Oxford University Press.

Das, S. K. 2013. *Governing India's Northeast: Essays on Insurgency, Development and the Culture of Peace*. New Delhi: Springer.

Escobar, A. 1995. *Encountering Development: The Making and Unmaking of the Third World*. Princeton: Princeton University Press.

Evans, P. 1989. 'Predatory Developmental and Other Approaches: A Comparative Political Economy Perspective on the Third World State'. *Sociological Forum* 4(4): 561–87.

Fernandes, W. 2005. *Tribal Customary Laws and Formal Law Interface in North East India: Implications for Land Relations*. Paper presented at the Seminar on Ethnicity, Identity, Social Formation and National Building with Special Reference to North Eastern India, Dibrugarh University, 26–27 March.

Frank, A. G. 1966. 'The Development of Underdevelopment'. *Monthly Review* 18(4): 17–31.

Goswami, A. 1981. 'Assam's Industrial Development: Urgency of New Direction'. *Economic and Political Weekly* 16(21): 953–56.

Grosfoguel, R. 2000. 'Developmentalism, Modernity, and Dependency Theory in Latin America'. *Nepantla: Views from South* 1(2): 347–74.

Gudynas, E. 2010. 'El nuevo extractivismo del siglo XXI' (The New Extractivism of the 21st Century). *Memoria. Revista de Política y Cultura* 242: 12–17.

Hussain, M. 2008. *Interrogating Development: State, Displacement and Popular Resistance in North East India*. New Delhi: SAGE Publications.

Kashyap, S. G. 2018a. 'Northeast at Heart of Act East Policy, Says PM'. *The Indian Express*, 4 February

———. 2018b. 'Replicate Yunnan, Mekong Models to Make Northeast ASEAN-India Hub: ADB'. *The Indian Express*, 5 February.

Kelly, R. E. 2008. 'No "Return to the State": Dependency and Developmentalism against Neo-Liberalism'. *Development in Practice* 18(3): 319–32.

Kelly, J. D., and M. Kaplan. 2001. 'Nation and Decolonisation: Towards a New Anthropology of Nationalism'. *Anthropological Theory* 1(4): 419–37.

Khosla, M. 2014. *Letters for a Nation from Jawaharlal Nehru to His Chief Ministers: 1947–1963*. New Delhi: Penguin.

Kohli, A. 2004. *State-Directed Development: Political Power and Industrialisation in the Global Periphery*. Cambridge: Cambridge University Press.

Krugman, P. 1991. 'Increasing Returns and Economic Geography'. *Journal of Political Economy* 99(3): 483–99.

Maddison A. 1995. *Monitoring the World Economy 1820–1992*. Paris: OECD Development Centre.

Malgavkar, P. D., and B. M. Ghiara. 1975. 'Regional Development: Where and How?' In *Readings on Micro-level Planning and Rural Growth Centres*, edited by L. K. Sen. Hyderabad: National Institute of Community Development.

Mathur, N. 2015. *Paper Tiger: Law, Bureaucracy, and the Developmental State in Himalayan India*. Cambridge and Delhi: Cambridge University Press.

Mi, J. 2006. *Neoliberal Developmentalism: State-led Economic Liberalization in China*. Ph.D. Thesis, Cornell University.

Misra, T. 1980. 'Assam a Colonial Hinterland'. *Economic and Political Weekly* 15(32): 1357–64.

Murphy, C. N., and E. Augelli. 1993. 'International Institutions, Decolonisation and Development'. *International Political Science Review* 14(1): 71–85.

Naqvi, S. N. H. 2015. *Economics of Development: Towards Inclusive Growth*. New Delhi: SAGE Publications.

Nee, V. 2000. 'The Role of the State in Making a Market Economy'. *Journal of Institutional and Theoretical Economics* 156(1): 64–88.

Nigam, A. 2009. 'Empire, Nation and Minority Cultures: The Post-national Movement'. *Economic and Political Weekly* 44(10): 5.

NITI Aayog Report. 2017. *Three Years Action Agenda: 2014–15 to 2019–20*. New Delhi: Government of India.

Patnaik, P. 2015. 'From the Planning Commission to the NITI Aayog'. *Economic and Political Weekly* 50(4): 1–3.

Pereira, M. 2005. *Globalisation and Changing Land Relations in North East*. Paper presented at the Seminar on Impact of Globalisation on North East, Himalayan Research Institute, 10–11 March.

Pieterse, J. N. 2010. *Development Theory: Deconstructions/Reconstructions*, 2nd Edition. New Delhi: SAGE Publications.

Postero, N. 2017. *The Indigenous State: Race, Politics and Performance in Plurinational Bolivia*. California: University of California Press.

Ramesh, B. P. 2016. 'Migration and Marginalisation: A Study of North East Migrants in Delhi'. In *Internal Migration in Contemporary India*, edited by Deepak K. Mishra. New Delhi: SAGE Publications.

Rao, N. C. 2015. 'Disadvantaged Regions and Social Groups: Is There a Way Out?' *Indian Journal of Agricultural Economics* 70(3).

Report. 2015. *Basic Statistics of North Eastern Region, 2015*. Shillong: Government of India, Northeastern Council Secretariat.

Rosenberg, D. 1981. 'The Theory of Peripheral Capitalism, Reviewed Work(s): Modern Greece: Facets of Underdevelopment by N. Mouzelis'. *Sociology* 15(4): 603–11.
Rothbard, M. N. 2004. *Man, Economy and State with Power and Market*. Auburn: Ludwig Von Mises Institute.
Roy Burman, B. K. 1989. 'Problem and Prospect of Tribal Development in North East India'. *Economic and Political Weekly* 24(13): 693–97.
Saad-Filho, A., and D. Johnston. 2005 *Neoliberalism: A Critical Reader*. London: Pluto Press.
Sanyal, K. 2007. *Rethinking Capitalist Development: Primitive Accumulation, Governmentality and Post-colonial Capitalism*. London: Routledge.
Scott, J. 2009. *Art of Not Being Governed: An Anarchist History of Upland Southeast Asia*. Yale: Yale University Press.
Singh, J. 2018. 'Frontier Becomes Mainland'. *The Indian Express*, 16 March.
The Economist. 2012. 'The Rise of State Capitalism'. *The Economist,* 21 January.
Turnock, D. 1967. 'The Region in Modern Geography'. *Geography* 52(4): 374–83.
Wallerstein, I. 1992a. 'The Concept of National Development, 1917–1989: Elegy and Requiem'. *American Behavioral Scientist* 35: 517–29.
———. 1992b. 'The Collapse of Liberalism'. In *The Socialist Register 1991*, edited by R. Miliband and L. Panitch. London: Merlin.
Witsoe, J. 2012. 'Everyday Corruption and the Political Mediation of the Indian State'. *Economic and Political Weekly* 47(6): 47–54.

PART I

Between Subsistence and Surplus

Chapter 1

Traditional Economy, Sustainability and Subsistence
Understanding India's North East

Tiplut Nongbri

A major issue that dominates contemporary discourse on India's North East is the issue of development or, more precisely, the dearth of development. The region consisting of the states of Assam, Arunachal Pradesh, Manipur, Meghalaya, Mizoram, Nagaland, Sikkim and Tripura is collectively seen as economically backward and characterized by an acute development deficit. Many attribute the region's underdevelopment to its locational disadvantage, landlocked and remote from the mainland, and the nation's economic and political centre. Some lay the blame at the doorstep of the central government, accusing it of neglect and failure to transform the rich natural resources that abound in the region into wealth. As a result, despite its vast endowment, practically all the states in the region are deficient, in varying degrees, in all parameters of development. What is a matter of serious concern is that this spectre of underdevelopment that haunts the region comes against the backdrop of a once self-sufficient and prosperous economy.

Though detailed information on the state of the economy in the distant past is lacking, the following observation made by the British historian, Edward Gait, in his widely read book *History of Assam*, is illuminating:

> Assam has been described as a country where there is no undue poverty or distressing starvation (*akala nai, bharalsnai*) and that indicates in a nutshell the general economic condition of the kingdom. Under the Ahom rulers the country was on the whole prosperous. It had developed a good system of agriculture, industry and trade. The existence of a strong and well organized central authority contributed not a little to make the country rich and self sufficient. That there was great economic progress has been attested to by the Muhammadan writers and the later British captains. Although the country was confronted with the Moamaria rebellion during the reign of Lakshminath Singh and Gaurinath Singh which was regarded as a disastrous period in Ahom history, there was no continuous economic crisis worth mentioning. (Gait 2010, 268)

Views on the same line have been expressed on tribes inhabiting the hill districts of the (Assam) Province. Commenting on the economic condition of the Khasis during the colonial period, B. C. Allen notes:

> The people as a whole are well to do. They are enterprising and industrious and are not hampered by the spirit of conservatism which in many parts of India is so ill fated to all progress. On the southern slopes of the hills, the Khasis prior to the earthquake made large profits from lime, oranges and areca nut. Since that date their profits have been reduced but still considerable. The fact that the headquarters of the Administration are located in Shillong puts a large sum of money in circulation from which the people in the neighbourhood cannot fail to reap their profit. The Khasi have succeeded in keeping nearly the whole of the trade in their hands, this in itself must be a considerable source of wealth. (Allen 1905, 88–89)

These excerpts from two well-known texts focused on two different sites and points of history throw interesting light on the economic condition of the entity designated today as North East India. However, the sharp contrast in the picture represented in the above lines and contemporary understanding of the same call for close scrutiny of the economic practices prevailing in the region prior to Independence. The exercise is necessary not only to understand the nature of the economy, which is broadly defined as 'traditional', the institutional arrangements on which it was based and the process of change that ensued, but also to look for possible clues that could help the people restore their self-sufficiency and rebuild their economic life with least damage to the environment from which they draw their sustenance or compromise the interest of the future generation. Of course, this would not be an easy task. The dearth of recorded information on the early period of the societies that constitute the region makes the attempt of tracing the contours of the traditional economy highly arduous. A related problem is conceptual: What constitutes traditional economy? Is it specific to a particular period of history? Given that change is an inherent aspect of human life can we speak of traditional economy as a static entity immune to the ravage of time?

Within the limits articulated above, this chapter focuses its attention on the livelihood practices that existed in the region during the colonial and pre-colonial period, remnants of which can be found vibrant and alive among many indigenous communities in Asia and Southeast Asia even today. The analysis is based on the information drawn from the accounts left by colonial administrators working in erstwhile Provinces of Bengal and Assam, academic literature on the region and personal observations and insights derived from years of research on the northeastern region.

HISTORICAL BACKDROP

To begin with, though the northeastern region on which this chapter focuses has generally been looked at as a single political entity by planners and policymakers, it is by no means homogenous but marked by sharp variations in physical as well as in cultural, political and economic terms. Historically, while the Brahmaputra Valley which constitutes the centre of Assamese polity and culture has been a site of social and political encounters, as successive waves of invaders from the East and the West descended on the rich and fertile plain to conquer the land and subdue its people, the hill areas which are largely inhabited by the so-called wild and primitive tribes have remained relatively undisturbed. Though politically exclusive, the hill men were by no means a reclusive race; evidence exists that suggests that tribes traditionally had trading relations with their neighbours in the plains[1] as well as with those on the other side of the border. However, the British policy of laissez faire and least intervention adopted in the administration of tribes not only broke the link but also served to keep the hill areas in perpetual isolation. Viewed as a frontier in colonial discourse, the area was kept outside the purview of general laws applicable in the rest of the colony.

The protectionist policy extended to the hill areas left a deep impact on their economy. It not only inhibited the flow of private capital into the area but also curbed the free exchange of goods that traditionally existed between the inhabitants of the hills and the communities in the plains to protect British interests, a process that deepened the difference between the hills and the plains, the tribes and non-tribes. Many scholars attribute the truncation of Assam in post-Independence India to this process. The issue however is beyond the scope of this chapter to address.

LIVELIHOOD STRATEGIES AND PRACTICE: A HISTORICAL ACCOUNT

A perusal of the writings left behind by colonial administrators and ethnographers serving in the region reveal that Assam (the northeastern region in contemporary parlance) was characterized by what may be described as an 'integrated economic system', in which households engaged in multiple activities at one and the same time, combining agriculture with other trades depending upon the physiographic condition, customs and culture of the place they lived in. The earliest and most comprehensive account of these activities can be found in W. W. Hunter's *Statistical Account of Assam* (1998) a two-volume compendium on a variety of subjects ranging from the description of the physical characteristics of the districts, to population, diseases and pestilence and to State revenue and expenditure. The *Account*, covering 12 districts and published in 1879, was based on information personally gathered by Hunter from district officers over a period of 4 years (1869–73) and through visits to some of the districts as part of his duties as the Director-General of Statistics, Government of India. Other documents that yielded rich information included A. J. M. Mills' Report on Assam,

1853; Alexander Mackenzie's *History of the Relations of the Government with the Hill Tribes of the Northeast frontier of Bengal*, 1884; Report on the Administration of Assam, 1902–1903; district gazetteers; and ethnographic studies on specific tribes.

From the information sourced, it is revealed that though Assam possessed huge deposits of coal, petroleum and other minerals, none of these was worked upon by the people;[2] the main source of livelihood for the majority of the population was agriculture combined with manufacturing, trade and collection of products from forests. Broadly, two kinds of agricultural systems could be discerned, settled agriculture largely practised in the lowlands of the Barak and Brahmaputra Valleys and *jhum* or shifting cultivation predominantly practised by communities inhabiting the hills and the riverine and weed-infested tracks in the valleys.

The Brahmaputra Valley with its rich alluvial soil and vast expanse of land was highly conducive for settled agriculture, for producing crops such as rice, mustard, Indian corn, pulses, sugar cane and so on in abundance. This ensured not only good returns for the household but also revenue for the State, which explains why this was also the region with highly developed State formation. The abundance of land and high soil fertility enabled people to grow practically everything they needed. Rice, the staple food of the people in the region, was the main crop. Rice came in different varieties, which variety would be sown was determined by the nature of the land—dry or marshy—and the season. Some of the widely cultivated varieties were *Aus* rice, sown broadcast on high dry lands in January and February and reaped in May and June; *bao* rice, sown broadcast during February and March and reaped in June and July; and *Sali* rice, sown in June, transplanted in July and August and harvested in December and January (Hunter 1998, 45). In some districts, pulses and mustard were grown as second crops on dry lands where rice was sown. Crop was sown both for consumption and for sale. Ordinarily, each village was self-sufficient in its food production. Peasants generally produced enough food crops to meet the needs of the family with a little surplus, which they exchanged in local *hats* for salt, ghee, sugar, piece goods, brass utensils and sundry items.

Whereas settled agriculture was the hallmark in the Brahmaputra and Barak Valleys, the over-active monsoon and turbulence of rivers during the rainy season made permanent cultivation untenable in the riverine tracks or *chapari* lands. Similarly, in the sub-mountain region the nature of the land was such that it induced people into an itinerant form of agriculture.

Communities in the hills predominantly subsist on *jhum* or shifting cultivation. The rugged topography, thin topsoil and poor irrigation facilities made settled agriculture a near impossibility in most districts except in lowlands or gentle slopes where rice and other crops were grown on well-constructed terraces. In *jhum*, a patch of forestland was selected and cleared by axing down the trees and scrubs and left to dry. The dried vegetal remains were then burned into ashes upon which seeds were sown with the aid of simple tools. No plough or animal power or fertilizer was used in shifting cultivation. The ashes from the burned vegetation served as manure, enabling the growth of a variety of crops on a single plot. Crops such as rice, maize, millet, beans, gourds, mustard, yam and cotton were grown on the cleared plot. A distinctive feature of shifting cultivation was rotation of the land as opposed to rotation of crops characteristic of settled cultivation. The land was put into use for 2 or 3 years or till fertility lasted, after which it was abandoned and the farmer moved to another plot to allow the land to regenerate before returning to it. In general, the period between cultivations or the 'fallow cycle' varied from 8 to 15 years, depending upon population pressure and the ability of the land to recover (Hunter 1998, 191, see also Allen et al. 2001, 63).

Because of the frequent abandonment and moving of sites, shifting cultivation is traditionally associated with community land ownership, in which villagers had occupancy rights but no proprietary rights over the plot they cultivate. Once a land was left fallow, other villagers could stake a claim to it. But the occupation of land was never arbitrary, a system was usually in place in which each household was allotted a plot according to its needs by the head of the village, who along with the council of elders also regulated its use. In general, membership in a village was mandatory for entitlement to a *jhum* plot.

Shifting cultivation is the oldest form of agriculture practised by humans. It is a mode of livelihood that marks the transition from food gathering to food production and is primarily geared towards subsistence than mass production of food. The people usually grew crops that met the requirements of the household, rather than catering to the market. Among many communities in North East India, the practice co-existed with collection of products from the forest. Although no caste or tribe solely depended on forest produce to satisfy their needs, the forest with its vast stores of lac, beeswax, honey, cotton, silk, black pepper and aromatic leaves constitutes an important lifeline for families whose yield from cultivation was too meagre to meet their needs. Tribes such as the Abors, Singhphos, Khamtis, Mishmis, Mikirs, Miris, Garos and Nagas traded in jungle products as a subsidiary occupation.

Manufacturing was another important source of income for a large segment of the population. During the period under investigation, manufacturing in Assam and the surrounding hills basically operated as an aspect of the domestic economy. To bolster household income and as a means to meet the family's requirements for clothing, tools and other items of daily needs, many enterprising individuals took to making things at home, resulting in the rise of manufacturing as a lucrative and vibrant industry. Assam was particularly reputed for its weaving industry, producing silk cloth of very superior quality that was much in demand especially by the wealthier class. Basically operating as a cottage industry, practically every home had a loom where the womenfolk weaved clothes for the family. The entire operation from the rearing of silkworms, to spinning and dyeing of the yarn, to weaving was carried out by individuals in the family without the aid of imported capital or labour. Of the varieties of silks produced, the most often mentioned included *pat* silk made from silks of worms fed on the leaves of mulberry trees; *muga* silk, made from silks of worms fed on *sum* and *soalu* tree; and *erid* silk made from the silks of worms fed on castor oil plants (Hunter 1998, 200).

Coarse cotton cloth for daily use and for use by the poorer classes was also widely produced. Like silk, the production of cotton cloth was a holistic affair, the individuals involved in the activity carried out all the vital tasks, from cultivation of the cotton tree, to plucking the pods from the tree, to spinning. Though, not in the same league as silk, cotton had its own place in Assamese society, a fact illustrated by the humble *gamcha*,[3] which today has become a symbol of Assamese identity.

Weaving as a craft was also widely practised in the hills inhabited by tribes. Like their neighbours in the plains, most tribes clothed themselves with materials woven and fashioned by the women of the family. To most of the communities in the region, clothes were not simply things to cover the body but also a marker of their identity and status. Among the Nagas, each tribe was marked by the colour and pattern of the clothes they wore. In the words of Allen

> The miniature kilt worn by the Angamis as a loin cloth is made of dark blue thread and is often embroidered in cowries. Their outer cloth has generally a dark blue body, with a broad border of green and orange or red and yellow stripes . . . The Semas and Lhotas generally wear cloths made of broad stripes of white and blue, while blue and red is the favourite colour of the Aos. The Kacha Nagas affect a white cloth, with a narrow border of madder and blue. (Allen 1905, 50)

Clothes also marked the distinction between clans and the social position of the wearer. Among the Tangkhul Nagas, the designs that adorned the costume of a chief or a person of honour who had given the 'feast of merit' to his country folks were barred for the use of common people.

Though weaving, as an activity, appeared to have emerged as a strategy to meet the requirements of the household, it contributed significantly to the growth of trade. A perusal of items traded in the valley reveals that silk constituted an important item of export. Assam silk, in particular, was a much sought-after item both in the home market and in the markets of Bengal. *Muga* silk was a highly valued item among the southern tribes, such as, the Khasis, the Jaintias and the Garos (Government of India 1882, 45).[4] Similarly, in the Naga Hills, huge quantities of clothes from the Ao villages were sold to tribes like the Phoms and Konyaks who lacked weaving skills. According to J. P. Mills, 'In these villages, cloths of patterns specially admired by their trans-frontier neighbours, but no longer worn by the Aos, are made expressly for this trade' (Mills 1926/1973, 104).

Other important items of manufacture included jewellery, pottery, knives, *daos*, mats, baskets and so on. Most of the articles were made from materials primarily sourced from the local bio-region. For instance, making judicious use of canes and bamboos that grew in profusion in many parts of the valley and in the adjoining hill districts, mats and baskets of various descriptions were manufactured as part of the local industry. From large baskets for storage, to sieves and trays for winnowing the grains at harvest, to *japis* (wide-brimmed hats) to protect the cultivator from the sun and rain as he toiled in the field, all were manufactured locally. The same was the case with other items. From pottery to tools, the basic ingredients were sourced from the local environment. As manufacturing was basically a home-based activity intended to meet local needs, there was no hereditary class of manufacturers in Assam (Hunter 1998, 201). Except for the Marias, a caste of brass makers who formed a distinct community and almost entirely depended on this trade for their livelihood, most families, which engaged in manufacturing, combined the activity with agriculture.

During the Ahom period, gold washing provided an important source of livelihood for many. Gold was extracted from the sands of Brahmaputra by washing the silt and taking out the gold particles embedded in it. Of the gold-producing districts, Lakhimpur and Darrang on the northern banks of Brahmaputra have been reported to yield the largest quantity. However, unlike manufacturing, which was primarily a home-based enterprise, 'gold washing was done by a guild known as Sonow Khel, who paid to the Government a tax of four *annas* weight or five rupees worth of gold per annum' (Gait 2010, 272). Gold washing as an economic pursuit, however, suffered a decline with the entry of the British. The high tax levied by the government and the strenuous process of washing huge quantities of sand for a small amount of gold made the activity economically unviable for its continuance.

In the Khasi and Jaintia Hills, extraction of iron was a vital part of the traditional economy, a practice that continued well into the colonial period. The ore was obtained by washing the excavated earth to separate the grain from the sand. The extracted ore was then taken to the woods for smelting and the product was exported to markets in Assam and Sylhet both in the raw and in the manufactured form. According to information provided by Captain Lister in his letter to A. J. M. Mills, 20,000 maunds of iron ore were exported from the Khasi and Jaintia Hills annually into the plains of Assam and Sylhet (Mills undated, 39). The presence of iron also led to the establishment of a flourishing manufacturing industry, which provided large segments of the population, especially in the Khasi uplands where the activity was widespread, with an important source of income.

Like gold washing in the plains, the incursion of colonialism into the hills rang the death knell for iron trade. Though iron from the Khasi Hills was a much sought-after product because of its greater malleability (Hunter 1998, 235), the arrival of cheap pig iron from England pushed the Khasi ore out of the markets of Assam and Sylhet.

ANALYSIS AND DISCUSSION

The account presented in the foregoing paragraphs broadly brings out the livelihood practices that existed in early colonial and pre-colonial Assam and the surrounding hills. The account however tells us little about how the economy fared in the wake of social change. The extension of the colonial rule and the vast changes it effected in the administration of the land and forests, taxation and revenue could not have left the traditional economic practices unaffected. However, except for stray and fragmented information on certain issues, information on the process of socio-economic transformation in the region is conspicuous by its absence. Commenting on the matter, historian Manorama Sharma of the North-Eastern Hill University declares that the problem has less to do with the paucity of sources as with the way in which history is written, which was concerned more with the narration of facts than with interpretation. She comes out strongly against the imperialist tradition, exemplified by Gait's work *History of Assam*, for its preoccupation with dynastic and political history and for treating dynasties as the sole source and vehicle of change. She is equally critical of the nationalist ideology for its fixation with Indian culture and glorification of that culture without much critical assessment of historical reality (Sharma 2004, 4–5).

Sharma's[5] umbrage is basically directed at the works of historians, which she avers are devoid of conceptual framework and therefore blind them to 'the link between the information provided in the sources and the process of socio-economic transformation' (Sharma 2004, 4–5). The same can be said of the large body of works left behind by the colonial masters, on which this chapter is based. Today, a large volume of this material is available in the published form. However, as bulk of the works was originally compiled as government reports, gazetteers and ethnographic accounts on specific tribes, commissioned by the administration primarily to advance the economic and political interests of the empire than for academic purpose, the information collected and presented is more in the nature of a descriptive account devoid of analysis. As a result, though many of the works contain a wealth of information on diverse aspects, customs, culture, diet, dress, occupation, religion, kinship and political institutions, they tell us very little about how the people respond to the forces of change, how they structure their relations or what are the social and structural mechanisms which make the societies work.

A major problem with the information provided in colonial accounts is the absence of people from the narrative. The facts are not only presented in a cut-and-dried fashion divorced from the people on whom they are based, but also treated as static and unchanging, insulated from the world around. This is particularly true of information pertaining to the economy. There is a tendency to treat the economy as an autonomous institution unrelated to other spheres of life; therefore, economic behaviour can be read and presented on its own, without relating it to the norms, values, customs and practices or experiences and expectations of the concerned people. This perspective goes against the functionalist view of society advanced by sociologists (Durkheim 1933, 1938; Parsons 1951; Radcliffe-Brown 1952), who view society as an interactive whole or a 'system' made up of different parts or sub-systems which are in constant interaction with each other, such that a change in one part leads to a change in other parts. Viewed thus, we cannot hope to understand economic behaviour unless we relate it to the social, economic and political processes and to the norms, values and culture of the people and society within which it is embedded. This is especially true of simple or small-scale societies like many of those in North East India and other parts of South and Southeast Asia, where society is more cohesive and the hold of tradition firmer.

When we apply the functionalist perspective to the livelihood practices documented in the earlier section of this chapter, the data assume new significance. To begin with, it would be well to recognize that the livelihood practices, which constitute a key element of the economy, are not genetically derived but represent a process of adaptation to the physical environment and are shaped, in part, by the socio-cultural system within which they are embedded. Both settled agriculture and shifting cultivation discussed earlier are illustrative of this fact. The favourable combination of geography and hydrology in the lowlands of the Brahmaputra Valley made settled cultivation the ideal choice. Similarly, the physiographic conditions in the hills with their rugged terrain and poor soil characteristics made shifting cultivation the best form of land use that could guarantee food security to people.

Unfortunately, shifting cultivation is one of the most misunderstood and maligned livelihood strategies worldwide. It has not only been labelled 'primitive', 'uncivilized', 'unscientific'[6] and ecologically hazardous but has also been at the heart of governments' attempts internationally to eliminate the practice and replace it with alternative modes of cultivation. In 1957, FAO declared shifting cultivation as the most serious land use problem in the tropical world (FAO 1968, cited in Erni 2015, 8). For more than a century, colonial and post-colonial governments in Asia have devised policies and laws to eradicate shifting cultivation, in the name of forest conservation and development (Erni 2015, 8).

Studies conducted on the subject have challenged the perception that shifting cultivation is ecologically unsafe (Christanty 1986; Dove 1985; Ramakrishnan 2001). Shifting cultivation not only has an in-built mechanism for conservation but was also found to be an ideal solution for agriculture in the humid tropics (Christanty 1986).

Studies from North East India reveal that among many communities, shifting cultivation is accompanied by a number of sustainable practices. In Meghalaya where 83 per cent of the indigenous population engaged in agriculture, farmers adopted tree-based cultivation and conservation-linked harvesting techniques to minimize the negative effect of shifting cultivation (Jeeva et al. 2006). Traditional tree-based farming practices, in which varieties of crops are grown along with ecologically and culturally valued trees, 'help in conserving and improving the field, optimizing the combined production of forest and agricultural crops' (Jeeva et al. 2006, 11). To improve soil fertility, during the harvesting of grains, only the ear heads are plucked and the straw is left in the field to decompose naturally, so that when it rots and gets fused with the earth, it enhances soil quality. Indeed, so strong was the people's concern for the environment that use of the sickle for reaping is traditionally taboo[7] among the Khasis (Gurdon 1907/1975). Among the Aos of Nagaland, farmers construct vegetative bunds along the contours of the field, as part of fallow management, to reduce soil erosion and water run-off and quicken the regeneration of the vegetation after the land is abandoned (Jamir 2015, 161–202). Among the Angamis where land was too elevated, farmers successfully adapted terrace cultivation to shifting cultivation, in which terraces were constructed at different levels on steep slopes and were held up by stonewalls, where rice and other crops were grown (Report on Administration of Assam 1903, see also Allen et al. 2010, 63). These practices not only point to the deep knowledge indigenous people had of nature, drawn as it was from their close and intimate interaction with the natural world, it also suggests ecological prudence.[8]

Even in areas where settled agriculture was in place, close examination of the data presented reveals that by and large the practice was underlined by strong moral and ecological principles. Although exact figures on the acreage under cultivation by households are not available, from the conditions of the peasantry and the frequent observations made by British officials about the 'indolent'[9] habits of the Assamese farmer (see in particular Hunter 1998, 366, 369; Mills 1980, 5), one can infer that colonial and pre-colonial Assam did not engage in extractive farming, notwithstanding the coercive attempts made by the

Ahom rulers to induce people to clear more jungle and grow more crops (Gait 2010, 269). Simple in habit and with limited wants, each family took only that much land that the family's labour power could manage to work on to fulfil the requirements of the household. They supplemented what was deficient by engaging in small-time manufacturing or by collecting products from the forest, which they traded in local *hats* for items they lacked. Indeed, the long chain of markets that existed along the foothills mainly thrived on bartered goods, which comprised surplus from the farmer's field and loom, forest products of various kinds gathered by poor peasants and tribes in the hills and imported items brought in by travelling salesmen.

The livelihood practices that prevailed in the region point to a system that accorded high value to self-reliance and self-sufficiency. By relying on simple technology and self-help, the people not only sought to produce everything that the household needed, but also made judicious use of materials available in the local environment, a fact that comes out sharply in manufacturing. From rearing of silkworms, to growing cotton, to dyeing, spinning and weaving, everything was carried out within and by the household. Raw materials that could not be grown or prepared at home were sourced from the local bio-region.

In the final analysis, what stood out in livelihood practices focused in the discussion was the role of trade in bridging the link between the local and external economies. Even as people sought to manage their life in accordance with the requirements of the natural environment and the socio-cultural milieu within which they were embedded, they were organically linked with the outside world through the exigency of trade. Mention has already been made of trade in farm surplus and in jungle products carried out through local *hats* and markets situated along the foothills. Trading relations also traditionally existed between Assam and communities across the frontier (Mackenzie 1884/2001, 15–16). Facilitating the relations were passes or *duars* in the Himalayan range, bordering Bhutan and Sikkim, which served as passageways through which goods and people moved, taking trade through the heartland of Bhutan into Tibet and China (Barpujari 1996, 275).

Trade not only meant exchange of goods but also the transfer of ideas, knowledge, skills and tastes between peoples. Local narratives are rich with stories of people spending weeks on the move, negotiating treacherous mountain passes and tiger-infested jungle tracks to bring back luxury items such as gold, coral beads, pearls and expensive Chinese and Burmese silks, in lieu of lac, cotton, *muga* and *endi* threads, black pepper, honey and so on. Trade has also led to the emergence of a class of people who made their living by acting as intermediaries in intra- and trans-border trade. Some of the frontier tribes such as the Abors, Khampas Khamtis, Mishmis, Nishis and Singphos acted as middlemen between different groups of traders operating within and beyond the border (Ganguly 2000, 13). On the southern part, tribes like the Nagas and Lushais and the Meiteis of Manipur had direct trade relations with the people of Burma and neighbouring countries (Ganguly 2000, 13). On the other hand, the Khasis and Jaintias traded with Sylhet and, according to local stories, with China and Tibet. All in all, the network of trade that existed provided Assam and her people a natural outlet for their surplus and a source to draw from to compensate for the deficits. Trade also provided the people the platform to maintain relations with their neighbours within and across the frontier.

ROOTS OF UNDERDEVELOPMENT

The facts presented in the discussion strongly challenge the popular view that Assam and the northeast hills were isolated entities cut off from the outside world. The data also raise pertinent questions about the state of the economy and its underdeveloped condition in present times. The historical data we were privy to neither talked of poverty nor debt, the two basic ingredients in the underdevelopment recipe. On the contrary, frequent references were made in colonial writings to the contented state of the peasantry, their strong disinclination to wage labour and aspiration to be *bhala manus* or gentlemen (Hunter 1998, 48), farmers with a field and a plough of their own capable of fulfilling the requirements of the household. References were also made to the vast expanse of uncultivated land and rich mineral resources, waiting to be tapped (see in particular Allen et al. 2010, 79–80). These facts do not point to an economic State that was impoverished or incapable of meeting the needs of the people. If that were the case, what then accounts for the underdevelopment, or what some scholars term 'crisis of development' (Bhaumik 2009; Uberoi 2010), that plagues India's North East in present times? Clearly, the fault does not seem to lie at the door of the traditional economy. Hence to arrive at the root of the matter we need to turn the lens elsewhere, more appropriately to the forces of change that rocked the region in the nineteenth century.

The 'underdevelopment' of North East India cannot be disassociated from colonialism. The advent of the colonial rule with its thirst for power and revenue, and its ideology of improvement, were to put the traditional economy under serious threat. The small-scale subsistence-based economy, which was the hallmark of Assam and the hills, was antithetical to the British's idea of progress, for whom progress meant extracting the maximum from nature to maximize profit. Hence the vast expanse of uncultivated land in the province was seen as 'wastes', which needed to be put under crops or transformed into plantations to render them productive. That these perceived wastes had their own use critical for the survival of the people and their time-tested economic system was oblivious to the colonial administration. The discovery of tea in upper Assam in the 1830s and Britain's ambition to break the monopoly of China in the world tea market added urgency to Britain's quest for reforms in the province. The wasteland settlement policies that ensued and the opening up of Assam to foreign capital to promote the establishment of tea plantations led to drastic effects not only on the Assamese peasantry but also on tribes in the hills.[10] At the same time, the introduction of money economy and increase in taxation on lands (Barpujari 1996, 224–25) added to the burden of an already stressed agrarian population, that it induced many farmers to grow opium for cash at the cost of other crops (Guha 1991, 166). The economic stagnation that followed reduced Assam into a market for imported goods.[11]

The revenue-oriented and resource-intensive policies of the British set the tone for the underdevelopment of India's North East. There was no space for subsistence farming or small-scale manufacturing in its scheme of things. The ideology of improvement, with its inherent bias for profit, also worked against the interest of the peasantry and the artisans. There was also no space for the kinds of economics practised in the hills. The hill areas had little in the form of revenue to offer to the British. Though blessed with immense resources, the poor means of communication and difficult terrain acted as a constraint for the British to exploit them, let alone invest in them, leading to their utter neglect and isolation that were reinforced by the policy of non-interference and inner-line regulation.[12]

TRADITIONAL ECONOMY, RESILIENCE AND CHALLENGES IN CONTEMPORARY TIMES

Notwithstanding the odds ranged against it, the traditional economy has exhibited a tremendous capacity to survive. Not only in North East India but a large number of communities in South, East and Southeast Asia continue to rely on the traditional economy for their subsistence. Rooted in tradition and customary practices, the traditional economy has shown remarkable ability to withstand the forces of change. What added to the resilience of the traditional economy are its basic characteristics: small-scale operation geared to subsistence, use of simple technology that causes least disruption to the environment, lack of specialization which ensured the easy transfer of skills from one generation to the next without having to go in for specialized training of the kind that is mandatory in industrial production and cooperative and egalitarian ethos. These characteristics are at sharp variance with the ideology of improvement and its post-colonial successor, the State-centred development paradigm, and its compulsive obsession with economic (read material) growth and progress, at the cost of well-being of the people and stability of the environment. If the processes in the recent years are any indicator, the vulnerability of the traditional economy has increased manifold. This, however, is an issue that requires a separate paper altogether.

Suffice it to say, there is hardly any room for traditional economy in the model of development followed by states today. Notwithstanding the much-hyped concept of 'sustainable development' put forward in the report by the United Nation's World Commission on Environment and Development *Our Common Future* (UN WCED 1987) and the 'sustainable livelihoods approach' advanced by liberal-minded economists (see, in particular, Chambers and Conway 1992), the traditional economy remains a largely neglected sector. In the context of India's North East, this finds vivid reflection in the *North Eastern Region 2020 Vision* document (Government of India 2007), a roadmap for the development of the northeastern states, jointly crafted by the Ministry of Development of Northeastern Region and the North Eastern Council, a statutory body constituted under an Act of Parliament to coordinate development activities in the northeastern states. While the document comes up with an impressive list of strategies to usher 'peace, progress and prosperity' so that the region 'catches up with the rest of the country', the model of development envisaged continues to be suffused with the ideology of improvement unmindful of people's wisdom and time-tested practices. What is worrisome is in its bid to accelerate growth, the architects of the *Vision* document had little option to offer other than the much-critiqued approach of damming the rivers and mining the land to extract the hydrological and mineral wealth that abound in the region. Professing to know what the people want the document states, '[T]he people would like to see the large river systems converted into a source of prosperity. Mineral wealth can be used to create employment and increase income' (p. 17). Not to speak of the likely effect such a strategy can have on the environment, who benefits from it is anybody's guess.

What really takes the wind out of the traditional economy is the document's call for structural change in the economies of all states, which entails a double shift from *swidden* to settled agriculture and from the production of food crops to cash crops (Government of India 2007). How this will affect the livelihood of the poor time alone can tell. Settled cultivation and cash cropping may have their advantage, but in a scenario where large segments of the population depend on the produce of land for their sheer survival, such a shift can have disastrous effects. It is also pertinent to note that North East India is severely deficient in food with bulk of its requirements coming from imports, a fact clearly brought out by the Shukla Committee in its report *Transforming Backlogs in Basic Minimum Services and Infrastructural Need* (Planning Commission 1997). The *2020 Vision* document not only appears to miss out on this vital fact but also ignores the principles of self-sufficiency and self-reliance that underline the traditional economy.

NOTES

1. During the Ahom rule, several frontier chiefs received grants of *khats* as well as allotted *paik* land or fishing waters on the plains from the Ahom kings like ordinary Assamese nobility (Mackenzie 2001, 91).
2. On this, see Hunter 1998, Vol. I, 137, 200, 259; Vol. II, 196, 234–35. From the record, the only minerals in Assam worked upon on a commercial scale were coal, limestone and petroleum oil carried out by the British. The most extensive were in Lakhimpur and Sibsagar Districts. In 1903 there were five mines worked upon by the company under the supervision of nine Europeans. As no labour was available locally, the labour force had to be brought from outside (Allen et al. 2001, 79). Grants were also given to anyone willing to mine coal (personal communication, Ms Rani, coal mine owner, Sohra). In the Khasi Hills the British took a lease from the Cherra chief to mine the rich coal deposit in their land (Allen et al. 2001, 79, also Hunter 1998, 234–35). The other reported case of mining was limestone in southern Khasi Hills. Here too there was little involvement by the locals. Professor Syiemlieh opined that the Mughals were probably the first to have made use of the product, which was exploited by the British to make gains out of it (Syiemlieh 2004, 30). One of the earliest known exploiters of the product was Robert Lindsay, who was appointed Commissioner of Sylhet in 1778. To carry out trade, Lindsay made Pandua his base and made considerable fortune out of it (on the latter see Lindsay 1849, 176).
3. This is a long narrow piece of cotton cloth about 1.5 yards long and three-fourths of a yard wide with red borders and elaborate weaves on the fall. It can be used both as a towel and as a scarf.
4. Report for the Administration of the Province of Assam 1892–93, Reproduced in *Physical and Political Geography of the Province of Assam*, Shillong, 1896.
5. Sharma also questions the relevance of the oft-used word 'pre-colonial' in the context of the North East as there is no uniformity in the process of historical development in the region. For instance, while 1826 marks the end of the pre-colonial phase for Assam, most of the societies in the hills were still in the pre-colonial phase (Sharma 2004). In the absence of a more suitable equivalent, we are constrained to retain the term 'pre-colonial' in this chapter.
6. The report for the administration of the Province of Assam describes shifting cultivation as a 'barbarous system of agriculture', reproduced in *Physical and Political Geography of the Province of Assam* (Province of Assam 1896, 26).
7. Use of iron in the construction of houses was also considered as *sang* or taboo among the early Khasis. For more on this, see Syiemlieh (2004).
8. Shifting cultivation was not simply a livelihood strategy or a form of land use that evolved in certain ecological conditions, it was a way of life underlined by strong communitarian and egalitarian ethos. As a way of life, shifting cultivation was closely tied up with the socio-cultural life of the people. Practically

in all societies that practise shifting cultivation as a mode of livelihood, feasts, festivals, ceremonies and rituals revolved round the practice.
9. In this context Hunter wrote, '[A]lthough the soil is very fertile, yet owing to the paucity of population and the *excessively indolent habits of the people*, only sufficient grain is raised to meet the wants of the local population' (Hunter 1998, 369, italics added). Hunter also attributed the Assamese's reluctance to take up wage work to their indolence: '[T]he people are averse to working for daily wages, as they affirm that by doing so they will compromise their respectability. *The most probable cause, however, of this repugnance is their natural indolence*' (Hunter 1998, 366, italics added). It would be pertinent to note that while the so-called indolence of the Assamese peasantry was an expression of their freedom from wage labour, it also gave legitimacy to the British population policy of importing a large number of migrant labourers from Bengal to work on the wastelands of Assam to render them productive.
10. The encroachment of plantation space into the hills generated a series of conflicts with frontier tribes centring on rights over land, giving rise to frequent attacks on British outposts and raids on inhabitants in the plains (see in particular Mackenzie 2001, 97).
11. Colonialism also had a crippling effect on manufacturing. Except for weaving which was widely pervasive and had a wide market, most of the crafts struggled to survive. As many of the crafts were practised by a small number of people, with limited capital and technological know-how, their products could not compete with cheap industrial goods that flooded the market. Some of the activities that flourished in the pre-colonial and early colonial period fell into disuse altogether. Gold washing and iron smelting, popular in many districts in Assam and among the Khasis and Nagas, respectively, disappeared with the arrival of the British, putting iron- and gold-based crafts under serious threat. The decline in handicrafts not only entailed a loss of livelihood, it also meant the loss of indigenous knowledge. A chilling example of this can be seen in dyeing, an activity closely associated with weaving and the manufacture of cloth. According to Saikia, out of over three hundred known varieties of plants traditionally used in dyeing in Assam, the use of only three or four varieties has survived and less than 10 per cent of the people can identify local plants that have dyeing properties (Saikia 2000, 53).
12. The effect of the inner-line regulation on the hill tribes comes out sharply in Singh's study of the Lushais. See, in particular, pages 27–29 in Singh (1996).

REFERENCES

Allen, B. C. 1905. *Assam District Gazetteers*, Vol. X. New Delhi: Gian Publications.
Allen, B. C., E. A. Gait, C. G. H. Allen, and H. F. Howard. 2001. *Gazetteer of Bengal and North-East India*. Delhi: Mittal Publications.
———. 2010. *Gazetteer of Bengal and North-East India*. Delhi: Mittal Publications.

Barpujari, H. K. 1996. *Assam in the Days of the Company*. Shillong: North-Eastern Hill University.
Bhaumik, S. 2009. *Troubled Periphery, Crisis of India's North East*. Delhi: SAGE Publications.
Chambers, R., and G. R. Conway. 1992. *Sustainable Rural Livelihoods: Practical Concepts for the 21st Century*, Institute of Development Studies Discussion Papers, 296. Cambridge: Institute of Development Studies.
Christanty, L. 1986. 'Shifting Cultivation and Tropical Soils: Patterns, Problems and Possible Improvements: A Human Ecology Perspective'. In *Traditional Agriculture in Southeast Asia*, edited by Gerald G. Marten, 132–58. Boulder/London: Westview Press.
Dove, M. R. 1985. 'The Agroecological Mythology of the Javanese and the Political Economy of Indonesia', *Indonesia* 39: 1–36. Cornell Southeast Asia Programme.
Durkheim, E. 1933 [1893]. *The Division of Labour in Society*, translated by G. Simpson. New York: Macmillan.
———. 1938 [1895]. *The Rules of Sociological Method*, translated from the French Edition by Sarah A. Soloway and John H. Mueller and edited by George E. G. Catlin. New York: The Free Press.
Erni, C. (ed.). 2015. *Shifting Cultivation, Livelihood and Food Security: New and Old Challenges for Indigenous Peoples in Asia*. Bangkok: FAO/UN, IWGIA & AIPP.
Food and Agricultural Organisation. 1968. *Yearbook of Forest Products 1967*. Rome: Food and Agricultural Organisation of the United Nations.
Gait, E. 2010. *A History of Assam*, Fifth Indian Reprint. New Delhi: Surjeet Publications.
Ganguly, J. B. 2000. 'The Border Trade in North-East India, the Historical Perspective'. In *Border trade, North-East India and Neighbouring Countries*, edited by Das Gurudas and R. K. Purkayastha, 12–19. Delhi: Akansha Publishing House.
Government of India. 1882. *Assam Administrative Report*. Government of India.
———. 2007. *Peace, Progress and Prosperity in the North Eastern Region Vision 2020*.
Guha, A. 1991. *Medieval and Early Colonial Assam, Society, Polity, Economy*. Calcutta and New Delhi: K.P. Bagchi & Co.
Gurdon, P. R. T. 1975 [1907]. *The Khasis*. Delhi: Cosmo Publications.
Hunter, W. W. 1998 [1879]. *A Statistical Account of Assam*, Vol. 1 and 2, Indian Reprint. Guwahati and New Delhi: Spectrum Publications.
Jamir, A. 2015. 'Shifting Options, a Case Study of Shifting Cultivation in Mokokchung District in Nagaland, India'. In *Shifting Cultivation, Livelihood and Food Security: New and Old Challenges for Indigenous Peoples in Asia*, edited by Christian Erni, 159–202. Bangkok: FAO/UN, IWGIA & AIPP.
Jeeva, S. R. D. N., R. C. Laloo, and B. P. Mishra. 2006. 'Traditional Agricultural Practices in Meghalaya'. *Indian Journal of Traditional Knowledge* 5(1): 7–18.
Lindsay, L. 1849. *Lives of the Lindsays: A Memoir of the Houses of Crawford and Balcarres*, Vol. III. London: John Murray, Albemarle Street.

Mackenzie, A. 2001. *The North East Frontier of India*. Delhi: Mittal Publications. (Reproduced from 1884 edition titled *History of the Relations of the Government with the Hill Tribes of the Northeast Frontier of Bengal*)

Mills, A. J. M. (undated). *Report on the Khasi and Jaintia Hills, 1853*. Shillong: North-Eastern Hill University.

———. 1980. *Report on Assam*. Delhi: Gian Publications.

Mills, J. P. 1973 [1926]. *The Ao Nagas*. Bombay: Oxford University Press.

Parsons, T. 1951. *The Social System*. Delhi: Amerind Publishing Co. Ltd.

Planning Commission. 1997. *Transforming Backlogs in Basic Minimum Services and Infrastructural Need*. New Delhi: Planning Commission, GOI.

Province of Assam. 1896. *Physical and Political Geography of the Province of Assam*. Shillong: Assam Secretariat Printing Office.

Radcliffe-Brown, A. R. 1952. *Structure and Function in Primitive Society, Essays and Addresses*. Glencoe, IL: The Free Press.

Ramakrishnan, P. S. 2001. *Ecology and Sustainable Development*. Delhi: National Book Trust of India.

Saikia, R. 2000. *Social and Economic History of Assam, 1853–1921*. Delhi: Manohar.

Sharma, M. 2004. 'Socio-economic History in Pre-colonial North-East India'. In *Society and Economy in North-East India*, edited by M. Momin and C. A. Mawlong, 1–20. New Delhi: Regency Publications.

Singh, D. 1996. *The Last Frontier, People and Forest in Mizoram*. New Delhi: Tata Energy Research Institute.

Syiemlieh, D. R. 2004. 'Technology and Socio-economic Linkages among the Khasi-Jaintias in Pre-colonial Times'. In *Society and Economy in North-East India*, edited by M. Momin and C. A. Mawlong, Vol. 1, 21–34. New Delhi: Regency Publications.

Uberoi, P. 2010. 'Development Issues in India's North East'. Paper for India-China Cooperation Forum, Kunming.

UN WCED. 1987. *Our Common Future*. Oxford: Oxford University Press.

Chapter 2

The Post-colonial Market
India's North East*

Samir Kumar Das

> *I see economics as a subdiscipline of the social sciences, alongside history, sociology, anthropology, and political science.*
>
> —Piketty (2014, 583)

The existing literature on the economic history of the market in India's North East seems to have been oscillating between the twin extremes

---

* I thank Bhagat Oinam, Anjan Chakrabarty, Rakhee Bhattacharya, Vijayalakshmi Brara and H. Srikanth for bringing a number of readings to my attention and also making them available to me. Two earlier versions of this chapter with the titles 'The Social in the Agricultural Societies: Ethnographies on the Institutional Crisis in India' and 'Market and Social Movements in India's East and the Northeast' were presented at the international seminar on 'Agriculture and Human Development in India: Indigenous Practices, Scientific Views and Sustainability' organized by the Regional Centre of Guwahati, Indira Gandhi National Open University, and Indian Institute of Technology Guwahati in Guwahati on 8 and 9 September 2017 and at the seminar on 'Social Movements: Micro and Macro Dimensions' organized by the Department of Political Science under the UGC DRS (Phase III) Programme, University of North Bengal, on 20 March 2018, respectively. I gratefully acknowledge my indebtedness to Sujata Dutta Hazarika, Dyutis Chakrabarty and Soumitra De for inviting me and offering their comments on the chapter. Lapses, if any, are entirely mine.

of the albeit regrettably halting and interrupted progress of market forces—the market being regarded as the prerequisite of economic development—and the 'lived spaces of the communities' facing 'the threat of extinction' in India's North East thanks to the relentless development of market forces accelerated in recent times with the advent of the forces and processes of globalization. On the one hand, Ganguly, for instance, argues that the introduction of the colonial rule in then undivided Assam marked 'a revolutionary transition' in terms of its development of agriculture and industry or the rule of law and political stability or in the extraction and utilization of forest resources. The rule, according to him, suffered from 'many structural constraints that eventually slowed down and at times effectively impeded the growth of market forces in the region' (Ganguly 2006, 100). On the other hand, the development of market forces is believed to have resulted in what Chakraborty calls 'somatic detachment' of the market from the 'lived spaces' of the communities (Chakraborty 2018, 82). The market and societies of the region—organized predominantly as the latter are in accordance with the community principle—take on two parallel trajectories with consequences that only turn out to be adverse for these societies. 'Collective right', observe Mishra and Upadhyay, while introducing a collection of recently published essays on the economies of the North East, 'need to be protected both from the onslaughts of capital and from local elites' (Mishra and Upadhyay 2017, 15). Social movements are viewed basically as an antithesis of the market or to be more apt its excesses. However, it is true that a great many social movements in contemporary India or even outside (the World Social Forum being just an instance) are directed against the excesses the market commits in its newly found globalizing zeal—whether in terms of destruction of the environment and its critical and life-bearing resources or in terms of market asymmetries and colonial extraction endemic in it or even otherwise—and thus takes a toll on human lives and livelihood. Farmers' suicides and land acquisition are just two among many such instances in our country.

In a sense the above two arguments are only reflective of two divergent perspectives on the ongoing development debate hitting as it were an irresolvable stalemate particularly in recent years. While the former calls for doing away with the 'constraints' that stand in the way of the unfettered development of market forces, the latter envisages a development scenario for the region that accords due recognition to the regime of 'collective rights' of the tribal[1] and ethnic communities through an elaborate paraphernalia of institutions, laws and regulations. The unrestrained and unregulated penetration of market forces is believed to spell a sure disaster for the societies of the North East in the near future.

This chapter inspired as it is by the forceful comment of Piketty cited in the epigraph argues that the relation of the market to the societies and communities of the region is, to say the least, much more complex than what is commonly understood by both these streams of scholars and commentators, and the complexities involved in their relationship need to be unpacked in a much more subtle and nuanced way. While the unbridled development of markets in different parts of the North East and their integration into the global political economy are widely regarded in official circles as the recipe for revitalizing the economies of the region, the post-colonial, as we argue in this chapter, keeps the societies of the region from being completely 'colonized' by the market mantra and thus being converted into unabashed market societies. The prefix 'post-colonial' is deployed here in order to understand the complex nature of the development of markets in India's North East.

In this chapter, I propose to unpack the complexities involved in the penetration of market forces and concentrate on at least three moments in this unpacking exercise. I define 'moment' more in the Hegelian sense of a specific combination of forces than as a determinate chronological stage in the evolution of the market in the North East as is commonly understood by the economic historians. First, we may refer to the moment of 'market society'. In a region like the North East, it is marked by the mediation of the State[2] and consequently a surge of policies undertaken both by itself and other non-State actors—commonly known as 'Look East' or 'Act East' in their combination—that are aimed at converting India's North East into a vast and gigantic market firmly integrated into the global one. The second moment marks the arrival of an ethnically configured market manifested through such ethnic practices as laying the monopoly claim to the newly emerging market, thereby often violently repudiating the claims of others or boycotting the goods and services produced and marketed by others. The third is what may—borrowing from E. P. Thompson and others—be called the moment of 'moral economy' for it is characterized by the overpowering sense that those who are resorting to the ethnic and community practices do so in the spirit of 'defending the traditional rights and customs' of their community in times of crisis. Often as we will see later the community spirit is imbibed and invoked as a means of countering market collapse, failures or shutdowns.

TOWARDS A MARKET SOCIETY

The moment of market society is marked by the introduction of a wide combination of policies meant evidently for the insertion of the region's societies into the evolving global market economy. Never before has the region been subjected to such intense policy experimentation as it is now. Certainly this trend towards governing the region through the unleashing of market forces has been facilitated by a heavy dose of such neoliberal policies as have been announced since the early 1990s through such packages as 'Look East' and its new avatar 'Act East', 'North East: Vision 2020' (2005), 'Industrial and Investment Policy of the North East, 2007', and so on. Also important are the policies and policy resolutions such as the 'Industrial and Investment Policy of Manipur 2013', the 'Industrial and Investment Policy of Assam 2014' and 'Nagaland Vision 2030' and so forth that are adopted by the respective states of the region to complement them. Besides these policies, policy advocacy papers such as 'PWC Report commissioned by FICCI North East Advisory Regional Council, 2013', *North East Region-Initiatives (NER-I)* (2016) and *Emerging North-East India: Economically and Socially Inclusive Strategies* (2015) prepared by investment banks, economists and consultants, think tanks and eminent individuals alike are of utmost importance.

Neoliberal market reforms in the region, first of all, are geared to the task of tapping the region's natural resources hitherto used and maintained as commons and subjecting them to the rule of private property and market forces. The 'Industrial and Investment Policy of Manipur' (2013), for instance, promises to provide an investor-friendly environment, extend institutional support, facilitate credit flow from banks and financial institutions and offer attractive incentive packages for optimum utilization of the state's existing resources. Such an investor-friendly environment can be created only by way of providing easy access to industrial infrastructure and developing market linkages, by utilizing locally available raw materials and drawing on the intellectual support from local universities and technological institutions. The most aggressive advocacy in this direction has been made by the FICCI-KPMG report that calls for reinstating the suspended provisions of 30 per cent capital investment subsidy, income tax exemption, excise duty refund and interest subsidy as a means of ensuring the 'ease of doing business' (FICCI-KPMG 2015, 27). The same document also pleads for a change in the existing land policies and calls for ease in land acquisition. It is argued that 'enabling conditions' must be created so that the region's economy becomes competitive and can engage with the global economy. This first of all requires 'protection of people's property rights'. While development and economic progress are left to private sector initiatives, such initiatives can thrive only when the inalienability of property rights is established and guaranteed. Insurgency and violence are considered by it as a direct threat to the safe and secure enjoyment of such rights. The headway that tourism in Sikkim could make in recent years is 'due to the lack of any insurgency in the State' (MDoNER 2005, 165). The whole idea is to trump insurgency and violence by rapid economic development that can make good the lost time and help resolve the crisis. Most importantly, the 'demand and supply networks' are expected to develop 'across the border', that is to say, on a trans-border scale, eventually paving the way for integration of the region's economy with the global market economy (Mishra and Upadhyay 2017, 8).

Second, policy reforms are keyed to the objective of reducing dependence on agriculture and shifting the economic fulcrum away to micro-, small and medium-sized (MSM) industries. One must remember that the large industries of the region continue to be agro-based industries. Significantly, 'the Industrial and Investment Policy of Manipur 2013' points out that the new thrust towards MSM is issued from the urge of 'preserving tradition and heritage of Manipur'.

Third, new policy reforms emphasize on the necessity of exposing the North East to the 'powerhouse' economies of the Southeast and wherever possible East Asia and to derive the benefits of such exposure. Although what is called the 'Look East Policy' dates back to the early 1990s, India's North East started figuring in it only since 2008. In simple terms, the realization that the region's development is integrally connected to the prospects of our Look East Policy came much later. Why did it take so long for policymakers to realize the region's importance in Look East Policy? Sood provides the answer:

> The Indian government's hesitation to project the North East in its Look East Policy can be traced to five factors. First, an overstress on security/strategic considerations, rather than a development perspective in development efforts was all along one of the dominant paradigms of the Indian government in dealing with the North East in the post-Independence period. Second, prolonged and uninterrupted militancy led by groups such as the National Socialist Council of Nagaland, United Liberation Front of Assam, People's Liberation Army and the National Democratic Front of Bodoland weighs heavily in rebuilding the Stilwell road across the thick hills and mountains of Myanmar. This could turn out to be a haven for numerous militant groups of the North East and thus involve high security risk. Third, the aggressive economic expansion of China to Southeast Asian countries such as Myanmar is perhaps a threat in terms of flooding of the Indian market with cheap Chinese goods. Fourth, it was also apprehended that the road could facilitate import of vices such as drugs and AIDS/HIVs. Finally, mainland India's trade with the Southeast Asian countries has traditionally been by sea. Even now it is cheaper and easier to trade with these countries by sea rather than by land. (Sood 2017, 41)

All this, it must be noted, was complemented by the overwhelming sway of what came to be known as the 'culturalist paradigm' in India's policy thinking towards the North East, according to which the region—the tribal-inhabited areas in particular—was sought to be kept from the destructive influences of development taking place in the so-called Indian 'mainland'. The isolation of tribes was regarded as a guarantee against any possible 'destruction of their traditional way of life' that might occur thanks to the whirlwind of development.

Verrier Elwin, the main architect of this policy, sums it up in the following terms:

> [The] policy may be summarized as one which approaches the historical development of tribal life and culture with respect and the people themselves in a spirit of affection and identification that eliminates any possibility of superiority. It would not ignore the past, but would build upon it. It would bring the best things of the modern world to the tribes, but in such a way that they will not destroy the traditional way of life, but will activate and develop all that is good in it. (Elwin 1989, 241)

The anxiety that fast and rapid development might turn out to be dangerous to the simple, homogeneous and closely knit tribal societies was too deep-seated to be removed from the minds of policymakers. As Elwin warned:

> When a man breaks a long fast, he is not immediately given a full meal, he takes a sip of orange-juice. Otherwise he may fall seriously ill. To learn from history, to follow the universally accepted principles of sociological science, to dig firm foundations is not to delay progress, it ensures that real progress will be made. (Elwin 1989, 235)

Extending the same analogy, one may say that the Look East Policy was offered as it were as a 'full meal' to the region for the first time without however initiating at the same time any major change in the hitherto existing isolationist policy regime. The internal reforms that such a policy necessitated were never carried out, let alone to their logical end.[3] The Look/Act East Policy is predicated on the assumption that the development in the North East is integrally connected with the development of the neighbouring sub-region lying in the critical cusp, spanning between South and Southeast Asia. Haokip describes this development imperative as one of the 'cooperative endeavours' and 'sovereignty bargains that India must engage' (Haokip 2015, 151). While centuries-old historical and spatial continuities are invoked in order to find out a market in these countries for goods and services produced in India, the resultant economic prosperity is expected to generate employment and wean the youth away from the 'insurgency industry'—the only booming industry in the North East. The overall economic prosperity of the region is likely to prevent the neighbouring countries from dumping their 'excess' population on India. In simple terms, it envisages a critical turnaround only by putting the region's economy on a fast track. The idea is to tap the resources of the region in a way that these can be marketed by way of improving connectivity and logistics and ensuring institutional reforms particularly with the twin objective of opening the region to the 'powerhouse' economies of Southeast Asia and securing the institution of private property in the otherwise troubled region of the North East. While marketization of resources is expected to make the economies of the region competitive, so long as prices are determined in the global market, poor and backward hill states of the region have 'no role to play in determining them' (Chakraborty 2010, 5).

In sum, societies of the North East are called upon to adjust to the laws of the market and orient them accordingly if the region were to benefit from the forces and processes of globalization and not the other way round. This is what Polanyi calls the 'market society', which he vociferously critiques and dismisses as an aporia in his magnum opus *The Great Transformation*:

> ...[T]he control of the economic system by the market is of overwhelming consequence to the whole organization of society: it means no less than the running of society as an adjunct to the market. Instead of economy being embedded in social relations, social relations are embedded in the economic system. The vital importance of the economic factor to the existence of society precludes any other result. For once the economic system is organized in separate institutions, based on specific motives and conferring a special status, society must be shaped in such a manner as to allow that system to function according to its own laws. This is the meaning of the familiar assertion that a market economy can function only in a market society. (Polanyi 1957, 57)

The market would not lose much, according to policymakers and advocates, if it cannot make any headway in the societies of the North East. Development will give the North East a miss if the societies of the region are unable to keep pace with the rapid growth of market forces. Most of the documents mentioned above keep the market on a high pedestal where it will not be affected by the slow-moving societies of the region. Today the market—and not the State—has occupied the 'commanding heights' of the economy. As Bhattacharya observes:

> India and [the] countries that share borders with the Northeast region constitute a market of about 2.81 billion people which is roughly 40 percent of the world population. Thus the role of market and trade can emerge as a strong force to transform India's Northeast. (Bhattacharya 2018, 56)

I see these policies and advocacies as a plea for the complete marketization that threatens to turn the entire North East into a market.[4] Thus, an author recently has argued that 'it is in [North East's] interest to extend all possible support to these initiatives' (Yhome 2015, 27). It is important that the North East appreciates the importance of market forces sooner. The states of the region must take all necessary steps in order to be able to reap the benefits that are expected to flow once these policies are fully implemented.

In other words, a body of people is expected to come into existence on the basis of their unwavering belief in the infinite possibilities of market development of this kind. By being rendered eligible for being part of a developing market society, thanks to these policy reforms and advocacies, the people turn into mere objects of the market. I argue that it is not the people as a body who initiate the market, it is the neoliberal market that frames them as its objects and inserts them into its own global scheme of things (Das 2015b, 2). The people are meant for the market, not the market for the people.

AN ETHNICALLY CONFIGURED MARKET

The evolution of the market in the North East—howsoever perfect it seeks to become—cannot effectively disembed itself from the larger society. In other words, while the market is supposed to be perfectly competitive particularly in our era of globalism, there is reason to believe that the market in many parts of the North East is socially and ethnically configured. Sen doubts if there is ever any market in history that exists in its complete abstraction from the larger society.

In his extremely insightful paper, he describes the relationship between 'economic' and 'non-economic elements' in the constitution of the market as 'dense' (Sen 1989, 24). In other words, there is what I called an 'ethnic dimension' to the development of market forces (Das 2005, 65–69). A community's claim to autonomy is often expressed through some form of control over non-replenishable and life-bearing resources (such as timber, oil, coal, uranium, water and agricultural land, etc.) that are located within a particular territorial space that it perceives as its 'homeland'. At one level, it is expressed through a community's desire of immediately ending the extraction of resources by the outside forces for the market. Insurgent groups of the region term this extraction 'colonial' and view the Indian State as 'an outside agency'.

Ethnic Monopoly

Even student organizations such as the All-Assam Students' Union (AASU) and Khasi Students' Union (KSU) are vehemently opposed to the flow of crude oil from Assam's oilfields and felling of trees in the rainforests of Meghalaya, respectively. KSU took a similar stand in their opposition to the planned uranium mining in Domiasiat in West Khasi Hills. Paul Lyngdoh the former KSU President for example observed in a BBC interview: 'our people cannot suffer because India wants *our* uranium'.[5]

Examples of this kind are certainly not rare. The United Liberation Front of Assam (ULFA)— the largest insurgent organization operating in Assam since it was born in 1979[6] —expressly asked the Oil and Natural Gas Commission (ONGC) in March 1996 to 'undo the environmental disaster' it had caused to 'Sibsagar (sic) and Jorhat Districts' in upper Assam. In the same statement, it issued a warning to the game hunters in Pabitora Reserve Forest against poaching white-winged wood ducks—a rare and near-extinct bird species in the world. Back in 1996, it observed: 'Assam's natural resources are being ruthlessly exploited to serve the interests of outside capitalists'. In March 2003, ULFA claimed responsibility for having organized the serial blasts that struck the Digboi oil refinery's main storage tank and the gas pipeline in Dibrugarh and justified it as an act of protest against 'economic exploitation ... since the days of (British) Raj'. Similarly in October in the same year, ULFA, for example, urged the tea majors set up in Assam to share the profits accrued from the region with its people.

While insurgent groups of the region criticize extraction by outside forces including the Indian State for selling the resources in the open market on the ground that the latter is an outside agency, they are not opposed to the idea of extraction as such if it is carried out by the insiders. A youth organization like the Jaintia Unemployed Youth Labourers Union (JUYLU) in the Jaintia Hills of Meghalaya demanded preference for Jaintia youth in coal extraction over others and *bandhs* (strikes) were organized in collieries on such a demand.[7] Elsewhere, we called it *ethno-ecologism*, a syndrome that tends to subordinate ecological concerns to an ethnic community's abiding quest for exercising control over its resources in a bid to exclude others (Das 1997, 21–35).

Ethnic Exclusion

That market is enmeshed in the society within which it functions and vice versa is nowhere more eloquently seen than in the history of Manipur. Indeed, the *keithels* (markets) of Manipur have a long history. Khwairamband bazaar—popularly called *sanakeithel* (*sana* in *Meitei* means 'golden')—is situated at the heart of the city Imphal. It is considered 'the largest shopping centre of Asia being exclusively run by women' (Asem 2011, 73). Asem's reasonably large survey on women vendors and shopkeepers of the market—perhaps the only of its kind conducted on the *keithels* so far—points to the socially enmeshed nature of these markets. For one thing, the division between the household and non-household labour of women, for all practical purposes, is blurred with a lot of complicated relationships developed between them, with the effect that women try to ensure that they do not compromise on their household responsibilities while taking part in market activities. Thus to cite an instance, while traditional institutions of financial support have by all accounts effectively disappeared in the state, women still prefer to depend on informal sources of financial support mostly from within the family or even the extended family that is 'engaged in the occupation for generations' to modern banking institutions for 'continuation or expansion' of their economic activities (Asem 2011, 102). According to Brara, there is a strong ethic prevailing in Manipur in favour of 'Manipuri women' earning for their family and 'one who is not economically productive is considered as lazy' (Brara 2017, 75). For another, their 'urge and commitment to participation in organizations for collective action' is stronger than the women who are not involved in the market as shopkeepers. They look upon 'the [social and political] organisations as ones providing them power to independently articulate and work for social cause' (Asem 2011, 135). The 'power' they wield through their involvement in a variety of such organizations (like *Meira Paibis* or women torchbearers and vigilante groups campaigning against alcoholism, substance abuse and army atrocities, etc.) helps them keep free from 'police hassles' but in articulating their 'political' demands (Brara 2017, 75). *Keithels* also constitute sites for seeking justice both within the market and without. For one thing, in the all-women market, disputes are settled not by men but by the transgendered people. For another, they played an important role during the *Nupi Lans* of the last century—the rebellions in which the women pinched by food shortage and prolonged hunger stormed the stockyards and granaries and forcibly wrested away crops and distributed them among themselves (Indramoni 2017).

If market forces are seen to take on an ethnic character thanks to the control sought to be exercised by any particular community over the market, such a character is further reinforced when a community decides to boycott the goods and services produced or distributed by others. Thus, to cite an instance, the first phase of a boycott of 'India-made' goods in Manipur began in 2004, although boycott was never very strong and effective in the subsequent phases as it was in its first phase. *Apunba Lup*—the conglomerate of 32 civil society organizations—spearheaded a stir demanding the repeal of the Armed Forces Special Powers Act (AFSPA) (1958) in Manipur. It gave a call to the Manipuris (the valley-based *Meiteis*) to boycott coke and packaged aerated water in the first phase. According to reports, the agitators demanding withdrawal of the AFSPA blocked roads at Tera, Kwakeithel, Imphal West District, Wangkhei in Imphal East District and Bishenpur. By that time, the state government had already withdrawn AFSPA from seven assembly segments in the Imphal municipal area on a trial basis. The move, however, did not satisfy the protestors.[8]

In its second phase, a section of militants imposed a prohibition on school uniforms stitched in Western or Indian styles such as denims for girls, T-shirts and salwar-kameezes, while articulating their resistance to the AFSPA. On 6 January 2005, the Meitei-insurgent *Kanglei Yawol Kanna Lup* (KYKL), a militant outfit fighting for an independent homeland for the majority Meitei community in Manipur, asked heads of educational institutions in the state to impose the *eeyongphi phanek* (the traditional Meitei dress) as the uniform for girl students of classes IX and X from the academic session in 2006. The diktat that came after a similar edict in September 2004 failed to elicit the desired response from teachers, students and their parents. KYKL's 'Operation New Kangleipak' (*Kangleipak* is Manipur's historical name) mainly targeted the state's education system, which the group believes is riddled with corruption. Violators of the organization's 'moral code' have been punished across an expanding area of influence of the organization. In a statement issued by KYKL on 6 January 2005 it made references to the integral nature of Manipur's cultural values and the restoration of the independence and dignity of Manipuri society, declaring:

> [F]or a society struggling to maintain its identity and achieve self-determination, it was essential to lay the foundations for a self-sufficient economy. The imposition of the phanek as school and college uniforms was a tiny step in this direction. It would provide better employment and income for the state's handloom weavers. (quoted in Routray 2005)

There have also been instances where student organizations in the state, such as The All Manipur Students' Union (AMSU), have come out openly in support of the group's initiatives for 'cleansing' the educational system. In the words of Kharsyntiew (2017, 129), this implies an 'identity-based challenge between the region and the [Indian] mainstream':

> Years of restriction imposed on Northeastern peoples' lives have prompted the youth of the region to open up to alternative channels of

protest that are non-violent, yet effective, for they operate despite the militants' diktat and against the Indian state. (Kharsyntiew 2017, 128)

On 6 August 2017, Thongam Biswajit Singh—Textile, Commerce and Industry Minister of Manipur—made it clear that handloom products of the state would be mandatory as school uniforms as well as for the employees of the government departments. He also pointed out that free education would start soon as most women weavers in the state are illiterate. Entrepreneurs, as he claimed, are ready to invest in the handloom sector in the state, and the government, according to him, is also weighing the feasibility of signing memorandums of understanding with some of the investors with the aim of improving the state economy. Explaining the rationale for the selection of beneficiaries for the Pradhan Mantri (Prime Minister's) Employment Generation Programme, the minister also announced that projects under the scheme will be granted to clusters instead of individual weavers. This, according to him, will help in promoting handlooms in the state.

THE MORAL ECONOMY

What is commonly known as 'the mode of production debate' in Indian agriculture revolves around the question of intrusion of market forces in agriculture and the impediments agricultural societies face in their evolution into a fully contractual society in the countryside. A contract society is usually regarded as the site where market forces are supposed to be nested. In this chapter, I rather propose to shift the focus away by arguing that the evolution of a contract society in the countryside historically depends, not so much on its capacity of destroying the pre-existing society and its forces but, on the capacity of the society at large to bring the contractual society into existence in the first place and organize itself in a way that can absorb the shocks and vicissitudes, the failures and collapse, interruptions and shutdowns of a fully contractual society in general and of markets in particular. The way society responds to and copes with them without letting them destroy it is described eloquently by Karl Polanyi as the 'counter-movement' for it is called upon to operate against the unbridled movement of market forces.

We therefore need to unearth not the history of the evolution of contract society but the history of the society that makes possible not only such an endless series of contracts and market exchanges to take place and be executed in the society but absorbing and withstanding their collapse, failures and shutdowns. Is it the continuing series of contracts that holds the society together or the society that makes it possible for the otherwise conflicting parties to arrive at a compromise through the instrumentality of contracts? The society, in other words, is prior to the contract and we seek to trace the history of the society that per se is not a contract society but that may facilitate the formation of a contract society. This is the reason why Polanyi's argument that market society cannot come into being without the mediation of the society and the political institutions is being 'resurrected' in the twenty-first century—a time when the neoliberal thrust towards complete marketization is more deeply felt across the world. With the 'retreat' of the State in our era of globalism, social networks and relationships seem to play a crucial role in sustaining the market forms. As Bugra, one of Polanyi's more contemporary critics, observes:

> In the contemporary context, where political power becomes 'diffused' and 'de-centered', where new forms of 'governance' render the boundaries of the realm of redistribution fluid, it is probably not very surprising to see that forms of resistance to the market themselves become less focused as to whom they address their complaints and demands. One outcome of this situation is the localization of political engagement, which comes to concentrate on problems of immediate concern to the daily life of the local community and its improvement. Along with community engagement to improve the provisioning of public services, we also witness the increasing importance of certain networks that challenge the market system through the values and alternative lifestyles that characterize their daily existence. (Bugra 2007, 184)

In simple terms, the recent drive towards rapid marketization turns our attention away from these varieties of networks that have the potential of acting as safety valves against the dangers of abstracting the market from the larger social forces (Hann and Hart 2009, 1–16). In India, the *samaj* (or society), as the recent historical-anthropological writings point out, was kept at a distance from the State with the effect that it was possible for it to retain some amount of autonomy and independence from the State. The decisions that affect the society were taken by the society itself. The isolation of the social from the political enabled the former to survive the incredibly whirlwind changes in political regimes in the regional or central capital (Rudolph 1987, 731–46). It is only with the advent of the modern State that this autonomy came under attack, resulting in the growing politicization of the society. The social is not the contractual—it is what can survive the highs and lows, ebb and flow of market forces and the market society that it entails.

Life in Darjeeling Hills came to a grinding halt for about 104 days reportedly with the complete shutdown of its markets in 2017. The shutdown was part of the movement—the third in recent years since the early 1980s—for a separate Gorkhaland, consisting of Darjeeling Hills and parts of North Bengal that secured a new lease of life as the Government of West Bengal considered the proposal for making 'Bengali' mandatory as the third language (besides the mother tongue and English) at the school level across the state. How did people survive for such a long period when the strike, by all accounts, was successful, I wonder? While food is mostly perishable and no amount of stocking could help them survive for such a long period, there might be few in the hills who had the means of stocking up provisions. I have not come across any work on this till now excepting some sporadic newspaper reports. It certainly calls for some serious ethnographic work in future. The prolonged market shutdown seemed to have elicited basically two kinds of responses or a combination of them. The first—and indeed the much talked about response—was that the shutdown led to an anarchy of sorts in which there was 'a war of all against all', in the sense that the unscrupulous traders and businessmen made their fortunes by way of clandestinely stocking up and selling their commodities at a premium price which only the few and very rich could afford to buy. There were stories of striking leaders swooping on the trucks ferrying public distribution materials, looting them before they could reach those who might have been in acute need of them. During the day, pro-Gorkhaland picketers would restrict travel in the hills, while in the plains, the Bengal police reportedly would check vehicles and disallow those carrying food to the hills. Many pro-Gorkhaland leaders accused the West Bengal government of blocking the supply of essentials to the hills in a bid to starve them to death.

The second response was that people would secretly buy the necessary commodities whether from across the adjoining areas of Sikkim or even from Siliguri at night, hiring vehicles from the hills at exorbitantly high fares. The vehicle owners would thus make money by unfairly hiking the fare. Most common people also depend on the army canteens of Sukna and Jalapahar, and these canteens had reportedly been generous towards needy villagers who were visibly in distress. Little ethnographic work has so far been conducted on how people could thrive on limited rations, how people helped each other on the basis of trust and neighbourliness accumulated over the decades instead of fighting among themselves and how they would distribute the vegetables grown in the backyard of their huts in a gesture of goodwill towards the members of their community. The Gorkhaland strike also brought about changes in the mode of living by way of threatening to throw particularly the poor and the marginalized sections of the people back into the era of hunters and gatherers. As Dutta reports: 'With food shortages in the hills becoming severe with every passing day, many people, especially in the far-flung villages, are forced to make long treks to forage for bamboo shoots and ferns in the forest' (Dutta 2017). Sometimes, social service organizations chipped in and distributed cauliflowers and other vegetables collected from the Manebhanjan side to the city dwellers. Dutta also reports: 'While there are reports of opportunists selling foodstuff at exorbitant prices, there are also instances of social and political organisations distributing rations for free' (Dutta 2017). Another report, for example, points out how subscriptions are raised from the rich, essential items are purchased with the money thus collected and then redistributed among the most needy in the society. Arbin Subba's is a first-hand account:

> With likeminded friends, I have formed a loose group called the Darjeeling Initiative (DI). We are distributing free rations in the villages … Pooling their own money with donations from the well-off, Subba and his friends are buying food stocks from the plains, where they have contacts, and distributing packets containing 10 kg rice, 500 gm lentils

and edible oil in hill villages.... Since July 5, we have reached 224 households covering 14 villages in Okayti, Durpin and Thulung Gaon in Mirik subdivision. Today, we reached out to at least 100 households in Nagri. (Anonymous 2017, 1)

E. P. Thompson argues that people's responses and practices in times of acute crises such as market failures, shutdowns and complete collapse are informed by what he describes as 'the belief that they were defending traditional rights or customs; and, in general, that they were supported by the wider consensus of the community' (Thompson 1971, 78). Such practices of mutual help, as underlined earlier, would certainly go a long way in riveting the bonds of unity at a time when the disappearance of the market threatens to sweep away the community by way of indulging in looting and plunder, setting one off against another and unleashing the war of all against all for sheer survival. In a sense, defending community rights acquires unprecedented importance when it becomes synonymous with the survival of one, one's family, one's kith and kin, neighbours, villagers and so forth. As James Scott observes:

> Patterns of reciprocity, forced generosity, communal land and work sharing help[ed] to even out the inevitable trough in family's resources, which might otherwise have thrown them below subsistence. The proven value of these techniques and social patterns, is perhaps what has given the peasants [of Southeast Asia] a Brechtian tenacity in the face of agronomists, and social workers who come from ... [outside] to help them. (Scott 1976, 3)

Darjeeling also seems to have shown the 'tenacity' for more than 100 days and not a single hunger death was reported during this period.

CONCLUDING OBSERVATIONS

Bayly's magisterial work on the history of bazaars in India shows how markets evolved in late-Mughal and early colonial India in response to the 'events and interests of the non-European world', and the regional specificities that became prominent with the decline of the central Mughal Empire made their mark in the articulation of market

(Bayly 1983, 2). Significantly Bayly prefers to retain the non-English word 'bazaar' in order to highlight its socially and regionally embedded character. While the creation of a market society modelled on abstract market principles—as we have argued earlier—is an aporia, one must acknowledge that it is indeed a powerful aporia that continues to drive policymakers and advocates alike working on the region. The market, as Applbaum summed up when preparing his state-of-the-art survey on the economic anthropology of the market, is not 'a universal truth'. To borrow his words of course used in the more general context, its persisting hegemony on the architects of the Look/Act East Policy speaks of its influence as 'a specific cultural theory or ideology' (Applbaum 2005, 284).

As we keep unpacking the abstract market, we come to realize that its unfettered growth anticipated in the Look/Act East Policy is neither inevitable nor irreversible as much as the market is seen to be grounded in the ethnic matrix of any given society. The socially and ethnically grounded nature of the market, as Akhil Gupta reminds us, marks the arrival of the post-colonial for it helps 'counter the 'teleologies of metanarratives' of the market that continue to inform our policies and practices including the present Look/Act East Policy. The post-colonial articulations of the market make such 'macrological processes' as nationalism, global market and global capitalism 'uncertain' as much as they 'shake one's confidence in pronouncing the direction in which [each of them is] heading' (Gupta 1998, 12). One must realize that the penetration of market forces seldom takes on only one direction.

NOTES

1. Such terms as 'tribe' and 'tribal' are used freely in India both in official circles and in popular parlance without any of their necessarily pejorative associations.
2. We use the term 'State' with 'S' in upper case to refer to the Indian State, while the term 'state' with 's' in lower case is reserved for referring to the states of the Indian Union.
3. I have discussed some of these much-needed reforms in Das (2008, 149–65).
4. I have discussed it in Das (2015a, 178–84).
5. Interview with Subir Bhaumik, BBC correspondent, on 5 May 2003, emphasis added. See Bhaumik (2003).
6. For details, see Das (1994).

7. Prasenjit Biswas appropriately designates it as 'counter-appropriation' and shows how the subjugated becomes a collaborator to the very process of subjugation. See Biswas (2004).
8. http://www.rediff.com/news/2004/aug/16mani.htm (accessed on 16 March 2018).

REFERENCES

Anonymous. 2017. 'How Darjeeling Is Coping with the Strike'. *The Telegraph* (Siliguri), 17 July.

Applbaum, K. 2005. 'The Anthropology of Markets'. In *A Handbook of Economic Anthropology*, edited by James G. Carrier, 275–89. Cheltenham: Edward Edgar.

Asem, S. 2011. *Women Market Participation and Empowerment*. Foreword by Amar Yumnam. New Delhi: Akansha.

Bayly, C. A. 1983. *Rulers, Townsmen and Bazaars: North Indian Society in the Age of British Expansion 1770–1870*. New Delhi: Oxford University Press.

Bhattacharya, R. 2018. 'Insider or an Outsider: Where Is the Northeast in India's Act East Policy?' In *Mainstreaming the Northeast in India's Look East and Act East Policy*, edited by A. Sarma and S. Chowdhury. Singapore: Palgrave Macmillan.

Bhaumik, S. 2003. 'Tribes Dig in to Fight Uranium'. Retrieved from http://news.bbc.co.uk/2/hi/south_asia/3000991.stm

Biswas, P. 2004. 'Insurgency and Regional Underdevelopment: Philosophical Issues in Youth Movement of Northeast India'. Unpublished paper. Mimeo.

Brara, V. N. 2017. 'Culture and Indigeneity: Women in Northeast India'. *Explorations: e-Journal of the Indian Sociological Society* 1(1): 72–90.

Bugra, A. 2007. 'Polanyi's Concept of Double Movement in the Contemporary Market Society'. In *Reading Karl Polanyi for the Twenty-First Century: Market Economy as a Political Project*, edited by A. Bugra and K. Agartan, 173–89. New York: Palgrave Macmillan.

Chakraborty, G. 2010. *Encountering Globalization in the Hill Areas of North East India*, 15. Occasional Paper 23. Kolkata: Institute of Development Studies.

———. 2018. 'Look East Policy and Northeast India: Is It a Conjectured Vision?' In *Mainstreaming the Northeast in India's Look East and Act East Policy*, edited by A. Sarma and S. Chowdhury. Singapore: Palgrave Macmillan.

Das, S. K. 1994. *ULFA: A Political Analysis*. Delhi: Ajanta.

———. 1997. 'Ethno-Ecologism: A Reconsideration of the Assam Movement (1979–1985)'. *Journal of Politics* IV: 21–35.

———. 2005. 'The Ethnic Dimension'. *Seminar*, Special Issue on 'Gateway to the East: A Symposium on Northeast India and the Look East Policy', 550: 65–69.

———. 2008. 'Between South and Southeast Asia: Recasting India's Northeast in the Age of Globalization'. In *Society, Politics and Development in North East India, Essays in Memory of Dr. Basudeb Datta Ray*, edited by A. K. Ray and S. Chakraborty, 149–65. New Delhi: Concept.

Das, S. K. 2015a. 'A Requiem for Social Science in India's Northeast'. *Eastern Quarterly* 11(III–IV): 178–84.

———. 2015b. 'Developmental State and Its Sovereign Gaze'. In *Democracy and Development in India's North-East: Challenges and Opportunities*, edited by L. S. Gassah and C. J. Thomas, 2. Delhi: Blackwell.

Dutta, D. 2017. 'Food Shortages Intensify in Darjeeling Hills, but the Statehood Movement Remains Strong'. Retrieved from https://scroll.in/article/845386/food-shortages-intensify-in-darjeeling-hills-but-the-statehood-movement-remains-strong

Elwin, V. 1989. *Philanthropologist: Selected Writings*, Edited by N. Rustomji. Delhi: North East Hill University Publications/Oxford University Press.

FICCI-KPMG. 2015. *Emerging North-East India: Economically and Socially Inclusive Strategies*. New Delhi: FICCI-KPMG.

Ganguly, J. B. 2006. *An Economic History of North East India (1826–1947)*. New Delhi: Akansha.

Gupta, A. 1998. *Postcolonial Developments: Agriculture in the Making of Modern India*. New Delhi: Oxford University Press.

Hann, C., and K. Hart. 2009. 'Introduction'. In *Market and Society: The Great Transformation Today*, edited by C. Hann and K. Hart, 1–16. Cambridge: Cambridge University Press.

Haokip, T. 2015. *India's Look East Policy and the North East*. New Delhi: SAGE Publications.

Indramoni, N. 2017. 'Development of Market in Manipur'. Unpublished paper. Mimeo.

Kharsyntiew, T. T. 2017. 'Youth Fashion and the Identity of Resistance in Northeast India'. In *Geographies of Resistance: Explorations in Northeast Indian Studies*, edited by M. Vandenhelsken, M. Borkotoki-Rushcheweyh and B. G. Karlsson. Abingdon: Routledge.

Ministry of the Development of the North East Region (MDoNER). 2005. *North East Region: Vision 2020*, Vols. 1–2. New Delhi: Government of India.

Mishra, D., and V. Upadhyay. 2017. 'Introduction'. In *Rethinking Economic Development in Northeast India: The Emerging Dynamics*, edited by D. Mishra and V. Upadhyay, 1–18. New Delhi: Routledge.

Piketty, T. 2014. *Capital in the Twenty-First Century*, Translated by A. Goldhammer. Cambridge, MA: The Belknup Press of Harvard University Press.

Polanyi, K. 1957/1044. *The Great Transformation: The Political and Economic Origins of Our Time*, Foreword by R. M. McIver. Boston: Beacon Press.

Routray, B. P. 2005. 'The Militant Moral Police', 14 January. Retrieved from https://www.outlookindia.com/website/story/the-militant-moral-police/226217

Rudolph, S. H. 1987. 'Presidential Address: State Formation in Asia — Prolegomenon to a Comparative Study'. *The Journal of Asian Studies* 46(4): 731–46.

Scott, J. 1976. *The Moral Economy of the Peasant: Rebellion and Subsistence in Southeast Asia*. New Haven: Yale University Press.

Sen, A. 1989. *On Economic Man*. Occasional Paper No. 112. Calcutta: Centre for Studies in Social Sciences.
Sood, A. 2017. 'Integrating Northeast with Southeast Asia'. In *Rethinking Economic Development in Northeast India: The Emerging Dynamics*, edited by D. Mishra and V. Upadhyay, 32–49. New Delhi: Routledge.
Thompson, E. P. 1971. 'The Moral Economy of the English Crowd in the Eighteenth Century'. *Past and Present* 50(1): 76–136.
Yes Institute, Yes Bank. 2016. *North East Region—Initiatives (NER-I)*, Yes Institute, Yes Bank, Emerging North East: Establishing North East India as Future Economic Hub. New Delhi: Yes Bank Limited.
Yhome, K. 2015. 'From "Look East" to "Act East": What It Means for India's Northeast?' *Eastern Quarterly* 11(1–2): 18–29.

PART II

Developmental Impacts on People

Chapter 3

Developmentalism and Consequences
Displacement and Marginalization in India's North East

Walter Fernandes

The present chapter is based on studies on 'Development-Induced Displacement and Deprivation 1947–2010' (DID) in several states of India. This all-India effort was made in order to understand the nature and extent of DID in the name of national development and the paradigm that guides it. Studies indicate that its extent has been enormous since the First Five Year Plan and that in the pattern that decision-makers opted for, development and displacement are two sides of the same coin. Its main reason is that most decision-makers view development only as economic growth and infrastructure building. While focusing on economic growth, its adherents do not accord adequate importance to people. They believe that DID is a sad but inevitable by-product of development. This approach is what Mahatma Gandhi opposed as developmentalism. The second school of thinkers believe that development should be inclusive, that is, it should include economic and social growth, as well as infrastructure building and the environment. None of them can be sacrificed for the others.

Research and field experience including the above studies indicate that one of the results of developmentalism is impoverishment and marginalization of the enormous number of persons displaced (DP) in the name of national development and of the project-affected persons (PAP), that is, people deprived of sustenance without physical relocation. One possible conclusion from it is that one class pays the price of development for another class. That turns the pattern of development into a human rights issue. Those who opt for inclusive development believe that to benefit all the classes the starting point of development should be the Supreme Court's interpretation of Article 21 of the Indian Constitution on right to life as every citizen's right to a life with dignity. Those who pay the price of development would thus have a right to its benefits. Applying this interpretation of the apex court to its analysis, this chapter begins with the background of the present development paradigm. It is followed by some all-India data on displacement and an analysis of the situation in India's North East where studies have been done in four states and are in an early stage in the remaining four.

THE PATTERN OF DEVELOPMENT

The pattern of development is a basic component in the study of displacement and developmentalism. Though the present pattern of development evolved after 1947, it originated in the colonial age which some authors call the first stage of globalization. Though the term 'globalization' is recent, its reality has existed for five centuries, from the 'discovery of new worlds' by Christopher Columbus and Vasco da Gama. Direct colonial control of much of Asia, Africa and the Americas by West European countries was its major consequence. The second phase, the neo-colonial economy or the Cold War began after most of Asia and Africa attained political independence. But the Global North (colonial rulers) continued to control their economies in a new form. It did not require direct colonial occupation because the North could control the economies of the South (former colonies) by using the financial and legal institutions built during the first phase. The third phase began with the end of the Cold War and the fall of the Soviet Union. The only remaining superpower imposed a single economy on the rest of the world by using the Bretton Woods Institutions built during the first two phases (Amin 1999, 22–23). There is continuity in change in these phases. Common to them is first the domination-dependency syndrome in North-South relations, second camouflaging the North's economic interests behind an ideology and third the North introducing legal changes and building new institutions in the South in order to change its economy to suit its own needs. The main difference is in the type of colonialism, the legal regimes and institutions built for this purpose.

The Paradigm and the Laws

Without going into their details, one mentions these phases only as a background to the development paradigm which originated in pre-1947 economic and legal changes. Among the legal changes, land laws had the greatest impact on the whole of India. They are symbolized by the Land Acquisition Act 1894 (LAA) which was in force for 119 years till the Indian Parliament enacted a new law in 2013. LAA was basic to the colonial enterprise which was legitimized in the name of Europe's mission of civilising education. In reality its objective was to change the economy of the colony to suit the needs of the European industrial revolution (Rothermund 1992, 11–12). For this purpose it had to first de-industrialize the colony and turn it into a captive market for its finished products. The next step was land and forest laws that were enacted in order to facilitate capital formation for the industrial revolution through high taxes and transfer of land to British-owned plantations, mines and other raw material producers and transporters (Rothermund 1981, 83–84). The foundation of the legal changes was laid by the feudal zamindari or Permanent Settlement Agreement 1793 meant to enhance tax collection for capital formation. These laws are based on the principle of the State's eminent domain that enables the State to acquire even private property for a 'public purpose' without the owner's consent (Ramanathan 2008, 28–29).

Such colonial interventions dispossessed the common property resource (CPR) dependants and others sustaining themselves as service providers on land belonging to other legal owners. There is difference of opinion on the exact number affected by the changes but scholars have identified most of their impacts. One of them is that individual ownership-based colonial land laws turned a large number of service providers, particularly Dalits (Scheduled Castes, SCs) into cheap labour. The CPR-dependent tribes lost most of their land initially because of the Permanent Settlement Agreement 1793 and later through acquisition for mining and other projects. Forest laws and mining added to their dispossession and impoverishment (Areeparampil 1996, 12–14). An attack on the material resources was lower in much of the North East where the foreign ruler needed taxes, not land. They required land only in Assam for tea plantations and later for petroleum exploration. So the attack in this region was mainly on people's culture and identity. Their material resources felt the impact after Partition when land was acquired to rebuild the transport and defence infrastructure (Fernandes and Borgohain 2017, 62–64). Not surprisingly most tribal regions witnessed revolts against the foreigner for protection of their resources. But in the North East the reaction was mainly to protect people's identities (Aosenba 2002, 12–20).

Land and the Legal System in the North East

In the North East, movements to protect land began much after Independence and many of them took the form of ethnic conflicts or turned against the Bangladeshi and Bihari immigrants to the region. Studies of the process leading to immigration reveal that land laws facilitate it. Its pull factors are the legal regimes in the region and unskilled jobs as construction workers, rickshaw pullers and so on that the local people do not take up easily. Land in the region is fertile and much of it belongs to tribes who run their civil affairs under their community-based customary law. But the laws recognize only individual ownership and treat land without *pattas* as State property. This interface of the two systems creates a disjunction between the legal and social realities and facilitates land alienation by making it easy for immigrants to encroach on tribal CPRs and for the State to appropriate the sustenance both in the tribal and in the non-tribal areas. But more tribal than non-tribal land has been lost to both migrants and local non-tribal population because Assam has reduced both the number of tribal blocks from which land cannot be alienated, from 35 in the 1950s to 25 in 2005, and the size of those that remain (Shimray 2006, 17–18).

Though the conflicts are recent, the process of alienating land began in the colonial period. It can be traced back to Assam Land Rules 1938 that were meant to help the British regime acquire land at a low price for tea gardens. Later they were used to help migrants encroach on it. Resentment against it was strong but it became an issue when post-1947 low investment in the secondary sector continued people's high dependence on land. Its alienation thus became basic to conflicts. The locals consider immigrants also a threat to their language, culture and identity (Datta 1990, 32–33). But land too plays a role.

DISPLACEMENT, THE ROLE OF LAND LAWS AND THE PARADIGM

While immigration is an emotional issue, the role of land laws and their impact on CPRs is much more visible in DID than in other areas. It also shows the nature of the development paradigm.

The Type of Development-induced Deprivation and Displacement in the North East

Though the Five Year Plans were launched in 1951, investment in the North East began only in the 1960s. Many reasons are given for the delay such as the need to wait till Partition refugees were resettled or the fear that India may not be able to protect their enterprises from a Chinese attack. One does not need to go into its details. Of greater importance than its reasons is the type of investment and DID in the region. Both of them have been conditioned by Partition so land takeover has been mainly for transport, security and refugee rehabilitation. Because of the creation of new borders, a security apparatus had to be built in the region. Roads and rail lines were built through North Bengal and Assam to replace the routes that had till then passed through East Pakistan. As a result, except for water resources in which the region abounds, most land acquisition has been for defence, transportation and refugee rehabilitation and it began immediately after Partition. Investment has been low in productive sectors. To some extent this pattern continues the pre-1947 trend of treating the region as a buffer zone between China and Burma. Later Assam also became a source of raw materials for tea and petroleum. The type of investment leaves one with the impression that a role has been assigned to each area in the North East—Assam is for petroleum and tea, Meghalaya for limestone, coal and uranium and so on (Fernandes, Pala, et al. 2016, 30).

The study of DID in Assam, 1947–2000, shows the role of the CPRs and the hiatus between the legal and social reality. Since the law treats the CPRs as State property, it does not keep a count of what is used for the projects. Its result is that while by official count all the projects that included water resources, refugee rehabilitation, environment protection, defence, transport and industries used 391,772.9 acres (1947–2000) and displaced 310,142 people, the study showed that not less than 1,405,809.38 acres were taken over and 1,916,085 people deprived of livelihood during these decades (Fernandes and Bharali 2011, 217–20). Thus, not less than 1,014,036.48 acres (72.13%) of land, all of it CPRs, are missing from official files because they are considered State property. Officials claim that they need not keep records of the CPRs or count the number of persons that their acquisition of State property deprives of sustenance. In so doing they deprive not fewer than 1,605,943 people of their sustenance without alternatives and without including them in the list of DP-PAPs.

More importantly, most of the 16 lakh persons not counted as DP-PAPs belong to rural poor classes. The caste tribe of only 1,025,336 of the 1,916,085 DP-PAPs was identified and 40.6 per cent of them are tribal. There are indications that around 50 per cent of the 884,032 DP-PAPs whose caste tribe is not known are tribal, who are 12.4 per cent of Assam's population. Some 150,000 land losers to environment protection are fish workers from the riverbanks or islands but no official records on them exist. Data are not available also on the CPR dependants of other projects such as dams, industries and refugee rehabilitation. One sees a similar situation in the remaining northeastern states. In Tripura, for example, much of the land used is CPRs and most of its land losers are tribal and they are not counted. For example, the Dumbur Dam displaced 8,500–9,000 families (45,000–50,000 persons) but counted only 2,361 *patta*-owning families (13,000 persons) as displaced (Debbarma 2008, 122–23). Because of the influx of East Pakistani refugees immediately after Partition and a much larger number of immigrants later, the State's tribal proportion declined from 51.8 per cent in 1951 to 31 per cent in 2011 but they are 56.66 per cent of its 176,828 DP-PAPs (Fernandes and Bharali 2010, 75). In Mizoram and Meghalaya, the proportion of the commons is low because of both poor record keeping and their land classification is different from that of the formal law. So it is not easy to record their sustenance in the language of formal law (Nongkynrih 2008, 34–35). As a result, much of the land they lost is not counted. Almost all the land taken in Nagaland is common and all the four lakh DP-PAPs of Meghalaya, Mizoram and Nagaland are tribal.

The Law and Land Loss

The development paradigm is basic to the priority accorded to infrastructure building over people's welfare and the land laws facilitate its process of land alienation. For example, the CPRs account for over 70 per cent of land used by development projects or encroached upon by immigrants in India's North East. In Assam much of that land is in tribal blocks that have been removed from the list. Moreover, even private land in the State is divided into permanent and periodic (*eksonia* or annual) *pattas*. It is a relic of the colonial system that was built on pre-British Ahom law, according to which all land belonged to the king. He allotted some land to each family in return for a tax or a month of free labour. It provided to the family security of subsistence without security of tenure. The British rulers accepted its first part that all land belonged to the king and treated all of it as Crown property but ignored the second part of distribution. It became the basis of Assam Waste Land Settlement Rules 1838 which enabled the colonial regime to acquire land for tea plantations at a very low price. They were turned into Land Reforms and Land Revenue Rules (LR&LR) 1886 in order to consolidate the system (Bora 1986, 46–49, 54–55).

The 1960 Tripura and Manipur Acts are exact replicas of the Assam 1886 rules. To limit oneself to Tripura Land Revenue and Land Reforms Act (TRLR&R) 1960, its declared objective was to reform the feudal system but some analysts state that it was meant also or possibly primarily to facilitate the transfer of tribal land to rehabilitate the

1947 East Pakistani refugees and later immigrants who had come in search of land. Whether it was its covert intention or not, in practice, the TRL&R 1960 had precisely that consequence. The Act recognized only land with individual *pattas* that was registered. Most tribal land was CPRs. The little individually owned land could not be registered both because of their high level of illiteracy and because they did not have records. Its net result is that apart from the land that the refugees occupied on an emergency basis immediately after Partition, the tribes lost 20–40 per cent of their land to the immigrants in the 1960s (Bhaumik 2003, 83–84).

Coming back to Assam, as a result of such laws, according to an estimate, even today, over 50 per cent of private land continues to be under *ek-sonia pattas* or CPRs. Studies, for example, of the Nagaon Paper Mill at Jagi Road show that the State accepts the *ek-sonia-patta* as the norm though a 1948 law abolished that system. In 1967 the Forest Department allotted two acres of land each to some tribal families in return for 5 days of free labour a year for plantation work, thus continuing the pre-Independence hidden contract system. The Nogaon Paper Mill displaced them in 1972, paying them ₹3,000 per acre of *ek-sonia patta* against ₹8,000 for permanent *patta* (Bharali 2009, 59).

The Development Paradigm and Displacement

Post-1947 displacement has to be studied in the above context as well as the development paradigm that the rulers opted for. This era has many more DP-PAPs than that prior to it. A big proportion of them have presumably been impoverished. Their sustenance was acquired in the name of national development under the eminent domain-based laws. Some analysts believe that by accepting the eminent domain as its basis, the paradigm legitimizes displacement and by implication, the impoverishment and marginalization of the DP-PAPs. That and the alarming number of post-1947 DP-PAPs turn displacement into a human rights issue. Thus, a development-displacement contradiction arose though the conscious ideology of the planners was of inclusive development, of welfare and 'benefits reaching all'. Despite this thinking in practice consciously or unconsciously they accorded priority to economic growth over human development and opted for a resource-intensive pattern of development based on sophisticated technology.

Its main reason seems to be that most freedom fighters who became India's post-1947 leaders attributed Western progress to technology alone. Based on this understanding of development they assumed that technology would solve the social problems of illiteracy and unemployment in India too. In order to achieve it they kept intact the laws that the colonial regime had enacted to exploit the resources of the colony for its own benefit. Independent India declared herself a welfare State but because the leaders attributed Western progress to technology alone, by and large they accorded priority to economic efficiency. They were convinced that since India lagged behind the West, she should do in a few decades what the West took a century to do and that the benefits of this model of development would eventually trickle down to every citizen (Vyasulu 1998).

That is the apparent contradiction between their ideology and the paradigm they opted for. But one cannot deny that much thinking had gone into its choice. People like Gandhi and Nehru knew that Western progress depended not merely on technology but also on the exploitation of its working class at home and of the colonies abroad. However, Nehru as well as P. C. Mahalanobis, the brain behind the mixed economy, thought that technology under the social control of the State would undo these negative components and solve India's socio-economic problems. In fact the social conscience of Nehru insisted that India should ensure industrialization within a democratic framework without the capitalist exploitation of workers or socialist dictatorship (Nehru 1946, 64–65).

Mahatma Gandhi disagreed with this approach. Because the colonizing countries had become rich by exploiting their colonies, he cautioned the leaders against following the Western path. He opposed not industries but industrialism, that is, developmentalism based on the types of technologies and a consumption pattern that are beyond the reach of the majority. He feared that if a small country like England could impoverish half the world in order to ensure a rich lifestyle to its citizens, by following this path, a big country like India would impoverish many more people. So he opted for a country based on a village republic and grassroots-level development (Gandhi 1948, 26). Some of his followers added that since India did not have colonies, its middle class would impoverish the poor for their own comforts.

An accompanying assumption of the planners was that to achieve the objectives of development, apart from accepting the best technology, India had to modernize herself, change her traditions and free herself from superstition. Most leaders were also aware of their social obligations but as stated above, they assumed that by taking control of the heights of the economy through the public sector, the State could ensure social equity (Vyasulu 1998). That explains why during the first decade of Independence the discussion was around nation-building, by which one meant that the benefits of development would eventually reach every Indian though initially some problems would arise. This conviction was based on the mixed economy as suggested by the Bombay Plan 1945 prepared by a group of nascent entrepreneurs like the Tatas and Birlas. One of its fundamental principles was that since the private sector lacked the wherewithal to invest in long gestation infrastructure like steel and power, the State should build it with the taxpayer money and leave the profit-making consumer industries to private entrepreneurs. Its framers were clear that the benefits of development should reach everyone but its approach was purely economic. They viewed development only as infrastructure building and economic growth. Within that perspective they gave an idealistic vision of every Indian having at least 30 yards of clothes and a family having a house not less than 100 square feet. But they did not specify the means of how the benefits would reach every Indian (Joseph 2014).

The planners thus combined developmentalist thinking and modernization with sophisticated technology. In so doing despite their social conscience they almost ignored India's caste- and gender-based inequality that ensures that the benefits of development reach the already powerful unless steps are taken to move towards an equitable society. As Dr B. R. Ambedkar said, while presenting the Constitution to the Constituent Assembly, the document he presented ensured political democracy. But economic and social democracy requires the type of development whose benefits can reach every citizen. With that in view he supported fast industrialization, not because of priority accorded to technology but with the hope that industries would produce revenue that can be used for the education and health care of the poor and that the jobs they would create would take the poor, Dalits in particular, away from bondage and exploitation to alternative employment (Ramaiah 2013, 139–40). Thus, he anticipated, without being aware of it, the apex court interpretation of Article 21 on right to life as every citizen's right to a life with dignity (Vaswani 1992, 158). This thinking should have guided planned development but in practice it did not because in reality two schools of the emerging development economics of the 1950s seem to have clashed in the choice of the paradigm. On one side the school led by Arthur Lewis argued that economic development is a process of capital accumulation and transferring labour from low-productivity traditional agricultural occupations and other occupations to high-productivity modern industry and capital accumulation which are basic to it. On the other side the school led by Paul Romer and R. E. Lucas stated that long-term development and economic growth are determined by investment in education and human capital formation. Lucas attributed the huge difference in per capita incomes of nations to the extent of investment in human capital (Sarkar 2007, 1434).

These schools were presented as opposite poles and despite the social thinking of its leaders India opted for the former, that is, a technology and economic growth model, with the hope that it would solve the socio-economic problems of its people. Based on this option, the country borrowed money and sophisticated technology from the West as 'foreign aid' to build capital-intensive projects. The planners believed in the trickle-down theory and ignored the fact that access to the benefits of such inputs requires cultural, psychological and social preparation through formal education and technical training. During Independence literacy, was low in India as a whole and much lower in the tribal and Dalit communities, especially women, among them. Most of those who had access to education belonged to the dominant castes and classes.

Social inputs were required to change this unequal society. Instead of focusing on them, India combined technology with welfare measures such as making free education and jobs available in the public sector to members of SCs and Tribes. Such benefits can reach only those who enter the school. A majority of the scheduled communities are unable to reach the classroom and are, therefore, excluded from it (Mencher 2013, 88–89). In other words, reservations, like the remaining inputs, made services available to the scheduled classes but in the absence of other enabling measures, only a small minority could gain access to them. Indications exist that in the absence of social change, trickle down has not worked and the benefits of development have reached the middle and upper classes but poverty has increased among the powerless (Kurien 1997, 134–35). With its greater profit orientation, the liberalized economy further neglects the social arena with no questions asked about who pays its price and who gets the benefits.

DISPLACEMENT IN INDIA AND ITS NORTH EAST

Signs of priority accorded to economic growth over social inputs are visible, among others, in the extent of land acquired, the number of DP-PAPs, the predominance of subalterns among them, poor rehabilitation and most importantly, impoverishment and marginalization of a large proportion of them. While it is true also of India's North East, both development and displacement are substantially different in the region from the rest of India. Development projects were launched in the North East not with the First Five Year Plan but only in the 1960s. According to one view the main reason of this delay in investment began after resettling Partition refugees. Others think that its main reason is focus on security. The North East has witnessed international wars, nationalist struggles, ethnic conflicts and the influx of refugees and immigrants. As a result, protecting borders gains priority over development. Also, natural and human-made disasters cause internally displaced persons (IDPs) in the region. However, DID, more than any other component, represents the impact of developmentalism.

Internally Displaced Persons

IDPs are persons displaced by disasters, conflicts or development projects who do not cross international boundaries. They become refugees when they flee to another country. A refugee is 'an uprooted, homeless, voluntary or involuntary migrant who flees his or her native country, usually to escape danger or persecution because of one's race, religion, or political views, and who no longer is protected by his or her former government' (Schmitz 2003, 33). India's North East has had a large number of refugees as well as conflict IDPs. The former belong mainly to Partition though others too have come, for example, from the Chittagong Hill Tracts of Bangladesh and the Chin State of Myanmar. Conflict IDPs have been, among others, the cause of the Anti-Foreigner Assam Movement, 1979–1985, the Tribal-Bengali tension in Tripura in the 1980s, the Kuki–Naga conflict in Manipur in the 1990s (Kashena 2017), the Mizo-Bru conflict in Mizoram (Haokip 2002, 248), the Boro-Santhal conflict in Assam in 1996, 1998 (Vandekerckhove 2010, 42–44) and 2014 (Saikia 2012, 12), the Bodo-Bengali Muslim conflict of 1993 and 2014 (Fernandes 2012), the Hmar-Dimasa tension of 2003, the Karbi-Dimasa conflict of 2005 (Mangattuthazhe 2008), the Bru-Mizo conflict of 1997 and 2009 and others elsewhere. The exact number of conflict IDPs is not known. The figures from the IDP camps put their total at around two million in the last two decades. But a much bigger number of them flee to their relatives' houses during a conflict and their number is not known. Apart from IDPs, a certain number of Rohingyas from Myanmar seem to have entered Manipur and possibly Mizoram but their number and status are not known. Mizoram has an estimated 100,000 Chin migrants. Initially they came as refugees fleeing the ethnic conflict with the Myanmar union government. Today most of them seem to be economic migrants rather than conflict refugees (Fernandes et al. 2015, 29).

Natural disasters force a much bigger number of people to move out of their habitat involuntarily. Such disasters are not always purely natural. The Assam floods, for example, are natural but human interventions such as real estate speculators encroaching on its water bodies, cutting of hills for building activities and massive deforestation in the catchment area of Brahmaputra intensify their consequences and turn what would be intense floods into disasters (Bandyopadhyay 2007, 5–7). Also these human-made disasters and conflicts are examples of impacts of developmentalism on people. Because of the view of natural resources as only a raw material to produce other goods, resources like forests are over-exploited. It results in environmental degradation. A major alert was sounded around it in the 1980s when the Moore Island was born in Bay of Bengal because of soil erosion caused by deforestation. Professor Madhav Gadgil calculated that in that decade the country lost 5,334 million tonnes of soil per year because of deforestation, 29 per cent of it 'exported' to Bay of Bengal. The Moore Island it formed led to an Indo-Bangladesh dispute for its ownership (Gadgil 1989, 374). The soil that was not washed out to the sea remained in India, and by 1980, the riverbed of the Ganga rose by 5 metres and that of the Brahmaputra by 1.98 metres (CSE 1987). It has risen further after it.

The rise in the level of Brahmaputra, the biggest river of India, because of deforestation, explains the higher intensity of floods from the 1980s in the North East. Madhav Gadgil attributes deforestation in the North East from the 1980s to the sequential exhaustion of natural and mineral resources. Deforestation began in the nineteenth century in western and southern India and moved north and eastwards. After denuding the forests in Jharkhand and Orissa in the 1980s, the attack on those of Uttaranchal and the North East began (Gadgil 1989, 367–68). Floods certainly existed in the past to. In fact, they were an annual event in Assam but today they have become more frequent and intense. For example, in 1953 they affected 410,000 persons in Assam but in 2007 they displaced some 4,000,000 persons. Their nature too has changed. Till the 1970s floods used to occur in one stage every July and were part of Assam's ecology on which its agricultural system was built. It explains why Bihu, the harvest festival, is celebrated in January, not in September, though Assam and the rest of the North East depend mainly on the southwestern monsoons. In the past the farmer would sow the first crop in May–June. In July the floods would wash away much of it but would also bring silt that functioned as a soil nutrient. Whatever paddy survived the floods would be allowed to grow. The farmer would replant the rest and fertilize it with silt and reap it in December (Bharali 2007).

It changed with the floods becoming more destructive. In the 1990s they came in two stages, in July and September, instead of the earlier single stage in July. Today they come in three or four stages even up to the month of October. Moreover, the silt that they bring is only sand so it no longer functions as a soil nutrient. The floods thus render the land non-cultivable. According to some studies 7 per cent of land in Assam has been lost permanently to erosion. Moreover, because the floods displace many more persons than in the past, the affected persons do not have reserves in the form of seeds for a second crop or food for the lean season since impoverishment that frequent floods cause forces them to consume even the seeds. Sand that covers much of their land renders it infertile. As a result, even the second crop does not give them adequate food for the whole year. Moreover, traditional coping mechanisms that depended on a different frequency and intensity of hazards are no more viable. But their victims are unable to develop new techniques to cope with them. As a result, their economic and health status deteriorates (Dekens 2007, 10–11).

To the disaster and conflict-induced IDPs, one may add process-induced and indirect IDPs. Process-induced IDPs are persons living in a traditional economy whom technological changes deprive of their sustenance and force to migrate. For example, thousands of potters migrated when household pottery was replaced by cheap plastic (Ravinder 2004). Indirect IDPs are created by environmental or other impacts of projects such as fly ash generated by thermal, aluminium and other plants that destroy the land around them and render it unusable. Unable to sustain themselves on it, their dependants move out 'voluntarily' (Ganguly Thukral 1999, 11). Also noise and dust pollution and blasts in coal mines force people to leave their homes. In legal terms they leave of their own accord but the real cause is the forces let loose by the project (Fernandes, Thadathil and Dutta 2016, 17–18). Their number is enormous but no methodology has been developed to make a reliable estimate. So they are excluded from studies on DID.

To the above IDPs, one has to add those of droughts whose intensity and frequency too have increased. However, one does not know the number of their IDPs. One only knows that these processes are intrinsic to desertification which is not the same as deserts. The latter belong to a settled ecosystem and people have developed a lifestyle suited to them. The latter is a new and ongoing process thrust on the people by changes in the environment. Communities that had developed a lifestyle meant for their earlier environments are unable to adapt themselves to the new one. So many of them are impoverished and their lifestyle deteriorates.

Their impact is not seen in one event as in disasters but it is lasting (Dasgupta 2007, 30–33). Moreover, as seen earlier, most conflicts in the North East are caused by shortage of land and other natural resources resulting from over-use of resources like deforestation and consequent environmental degradation (Vandekerckhove 2010, 11–12).

Development-Induced Displaced Persons and Project-affected Persons

Thus, the number of conflict and disaster DPs is enormous. But the biggest damage is done by DID. Moreover, people have very little control over disasters and conflicts, even the ones that are human made. But specific to DID is the fact that land acquisition is planned so it should be possible for project authorities to ensure a humane process of deprivation and proper rehabilitation. In reality, the resettlement of the DPs is low and very few measures are taken for their rehabilitation. Moreover, though the eminent domain affects only private land, in reality project authorities behave as though the CPRs and all biodiversity are State property and treat their inhabitants as encroachers though that land that was their habitat for centuries before colonial laws recognized only individual ownership. It goes against the weakest among DP-PAPs as one can see in the difference between the official and real figure of land used and DP-PAPs in Assam (see above). Similar is the situation in seven states outside India's North East where studies were done on DID 1951–1995 or a longer period.

To begin with, North East's Tripura had 176,828 DP-PAPs from 209,336.39 acres, 1947–2000. In Mizoram more than 100,000 people were relocated by the security forces during the nationalist struggle for village reorganization in the name of national security. Because of that, Mizoram had 200,139 DP-PAPs from 52,104 acres, 1947–2000. Meghalaya had 136,206 DP-PAPs from 240,176.48 acres and Nagaland had 60,481 of them from 54,671.79 acres, 1947–2010. Sikkim had 85,689 DP-PAPs, 1975–2010, from 130,571.19 acres. Studies are in progress in Arunachal Pradesh and Manipur. When these studies are complete and those up to 2000 are updated, the total is expected to exceed 30 lakh DP-PAPs which is more than 7 per cent of the region's population (Fernandes et al. 2017, 246). Rehabilitation is all but non-existent. Moreover, most DP-PAPs are tribal. As stated earlier in Assam tribes are 12.9 per cent of the population but they are some 40 per cent of the DP-PAPs whose caste tribe is known and probably most of those whose caste tribes are not known. So in practice they are over 50 per cent of the DP-PAPs. At the national level, after studying 16 states including those of India's North East, one has reached an estimate of around 65 million DP-PAPs, 1947–2010, from 70 million acres. Forty per cent of them are tribal (Fernandes, Thadathil and Dutta 2016, 23–25).

An indication of a large number of DP-PAPs being CPR-dependent tribals is the close link between the type of land and its inhabitants. In Sikkim, Assam and the rest of the North East, data on the CPRs are scanty. This type of 25–30 per cent of land in Meghalaya, Mizoram and Nagaland could not be obtained. It is CPRs because private land is accounted for in the gazettes. It was included in the NA category since one was not certain whether it was revenue or forest land. In either case it was sustenance of communities like the tribes and the weakest of OBCs like fish and quarry workers. Many projects give a low number of DP-PAPs because they do not count the CPR dependants among them. For example, by official count, the proposed Pagladia Dam in the Nalbari District of Assam is said to displace a little over 18,000 persons when the reality is 105,000 because the tribes inhabiting the CPRs are not counted (Bharali 2004). One has already mentioned above the difference between the official and real count of the DP-PAPs of the Dumbur Dam in Tripura. CPRs are almost 50 per cent of the land used in Tripura, and almost all land in Meghalaya, Nagaland and Mizoram is common.

Rehabilitation is almost non-existent in the North East and is weak in the rest of India. Only Orissa (35.27%), Andhra Pradesh (28.82%) and Goa (40.87%) resettled more than 25 per cent of their DPs till 1995. Kerala resettled 13 per cent, 1951–1995, Gujarat around 20 per cent, 1947–2004, and West Bengal 9 per cent, 1947–2000. The numbers are negligible in the remaining states studied. Most of such families who have been partially rehabilitated are of settled agriculturists. The tribes depend on the CPRs and most of them are not even counted among DP-PAPs (Fernandes and Bharali 2011, 18). In the

North East out of some 3,000 files studied in Assam, one found a few components of rehabilitation like some jobs in only 10 projects. Two projects each in Tripura and Mizoram had rehabilitation packages. Of the eight states, only Arunachal has a rehabilitation policy of allocating a hectare of land to a displaced family but one saw no signs of it being implemented. Even if implemented it would be extremely inadequate because most tribes in Arunachal Pradesh sustain themselves on shifting cultivation. One hectare is adequate only for settled agriculture in which they are not trained. Moreover, only individual owners are counted in Arunachal Pradesh where most people sustain themselves on the CPRs. For example, the Environment Impact Report mentions that only 38 families were to be affected by the Lower Subansiri Dam in two villages and ignores 12 villages on the Right Bank. Moreover, these 38 families, all of them shifting cultivators, sustained themselves on 986 hectares but were given only 38 hectares with no preparation for the transition to settled agriculture (Menon 2008, 131–33). It is a recipe for their impoverishment.

Development-induced Deprivation and Displacement and Impoverishment

That brings one back to the paradigm that views development only as infrastructure building. Land is acquired for it under a law based on the State's eminent domain that confers on the State alone the power to define the public purpose and acquire even individual land without the owner's consent. Much of the common land is not included in the list so it does not count its dependants and also those who do not own the acquired land under the present law but sustain themselves on it as cultivators of the CPRs, wage labourers on land legally belonging to an individual owner or service providers to the village as a community as merchants, barbers and so on. They too are deprived of their sustenance but are not counted among the DP-PAPs. A few of its examples from North East have been given above. For example in Assam not even 25 per cent of land used and DP-PAPs are counted in the official list.

Land alienation in the name of development has increased with liberalization or globalization. An example is minerals that have become a major source of profit for the private sector. As the opening statement of the 1994 draft rehabilitation policy said, more land than in the past has to be acquired in order to encourage Indian and foreign private investment, much of it in the tribal areas for mining (MoRD 1994, 1.1–1.2). An example of this statement (though in a draft) being implemented is Meghalaya where a study of DID found only 586 acres used for mining till 2000. More that might have been used cannot be identified but it would not have exceeded 2,000 or 3,000 acres. But 25,747.53 acres were used for uranium and limestone mining during the 2001–2010 decade of globalization, 21,151.76 acres of it were forest land (Fernandes, Pala, et al. 2016, 358). Much of the land used for coal mining is not counted in this total because in Meghalaya coal is mined under the customary land-holding pattern. The community allots plots to individuals, some of whom also take private land on lease. No official records are kept. Mining is done with no safety measures, through 'rat holes' (D'Souza et al. 2013). That land is uncultivable when it is returned to the original owner.

It raises questions about the economy of the North East in which some 70 per cent of the population depends on the primary sector and over 20 per cent on the tertiary sector. The secondary sector is weak. As stated above, land alienated in the name of development exceeds 20 lakh acres in the four states studied and it has deprived more than 30 lakh people of their livelihood in these states. But the jobs lost in the primary sector have not been replaced. Rehabilitation is all but non-existent in the region. Environmental degradation is one more of its consequences. For example, in Meghalaya, deforestation by mining began in the 1970s and 56 sq. km of dense forests, and 28.9 sq. km of open forests were lost to mining and related schemes like settlements between 1975 and 2005 (Sarma and Kushwaha 2007). It deprives ordinary people of their livelihood resources for the profit of a few entrepreneurs.

Impoverishment is its consequence. It does not mean the poverty that many DP-PAPs live in before their deprivation. It refers to what results from the loss of their sustenance to the project. Many DP-PAPs belong to a semi-monetized economy but are forced to begin life in an alien (formal) system that treats their sustenance only as a commodity, for example, trees as timber though to the people they are edible fruits, flowers and leaves, medicines and other benefits (Dewan and Chawla 1999). Though the State and project authorities who acquire their sustenance are in a position to plan their rehabilitation, in practice, they do not do it since the eminent domain is their basis. The project authorities plan all the technical and financial details of the project but ignore the people who pay its price. It is basic to the paradigm that gives priority to economic growth and the infrastructure and is not so concerned about the people who pay its price.

Women and children pay a higher price of it than men and adults do. For example, in Assam, 56 per cent of the DP-PAP families kept their children out of school or withdrew them from it in order to turn them into child labourers and earn an income for the family since the parents had no work (Fernandes and Bharali 2011, 317–19). To joblessness which is only one of the features of impoverishment, one has to add landlessness, homelessness, marginalization, higher morbidity, lack of access to the CPRs, food insecurity and community disarticulation (Cernea 2000, 15–24). Ramaiah (1995) adds the adverse impact on their health caused by malnutrition, mental stress, poor air and water quality and higher work pressure because of paucity of resources. Areeparampil (1989, 19–20) calls it dispossession since land loss dismantles their traditional production systems and income without replacing them. One has to add to it marginalization which goes beyond impoverishment and is a result of alienation of their land which disrupts not merely their economy but also their social networks and cultural practices, causes social and cultural dislocation, loss of identity, spiritual beliefs, history, legends and myths attached to it (Pamei 2001, 1146). Such disruption affects also their psyche. Outsiders who come to the project's township consider the locals inferior. Slowly the DP-PAPs internalize this ideology and think of their own community as incapable of developing itself (Fernandes 2000, 212).

Infrastructure and Land Loss in India's North East

Priority accorded to infrastructure over people is visible in India's North East more after liberalization than before it. Immediately after Partition the effort was to replace the defence and transport infrastructure lost to Pakistan. Beginning from the 1990s private profit has overtaken the sector particularly through privatization of the social and health sector. One can see it in the educational, health as well as transport infrastructure. The region has some good-quality educational and health institutions but most of them are in cities such as Guwahati and Shillong. Very few good institutions exist in the hills or even in the rural areas of the plains. Most such good institutions are run by civil society or church agencies with no aid from the State. As a result the agencies that run such good institutions in small towns and rural areas have to charge fees which may be low but are too high for most poor parents to pay. It also means that they pay low salaries to their teachers and they find it difficult to retain them.

Similarly, improvement of transport has come to mean the Asian Highway and the Golden Quadrilateral. They are needed no doubt for creating links with the Association of Southeast Asian Nations (ASEAN) on one side and mainland India on the other. Urban transport may improve particularly in big cities but rural transport is neglected. As a result, even if some health and educational institutions exist in a few rural areas the people are unable to access them because of poor transport facilities between villages and with the district or sub-divisional headquarters where they exist. Its result is that most parents have no choice but to send their children to colleges in the cities of the region or outside it (Fernandes 2017, 42–43).

That is a threat to their land. The poor are excluded even from schools. But those who have land at times use it to earn income for their school fees. For example, when a school opened in the 1970s in the southern Angami area of Nagaland, many families went beyond their tradition of growing a single paddy crop in their terrace fields and vegetables in the *jhum* fields. They grew a second crop of potatoes to earn money for their children's school fees. But the amount they earned was inadequate when it was time to send their children for higher studies outside the State or region. To earn higher amounts for it, they begin to cut their village forests that they had protected till then (D'Souza 2001, 38). In most villages parents who want to send their children for higher studies outside the State sell their best land to richer members of the community. They do the same for health emergencies when they have to send the patient to cities within the region or outside the region. The sellers may be able to negotiate its price to some extent when they sell it for their children's college education. But in case of a medical emergency, to rush a patient to a city, they have no choice but to sell their best land at a throwaway price (Kekhrieseno 2009, 207–09). Land is their only resource and its sale sets the process of class formation, impoverishment and conflicts in motion. This process also shows the close link between the absence of rural infrastructure and land alienation. This vicious circle too is linked to the type of development that focuses on infrastructure without paying adequate attention to people's access to it.

The same holds good for trade with ASEAN, particularly Myanmar. The government restricts it to formal exchange between the countries and it is declining by the year. But the tribes divided by borders have been exchanging goods among themselves. In fact, they go beyond barter trade, cultural and social exchanges, for example, marital alliances. Also the people of divided tribes on the Myanmar side depend on the Indian side for medical emergencies and not infrequently for education. One found a fairly big number of such children in Mizoram, Manipur and Arunachal Pradesh. The researchers were told that the Government of India is aware of it but ignores it. However, both those who study in India and those who come for medical emergencies are considered illegal residents. Moreover, on the Myanmar side too, the sale of land is the mode of paying for education and medical emergencies. That can be prevented by recognizing the regular exchanges between members of the tribes on two sides of the border but it is not done (Fernandes et al. 2015, 179–81).

CONCLUSION

The discussion in this chapter shows the link between the development paradigm that has developmentalism as its base and people's impoverishment that results mainly from land alienation. The national leaders wanted its benefits to reach every citizen. However, the sophisticated technology-intensive pattern that they opted for made infrastructure and economic growth available but not accessible to the majority. This contradiction arose because the decision-makers did not take the caste- and gender inequality-based Indian society into consideration. The eminent-based laws intensified this process. A solution has to be found in the direction of making the benefits of development accessible to everyone. The law has to be changed no doubt. But much more important is to change the paradigm on which development is based at present and the society that goes against inclusive development.

REFERENCES

Amin, S. 1999. 'Globalisation Yesterday and Today'. In *Colonialism to Globalisation: Five Centuries after Vasco da Gama*, edited by W. Fernandes and Anupamadutta, 22–26. New Delhi: Indian Social Institute.

Aosenba. 2002. *The Naga Resistance Movement Prospects of Peace and Armed Conflict*. New Delhi: Regency Publication.

Areeparampil, M. 1989. 'Industries, Mines and Dispossession of Indigenous Peoples: The Case of Chotanagpur'. In *Development, Displacement and Rehabilitation: Issues for a National Debate*, edited by W. Fernandes and E. G. Thukral, 13–38. New Delhi: Indian Social Institute.

———. 1996. *Tribals of Jharkhand: Victims of Development*. New Delhi: Indian Social Institute.

Bandyopadhyay, C. 2007. *Disaster Preparedness for Natural Hazards: Current Status in India*. Kathmandu: International Centre for Integrated Mountain Development.

Bharali, G. 2004. 'Dam Threat to Livelihood'. *The Telegraph: North East*, 29 November.

———. 2007. 'Prakrotik Durjyoton Kiman Prakrotik?' *Dainik Janambhumi*, September 8.

———. 2009. *Social and Environmental Cost of Development-Induced Displacement: An Appraisal of Cost-Benefit analysis in Assam*. PhD Thesis, Department of Economics, Dibrugarh University.

Bhaumik, S. 2003. 'Tripura's Gumti Dam Must Go'. *The Ecologist Asia* 11 (1, January–March), 84–89.

Bora, A. K. 1986. *Pattern of Land Utilization in Assam*. Delhi: Manas Publications.

Cernea, M. M. 2000. 'Risks, Safeguards and Reconstruction: A Model for Population Displacement and Resettlement'. In *Risks and Reconstruction: Experiences of Resettlers and Refugees*, edited by M. M. Cernea and C. McDowell, 11–55. Washington, DC: The World Bank.

CSE. 1987. *The Wrath of Nature: The Impact of Floods and Droughts on Floods and Droughts*. New Delhi: Centre for Science and Environment.

D'Souza, A. 2001. *Traditional Systems of Forest Conservation in North East India: The Angami Tribe of Nagaland*. Guwahati: North Eastern Social Research Centre.

D'Souza, A., M. Pereira, R. Chymrang, W. Lngkhoi, W. Shylla, R. Sangma, and R. Thabah. 2013. *Welfare of Children in Coal Mining Areas of Meghalaya*. Guwahati: North Eastern Social Research Centre (mimeo).

Dasgupta, R. 2007. *Disaster Management and Rehabilitation*. New Delhi: Mittal Publications.

Datta, B. 1990. 'Ethnicity, Nationalism and Sub-Nationalism, with Special Reference to North-East India'. In *Nationality, Ethnicity and Cultural Identity in North-East India*, edited by D. Pakem, 36–44. New Delhi: Omsons Publications.

Debbarma, S. 2008. 'Refugee Rehabilitation and Land Alienation in Tripura'. In *Land, People and Politics: Contest over Tribal Land in Northeast India*, edited by W. Fernandes and S. Barbora, 113–27. Guwahati and Copenhagen: North Eastern Social Research Centre and International Work Group for Indigenous Affairs (IWGIA).

Dekens, J. 2007. *Local Knowledge for Disaster Preparedness: A Literature Review*. Kathmandu: International Centre for Integrated Mountain Development.

Dewan, R., and M. Chawla. 1999. *Of Development Amid Fragility: A Societal and Environmental Perspective of Vadhavan Port*. Mumbai: Popular Prakashan.

Fernandes, W. 2000. 'From Marginalisation to Sharing the Project Benefits'. In *Risks and Reconstruction: Experiences of Resettlers and Refugees*, edited by M. M. Cernea and C. McDowell, 205–26. Washington, DC: The World Bank.

———. 2012. 'Violence in Assam: Land, Identity and Immigration'. *Infochange*, October.

———. 2017. 'Land Alienation and Rural Development in Northeast India'. *E-Journal of the Indian Sociological Society* 1(1): 31–47.

Fernandes, W., and G. Bharali. 2010. *Development-Induced Displacement 1947–2000 in Meghlaya, Mizoram and Tripura: A Quantitative and Qualitative Database on Its Extent and Impact*. Guwahati: North Eastern Social Research Centre (mimeo).

———. 2011. *Uprooted for Whose Benefit? Development-Induced Displacement in Assam 1947–2000*. Guwahati: North Eastern Social Research Centre.

Fernandes, W., and B. Borgohain. 2017. *Journals of Dispute: Media Coverage of Conflicts in the Northeast*. Guwahati: North Eastern Social Research Centre.

Fernandes, W., T. Das, Z. Goan, T. N. Lin, and F. Kashyap. 2015. *Relations across Borders: Communities Separated by the Indo-Myanmar Border*. Guwahati: North Eastern Social Research Centre and Yangon: Animation and Research Centre-Myanmar.

Fernandes, W., V. Pala, G. Bharali, and B. Dutta. 2016. *The Development Dilemma: Displacement in Meghalaya 1947–2010*. Guwahati and New Delhi: North Eastern Social Research Centre and Indian Social Institute.

Fernandes, W., G. Thadathil, and B. Dutta. 2016. *Development-Induced Displacement in Meghalaya 1947–2010*. Guwahati: North Eastern Social Research Centre and Siliguri: Salesian College.

Fernandes, W., B. C. Mughavi, M. Pienyu, A. Achumi, M. Yanthan, and T. Fidelia. 2017. *The Challenge of Development: Displacement in Nagaland 1947–2010*. Guwahati: North Eastern Social Research Centre and Jakhama: St Joseph's College.

Gadgil, M. 1989. 'Forest Management, Deforestation and People's Impoverishment'. *Social Action* 39(4): 357–83.

Gandhi, M. K. 1948. *Cent Per Cent Swadeshi*. Ahmedabad: Navjivan Publishing House.

Ganguly Thukral, E. 1999. 'Bottom-Up'. *Humanscape* 6(11), 10–12.

Haokip, T. 2002. 'Ethnic Conflicts and Internal Displacement in Manipur'. In *Internally Displaced Persons in Mizoram*, edited by C. J. Thomas, 248–49. New Delhi: Regency Publication.

Joseph, M. 2014. 'An Experiment with Socialism Finally Ends: Narendra Modi to Replace India's Planning Commission'. *The New York Times*, 20 August.

Kashena, A. R. 2017. *Enduring Loss: The Kuki-Naga Conflict in Manipur*. Guwahati: North Eastern Social Research Centre.

Kekhrieseno, C. 2009. 'Changing Land Relations and Angami Society'. In *Angami Society at the Beginning of the 21st Century*, edited by K. Kikhi, A. D'Souza, and V. Hibo, 191–217. New Delhi: Akhansha Publishing House.

Kurien, C. T. 1997. 'Globalisation: What Is It About?' *Integral Liberation* 1(3): 133–40.

Mangattuthazhe, T. 2008. *Violence and Search for Peace in Karbi Anglong, Assam*. Guwahati: North Eastern Social Research Centre.

Mencher, J. 2013. 'On Being an Untouchable in India: A Materialistic Perspective'. In *Life as a Dalit: Views from the Bottom on Caste in India*, edited by S. Mitrachanna and J. Mencher, 81–115. Los Angeles: SAGE Publications.

Menon, M. 2008. 'Land Alienation Due to Large Hydro-Power Projects in Arunachal Pradesh'. In *Land, People and Politics Contest Over Tribal Land in Northeast India*, edited by W. Fernandes and S. Barbora, 128–41. Guwahati: North Eastern Social Research Centre and IWGIA.

MoRD. 1994. *The Draft National Policy for Rehabilitation of Persons Displaced as a Consequence of Acquisition of Land*. New Delhi: Ministry of Rural Development, Government of India (Second Draft).

Nehru, J. 1946. *The Discovery of India*. London: Oxford University Press.

Nongkynrih, A. K. 2008. 'Privatization of Communal Land of the Tribes of North East India: A Sociological Viewpoint'. In *Land, People and Politics Contest Over Tribal Land in Northeast India*, edited by W. Fernandes and S. Barbora, 16–37. Guwahati: North Eastern Social Research Centre and IWGIA.

Pamei, A. 2001. 'Havoc of Tipaimukh High Dam Project'. *Economic and Political Weekly* 36(13): 1045–148.

Ramaiah, S. 1995. *Health Implications of Involuntary Resettlement and Rehabilitation in development Projects in India*, Vol. I. New Delhi: Society for Health Education and Learning Packages.

Ramaiah, A. 2013. 'Dalits to Benefit from Globalization Lessons from the Past for the Present'. In *Life as a Dalit: Views from the Bottom on Caste in India*, edited by S. M. Channa and J. P. Mencher, 135–54. New Delhi: SAGE Publications.

Ramanathan, U. 2008. 'The Land Acquisition Act 1894: Displacement and State Power'. In *India: Social Development Report 2008: Development and Displacement*, edited by H. M. Mathur, 27–38. New Delhi: Council for Social Development and Oxford University Press.

Ravinder, Dr. 2004. *Policy-Induced Displacement: A Case of Sheep and Goat Rearing Communities in Andhra Pradesh*. Paper Presented at International Seminar on Development and Displacement: Afro-Asian Perspectives, Department of Political Sciences and Regional Centre for Urban and environment Studies, Osmania University and Human Rights Education Programme, Dr. B.R. Ambedkar Open University, 27 and 28 November.

Rothermund, D. 1981. *Asian Trade and European Expansion in the Age of Mercantilism*. Delhi: Manohar.

———. 1992. '500 Years of Colonialism'. *Social Action* 42(1): 1–15.

Saikia, A. 2012. 'The Historical Geography of the Assam Violence'. *Economic & Political Weekly* 47(41): 15–18.

Sarkar, A. 2007. 'Development and Displacement: Land Acquisition in West Bengal'. *Economic and Political Weekly* 42: 1435–42.

Sarma, K., and S. P. S. Kushwaha. 2007. 'Coal Mining Impact on Land Use and Land Cover in Jaintia Hills District of Meghalaya: India Using Remote Sensing and GIS Technique'. Retrieved from http://www.csre.iitb.ac.in/~csre/conf/wp-content/uploads/fullpapers/OS5/OS5_17.pdf

Schmitz, P. G. 2003. 'Psychological Factors of Immigration and Emigration'. In *Migration: Immigration and Emigration in International Perspective*, edited by L. L. Adler and U. P. Gielen, 23–50. Westport: Praeger Publishers.

Shimray, U. A. 2006. *Tribal Land Alienation in North East India: Laws and Land Relations*. Guwahati: North Eastern Social Research Centre and Indigenous Women's Forum of Northeast India.

Vandekerckhove, N. 2010. *No Land, No Peace: Dynamics of Violent Conflict and Land Use in Assam, India*. Ghent: Ghent University.

Vaswani, K. 1992. 'Rehabilitation Laws and Policies: A Critical Look'. In *Big Dams, Displaced People: Rivers of Sorrow Rivers of Change*, edited by E. G. Thukral, 155–68. New Delhi: SAGE Publications.

Vyasulu, V. 1998. *The South Asian Model*. Paper Presented at the *International Conference Colonialism to Globalisation: Five Centuries After Vasco da Gama*. New Delhi: Indian Social Institute, 2–6 February.

Chapter 4

India's Developmentalism in Northeast Region and Its Consequences
Identity, Uncertainty and Migration

Deepak K. Mishra

India's northeastern region, with its ecological and social diversity, is often seen as a conflict zone, as a 'disturbed area', but in the past decades, major changes have also been observed in the region. For long the states located in the northeastern region, despite their significant diversity, are clubbed as part of a region that has been known for its political instability, insurgencies and economic backwardness. The mainstream approach towards this border region was marked by the overwhelming dominance of security concerns in almost all developmental interventions. In neoliberal India, there has been a shift towards policies aimed at the region, although there are significant continuities with the past (McDuie-Ra 2009). From being an 'enchanting frontier', the region has come to be seen as a 'gateway' connecting India with its eastern neighbours (Mishra and Upadhyay 2017). Despite the invocation of trans-border connections and high-profile policy enouncements such as 'Look East' and 'Act East' Policies (Das 2010; Haokip 2015; Sikri 2009), in concrete terms, the region continues to remain in the backwaters of economic development. In some ways, the economic performance of the states in the region worsened in the post-reform period, in which per capita income of the country as a whole has seen a remarkable turnaround (Dutta and Das 2017), with a rise in intra-regional disparities in the region (Bhattachraya 2011, 36–7).

The specificities of the region—that is, the mountain ecology in many of the states, the ethnic and institutional diversity and the geographical factors related to transport and communication networks regulating the flow of goods and commodities—have shaped the nature of economic transformation of the region. However, these specificities and their role in economic transformation can only be understood in a broader framework of development that examines the interconnections within the region as well as between the region and the national and international economies.

The objective of the chapter is to understand the way developmentalism has unfolded in the region with respect to the labour market and migration. It is difficult to generalize about a region that exhibits so much diversity. Parts of the region are characterized by such economic institutions that are common to most of the states of the country, while some forms of property relations are found in some parts of the region that are quite unique to the specific areas.

KEY ELEMENTS OF INDIA'S DEVELOPMENTALISM IN THE NORTHEAST REGION

The State approached India's North East with a lot of baggage from the colonial period. Not just that part of the region was simply under minimal governance, there were multiplicities of structures which defined the approach of the colonial government towards this region. The demarcation of the inner line was, for example, something unique to the region. Initial attempts to establish an infrastructure of governance in the region were marked by a remarkable degree of incompetence and a simple lack of understanding about the region and the people. The region was primarily seen as a frontier that was too distant to be seen and understood from the centres of power, but one which was too significant from the security point of view. From the vantage points of security, the region with its hostile terrain, linguistic and cultural diversity and porous borders posed formidable challenges to the newly independent nation. The security framework that dominated the thinking and approach towards the region in the initial decades contributed significantly to the long-term crisis of legitimacy that the Indian State continues to face, despite its formidable military and administrative presence now. However, it was not a simple narrative of a distant, alien power trying to establish control over a hostile people and their territory. The story of 'nation building' was far more complex than that. Although the processes through which the national freedom struggle attempted to articulate the vision of a shared future were also present in the region (Guha 2015), nevertheless, there were significant segments of populations who were simply outside these 'shared visions'.

In economic terms, Assam was among the states that already had a well-integrated economic base in tea, petroleum and mining industries. Despite the disruptions created as a result of Partition at the time of Independence, Assam's economy continued to play a major role in the early period of development. However, the early advantage did not contribute to further consolidation and expansion of the state's economy, partly as a result of the low priority accorded to the question of harnessing the state's economic potential through investment in key sectors of growth. Alongside, the economies of the hilly regions were marked by dependence on agriculture and allied activities, which included shifting cultivation, hunting and gathering and pastoralism. With poor administrative and economic infrastructure, the economies were mostly nature dependent and localized, although, historically some of the prominent trade routes passed through these hill tracts (Mishra 2013).

The post-colonial State adopted a range of strategies to strengthen its administrative, economic and military power in the region. However, key markers of the strategies were (a) cautious approaches towards assimilation in some parts of the region partly under the influence of the Nehru-Elwin policy; (b) escalation of conflicts in regions such as Nagaland and later other states, where insurgencies and secessionist movements started early; (c) emphasis of the creation of defence infrastructure in border areas following the war with China in 1962; (d) the creation of separate hill states and autonomous councils to accommodate identity-based assertions of diverse kind; (e) special economic packages to counter the allegation of fiscal negligence towards the region; and (f) the repositioning of the region in the framework of the Look (and Act) East Policy. The list is far from exhaustive, but it points to the diversity in the responses of the Indian State towards a conflict-prone and backward region. Without making any attempt to provide a comprehensive overview of developmentalism in the northeastern region, it would be important to underscore a few characteristics of this process, which have a significant bearing on the employment and migration scenario that have been discussed in the subsequent chapters.

First, the emphasis was to develop, consolidate and strengthen the governance infrastructure of the State in this relatively weakly administered region. As a result of the protracted investment in expansion and consolidation of State machinery, the presence of the Indian State is formidable. However, the strong military and administrative presence of the State co-exists with its inability to enforce the rule of law in various ways. Non-State actors of various kinds, for example, operate with impunity in various parts of the region, often contesting, substituting or restricting the actions of the State. Second, apart from various attempts to defeat and eliminate insurgencies through military action, attempts have been made to co-opt and accommodate particularistic demands within a framework of institutional diversity in governance. At times, it has helped the State consolidate its position through local stakeholders and collaborators. At the same time, such a framework has resulted in a 'crisis of citizenship', where civic rule is being replaced by a framework of ethnic competition and bargaining (Baruah 2003b; Harriss-White et al. 2013). Third, partly as a consequence of the above, the sphere of development intervention has itself been a site for contestation among conflicting interests of ethnic groups. The government sector in general, and public administration in particular, has been the medium of ethnic competition and distributional coalitions among competing interests. In the absence of the growth of employment opportunities in other sectors of the economy, competition for government jobs has intensified and access to these jobs has become synonymous with social mobility for a large section of the population.

Finally, with the low revenue-generation capacities of the small hilly states, they have been dependent on grants and aids from the central government to maintain public administration, manage conflicts among various groups and also invest in various development projects. The asymmetric federal structure and 'Special Category Status' to the states of the region have further facilitated the flow of funds to state governments. This chronic dependence has resulted in a kind of weak fiscal governance structure that has been termed 'cosmetic federalism' in the region (Baruah 2003a). In the neoliberal period, as the emphasis has shifted to the development of big-ticket development projects, such as hydropower, infrastructure and so on (Mishra and Upadhyay 2017), and with the participation of the private sector, the competition at the provincial level has further intensified.

THE ETHNIC ECONOMIC ORDER: CONSEQUENCES OF DEVELOPMENTALISM

Among the outcomes of the pattern of development in the region is the gross mismatch between the demand and supply of labour in the economy. Despite a few attempts to establish heavy industries in the region through the PSUs, weak forward and backward linkages, like elsewhere in the country, failed to create a shift of labour from agriculture to industry (Das 2017). First, the nature of investment was capital intensive and second, the limited employment opportunities that were created did not match with locally available skills. Moreover, with limited forward and backward linkages, such investments failed to create growth of employment in the local economy.

From 1980–1981 to 2012–2013, while the net domestic product (NDP) of India increased at a compound annual growth rate of 6.02 per cent, the net state domestic product (NSDP) of the north eastern region (NER) increased at a rate of 4.36 per annum (Dutta and Das 2017). Thus, during the period that India's economic growth was robust, the NER, despite some improvements, witnessed a growth rate that is below the national average. The secondary sector, including the manufacturing sector, grew at a sluggish rate, and its share in the NSDP declined in the post-reform period (Dutta and Das 2017).

THE EDUCATED UNEMPLOYED

This inability has been mentioned as one among many factors that contributed to the frustrations of the youth, which were manifested in the prolonged period of conflict in the region. In the meantime, access to education gradually expanded and the demand for jobs increased manifold.

The creation of smaller states was part of a process through which the Indian State attempted to accommodate the aspirations of various ethnic groups, in the backdrop of insurgencies and movements demanding secession from India. In economic terms these states were dependent upon fiscal assistance and grants in aid from the central government. While such a strategy was successful in creating a class of citizens who allied with the interests of the Indian State, the inability to create a productive base for the local economy meant that such support remained limited to a minority within these societies. Another fallout of this strategy was that whatever financial assistance was granted by the central government, it failed to transform the local economy. A significant portion of it went towards the purchase of goods and services produced elsewhere in the country or outside India.

Tables 4.1 and 4.2 suggest that total usual status unemployment is significantly high in Nagaland and Tripura and in North East India, and also in both these high-unemployment states, female unemployment and urban unemployment are comparatively higher.

The nature of unemployment becomes clearer in an age group-wise disaggregation, presented in Table 4.3. In the 15–59 age group, the rates of rural and urban unemployment for the region were found to be 5.07 and 9.25 per cent, respectively, while for the younger age group, 15–29, the rates were 15.18 and 26.03 per cent, respectively. Among young urban females, the unemployment rate was found to be as high as 37.8 per cent.

The unemployment rate among the younger age group by categories of educational attainment, presented in Tables 4.4 and 4.5, clearly points to the fact that, despite some state-level variations, by and large, the educated youth face severe unemployment in North East India. It is

Table 4.1 Usual Status Unemployment in States of North East India (15–59)

State	Rural	Urban	Male	Female	Total
Sikkim	1.04	2.28	1.48	0.94	1.25
Arunachal Pradesh	1.77	4.8	2.19	2.45	2.27
Nagaland	16.31	24.01	17.01	21.89	18.7
Manipur	2.83	7.68	3.48	5.07	3.98
Mizoram	1.92	5.22	2.62	4.54	3.34
Tripura	11.21	26.4	7.55	26.89	13.6
Meghalaya	0.4	2.96	0.82	0.81	0.81
Assam	4.7	5.74	4.62	5.77	4.81
North East	5.07	9.25	4.82	8.46	5.66

Source: 68th Round NSS, 2011–12.

Table 4.2 Usual Status Unemployment (15–59): Rural and Urban

	Rural		Urban	
State	Male	Female	Male	Female
Sikkim	1.06	1.03	3.03	0.26
Arunachal Pradesh	1.81	1.71	3.71	9.03
Nagaland	15.84	17.07	19.23	36.5
Manipur	2.64	3.22	5.98	12.15
Mizoram	1.35	2.79	4.17	7.16
Tripura	6.68	21.2	12.24	56.87
Meghalaya	0.41	0.38	2.57	3.75
Assam	4.51	5.64	5.51	7.31
North East	4.5	6.95	6.74	18.3

Source: 68th Round NSS, 2011–12.

Table 4.3. Usual Status Unemployment in North East India by Age Groups

Age Group	Rural			Urban		
	Male	Female	Total	Male	Female	Total
15–19	18.76	20.77	19.28	22.04	34.58	25.6
20–24	17.64	25.36	19.8	36.92	51.18	40.75
25–29	9.75	8.56	9.46	12.57	30.95	17.66
15–29	**14.29**	**17.7**	**15.18**	**21.58**	**37.8**	**26.03**
30–34	1.49	4.09	2.24	6.11	18.66	8.51
35–39	0.35	1	0.5	0.88	9.98	2.71
40–44	0.05	0.25	0.09	0.11	2.99	0.65
45–49	0.03	0.02	0.02	0.22	5.15	1.29
50–54	0.12	0.17	0.13	0.17	0	0.15
55–59	0	0	0	0.15	0	0.11
15–59	**4.5**	**6.95**	**5.07**	**6.74**	**18.3**	**9.25**

Source: 68th Round NSS, 2011–12.

evident that the graduation and above category, and also those having diplomas/certificate course degrees and with up to secondary education in some states, have very high levels of unemployment. Among the educated youth, in age group 15–29, and having an education up to graduation and above, the unemployment rates are higher than the working age population in almost all the states. When we consider North East India as a whole, it is found that, in the age group 15–59, the unemployment rate is the highest among those who have an educational attainment of graduation and above. Also, among all categories in the age group (total males, total females, rural, urban, rural males, rural females, urban males and urban females), the rate of unemployment is highest among those who have a graduation and above level of education, except urban males, where it is those having a higher secondary level of education who have a marginally higher level of unemployment. Such a trend is much more pronounced in the case of the highly educated in the age group 15–29. Also youth unemployment among

Table 4.4. Unemployment Rate by Education among the Working Age Group and Young Population in States

States	Age Group	Illiterates and up to Primary	Middle	Secondary	Higher Secondary and Diploma Courses	Graduation and Above	Total
Sikkim	15–59	0.41	0.58	2.08	0.12	11.08	1.25
	15–29	1.16	1.3	5.06	0.39	26.87	3.54
Arunachal	15–59	0.85	3.13	2.79	6.48	4.35	2.27
	15–29	3.32	9.06	6.71	17.47	21.58	7.71
Nagaland	15–59	1.44	2.00	11.56	28.08	50.24	18.7
	15–29	9.86	7.22	30.2	56.22	81.2	48.28
Manipur	15–59	0.58	3.46	2.27	6.36	10.35	4.00
	15–29	2.61	9.99	6.73	16.37	41.94	12.28
Mizoram	15–59	0.16	1.02	7.31	9.75	12.63	3.34
	15–29	0.28	2.7	16.56	27.2	33.46	8.88
Tripura	15–59	2.47	18.65	36.27	41.31	33.76	13.6
	15–29	9.71	34.21	60.53	68.63	65.9	32.61
Meghalaya	15–59	0.04	0.57	0.99	3.32	3.68	0.81
	15–29	0.00	0.24	0.25	4.78	3.52	0.74
Assam	15–59	0.73	4.61	11.46	13.13	12.23	4.82
	15–29	2.8	13.23	25.4	31.14	36.35	15.01

Source: 68th Round NSS, 2011–12.

Table 4.5 Unemployment by Educational Attainment of the Working Age Group and Young Population in North East India

Educational Attainment	Rural	Urban	Male	Female	Rural Male	Rural Female	Urban Male	Urban Female	Total
Age group 15–59									
Illiterate	0.93	0.7	1.36	0.16	1.41	0.11	0.33	1.36	0.92
Literate and up to primary	0.76	2.08	0.74	1.22	0.66	1.07	1.69	3.57	0.86
Middle	5.44	5.92	4.44	9.8	4.47	9.39	4.3	12.62	5.5
Secondary	12.01	7.61	9.13	21.89	9.96	23.3	4.88	17.25	11.24
Higher secondary	13.88	14.76	11.96	23.12	11.86	22.36	12.25	25.37	14.1
Diplomas/certificate courses	12.13	4.11	9.62	8.93	12.83	9.42	3.65	7.31	9.49
Graduation and above	17.06	16.79	12.48	32.8	13.19	31.89	11.68	33.67	16.93
Total	5.07	9.25	4.83	8.46	4.5	6.95	6.74	18.3	5.67

Age group 15–29

Educational Attainment	Rural	Urban	Male	Female	Rural Male	Rural Female	Urban Male	Urban Female	Total
Illiterate	4.14	2.86	6.17	0.63	6.32	0.48	0.99	7.03	4.11
Literate and up to primary	2.95	5.91	2.89	4.24	2.65	3.81	4.94	10.63	3.23
Middle	14.11	15.77	13.07	17.89	13.01	17.36	13.55	21.95	14.29
Secondary	25.37	21.35	21.74	38.89	22.44	39.11	15.14	37.76	24.93
Higher secondary	31.63	41.26	31.28	39.44	29.51	37.51	38.89	48.17	33.43
Diplomas/certificate courses	24.89	16.35	26.74	14.68	29.59	13.46	14.6	23.87	23.43
Graduation and above	44.24	45.88	42.95	48.39	44.84	43.27	40.77	54.72	44.99
Total	**15.18**	**26.03**	**15.25**	**20.52**	**14.3**	**17.7**	**21.58**	**37.8**	**16.63**

Source: 68th Round NSS, 2011–12.

those having diplomas or certificate courses, and those having education up to higher secondary, is much higher than those with less education. This points to the context where economic development of a particular nature, on the one hand, has expanded the access to education and, on the other hand, has failed to create enough job opportunities for educated youth. While part of the problem is similar to rest of the regions and states in India, that is, post-reform growth has been largely jobless growth, and skill deficits and mismatches have been limiting the scope of employment for the youth, the specific trajectories of development in the northeastern region, where the government sector and public administration have been among the primary avenues for employment, have also contributed to such a situation (Sahu and Kumar 2017). The creation of educational institutions for higher learning is often viewed as a way of addressing the developmental aspirations of specific communities and the creation of multiple tiers of administrative structures have been used as a way of providing access to the institutions and resources of the State.

LABOUR MIGRATION AND CITIZENSHIP

In the standard economics literature, migration is considered both as a characteristic and as an outcome of the development process. Mainly, it is considered as one of the equilibrating mechanisms through which the labour markets respond to spatial unevenness and mismatches in the demand and supply of labour as the economy develops. The causes of migration are typically explained in the framework of rationality of individual agents (migrant individuals or households), who respond to pull (demand-side) and/or push (supply-side) factors.[1] In development economics, following the dual sector models, migration from the less productive, agriculture sector to the more productive industrial sector was assigned a significant position in the process of economic development in less developed economies. Inter-regional and rural-urban differences in levels of development and employment opportunities, along with expected wage differentials, labour market conditions, costs of living and public transfers, have been identified as factors responsible for labour migration (Harris and Todaro 1970). Contrary to the earlier expectations of a Lewisian structural transformation, most of the migrant labourers are typically absorbed in the low-earning, low-productive urban informal economy[2] (Mishra 2016). Recent approaches to labour migration have emphasized the role of group decision-making (e.g., by households and families) rather than individual decision-making that leads to labour migration and have further argued that the objective of such migration may not be to maximize the expected income rather than minimize household-level risks (Stark and Bloom 1985). The livelihoods diversification approach has also contributed to the understanding of labour migration as the spatial reallocation of family labour (Ellis 2000). There is also greater appreciation of the role of social networks and ethnic bonding in determining the destinations, costs and outcomes of migration.

In the political economy framework, migration is seen as part of the structural processes of commodification of labour power as well as that of capitalist development. These theorists criticize the assumptions of atomistic and ahistorical individuals underlying the neoclassical approaches to labour migration and instead focus on the larger processes of social and economic changes that facilitate or constrain labour migration, often linking migrant labour to the concept of 'reserve army of labour' and the necessity of capital to control labour power (for a summary, see Shrestha 1988).

The migration to and from North East India, like elsewhere, is diverse in nature, in which both individual and structural factors tend to play a role. A specific aspect of migration in the region is the significance of the *State*, as an initiator, facilitator and controller of migration to and from the region. The role of the State is, however, not limited to the actions taken (i.e., its presence), but also to the actions that are not taken (i.e., its absence), deliberately or otherwise. The role of non-State actors, particularly powerful non-State actors such as insurgent groups, popular identity movements and pressure groups, is another dimension of the complex linkages between political contestations and labour migration in the region (Ghosh 2016; Singh 2010).

It is hardly surprising that the issue of migration to and from North East India has been at the centre stage of public discourse in the region. A comprehensive analysis of migration and its diverse implications is beyond the scope of the present exercise. The Northeast region, historically, has been a relatively less densely populated region in India. Migration to the region has a long history. During the colonial period there were attempts to settle migrant peasants in the plains of Assam with the objective of increasing land revenue. In the post-Independence period, there were various episodes of migration to the region as a result of Partition. Among the involuntary migrations to the region are the migrations of Chakma-Hajong, Tibetan and other refugees. The issue of international migration, particularly illegal migration to Assam and other states of the region, has been a vexed issue, which has not been considered here.[3]

Internal migration from other states to the states of North East India is also a complex issue, one that deserves attention. The development of the wage labour market is often part of the broader process of commercialization of the economy, which itself is seen as a manifestation of the emergence of a capitalist or market economy. The political economy literature, following the writings of Marx, Lenin and Kautsky, identifies two processes through which labour markets can emerge, that is, primitive accumulation and the differentiation of peasantry.[4]

The so-called primitive accumulation, however, has been found to be an enduring feature of capitalism (Adnan 2017, 77).[5] In the classic sense, primitive accumulation has led to 'double transformation', that is, on the one hand, land is concentrated in the hands of capitalists or it is made available to them through land leasing by the landlords; on the other hand, a class of wage labourers emerge from the ranks of independent producers. Peasant differentiation, operating through the normal process of expanded reproduction under capitalism, also creates a process through which a class of pauperized peasants gradually join the ranks of landless wage labourers. While both the processes have certainly been part of the process of agrarian change in North East India, in the thinly populated hilly states, such as Arunachal Pradesh, the wage labour market has not emerged through these internal dynamics; rather, it has been created through direct interventions by the State (and later by individual employers) *from above*.

Since the labour market in many of the hilly regions of North East India was created through conscious State decisions[6] that were justified through developmental and security imperatives and not necessarily through the process of internal differentiation of peasantry, changes in the non-farm economy that were critical for creating a labouring class dependent on the labour market, the migrant labour market, emerged as a significant aspect of labour relations in the region. In Arunachal Pradesh, for example, the State was instrumental in bringing migrant labour from different parts of India for creating military and civil infrastructure (Mishra 2013). Market and State institutions complemented each other in the process of gradual integration of local economies (Mishra 2015b).

The basic data on migration in different states, from the NSS 64th round survey, which is the latest round with information on migration, has been presented in Table 4.6.[7] The information from the NSS data at the State level for smaller states in particular suffers with problems of small sample size. However, in the absence of alternative sources of data on these aspects, this information has been used for getting a broader picture. Sikkim, Mizoram, Assam and Nagaland are the states with relatively higher migrant shares in population. The data from the NSS 64th round suggest that 14.42 per cent of households reported migration of a family member in the past and of the total migrants, 46 per cent were temporary migrants whereas 54 per cent were permanent migrants (Irudaya Rajan and Chyrmang 2016). Unlike in many other parts of the country, rural to urban migration is not necessarily the dominant stream of migration in the states of the region (Table 4.7). In the case of the number of out-migrants per 1,000 persons, the states of Sikkim, Nagaland, Mizoram and Assam have relatively higher number of out-migrants per 1,000 persons (Table 4.8). Intra-district and intra-State migration are the dominant forms of out-migration in the region (Table 4.9).

Much of migration is related to marriage or associational migration. However, this has relatively less significance in the context of out-migration from North East India. Employment and studies were the reasons for migration, for 48.3 and 6.3 per cent of migrants, whereas marriage was the reason for migration in the case of 39 per cent of out-migrants (Table 4.10).

Table 4.6 Migration Rate in (per 1,000 Persons) Northeastern States

State	Rural			Urban			Total		
	Male	Female	Total	Male	Female	Total	Male	Female	Total
Sikkim	195	414	300	536	729	627	233	448	336
Arunachal Pradesh	11	5	8	38	27	33	17	9	13
Nagaland	62	92	76	320	329	325	121	148	134
Manipur	6	5	6	10	26	18	7	10	9
Mizoram	107	114	110	189	223	206	143	164	153
Tripura	57	163	110	112	201	156	66	169	117
Meghalaya	38	29	33	42	47	44	38	32	35
Assam	26	227	120	223	327	270	45	236	134

Source: National Sample Survey Report, 64th Round, 2007–2008.

Table 4.7 Distribution (per 1,000 Persons) of Internal Migrants by Migration Streams for States of North East India

State	Rural to Rural	Urban to Rural	Rural to Urban	Urban to Urban
Male				
Sikkim	632	95	152	122
Arunachal Pradesh	264	287	287	161
Nagaland	159	238	343	260
Manipur	514	135	203	149
Mizoram	328	40	333	300
Tripura	659	20	257	64
Meghalaya	581	251	118	50
Assam	492	35	357	117
Female				
Sikkim	738	78	110	74
Arunachal Pradesh	405	48	286	262
Nagaland	311	164	300	224
Manipur	307	30	376	287
Mizoram	290	53	336	321
Tripura	759	39	145	56
Meghalaya	605	155	144	97
Assam	836	40	90	35
All Persons				
Sikkim	700	83	125	92
Arunachal Pradesh	305	203	281	211
Nagaland	241	198	320	240
Manipur	394	80	303	223
Mizoram	307	47	335	311
Tripura	735	34	173	58
Meghalaya	593	208	128	71
Assam	774	39	138	50

Source: National Sample Survey Report, 64th Round, 2007–2008.

Table 4.8 Number of Out-migrants (per 1,000 Persons) in Northeastern States

State	Rural			Urban			Total		
	Male	Female	Total	Male	Female	Total	Male	Female	Total
Sikkim	70	93	81	138	133	135	78	97	87
Arunachal Pradesh	51	21	37	39	11	26	49	13	34
Nagaland	63	83	73	55	49	52	61	75	68
Manipur	51	21	37	36	23	30	48	21	35
Mizoram	43	38	41	58	43	50	50	40	45
Tripura	35	33	34	47	30	38	37	32	35
Meghalaya	35	20	28	23	14	18	33	19	26
Assam	43	49	46	38	45	41	42	49	45

Source: National Sample Survey Report, 64th Round, 2007–2008.

Table 4.9 Shares of Inter-district, Inter-state and International Out-migrants among Total Out-migrants in States of Northeast India (per 1,000 Population)

Present Place of Residence	North East	Sikkim	Arunachal	Nagaland	Manipur	Mizoram	Tripura	Meghalaya	Assam
Same state and within the same district	421	447	541	423	241	378	463	380	426
Same state but another district	391	294	264	441	382	463	250	397	409
Outside the state	182	211	190	134	372	156	259	209	163
Another country	6	49	3	1	5	3	28	14	2
Not known	0	0	2	0	0	0	0	0	-
Total	1000	1001	1000	1000	1000	1000	1000	1000	1000

Source: Author's calculation based on 64th Round of National Sample Survey, 2007–2008.

Table 4.10 Reasons for Migration of Out-migrants (Per 1,000 Individuals) in North East India

Reasons	North East	Sikkim	Arunachal	Nagaland	Manipur	Mizoram	Tripura	Meghalaya	Assam
In search of employment	113	55	212	54	113	130	33	22	128
In search of better employment	74	19	37	6	41	61	30	29	91
Business	49	14	54	4	45	49	30	15	57
To take up employment/ better employment	161	95	81	170	178	174	105	281	165
Transfer of service/ contract	73	62	223	141	239	169	292	136	25
Proximity to the place of work	13	26	15	24	15	11	5	4	13
All Employment Related	**483**	**271**	**622**	**399**	**631**	**594**	**495**	**487**	**479**
Studies	63	298	224	154	207	153	61	400	13
Marriage	**394**	**349**	**94**	**433**	**93**	**226**	**381**	**97**	**444**
Migration of parents/ earning members of the family	49	45	29	5	43	18	40	3	57
Others	11	37	31	9	26	9	23	13	7

Source: Author's calculation based on 64th Round of National Sample Survey Data, 2007–2008.

Table 4.11 Background Characteristics of Economic Out-migrants in North East India (percentages)

Characteristics and Sector	Rural	Urban	Total
Social groups			
Scheduled Tribe	29.25	34.36	29.92
Scheduled Caste	3.92	9.1	4.6
Other Backward Class	23.89	15.81	22.82
Others	42.94	40.73	42.65
Religion			
Hindu	54.12	63.68	55.38
Muslim	25.84	3.14	22.84
Christian	15.49	28.71	17.24
Others	4.55	4.47	4.54
Monthly per capita expenditure			
Quintile 1	17.25	1.57	15.18
Quintile 2	19.63	3.47	17.5
Quintile 3	21.31	7.5	19.48
Quintile 4	23.23	24.22	23.36
Quintile 5	18.58	63.24	24.48
Land possessed			
Less than a hectare	74.43	91.94	76.74
From one to four hectares	24.98	7.97	22.74
Four hectares and above	0.58	0.09	0.52

Source: Author's calculations based on the 64th Round of National Sample Survey, 2007–2008.

Among those who out-migrated for economic reasons (i.e., employment, business and education), 30 per cent were STs, 5 per cent were SCs, 23 per cent were OBCs and the rest were others. Nearly 76 per cent of the migrants own less than a hectare of land. At the same time, nearly 48 per cent of them (87 per cent in urban areas) belong to the two upper-most quartiles. It shows that out-migrants have a relatively higher standard of living (also see Irudaya Rajan and Chyrmang 2016). As the non-farm economy has played a significant role in inducing people to migrate, the migrant population despite having belonged to low land-holding categories have a significant presence in the high-consumption expenditure classes.

However, the dynamics of economic migration in the region is far more complicated in the region that can be distilled from the available secondary data. As mentioned, the consolidation and expansion of State administration, the development of infrastructure, including roads and communication networks, transport, construction and retail trade and business have expanded the scope of employment, and hence people have migrated from other states and districts to work in these sectors. There are local specific reasons for migration as well. For example, unlike elsewhere in the country, the shifting of entire villages to new settlements has been a feature of migration in the remote and relatively inaccessible parts of the region. In Arunachal Pradesh, people have shifted villages from high-altitude to low-altitude areas, with better infrastructure and road connectivity. In the past, the involuntary reorganization of villages in Mizoram during army operations against insurgents also led to displacement (Bhaumik 1996, 162).[8] The gradual decline of *jhum* cultivation and shift to settled agriculture have also led to migration in some of the hilly districts (Harriss-White et al. 2009). However, the concentration of civic amenities and infrastructure in the urban areas and in the administrative centres has induced migration from the surrounding villages. The uneven nature and concentration of the non-farm economy in some relatively large villages and administrative headquarters suggest such a pattern of development (see, for example, Mishra 2007).

The demand for labour in the expanding infrastructure sector in the region has attracted migrant labourers from different parts of India. In the border regions the army and its various units (such as the General Reserve Engineering Force [GREF] and Border Roads Organisation) have always been dependent on migrant labour from elsewhere. Some of these labourers are kept in specially designated 'labour camps'. Often they are not directly employed by the army but are employed through contractors. Given the underdeveloped labour markets and low population density in some parts, migrant workers have found work in the government sector, in the urban informal sector as well in agriculture. The emergence of this migrant labour force has played a significant role in creating a labour market from *above*, with significant implications for economic transformation of the region.

The small but economically powerful group of local elites has been able to establish business operations, such as timber trade, wood-based industries and tea estates, by employing migrant labourers. In the recent period, migrant labourers have been mobilized through contractors to work in road construction and hydroprojects in different parts of the region (Mishra 2018, forthcoming). Tenancy involving local, tribal landlords and migrant tenants have also been reported from some parts (Mishra 2015a, 2017). As the traditionally labour-intensive industries such as the tea estates in Assam have started shedding labour, the labour force has started to look for alternative employment opportunities in construction, agriculture and in different urban informal sectors (Mishra et al. 2012). On the basis of a micro-study in Assam, Irudaya Rajan and Chyrmang (2016) report that migration for studies is the predominant cause of migration, followed by marriage. In the preceding 4 years of the survey, 48.72 per cent of migrant households had received some remittances, and nearly 46 per cent of remittances were used for household consumption expenditure, followed by marriage and other ceremonies (30.77 per cent). This suggests a gradual move towards migration from agriculture and the rural areas.

Like elsewhere, migrants in North East India are a diverse group. They range from economically prosperous traders, businessmen, professionals, bureaucrats and high-end white-collar workers to hapless, unskilled workers working in the informal economy, without any social protection. In a situation of ethnic differentiation and conflict, workers' rights often take a back seat.[9] Informal workers, working with little protection, face discrimination and exploitation almost everywhere. In situations where citizenship rights are ill defined or weakly defended by the State, or civil society, it is the working poor who face harassment at the workplace as well as outside (Harriss-White et al. 2013). Capitalist labour relations impose certain limitations on the articulations of such demands, as identity-based fragmentation of the working classes tends to strengthen the ability of capital to control migrant workers. Unfortunately, due to the webs of *othering*[10] that have made identity-based hierarchical citizenship a durable feature of ethnicized development processes in most parts of the region, a significant section of migrant workers from within and outside the region faces insecurity, discrimination and isolation in diverse spheres of their work and existence.[11]

OUT-MIGRATION AND DISCRIMINATION

In the recent years, out-migration from the northeastern region to other parts of India, for studies, business and employment purposes, has increased, although there is a dearth of evidence to examine the details of this migration (Reimeingam 2016). The data on migration from the 2011 census suggest an increase in migration to the relatively developed southern states, and migration from the eastern states, West Bengal, Assam and Odisha, along with the migration from the densely populated states such as Bihar and Uttar Pradesh, is said to have contributed to this trend. The Economic Survey, 2016–2017, also takes note of the rising degree of mobility through alternative indicators of mobility and goes on to argue that language, which was considered to be one among the key barriers to inter-state migration in India, has started to matter less in migration decisions. Anecdotal evidence suggests that out-migration of the youth to metropolitan cities such as Delhi (and the NCR), Bengaluru, Chennai, Pune and Mumbai has increased substantially. There are niche employment opportunities, such as those in the hospitality industries, hospitals, shopping malls, call centres and so on, where migrants from the region have started to make their presence felt.

On the basis of a primary survey of migrants from the northeastern region to the NCR, Babu P. Remesh argues that

> the growing presence of youth from NER in urban centres is largely determined by the inadequacy of higher education system and the non-availability of employment opportunities that match with the aspirations of the youth in the native economies. Such a situation, coupled with

the social tensions (due to multiple reasons) necessitates the massive city-bound exodus of the youth in the region. (Remesh 2016, 90)

The study finds evidences of discrimination and harassment at workplaces, harassment in daily life and also in the areas where the migrants live, leading to increased vulnerabilities and marginalization of migrants in the city, and this is also supported by other studies (McDuie-Ra 2013). Although the neoliberal reconstruction of city spaces and access to new employment opportunities, McDuie-Ra (2013) argues, are 'connecting the frontier and heartland in relatively peaceful ways, embedded stereotypes towards ethnic and tribal communities from the north-east frontier still hold, unaffected by the neoliberal transformation of the city and its labour markets' (McDuie-Ra 2013, 1637). Although a simple framework of exclusionary urbanization might not explain the complexities of exclusionary inclusion of the migrants to the city, at times of crisis and conflict, such as the panic exodus of thousands of migrants from Bengaluru in 2012 following rumours of violence, these inherent social and ethnic divisions come to the forefront (Srivatsa and Kurup 2012). Even in states with better human development, migrants face new surveillance techniques where their citizenship rights remain 'inextricably linked to identities of class, caste and gender' (Prasad-Aleyamma 2018).

CONCLUSION

In the post-Independence period the Indian State attempted to develop an administrative and developmental architecture that was aimed at consolidating its presence and authority in this sensitive border region, and at the times attempts were made to integrate the pre-existing local institutional structures with the forma structures of governance. The resultant institutional diversity was, thus, not simply a relic of the past but was at least partly created and sustained by deliberate State policy (Harriss-White et al. 2017). Over the period such diversity has created vested interests and hence, ethnicization of governance and citizenship has emerged as a preponderant framework for developmentalism of the Indian State. The creation of smaller states and multiple layers of governance structures, primarily motivated by the need to accommodate ethnic demands and minimize conflicts, has been successful to some extent, resulting in a degree of legitimacy for the State but at the same time has perpetuated a regime of fiscal dependence.

By locating two important aspects of the labour market, such as educated youth unemployment and migration to and from the region, in the broader framework of ethnicized developmentalism, this chapter presents the complex linkages between the unfolding dynamics of development in the region and labour market outcomes. Although only selected aspects of the labour market have been dealt with in this chapter, nevertheless, it presents the ways the political economy of development has resulted in the expansion of education and public administration in the region. This lopsided development has led to inadequate job opportunities for the educated youth of the region, while on the other hand the process of migration of labour into the informal economy has continued. The ethnic division between the migrant population and the host population has led to endless cycles of nativist movements, often leading to violence against migrants. At the same time, due to lack of employment opportunities within the region, and conflict-induced insecurities, a section of the youth has started to move out of the region to find better education and employment opportunities in the cities. There are evidences of discrimination, harassment and unfair treatment towards migrants from the northeastern region at the urban destinations, which can be termed 'adverse inclusion' or 'exclusionary inclusion' of migrants from the region. As precarious employment without adequate social security has emerged as a fundamental feature of the labour market under neoliberalism, there is an urgent need for recognition of the basic economic rights of migrant citizens, including social securities and protection from harassment and discrimination, within and outside the region.

ACKNOWLEDGEMENTS

Financial assistance under the Jawaharlal Nehru University-UPE Scheme (Project ID 34) is gratefully acknowledged. The author is grateful to Krishna Surya Das for his research support. The usual disclaimers apply.

NOTES

1. For a comprehensive summary, see Greenwood (1997) and Constant and Zimmermann (2013). Recent commentaries on labour migration research include Ghatak et al. (1996), Taylor (1999) and Kolev (2013).
2. The informal economy, that is, 'the economic activity of firms and individuals that is not registered for the purpose of taxation and/or regulation by the state', is, however, not unregulated. It is regulated by the non-state means of regulations (Harriss-White 2003, 4). Breman (2016, 27) points out 'far from being a specific feature of a faulty and "backward" organizational regimen, informality is an expression of the state's inability and/or unwillingness to control capital and those who own it'.
3. The anxieties and apprehensions of host populations regarding illegal migration have, however, multiple implications for the living and working conditions of migrant workers in the region, who are legally citizens of India. Strong nativist mobilizations (Vandekerckhove 2009), prolonged conflicts involving host and refugee populations (Singh 2010) and the presence of marginalized, excluded and stateless populations (Ghosh 2016) have specific implications on the rights of the migrant workers, who, otherwise also, face discriminations and exclusions of diverse types.
4. According to Marx, 'The capitalist system presupposes the complete separation of the labourers from all property in the means by which they can realize their labour. As soon as capitalist production is once on its own legs, it not only maintains this separation, but reproduces it on a continually extending scale. The process, therefore, that clears the way for the capitalist system, can be none other than the process which takes away from the labourer the possession of his means of production; a process that transforms, on the one hand, the social means of subsistence and of production into capital, on the other, the immediate producers into wage labourers. The so-called primitive accumulation, therefore, is nothing else than the historical process of divorcing the producer from the means of production. It appears as primitive, because it forms the prehistoric stage of capital and of the mode of production corresponding with it' (Marx 1976, 874–75).
5. For a criticism of this view, see Levien (2013).
6. During the colonial period, it was to facilitate the growth of the plantation sector that labour from the Central Indian tribal belt and elsewhere was mobilized through the active connivance of the colonial state (Behal 2014; Mishra et al. 2012).
7. For a detailed analysis of the NSS 64th round data on migration in the region, also see Irudaya Rajan and Chyrmang (2016).
8. For a detailed description of involuntary displacement in the northeastern region, see Hussain (2008).
9. Although the issue of illegal migration from Bangladesh to North East India, specifically Assam, has not been dealt with in this chapter, the long-drawn

political conflicts on the vexed issue of illegal migration (and more recently around the issue of the NRC) have resulted in an atmosphere where rights of migrant workers are almost always framed with reference to the conflicts over illegal international migration. Quite apart from the specific complexity of the issue of illegal migration, such a situation of conflict and polarisation generally results in the fragmentation of workers' solidarity, more so in the case of migrant workers.

10. As claims over economic rights and privileges are structured around notions of 'sons of the soil' and 'outsiders', in the overarching framework of ethnic competition over resources and power, the dividing line between the 'sons of soils' and others keeps on shifting across different spatial scales and moral political contexts. With increasing mobility within the region, many of those who are identified as indigenous in one context are discriminated as others in another.

11. This does not imply that migrant workers do not benefit from migrating to the region. *Dalit* shoemakers from North India, for example, have been able to escape caste oppression in their villages, and many of them have been able to send some remittances which are used to build houses and repay old debts (Personal Interview, 2010; also see Harriss-White et al. 2014).

REFERENCES

Adnan, S. 2017. 'Land Grabs, Primitive Accumulation and Resistance in Neoliberal India: Persistence of the Self-Employed and Divergence from the "Transition to Capitalism"?' In *The Land Question in India: State, Dispossession, and Capitalist Transition*, edited by A. P. D'Costa and A. Chakraborty, 76–100. Oxford: Oxford University Press.

Baruah, S. 2003a. 'Nationalizing Space: Cosmetic Federalism and the Politics of Development in Northeast India'. *Development and Change* 34(5): 915–39.

———. 2003b. 'Protective Discrimination and Crisis of Citizenship in North-East India'. *Economic and Political Weekly* 38(17): 1624–26.

Behal, R. P. 2014. *One Hundred Years of Servitude: Political Economy of Tea Plantations in Colonial Assam*. New Delhi: Tulika Books.

Bhattachraya, R. 2011. *Development Disparities in Northeast India*. New Delhi: Foundation Books.

Bhaumik, S. 1996. *Insurgent Crossfire: North-East India*. Delhi: Lancer Publishers.

Breman, J. 2016. *At Work in the Informal Economy of India: A Perspective from the Bottom Up*. Delhi: Oxford University Press.

Constant, A. F., and K. F. Zimmermann. 2013. *International Handbook on the Economics of Migration*. Cheltenham, UK: Edward Elgar Publishing.

Das, K. 2017. 'Understanding the Sluggish Industrialisation Process in Northeast India: How Do the Industrial Policies Help?' In *Rethinking Economic

Development in Northeast India: The Emerging Dynamics, edited by D. K. Mishra and V. Upadhya, 315–36. London: Routledge.

Das, S. K. 2010. 'India's Look East Policy: Imagining a New Geography of India's Northeast'. *India Quarterly: A Journal of International Affairs* 66(4): 343–58. doi: 10.1177/097492841006600402

Dutta, M. K., and I. Das. 2017. 'Economic Performance of the North-Eastern Region in the Post-Liberalisation Period'. In *Rethinking Economic Development in Northeast India: The Emerging Dynamics*, edited by D. K. Mishra and V. Upadhyay, 50–68. London: Routledge.

Ellis, F. 2000. *Rural Livelihoods and Diversity in Developing Countries*. London: Oxford University Press.

Ghatak, S., P. Levine, and S. W. Price. 1996. 'Migration Theories and Evidence: An Assessment'. *Journal of Economic Surveys* 10(2): 159–98.

Ghosh, P. S. 2016. *Migrants, Refugees and the Stateless in South Asia*. New Delhi: SAGE Publications.

Greenwood, M. J. 1997. 'Internal Migration in Developed Countries'. In *Handbook of Population and Family Economics*, edited by M. R. Rosenzweig and O. Stark, Vol. 1, 647–720. Amsterdam: Elsevier.

Guha, A. 2015. *Planter Raj to Swaraj: Freedom Struggle and Electoral Politics in Assam 1826–1947*. New Delhi: Tulika Books.

Haokip, T. 2015. 'India's Look East Policy: Prospects and Challenges for Northeast India'. *Studies in Indian Politics* 3(2): 198–211.

Harris, J. R., and M. P. Todaro. 1970. 'Migration, Unemployment and Development: A Two-Sector Analysis.' *The American Economic Review* 60(1): 126–42.

Harriss-White, B. 2003. *India Working: Essays on Society and Economy*. Cambridge: Cambridge University Press.

Harriss-White, B., E. Basile, A. Dixit, P. Joddar, A. Prakash, and K. Vidyarthee. 2014. *Dalits and Adivasis in India's Business Economy: Three Essays and an Atlas*. New Delhi: Three Essays Press.

Harriss-White, B., D. K. Mishra, and A. Prakash. 2017. 'Inclusive Development, Citizenship and Globalisation: The Case of Arunachal Pradesh'. In *Rethinking Economic Development in Northeast India: The Emerging Dynamics*, edited by D. K. Mishra and V. Upadhyay, 136–50. London: Routledge (Taylor and Francis).

Harriss-White, B., D. K. Mishra, and V. Upadhyay. 2009. 'Institutional Diversity and Capitalist Transition: The Political Economy of Agrarian Change in Arunachal Pradesh, India'. *Journal of Agrarian Change* 9(4): 512 47. doi. 10.1111/j.1471-0366.2009.00230.x

Harriss-White, B., A. Prakash, and D. K. Mishra. 2013. 'Globalization, Economic Citizenship and India's Inclusive Developmentalism'. In *Citizenship as Cultural Flow: Structure, Agency and Power*, edited by S. K. Mitra, 187–210. Heidelberg: Springer.

Hussain, M. 2008. *Interrogating Development: State, Displacement and Popular Resistance in North East India*, Vol. 1. New Delhi: SAGE Publications.

Irudaya Rajan, S., and R. Chyrmang. 2016. 'Labour Migration in the North East'. In *Internal Migration in Contemporary India*, edited by D. K. Mishra, 96–153. New Delhi: SAGE Publications.

Kolev, A. 2013. "Labour Migration and Development: A Critical Review of a Controversial Debate." In *Perspectives on Labor Economics for Development*, edited by S. Cazes and S. Verick, 119–59. Geneva: ILO.

Levien, M. 2013. 'The Politics of Dispossession: Theorizing India's "Land Wars"'. *Politics & Society* 41(3): 351–94.

Marx, K. 1976. *Capital: A Critique of Political Economy*, Vol. I, 1990th edition. London: Penguin.

McDuie-Ra, D. 2009. 'Vision 2020 or Re-Vision 1958: The Contradictory Politics of Counter-Insurgency in India's Regional Engagement'. *Contemporary South Asia* 17(3): 313–30. doi:10.1080/09584930903108994

———. 2013. 'Beyond the "Exclusionary City": North-East Migrants in Neoliberal Delhi'. *Urban Studies* 50(8): 1625–40.

Mishra, D. K. 2007. *Rural Non-Farm Employment in Arunachal Pradesh: Growth, Composition and Determinants*, NLI Research Studies Series No. 075/2007. Noida: V. V. Giri National Labour Institute.

———. 2013. 'Developing the Border: The State and the Political Economy of Development in Arunachal Pradesh'. In *Borderland Lives in Northern South Asia*, edited by D. N. Gellner, 141–62. Durham: Duke University Press. doi: 10.1215/9780822377306-007

———. 2015a. 'Agrarian Relations and Institutional Diversity in Arunachal Pradesh'. In *Indian Capitalism in Development*, edited by B. Harriss-White and J. Heyer, 66–83. Abingdon: Routledge.

———. 2015b. 'Regions and Capitalist Transition in India: Arunachal Pradesh in a Comparative Perspective'. In *Mapping India's Capitalism: Old and New Regions*, edited by E. Basile, B. Harriss-White, and C. Lutringer, 87–112. Palgrave Macmillan.

———. 2016. 'Introduction: Internal Migration in Contemporary India—An Overview of Issues and Concerns'. In *Internal Migration in Contemporary India*, edited by D. K Mishra, 1–25. New Delhi: SAGE Publications.

———. 2017. 'Agrarian Transformation in Mountain Economies: Field Insights from Arunachal Pradesh'. In *Rethinking Economic Development in Northeast India: The Emerging Dynamics*, edited by D. K. Mishra and V. Upadhyay, 258–72. London: Routledge.

———. 2018. 'Desarrollo Hidroeléctrico y Derechos Comunitarios En El Himalaya Oriental, India. El Caso de Arunachal Pradesh' (Hydropower Development and Community Rights in Eastern Himalayas, India: The Case of Arunachal Pradesh). *Ecología Política* 55: 87–91.

———. Forthcoming. 'Himalayan Hydro-Criminality: Dams, Development and Politics in Arunachal Pradesh, India'. In *Wild East? Criminal Political Economies across South Asia*, edited by L. Michelutti and B. Harriss-White. London: UCL Press.

Mishra, D. K., and V. Upadhyay. 2017. 'Locating North Eastern Region in a Globalising India'. In *Rethinking Economic Development in Northeast India: The Emerging Dynamics*, edited by D. K. Mishra and V. Upadhyaya, 1–18. London: Routledge.

Mishra, D. K., V. Upadhyay, and A. Sarma. 2012. *Unfolding Crisis in Assam's Tea Plantations: Employment and Occupational Mobility*. New Delhi: Routledge.

Prasad-Aleyamma, M. 2018. 'Cards and Carriers: Migration, Identification and Surveillance in Kerala, South India'. *Contemporary South Asia* 26(2): 191–205.

Reimeingam, M. 2016. *Migration from North-Eastern Region to Bangalore: Level and Trend Analysis*, Working Paper 371. The Institute for Social and Economic Change, Bangalore.

Remesh, B. P. 2016. 'Migration and Marginalisation: A Study of North East Migrants in Delhi'. In *Internal Migration in Contemporary India*, edited by D. K. Mishra, 71–95. New Delhi: SAGE Publications.

Sahu, P. P., and R. Kumar. 2017. 'Employment Challenges in the North-Eastern Region of India: Post-Reform Trends and Dimensions'. In *Rethinking Economic Development in Northeast India: The Emerging Dynamics*, edited by D. K. Mishra and V. Upadhyay, 69–96. London: Routledge.

Shrestha, N. R. 1988. 'A Structural Perspective on Labour Migration in Underdeveloped Countries'. *Progress in Human Geography* 12(2): 179–207.

Sikri, R. 2009. 'India's "Look East" Policy'. *Asia-Pacific Review* 16(1): 131–45. Available at https://doi.org/10.1080/13439000902957624

Singh, D. K. 2010. *Stateless in South Asia: The Chakmas between Bangladesh and India*. Delhi: SAGE Publications.

Srivatsa, S., and D. Kurup. 2012. 'After Rumours, Northeast People Flee Bangalore'. *The Hindu*, 16 August. Available at https://www.thehindu.com/news/national/karnataka/after-rumours-northeast-people-flee-bangalore/article3776549.ece

Stark, O., and D. E. Bloom. 1985. 'The New Economics of Labor Migration'. *The American Economic Review* 75(2): 173–78.

Taylor, E. J. 1999. 'The New Economics of Labour Migration and the Role of Remittances in the Migration Process'. *International Migration* 37(1): 63–88.

Vandekerckhove, N. 2009. '"We Are Sons of this Soil": The Endless Battle over Indigenous Homelands in Assam, India'. *Critical Asian Studies* 41(4): 523–48.

Chapter 5

Development and Women Labour Market in India's North East
An Empirical Understanding

Archana Sharma

At the time of Independence India inherited an economy which was far behind the industrialized developed countries. There was more than one reason to identify the country as underdeveloped. India stepped into the path of development systematically with the launching of the First Five Year Plan in 1951, targeting a higher growth rate with the expectation that the benefits of the enhanced growth rate will percolate down to ameliorate poverty. Problems of unemployment and underemployment were also the other priorities. With the predominance of the public sector, the private sector functioned under the control of the government with a set of strict and lengthy licensing procedures. The strategy followed and resembled that of a developmental State which blended together with the conventional elements of capitalism such as private property, market economy and business elites and socialist elements such as national planning, public enterprises, government bureaucratic elites and egalitarian ideology (Hill 2007).

While the growth rate was quite promising in the initial period, particularly in the context of the poor state of affairs at the time of

Independence, very soon, it was identified that the growth rates were determined more by the vagaries of nature than by the then State developmental efforts. The problem of poverty persisted, and unemployment, inflation and other macro-parameters became uncontrollable. Regional inequalities cropped up, accompanied by other forms of inequalities, like gender inequality. The northeastern region continued to be conspicuous because of its economic backwardness in spite of the region being resource rich. On the other hand, the region with its topography, customs, traditions and culture, political upheavals, insurgency and many other issues like environmental degradation and natural disasters engaged the attention of policy planners. Eventually, in 1971, North Eastern Council was formed for regional planning, for better planning and for expediting growth of the seven states, namely, Arunachal Pradesh, Assam, Manipur, Meghalaya, Mizoram, Nagaland and Tripura. Sikkim was added to the group in 2002.

A technology-driven development agenda normally shifts the focus from agriculture to industries. As a result, the employment potentialities in the agricultural sector gets reduced. This obviously has a detrimental impact on women's employment as traditionally more women are employed in the agricultural sector. The urban industrial sector requires skilled and more productive labour. It is difficult for women to acquire such skills and hence they are less preferred in the urban industrial sector. Commercialization and mechanization of the agricultural sector reduces women's employment opportunities also within the agricultural sector (Rai 2008). As a whole, the development agenda is unable to address the problems and needs of women and other vulnerable sections of the society as well as of the peripheral regions. India's development experience also did not prove to be gender friendly.

That the benefits of development did not reach the majority of women, particularly the women in the informal sector, was revealed by the seminal work 'Towards Equality' (GOI 1974). The way Boserup's (1970) study on women's work rang a bell for the United Nations, so did this report awaken policymakers in India. This awakening was backed by women's movements and also the initiatives taken by the United Nations led to some major policy changes towards women in the country. Studies on women including women's work participation became a popular area of research and subsequent cutting-edge publications created a genre on women studies in the economic domain. However, most of these studies are confined to the major states of India and hence women's labour market interaction in the peripheral regions like the North East still has to be explored. Region-specific studies on women's work participation are all the more important because gender is a social construct and its form is region and culture specific (Bannerjee 2011).

Although at the global level women's roles in economic activities and development were recognized only in the 1970s, Indian planners were not blind to women's roles as productive workers. Much before Independence, a marked decline in women's work participation rates (WPRs) in India was pointed out in the 1920s by the renowned scholar D. R. Gadgil. The dramatic decline in women's WPRs in West Bengal between 1901 and 1951 was later raised and discussed by Ashok Mitra in his census report for 1951. In 1961, exactly 10 years after launching the First Five Year Plan, Indian Council of Social Science Research (ICSSR) published a report on the status of women's employment compared to that of men in India on the basis of tables constructed in the 1961 census. The document revealed the position of women in India's labour market in different political zones of the country that emerged under its federal structure. Among the five political zones, the eastern zone included the states of Assam, Manipur, Tripura, Nagaland, Sikkim and the North-East Frontier Agency (NEFA) of Assam in addition to three states of eastern India, namely, West Bengal, Orissa and Bihar. In 1961, the northeastern states Meghalaya and Mizoram were not different states but were part of Assam, and today's Arunachal Pradesh was known as NEFA. As such, the northeastern region/states did not figure in the census report separately and were clubbed together with the eastern states—Orissa, West Bengal and Bihar.

As all the states comprising the present northeastern region appear in one homogenous group in State imagination, the chapter has taken this consolidated report as a baseline of women's WPRs to understand the pattern of northeastern states. Whereas the mean sex ratio in WPRs was quite low in all the five zones, the western and southern zones had much higher values, and the eastern zone was in between. Rural household industries employed the majority of women in all the five zones at that point of time, with the sex ratio not being significantly different between the zones. The urban household industry employed much lesser women, which was followed by the rural and urban non-household industry. The mean sex ratios of workers in the eastern zone in these three industrial divisions were, respectively, 403, 163 and 78, the first two divisions being at the penultimate place and the third division in the bottom.

Within the rural non-household industries, the sex ratio of workers has been above 500 only in three major groups, namely, plantation, forestry and logging and foodstuffs. In the case of urban household industries, the sex ratio of workers was the highest in the cotton and textile industry, followed by the silk textile industry. Within urban non-household industries, the sex ratio of workers was the highest in the manufacturing of wood and wood products followed by construction, machinery and forestry and logging. In this major division of industries, cotton textiles can be identified as a woman-dominant activity. On the whole, women's WPRs in all the political zones of India were low and women were employed in traditional, low-paid, pain-staking jobs.

In 1991, the country embraced neoliberalism, stepping out from a technology-driven development State towards a knowledge-driven market society. Such policy changes and structural shifts raised expectations about women's WPRs and their respective opportunities in some quarters, while some others were critical and apprehensive about such economic changes. Without entering into any such debate, the chapter examines the realities of women's work participation with the help of data from National Sample Survey Office (NSSO).

The 1993–94 data have been looked at from two perspectives—as the end of the State development era and the beginning of the neo-liberal regime. The scenario in 1993–94 has been compared with that of the early period of development, as reflected in the ICSSR study analysed earlier. Though the NSSO data used for 1993–94 are not directly comparable with the census data used in the ICSSR study, the comparison could provide a glimpse of changes in women's WPRs in the North East over the developmental decades.

Then, taking the 1993–94 data as the baseline, the chapter has assessed the trend and pattern of women's work participation from 1993–94 to 2011–12 to find out the impact of liberalization on the position of women in the labour market in all northeastern states vis-à-vis the all-India average position in the post-liberalization period in the following structure.

1. The WPRs of women compared to that of men;
2. the types of work where more women than men are engaged; and
3. the sectoral distribution of economic activities of women vis-à-vis men.

WORK PARTICIPATION RATES OF MEN AND WOMEN: LOCATING INDIA'S NORTH EAST

Though the North East is imagined as one regional unit for administrative purposes, the present chapter has deconstructed it by taking its states as individual units to understand and examine the situation of each state separately. Without discarding the factors that have led to the recognition of these states as one region, each state is examined separately due to its different demographic composition. The manifestation of commonalities and the differences among these individual states in the North East are considered here as normal affairs like any other states in India. Though this might not have been true in the past, with rising differences in many fronts of socio-economic activities, such distinctions among the states of North East can no longer be ignored in the present-day context. The term 'North East' can be viewed more as a political construct which emerged since colonial times. Sometimes, it is felt that by clubbing these states as a region, they are treated as 'the other'—different from the mainstream. To break such barriers, it is more justified to see these states as independent unique entities within the Indian State.

It may be noted that the NSSO data provides information on the labour market of a particular area, be it a state, a country or a district. When the chapter talks about the labour market of the eight states of the northeastern region, it refers to the labour market participation of women and men within the state. In case of women in these states who have migrated to other states and are working there, such a scenario is not reflected in the estimated tables. Similarly, all the workers may not belong to the respective state(s), and many are also from outside. So, the larger picture of the NSSO data is on the labour market of each state and not necessarily of men and women separately of the states. There are men and women of northeastern states in different categories of jobs, including the high-valued ones, in other parts of the country and also abroad, which are not captured in this chapter. The analysis done in the following rather reveals some pertinent facts about labour market participation of men and women residing in the respective states.

As the first step of the exercise, we analyse the data for 1993–94. As per the data, the sex ratio of WPRs at the all-India level was marginally above 500 in rural areas and less than 300 in urban areas. In all the northeastern states, the female WPR was much lower than that of men. Arunachal Pradesh had the highest sex ratio in WPRs, with 822.9 in rural areas, followed by Meghalaya with 796.4 and Manipur with 645.7. In the lower scale, Tripura had the lowest rate, with 245.2, followed by Assam with 308.1. In the descending order, Mizoram comes next to Manipur, with 599.2, followed by Nagaland, with 492.0, and Sikkim with 339.2. The 1961 report on census data, as mentioned earlier, states that, 'in Eastern Zones and … 68 per cent … of the major industries have a sex ratio less than 500' (Mitra et al. 1979, 9). As such, sex ratios above 500 could be taken as an improvement but that level also was not be reached by four states of the North East. In case of the urban labour market, only Manipur and Mizoram had sex ratios above 500, the lowest being Assam with 174.2. It could therefore be inferred that women in the northeastern states did not enjoy the benefit of the expanding labour market during the developmental decades.

THE TYPES OF WORK: MEN AND WOMEN PARTICIPATION

With regard to the type of employment, the 1993–94 NSSO data show that very few women in rural areas had regular wages/salaried jobs. Women mostly were self-employed and more women worked as casual labourers compared to men at the all-India level, with sex ratios of 317.6, 1,015.6 and 1,144.9 for regular wages/salaried jobs, self-employed and casual labourers, respectively. In the urban labour market, the respective figures were 676.2, 1,098.3 and 1,582.8, which shows that although there may be differences in the number of women employed in different types of employment in urban areas, the relative positions of the three types of employment remain the same as in the case of rural areas, with casual labour and self-employment being the main resorts for women.

In contrast to the all-India scenario, in Assam, the sex ratio in salaried jobs in rural areas was more than those of self-employed and casual labour, but in urban areas, the sex ratio in casual labour was the highest followed by regular wages/salaried jobs. The sex ratios in casual labour and salaried jobs in both the rural and the urban areas were in favour of women, that is, above 1,000. In Arunachal Pradesh and Manipur, sex ratios in salaried jobs and casual labour were very low in both the rural and the urban labour market; it was higher in the case of self-employment. In the case of Meghalaya, the sex ratios in all three types of works were similar, but in the urban areas, the proportion of female self-employees was higher than that of male self-employees. In Nagaland, sex ratios were in favour of women in both regular wages/salaried jobs and among the self-employees in rural areas and only in regular wages/salaried jobs in urban areas. In Mizoram, sex ratios were in favour of women in the case of the self-employees in both the rural and the urban areas but low in other types of works. In urban areas, sex ratios were in favour of women in the case of self-employees and much below 500 in the other two types. In Sikkim and Tripura, sex ratios were in favour of women for self-employees in rural areas and in case of regular Wages/salaried jobs in urban areas. In Tripura, women's participation as casual labourers was also as high as 973.8 in rural areas and more than 1,000 in urban areas.

THE SECTORAL DISTRIBUTION OF ECONOMIC ACTIVITIES OF MEN AND WOMEN

The sex ratio of WPRs in both rural and urban India was the highest in the primary sector—in agriculture and allied activities—followed by secondary sector; the lowest sex ratio was in the tertiary sector. Within the secondary sector, manufacturing had the highest sex ratio. Within the service sector, other services which include domestic workers absorbed the highest number of women at the all-India level.

In case of both rural and urban Assam, the sex ratio was in favour of women in the primary and the secondary sectors, with the secondary sector having a higher sex ratio. Sex ratio in the tertiary sector was less than 500 in rural areas but as high as 988.3 in urban Assam. In both rural and urban areas within the secondary sector, manufacturing had the highest sex ratio, while 'other services' was at the top in case of the tertiary sector. In rural Arunachal Pradesh, the sex ratio was the highest in the primary sector and was in favour of women with a value above 1,000, but the sex ratio was less than 500 in the case of the secondary sector and less than 100 in the case of the tertiary sector, reflecting women's minimal presence in this sector. Within the secondary sector the sex ratio was the highest in the manufacturing sector and within the tertiary sector, 'other services' absorbed more women. In both rural and urban Arunachal Pradesh, the sex ratio was the highest in the primary sector but the sex ratio was much higher than that in rural Arunachal Pradesh; in urban areas the next position was occupied by the tertiary sector with a value above 1,000. Within the secondary sector the sex ratio was the highest in construction and within the tertiary sector, 'other services' have the highest sex ratio. In rural Manipur, the sex ratio was the highest in the secondary sector and in favour of women with a value above 3,000, but the sex ratio was less than 500 in case of the tertiary sector and a little less than 1,000 in case of the primary sector. Within the secondary sector the sex ratio was the highest in the manufacturing and within the tertiary sector, trade, hotels and restaurants absorbed more women. In urban Manipur, the sex ratio was highest in the secondary sector with manufacturing taking the most prominent position; the sex ratio in the tertiary sector was only 664.9 with trade, hotels and restaurants having the highest sex ratio. In both rural and urban Meghalaya, the sex ratio was highest in the primary sector followed by the tertiary sector; the secondary sector had the lowest sex ratio which was below 500 in rural Meghalaya. In rural Meghalaya, mining and quarrying had the highest sex ratios, followed by trade, hotel and restaurant; electricity and water; manufacturing and other services. Within the tertiary sector, trade, hotel and restaurants employed more women. In rural Nagaland the sex ratio was highest in the primary sector, followed by the secondary sector and the tertiary sector, respectively, but in urban areas the primary sector was followed by the tertiary and the secondary sectors, respectively. In rural areas, the only avenue which had a favourable sex ratio was mining and quarrying; there were no women in the other secondary sector activities. In the tertiary sector the highest sex ratio was in transport, storage and communications. In urban Nagaland, within the secondary sector, electricity, water and so on had the highest sex ratio followed by construction. Among tertiary sector activities 'other services' had the highest sex ratio. In rural Mizoram the sex ratio was the highest in the primary sector/agriculture followed by the tertiary and the secondary sector. The secondary sector had the lowest sex ratio which was only a little above 100, implying a marginal presence in this sector. As a whole, the sex ratio in the tertiary sector was only a little above 500 but it was very high in trade, hotels and restaurants. In urban Mizoram, the sex ratio was highest in the primary sector followed by the tertiary and the secondary sectors, respectively. The tertiary sector had a sex ratio of less than 1,000 with trade, hotels and restaurants having the highest sex ratio within the tertiary sector. In rural Sikkim the sex ratio was the highest in the primary sector/agriculture followed by the secondary and the tertiary sectors, respectively. In the urban areas sex ratio in the tertiary sector was the highest followed by the secondary sector. Within the secondary sector construction had the highest sex ratio. In the tertiary sector sex ratio was the highest in other services in both rural and urban areas. In both rural and urban Tripura, the sex ratio was the highest in the primary sector/agriculture followed by the secondary and tertiary sectors, respectively. Within the secondary sector manufacturing had the highest sex ratio in rural Tripura, while mining and quarrying took the lead in urban Tripura. In the service sector the sex ratio was highest in other services in both rural and urban areas.

From the analysis of data for 1993–94, it could be inferred that the employment pattern of women in majority of the northeastern states follows the all-India pattern; marginal differences in the composition of the workforce could be perceived within the eight states. The activity where sex ratio was higher in most of the northeastern states as well as in the all-India level was 'other services'. It may be noted that 'other services' includes domestic work. Trade, hotels and restaurants were other major employers in the tertiary sector in most of the states in the northeastern region. This may be treated as an indicator of the prevalence of the sexual division of labour even in the public domain. This also re-establishes the position reflected in the census data of 1961 that women workers were both more in the rural household sector and in low-paid jobs.

In the next step, we analyse the data on the same aspects for the post-liberalization period, on the basis of the NSSO data for five rounds, that is, 1993–94 (50th round), 1999–2000 (55th round), 2004–05 (61st round), 2009–10 (66th round) and 2011–12 (68th round) (Tables 5.1–5.9).

As evident from the data, the WPR in general for both men and women and across both rural and urban areas had a substantial decline between 1993–94 and 1999–2000 at the all-India level and even in the northeastern states of Arunachal Pradesh and Tripura. In case of other northeastern states, namely, in Assam, the WPR of rural males and urban females increased while it decreased for rural females and urban males. In Manipur, the WPR of both rural and urban males increased while the same WPR of both rural and urban females decreased. In

Table 5.1 *Work Participation Rates (Principal Status [PS] + Subsidiary Status [SS]) by Sex and Sex Ratios: All India (Rural and Urban), between 1993–1994 and 2001–2012*

Rounds	Rural			Urban		
	Male	Female	Sex Ratio	Male	Female	Sex Ratio
50th (1993–1994)	553	328	593.1	521	155	297.5
55th (1999–2000)	531	299	563.1	518	139	268.3
61st (2004–2005)	546	327	598.9	549	166	302.4
66th (2009–2010)	547	261	477.1	543	138	254.1
68th (2011–2012)	543	248	456.7	546	147	269.2

Source: GOI 1994, 2001, 2006, 2011 and 2014.

Table 5.2 Work Participation Rates (PS+SS) by Sex and Sex Ratios: Assam (Rural and Urban), from 1993–1994 to 2011–2012

Rounds	Rural			Urban		
	Male	Female	Sex Ratio	Male	Female	Sex Ratio
50th (1993–1994)	516	159	308.1	52.8	9.2	174.2
55th (1999–2000)	529	151	285.4	52.2	11.2	214.5
61st (2004–2005)	551	209	379.3	55.1	10.9	197.8
66th (2009–2010)	553	158	285.7	52.8	9.3	176.1
68th (2011–2012)	540	122	225.9	54.2	9.0	166.0

Source: GOI 1994, 2001, 2006, 2011 and 2014.

Table 5.3 Work Participation Rates (PS+SS) by Sex and Sex Ratios: Arunachal Pradesh (Rural and Urban), from 1993–1994 to 2011–2012

Rounds	Rural			Urban		
	Male	Female	Sex Ratio	Male	Female	Sex Ratio
50th (1993–1994)	497.0	409.0	822.9	515.0	101.0	196.1
55th (1999–2000)	422.0	310.0	734.6	399.0	100.0	250.6
61st (2004–2005)	500.0	410.0	820.0	461.1	148.0	321.0
66th (2009–2010)	499.0	293.0	587.2	438.0	148.0	337.9
68th (2011–2012)	483.0	278.0	575.6	457.0	127.0	277.9

Source: GOI 1994, 2001, 2006, 2011 and 2014.

Meghalaya the WPR of urban females marginally rose while there was a fall for all other categories. In Nagaland the WPR increased for all categories except urban females. In Mizoram, there was a fall in the WPR of urban males and females but an increase in the WPR of rural males and females. In Sikkim the WPR of both rural and urban women increased but the WPR of both rural and urban males decreased. Thus, the first bout of reforms did not lead to a positive change in the labour

Table 5.4 Work Participation Rates (PS+SS) by Sex and Sex Ratios: Manipur (Rural and Urban), from 1993–1994 to 2011–2012

Rounds	Rural			Urban		
	Male	Female	Sex Ratio	Male	Female	Sex Ratio
50th (1993–1994)	477.0	308.0	645.7	434.0	223.0	513.8
55th (1999–2000)	495.0	253.0	511.1	445.0	211.0	474.1
61st (2004–2005)	524.0	351.0	665.8	456.0	221.0	484.6
66th (2009–2010)	499.0	212.0	424.8	472.0	146.0	309.3
68th (2011–2012)	510.0	262.0	513.7	456.0	182.0	399.1

Source: GOI 1994, 2001, 2006, 2011 and 2014.

Table 5.5 Work Participation Rates (PS+SS) by Sex and Sex Ratios in Work Participation: Meghalaya (Rural and Urban), from 1993–1994 to 2011–2012

Rounds	Rural			Urban		
	Male	Female	Sex Ratio	Male	Female	Sex Ratio
50th (1993–1994)	619.0	493.0	796.4	500.0	189.0	378.0
55th (1999–2000)	557.0	418.0	750.4	393.0	197.0	501.3
61st (2004–2005)	572.0	478.0	835.7	454.0	303.0	667.4
66th (2009–2010)	580.0	371.0	639.6	468.0	214.0	457.3
68th (2011–2012)	527.0	391.0	741.9	503.0	202.0	401.6

Source: GOI 1994, 2001, 2006, 2011 and 2014.

market at the all-India level, while some of the northeastern states showed a positive trend.

The trend in the WPR beyond 1999–2000 did not follow the same direction as seen between 1993–94 and 1999–2000. The results broadly highlight that considering the trend in the case of the all-India

Table 5.6 Work Participation Rates (PS+SS) by Sex and Sex Ratios in Work Participation: Nagaland (Rural and Urban), from 1993–1994 to 2011–2012

Rounds	Rural			Urban		
	Male	Female	Sex Ratio	Male	Female	Sex Ratio
50th (1993–1994)	439.0	216.0	492.0	378.0	990.0	261.9
55th (1999–2000)	518.0	441.0	851.3	393.0	199.0	506.4
61st (2004–2005)	549.0	504.0	918.0	457.0	257.0	562.4
66th (2009–2010)	500.0	319.0	638.0	436.0	132.0	302.7
68th (2011–2012)	504.0	312.0	619.0	412.0	144.0	349.5

Source: GOI 1994, 2001, 2006, 2011 and 2014.

Table 5.7. Work Participation Rates (PS+SS) by Sex and Sex Ratio in Work Participation: Mizoram (Rural and Urban), from 1993–1994 to 2011–2012

Rounds	Rural			Urban		
	Male	Female	Sex Ratio	Male	Female	Sex Ratio
50th (1993–1994)	529.0	317.0	599.2	484.0	264.0	545.4
55th (1999–2000)	555.0	440.0	792.8	471.0	259.0	549.9
61st (2004–2005)	594.0	441.0	742.4	484.0	281.0	580.6
66th (2009–2010)	598.0	404.0	675.6	521.0	288.0	552.8
68th (2011–2012)	591.0	394.0	666.7	487.0	249.0	511.3

Source: GOI 1994, 2001, 2006, 2011 and 2014.

average, the WPR for rural males and females and urban females from 1993–94 to 2011–12 can be termed 'fluctuating decline' while for urban males it was a fluctuating increase. In Assam and Manipur the female WPR declined in both rural and urban areas while the WPR in both rural and urban males increased. In Arunachal Pradesh, the

Table 5.8 Work Participation Rates (PS+SS) by Sex and Sex Ratio in Work Participation: Sikkim (Rural and Urban), from 1993–1994 to 2011–2012

	Rural			Urban		
Rounds	Male	Female	Sex Ratio	Male	Female	Sex Ratio
50th (1993–1994)	563.0	191.1	339.2	580.0	136.0	234.5
55th (1999–2000)	502.0	241.1	480.1	519.0	200.0	385.3
61st (2004–2005)	554.0	318.0	574.0	545.0	168.0	308.2
66th (2009–2010)	556.0	309.0	555.7	601.0	150.0	249.6
68th (2011–2012)	580.0	487.0	839.6	609.0	273.0	448.3

Source: GOI 1994, 2001, 2006, 2011 and 2014.

Table 5.9 Work Participation Rates (PS+SS) by Sex and Sex Ratio in Work Participation: Tripura (Rural and Urban), from 1993–1994 to 2011–2012

	Rural			Urban		
Rounds	Male	Female	Sex Ratio	Male	Female	Sex Ratio
50th (1993–1994)	522.0	128.0	245.2	497.0	124.0	249.5
55th (1999–2000)	504.0	73.0	144.8	494.0	75.0	151.8
61st (2004–2005)	549.0	85.0	154.8	504.0	100.0	198.4
66th (2009–2010)	583.0	188.0	322.5	556.0	108.0	194.2
68th (2011–2012)	562.0	228.0	405.7	525.0	113.0	215.2

Source: GOI 1994, 2001, 2006, 2011 and 2014.

WPR in all categories except for urban females declined, and even for urban females there was a fall in the WPR in 2011–12 compared to 2009–10. In Meghalaya the WPR declined in rural areas but increased for urban males. In Nagaland, the trend in female WPR showed an upward trend in both rural and urban areas, up to 2004–05, and then the downturn continued till 2011–12. In Mizoram the WPR increased in all categories except in the case of urban females. In Sikkim the WPR increased in all categories. In Tripura the WPR declined in all categories except urban females.

At the all-India level, there was a clear decline in the sex ratio in work participation over time, except for a small rise between 1999–2000 and 2004–05. This applied to both rural and urban areas. Manipur revealed the same trend as the all-India pattern. In both rural and urban Assam, there was a decline in the sex ratio over the period, but there was an upward movement between 1999–2000 and 2004–05 in rural Assam and in rural Meghalaya. In urban Assam, the upturn was between 1993–94 and 1999–2000, followed by a continuous decline till 2011–12. In rural Mizoram the upturn continued till 2004–05 and in urban Mizoram the upturn continued till 2009–10 and then declined. In urban Arunachal Pradesh there was an upward movement till 2009–10 but rural Arunachal Pradesh showed a decline over the period, in spite of a considerable rise between 1999–2000 and 2004–05. Urban Meghalaya and rural Nagaland showed improvement till 2004–05 and then a downturn; urban Nagaland also had the same trend with a marginal improvement between 2009–10 and 2011–12. Both rural and urban Sikkim showed improvements in both male and female WPRs while Tripura showed an improvement in all other cases except in the case of urban females.

The trend in the sex ratio in work participation by types of employment in India and the eight northeastern states has a few encouraging developments, for example, the relative presence of female child labour has gone down in both rural and urban areas at the all-India level, Assam and Sikkim as well as in the urban areas of four other northeastern states, namely, Manipur, Meghalaya, Mizoram and Tripura. It increased in Arunachal Pradesh and Nagaland in both rural and urban areas. It may be noted that Arunachal Pradesh and Nagaland also have higher sex ratios in construction. An increase in the sex ratio in salaried jobs was seen in the case of all northeastern states except in Nagaland, Sikkim and urban Arunachal Pradesh.

As regards the sectoral distribution of workers, at the all-India level, the relative position of the three sectors, the predominance of manufacturing within the secondary sector and that of 'other services' in the tertiary sector remain the same even at the end of the period under consideration. Sex ratios increased in all the three sectors in rural India but decreased in urban India; the increase in the sex ratio of the secondary and tertiary sectors is not commensurate with the decrease in the primary sector. In both rural and urban Assam, the secondary sector had the highest rank in terms of sex ratio in 1993–94, it maintained its position in rural Assam in 1999–2000 but not in urban Assam. Thereafter, the primary sector took the lead followed by the secondary and tertiary sectors, respectively. The sex ratio in other services was high.

Both in rural and urban Arunachal Pradesh the predominance of the primary sector and 'other services' continued, although in urban areas trade, hotels and restaurants had a higher sex ratio in work participation than 'other services'—showing expansion of women's job opportunities in the hospitality sector. The sex ratio in construction increased in urban areas but declined considerably in rural areas. In both rural and urban Manipur, the secondary sector remained dominant followed by the tertiary sector, with the primary sector remaining at the bottom. Within the secondary sector manufacturing had the highest sex ratio, while in the tertiary sector, trade, hotels and restaurants employed more women than men in rural areas. In both rural and urban Meghalaya the primary sector employed more women than men, followed by the tertiary and the secondary sectors, respectively. In the secondary sector, manufacturing had the highest sex ratio while in the tertiary sector trade, hotels and restaurants had the highest sex ratios followed by 'other services'. The sex ratio in manufacturing however declined in 2011–12 compared to 1993–94, although there was an upward trend between 1999–2000 and 2004–05, and between 1993–94 and 1999–2000, it had fallen down considerably from 818.2 to 444.4. In rural Nagaland, the higher participation of women in the primary sector could be seen at the end of the period under study but the trend was not smooth; the sex ratio in the secondary sector increased between 1993–94 and 2009–2010 at such a rate that in 2009–10, the sex ratio in the secondary sector was even higher than that of the primary sector. While mining and quarrying had the highest sex ratios in 1993–94, the position was taken over by the manufacturing from 1999–2000 onwards. In urban Nagaland, the primary sector had the topmost position in terms of sex ratio followed by the secondary and the tertiary sectors throughout the period, but between 1993–94 and 2011–12, the sex ratio increased only in the case of the secondary sector. Within the secondary sector, manufacturing and, within the tertiary sector trade, hotels and restaurants had the highest sex ratios from 1999–2000 onwards. In rural Mizoram, the primary sector faced a decline in the sex ratio while in the secondary and the tertiary sector it increased. Within the secondary sector, construction had the highest sex ratio and in the tertiary sector trade, hotels and restaurants had the highest sex ratios, although there was a decline over time. In urban Mizoram, in terms of sex ratio, the primary, tertiary and secondary sector can be placed in the descending order if sex ratios are considered. Manufacturing in the secondary sector and trade, hotels and restaurants in the tertiary sector employ more women than men. In 2011–12, in both rural and urban Sikkim, the three sectors appear as primary, tertiary and secondary sector in the descending order. Sikkim's labour market is dominated by the secondary and tertiary sector. Over time, the sex ratio in construction decreased while it increased in trade, hotels and restaurants. In rural Tripura, the sex ratio is the highest in the secondary sector followed by the primary and tertiary sectors; manufacturing continues to be the dominant activity in the secondary sector while other services occupies the topmost position in the tertiary sector. In urban Tripura the primary, tertiary and secondary sectors appear in that order. The positions of other services and manufacturing continue to be at the top in the tertiary and secondary sectors, respectively.

CONCLUDING OBSERVATION

From the earlier, it can be seen that the trend and pattern of participation of women in the labour market in the northeastern states are not very different from the all-India pattern, although some differences could be perceived even within these eight states. The female WPR did not cross the 50 per cent mark in any state, the sex ratio in WPRs was above 500 for the entire post-liberalization period in Mizoram, both rural and urban, rural Arunachal Pradesh and rural Meghalaya. Assam and Tripura could never reach that level. Only Sikkim had a sex ratio of more than 800 in WPRs at the end of the period. Employment avenues in the region being limited, women have not been able to niche out a secured space within the labour market. The analysis justifies the need for addressing the issue of women's work participation from the perspective of each individual state, considering them not only as members of a region but also as the recipients or victims of the development pattern that took place in the respective states.

REFERENCES

Bannerjee, N. 2011. 'Reproduction and the Family'. In *Mapping the Field: Gender Relations in Contemporary India*, edited by N. Bannerjee, S. Sen, and N. Dhawan, Vol. I. Kolkata: Stree.

Boserup, E. 1970. *Woman's Role in Economic Development*. New York: St. Matin's Press.

Government of India (GOI), Ministry of Education and Social Welfare. 1974. *Towards Equality*. New Delhi: Report of the Committee on the Status of Women in India

Government of India (GOI), Ministry of Statistics and Programme Implementation. 1994. *Employment and Unemployment Situation in India, NSS Report 50th Round*. New Delhi: National Sample Survey Organisation.

———. 2001. *Employment and Unemployment Situation in India, NSS Report, 55th Round*. New Delhi: National Sample Survey Organisation.

———. 2006. *Employment and Unemployment Situation in India, NSS Report, 61st Round*. New Delhi: National Sample Survey Organisation.

———. 2011. *Employment and Unemployment Situation in India, NSS Report, 66th Round*. New Delhi: National Sample Survey Organisation.

———. 2014. *Employment and Unemployment Situation in India, NSS Report, 68th Round*. New Delhi: National Sample Survey Organisation.

Hill, R. C. 2007. 'Neoliberalism & Developmentalism: The East Asian Experience Taipei Discussion Forum'. 20 December. Retrieved from https://msu.edu/user/hilrr/TaipeiTalk

Mitra, A., A. K. Srimany, and L. P. Pathak. 1979. *The Status of Women: Household and Non-Household Economic Activity* (ICSSR Programme of Women's Studies-III). New Delhi: Allied Publishers Pvt. Ltd.

Rai, Shirin M. 2008. *The Gender Politics of Development*. New Delhi: Zubaan.

PART III

New Development at the Periphery

Chapter 6

Neoliberal Developmentalism
State Strategy in India's North East

Rakhee Bhattacharya

Various narratives on India's economic liberalization since the 1990s have largely produced a body of knowledge on both its policy approach towards an open economy and its outcomes, which are deeply intertwined with binaries such as 'growth and inequality', 'advanced and backward' and 'progressive and regressive' (see Ahluwalia 2002; Barua and Sawshey 2015; Chakravorty 2000; Chandrashekhar and Ghosh 2004; Ghosh et al. 1998; Hari and Hatti 2015; Jha 2004; Kundu and Varghese 2010; Kurian 2000; Misra 2015; Nayar 2008; Piketty 2013). This vast knowledge production in the last quarter century has reoriented the mainstream–margin and core–periphery debates of post-colonial times. India's North East has been precisely perceived as a backward peripheral space with negligible economic outcomes (see Bhattacharya 2011; Brunner 2010; Nayank 2009; Rajeev and Akhtar 2015; Singh 2009). This dominant discourse of measuring and scaling an economy and its progress, typically within the neoliberal 'flat world', has paid a little attention towards other theoretical debates such as (new) economic geography, which the economic thinker like Paul Krugman has contributed immensely in the 1990s to construct a powerful approach (Krugman 1991) to understand the spatial significance in economic progress. While emphasizing locational specificities, economic geography is an approach to integrate intra-regional and transnational economic affairs like trade and other engagements in the age of economic liberalization and then increase the returns to scale. India has paid attention to such spatial significance in its approach to economic integration with its neighbouring nations by relocating the space of margins like the North East. North East, a constructed geography of colonial capitalists, was largely a site for resource extraction and a subject of the 'periphery' for economic appropriation, mobilization and circulation (see Bhattacharya 2007, 2011; Goswami 1981; Misra 1980; Sachdev 2000). On the other hand, with the making of political boundaries between 1826 and 1947, this constructed geography was mapped with a set of the most complex external orientations and re-territorialized with about 98 per cent of international borders, and this forced the post-colonial securitist State to imagine the North East as a 'strategic borderland' of India (Bhattacharya 2014). With Radcliffe Border in 1947, the economic contiguity of this trans-spatial North East was disrupted heavily. Such evolving politics of territory and its realities also became paramount for spatial and temporal specificities of the North East along with State strategies and the 'logic of security' in post-colonial times. This had unheeded economic nationalism in the North East unlike other parts of India. The further closure of trans-spatial routes after the creation of Bangladesh in 1971 led to the isolated and cut-off geography of the North East, and the distance differentials between most of the North East towns and the nearest city Calcutta were increased by the galloping distance of 4,458 km. Left with a stress of a solitary 28-km connecting corridor through the town Siliguri of North Bengal, this new geography of the North East was also stereotyped as 'landlocked' and became a 'buffer' zone to protect India from external aggression. Without any proactive role of the developmental State, the North East was imagined as 'backward' and 'underdeveloped' in the post-colonial period (see MDoNER 2008; Planning Commission 1981, 1997; Strategy Report 2007).

During the 1990s, India made a structural shift in the economy, from a nationalist approach towards a neoliberal economy by opening and engaging at transnational spaces through multiple channels of connectivity, trade, market, innovation, capital and labour movement. India aimed at expanding its economy towards East and Southeast Asia, and the North East with its geographical proximity to those nations became a space of significance in State economic policy. This was re-imagined as a 'connecting gateway' for creating various transnational routes and market networks (FICCI 2004; Indian Chamber of Commerce 2013). Such 'market-conforming liberalization' though usually is a sign of the 'State's retreat' in any capitalist structure, but the developmental State of India made an effort to engage and augment the market in the North East by creating 'essential conditions' like transport and connectivity infrastructure. Thus, as the logic of State and market relations was restructured, the internal dynamics of the North East also gradually changed with the rising necessity of economic progress to ensure the well-being and 'catch up' with other parts of India. The State, in the process, has gained authority and control over the logic of development. As the spatial significance of the North East was understood by India's neoliberal State, its policy of international economic relations also eventually started to relocate the geography of the North East as a gateway to engage in sub-regional cooperation with various neighbouring nations. This strategy of new regionalism has pushed India to essentialize the North East as a subject of transnational theatre for commercial integration and neoliberal market expansion (NITI Aayog 2017). Developmentalism accordingly has also become a State strategy, where connectivity, capital and corridor are seen as initial conditions in the North East towards the idea of a trans-border Asian network. As this structural shift in policy space needs a new theoretical interrogation within a larger debate of State strategy, this chapter attempts to understand such changing State's perceptions of the North East and their significance in India's neoliberal approach. The chapter is built up within the conceptual frame of economic geography and its implications in market expansion at the transnational level. It also looks at the complexities of contemporary State patronage for new capital towards various developmental activities and its emerging social relations in the North East. Finally, in a suggestive note, it explores an endogenous approach towards transregional economic agglomeration in the North East and its neighbouring areas as a counter-strategy of market integration and its world view.

FROM NATIONAL TO TRANSNATIONAL: ROLE OF THE DEVELOPMENTAL STATE

With the changing strategy of State developmentalism in the 1990s, the North East for the first time in the post-colonial period was imagined with the idea of an open space through the unmaking of borders and 'thinning' of its barrier affects and then connecting with neighbouring nations through transnational economic interactions such as border huts, border trade, cross-border industry, cross-border routes and cross-border trades and supply chains. Such an idea of unmaking borders was to ensure large-scale economies, greater mobility and market expansion at the trans-spatial level and also address the issue of 'geographical isolation' of this space. Many new State projects on connectivity infrastructure development were proposed and some have been commissioned in the last two decades to create spatial connections with its neighbours and beyond. With such moves, the ideology of a nationalist-protectionist post-colonial State has transformed towards a transnational narrative of developmentalism in the North East.

This re-orientation of the State's role emerged in the larger changing context of the neoliberal economic order, where territorial delimitation was proposed through globalism to craft newer 'methods of commerce' and economic surplus by increasing and expanding the dependence on transnational economic activities through the geoeconomic strategies of various States. Such State projects in a country like India, as argued by Priya Chako, reflect the prioritization of the nation's economic growth and global competitiveness at both institutional and international dimensions. She argues that, prior to 1991, the national developmental State project was linked to 'geo-political social forms' to shape its global and regional multilateralism, which laid the path for a deeper shift in the 'national social order'. This engagement fluctuated according to the shifts in the legitimacy and viability of State projects in India, and the erosion began since the 1990s with greater introspection on economic openness, growth and competitiveness. This shift in the State project in India gave rise to new forms of global and regional engagements with the 'geo-economic social form' (Chako 2015), throwing new challenges to traditional geopolitical narratives. The theoretical debates on geoeconomics began about a quarter century ago in 1990 with the pioneering work of Edward Luttwak, *From Geopolitics to Geo-economics: Logic of Conflict, Grammar of Commerce*, where Luttwak constructed geoeconomics in the context of post-Cold War geopolitics and showed it as a system of inter-State rivalry and conflict, which is largely conducted through the 'grammar of commerce'. According to him, States will not disappear but reorient themselves towards geoeconomics to compensate for their decaying geopolitical roles in international relations (Luttwak 1990). This, according to Mikael Mattlin and Mikael Wigell (2016), appears to be vexing and is seen as the first theoretical approach to geoeconomics, and subsequently scholars such as Stulberg (2005), Sparke (2007), Youngs (2011) and Wu and Koh (2014) have expanded its scope as a form of 'State-craft'. States, according to them, remain the primary agent for any transnational economic ends and gains such as financial gains, mercantilism, energy and control over resources.

With the structural reforms in the 1990s, the Indian State has reoriented its role and activated many State projects towards an open-ended economy. It also has aimed to produce new geographies to qualify the 'grammar of commerce' at transnational spaces. As East and Southeast Asian economies were by then successful models of neoliberal economy, the State strategy moved towards engaging with these nations for greater commercial gains through trade, investment and mobility. This essentialized the production of new geographies, which could facilitate such flows and activities. The North East, having geographical proximity with these groups of nations, was re-imagined as a 'strategic location' to fulfil such a State agenda. Interestingly with fluid borders, transnational activities had always been an important aspect of the North East and its people, which were affected vastly due to various exceptional strategies of the securitist State, like the closing of borders, imagining it as a 'frontier' and halting regional cooperation in the post-colonial period. In 1991, the Look East Policy (LEP) was the first State strategy to change the perception of the North East. The LEP was an initiative of neoliberal India to establish transnational engagement beyond its old allies of the West towards East and Southeast Asia. The North East was seen as strategic borderland to connect both the ends; it became the 'Indo-ASEAN gateway' (Association of South East Asian Nations [ASEAN]), a subject of India's new regionalism, and it germinated the seed for geoeconomic significance and to aggrandize cross-border economic affairs, while the LEP became an interface of intra-regional and international relations of India. As this policy placed the North East as a new 'connecting gateway', developmental State began with various logistical goals. Unfortunately in the early 1990s, such changing perceptions of the State made no significant impact in this politically 'disturbed' space of North East (Bhattacharya 2017), and amidst various long-term unresolved questions, the geography of the North East could not become a meaningful 'gateway' in Indo-ASEAN relation in the era of LEP. Studies show that economic gains of India in the two successful decades of LEP were from those states and regions, which remained spatially far off from ASEAN but could ensure good governance, better infrastructure and a business-like approach. Thus LEP became highly 'region-specific' (Bhattacharya 2015), and western, southern and even northern states of India were key players in that economic engagement and had taken away India's lion's share of transnational economic activities. The production of various new geographical enclaves like special economic zones under the Special Economic Zone Act (2005) was aimed at surplus appropriation and created a new binary—progressive and regressive 'regions'—in India within the larger core–periphery structure. Rising regional disparities in the post-liberalization period further stereotyped the North East as a 'backward and regressive region' and therefore remained an 'outsider' in India's LEP (Bhattacharya 2017).

However, with a renewed State agenda on economic growth since 2014 and its policy transformation, like the Act East Policy, the North East once again gained State attention as being 'a heart of it' (Mukul 2018). India's economic growth agenda since 2013–14 in general was connected to various ongoing political economic challenges in the oil market and its volatility, labour market and its mobility, trade and investment with their low intensity, economic outcomes with less growth and joblessness of the youth. These issues have created constant pressure on the State to expand and integrate economies for larger returns and surpluses, and the concept of economic geography gained importance. The policy strategy of India accordingly moved towards 'internationalizing' the North East borderland to make transnational economic engagement and expansionism a reality. While doing so, the State also gradually started to lessen the logic of security in the North

East, and with careful negotiation and measures, India has started to revoke even its most draconian and contested security policy, the Armed Forces Special Power Act (AFSPA of 1958), in different states of the North East such as Tripura, Mizoram and Meghalaya in the last three years. This is significant and largely to send a signal towards a 'peaceful' North East, which is a prerequisite for the current State economic agenda (Bhattacharya 2018). With such a relative decline of security concerns and the simultaneous rise of economic concerns within the North East, improved relations with neighbouring States like Bangladesh and Myanmar, which are politically transforming, also became visible. State developmentalism thus is actively focusing on negotiating 'peace' and qualifying the North East as an interlinking geographical space, even by opening up the old routes and transits for intra-regional people, product and capital network. As the 'effect of geography', as discussed by some recent scholars such as Aaltola et al. (2014), Scholvin and Malamud (2014), is becoming increasingly important to organize both politics and economy, the North East, which was so far a 'prisoner of geography' is now likely to transform. This fast change also raises questions on many fronts, such as its long-term sustainability, or is it simply a transitory political configuration of forces of contemporary times? Can such transnationalism suggest any 'prognosis of (in) stability' in the North East and its relations with neighbouring areas, which largely affected the genesis of this space in post-colonial times? Lastly, while pushing such an aggressive agenda in North East, how effectively is the developmental State going to cope up and partner with people's interests and rights at the local level?

DEVELOPMENTALISM, NEW CAPITAL AND SOCIAL MAPPING

With a new normal in the North East through rapid logistical expansion and capital inflow by the developmental State, the larger question lies on how effectively local spaces interact and negotiate with such 'transformational' idea, both at structural levels and at social levels. Large financial capital is now in circulation within this space to create a robust connectivity network and receive investors' responses. For example, the road construction project alone has attracted huge capital since 2006, with a policy announcement on Special Accelerated

Road Development Programme in North East (SARDP-NE) by the Ministry of Transport and Highway. It was initiated with ₹40,000 crores to build 6,500-km roads with at least 2-lane roads in all 88 district headquarters of the North East and improve 'roads of strategic importance' in its border areas. Less than a decade later in 2014, the same ministry took a renewed policy initiative to multiply this road infrastructure network. A road construction company called National Highway and Infrastructure Development Corporation (NHIDC) of India was created to construct and commission a 19,903-km stretch of road in the North East and its border areas. With 13,400 km of more roads, this aims for a three times increase in total road length from the previous SARDP-NE. This ambitious road project in the North East aims to mobilize ₹1.41 lakh crore of capital for its civil work, and while meeting compensation and rehabilitation due to land acquisition, it needs to generate another ₹1.07 lakh crores. A large share of this huge capital is expected to be raised by the NHIDC from various global private players including the World Bank, Asian Development Bank (ADB), Japan International Cooperation Agency (JICA), German Development Bank (DEG) and other global agencies.[1] This road construction project of the contemporary developmental State merged with India's larger connectivity-EC project. The Bharat Mala Project, initiated in 2017 to build 50,000 km of roads in the country, covering all far-flung bordering areas of India, including both coastal and hilly boundaries, extensively covers the bordering states of the North East, particularly Sikkim, Assam, Arunachal Pradesh, Manipur and Mizoram. This is to create a connectivity-economic corridor with the neighbouring East and Southeast Asia and beyond. This road construction project is typically a Keynesian concept of State investment to address the symptom of a slow economy with the issue of joblessness and aims to create nearly 100 million man-days of jobs and generate 22 million in increasing economic activity across the country and beyond borders (*The Indian Express* 2016). This mega-road construction project aims to mobilize an investment of ₹6.92 lakh crores through various government and private funds such as debt funds, budgetary allocations, private investment, toll operator transfer model and so on along with global capital. This massive road infrastructure is seen as 'enhancing opportunities for business development with other nations and their agencies'. Thus, through such 'meaningful roles of multilateral organizations and institutions' even in the North East, the State aims to multiply transnational investment, trade and commerce. Various ongoing cross-border connectivity projects are also under fast-track modes, such as the 1,360-km trilateral highway, which aims to connect India, Myanmar and Thailand; Kaladan Multi-Modal Transit Transport Project, which aims to connect Kolkata and Myanmar via Mizoram; and the East West Corridor which aims to connect Gujarat and Southeast Asia via Manipur through the Mekong-India Economic Corridor (MIEC). On the other hand, Bangladesh has agreed to give the transit rights to India with the passing of the Land Boundary Agreement Bill in 2015. With this, many routes are functional for the North East to connect with neighbouring areas, and as reported by the Ministry of Road Transport and Highway, 24 more cross-border connectivity projects in the neighbours of the North East such as Bangladesh, Bhutan, Nepal and ASEAN are ongoing (*The Indian Express* 2018). The other modes of connectivity will also be operational and effective soon in the North East, as NITI Aayog, the State's think tank, has proposed the large-scale extension of railway links in the region, which currently cover only two state capitals, of Assam and Tripura, with approximately 2,600 km of railway lines. Similarly the concept of UDAN, a regional airport development and connectivity scheme was inducted in 2017 to bring larger air connectivity to the North East, which has currently only 11 airports and are not seen as enough for intra-State and inter-State air connectivity networks. Union Budget 2018–2019 allocated ₹1,000 crore for air connectivity networks in the space to transform the North East to the 'new energy centre of the country' (Mukul 2018). Also, the inland waterway transportation network, which used to be the strength of this region prior to 1947 as a traditional, cheap and fast mode of transportation, suffered immensely in the post-colonial period due to the closure of riverine routes in the context of national security. NITI Aayog has proposed to revive such traditional routes by emphasizing both Brahmaputra and Barak rivers of the North East as pivotal river connectivity routes once again and created the revival strategy along with the commencement of dredging and channel stabilization works. This is expected to create around 20 new ports in these two rivers and would act as 'ancillary facilities to enhance the connectivity across the region and bring down the freight movement costs'. This ambitious strategy of the developmental State to connect this 'cut-off' region is largely for neoliberal economic activities and creating a space for private players and multinational companies for larger returns and the appropriation of resources, like hydrocarbon and hydroelectricity, from different parts of the North East (Koijam and Yumnam 2015a). Telecom and digital connectivity is another thrust area of the developmental State in this 'hinterland', with about 8,621 targeted villages with a capital of ₹15,000 crores. This is part of India's flagship Bharat-net project (*The Indian Express* 2018). Such a massive aim for connectivity infrastructure is also to ensure economic development in the region. The mega-event, 'Advantage Assam'—The Assam Global Investors' Summit, which was held in 2018, is one such important event where regional and national leadership were at the same platform to woo global capital in the North East. The North East was projected with 'geostrategic advantages' for investors, with Guwahati as the actual epicentre of both a manufacturing hub and economic growth for the Southeast Asia and East Asian neighbours through investments, opportunities and transformation. Emphasizing on Assam as 'India's Expressway to ASEAN', the summit showed the importance of geography of the North East, even for neighbours such as Vietnam, Cambodia, Laos, Thailand, Myanmar, Nepal, Bhutan and Bangladesh. This extended transnational space has about 800 million people and signifies the potential of market expansion and economic integration. About 200 Memorandums of Understanding (MoUs) were signed to raise ₹1 lakh crores of capital to essentialize India's agenda on neoliberal developmentalism (Advantage Assam 2018). Similarly the first North East Development Summit took in Manipur in 2017, which aimed to expand trade, investment, connectivity and tourism in 'underdeveloped' areas of the North East through various global financial capital.

These events and promises to global investors in the North East are changing the perceptions of people with both hope and anxiety along with the changing social mapping. A large section of the population today expects a needful and gainful economic exercise in the North East, which was unheeding for a long period under the logic of security. NITI Aayog, in its 'Three Year Action Agenda', which was released in 2017, has laid down a concrete vision towards the North East with emphasis on infrastructure and transit connectivity, industry and global capital and the youth. To translate these aims into reality and for logistical expansion, the developmental State is working with local political forces of the North East, and also a careful negotiation with various local social groups has become important. Unlike the past, there is a threshold level in the acceptance of the current agenda of the State by many people within the North East. This has created space for the developmental State to negotiate and partner with various local voices in a gainful manner. Thus, many, who were strong resisting forces in the past, are now gradually partnering with the State with the hope of new beginnings and empowerment. State policy incentives for local economy and livelihood are acceptable for various social groups like women and the youth, who were earlier the subjects of resistance and violence. They are now the new subjects of participatory governance and beneficiaries of various inclusive government policies. Such groups now partner with the State to find their legitimate space and rights within a very 'governmentalised notion of empowerment' (Banerjee 2014) as they were so far either victims of traditional customary systems or trapped in economic 'underdevelopment'. Such new consolidation helps the State legitimize its larger agendas of surplus economy, cash cropping, the monetization of indigenous knowledge and tourism projects. They are gradually transforming the aspirations of the people and helping to connect North East local economy and knowledge to larger market spaces through physical infrastructure and scientific and digital innovations. As this has created space for economic integration, for many people in the North East, the State no longer is seen as a major perpetrator or enemy but an acceptable partner (Banerjee 2012) in this game change, and political democracy has also created space for such new partnership as well as cronyism. A unified political forum called *North East Democratic Alliance* is acting at various levels in the North East to gain support for such ideation, and political mandates and various leaderships in the North East are gradually moving towards this. For example, while attending Delhi Dialogue Forum in 2016 on *Connectivity: Creating Pathways to a Shared Future,* the chief ministers of Nagaland and Mizoram strongly expressed the key role of connectivity between Northeast and Southeast Asia as an 'enabler for prosperity, growth, peace and people-to-people contacts'.

In the 2018 Rajya Sabha elections in Tripura, the prime minister of India in his political campaign promised to provide Highway, Internet, Railway and Aviation (HIRA) to its people to change the development narrative of the State, and people of the State accordingly mandated for political change after 25 years. Similarly, in other states of the North East, the developmental State has become successful in partnering with local political and social forces, which in many ways endorse and accept such changes in the region.

While there is a sign of partnership and cronyism, there is also the other side of the debate, which evolves around the disruption in everyday life, traditional livelihood and moral and cultural aspects of the traditional and time-tested systems of the North East. A new form of anxiety has emerged at various societal levels for such 'transformative' State agendas and its partnership with various global financial agents for the appropriation of resources and economic gains (Koijam and Yumnam 2015b). These are many a time evolving into new forms of contestation as anti-development movements. They are unleashing and organizing through resistance, protests, obstruction and struggle for political effectiveness. This new form of indigenous struggle in contemporary North East has the potential to challenge this new role of the developmental State in the North East around the issues of rights and justice, which is increasingly posing threats to livelihood with displacement and marginalization. Thus, in the states of Manipur, Nagaland, Arunachal Pradesh, Tripura and Meghalaya, various such State projects were halted at various points of time due to local ethnic uprises. Some of the obstructions against such new developmentalism so far are noteworthy, like people's resistance on oil extraction in Changpang Village in Nagaland and dam construction in Mapithel and Tipaimukh. In 2013, the 'Indigenous Peoples Consultation on Dams and Natural Resources Protection in India's North East' was held in Agartala to discuss the issue of 'corporatization and militarization of indigenous land and resources', and accordingly, the 'Agartala Declaration' was made in that forum to resist dam construction in the North East. Thus, such social collectivities have already shown the potential to challenge such an agenda of the utilitarian State on developmentalism. In this regard, the developmental State needs to act more carefully and needs to strategize through an informed and accountable mechanism to gain the confidence of people. This can be done by making policy drafts available in the public domain for fair discussion, debates and consent. An ethical frame in the policy, according to XAXA, is important, where 'public purpose', compensation, people's involvement and environmental safeguards are essential to make such structural changes sustainable in the North East (XAXA 2014). If the response of people and policy initiatives can converge, such changes become sustainable to make market and society compatible to each other.

GEOGRAPHY AND THE TRANSNATIONAL MARKET

With the rising spatial significance in an open economic system, some approaches of market integration like agglomeration economies are gaining importance, where firms, people and production centres are located in a contiguous vicinity in cities and industrial clusters and even across the borders, accessible through the transport infrastructure network. Theoretically, as argued by Ottaviano, with Krugman's scholarly contribution, both transnational trade and economic geography are intertwined, which emphasizes that the same basic forces simultaneously determine specialization across countries for a given international distribution of factors of production (trade theory) and the long-run location of those factors across countries (economic geography). New economic geography thus has focused on 'macro-heterogeneity' across locations, showing how this can be endogenously generated by various micro-economic decisions of similar groups of people, firms and industries at local spaces towards agglomeration economies (Ottaviano 2010). Usually agglomeration economies operate with an agreed set of modalities, having a synergy of both partnership and ownership among local, regional, national and global players and industries, which is also typically successful in urban landscapes.

The geography of the North East being a subject of India's intra-regional and transnational economic relation now, various local, regional, national and global economies and institutions are increasingly intersecting through its trans-boundary spaces. In this new dynamics, the State subsequently aims to gain through high-valued 'trade network for energy, food-grains and digital links', and the North East is expected to be 'the catalyst for the deeper engagement' of India with its neighbouring nations. The current data show that in India's ongoing international trade, the North East has made no significant contribution yet. India's trade volume with its Eastern neighbouring nations is only 5 per cent of its total international trade, and interestingly, 95 per cent of such trade activities have been taking place from regions other than the North East (NITI Aayog 2017). To overcome such acute trade disparity at the regional level, the State's approach to multiple logistical expansion can be effective to make the geography of the North East economically efficient. These logistical expansions are also expected to relocate the political borders across this entire sub-region, having contiguous land and geography for larger economic growth, circulation and gain, and the North East market will be relocated beyond borders. Amidst such State enthusiasm, local engagements and expectations also have to be mapped, and in this regard, an idea of exploring the endogenous growth model (Romer 1986, 1990) can be useful. As the space has its own strength in various economic activities, including its traditional activities, some sectors like the plantation economy can be investigated for creating an endogenous growth model through cross-border agglomeration with neighbouring areas of the North East. This can help create a competitive and self-reliant regional economy and conquer the stigma of being a 'periphery' and address the existing challenge of dependency, sub-optimality and market fragmentation in the region. Recent works on economic geography highlight the importance of such agglomeration economies as key determinants where firms and people can locate and relocate. Studies in some parts of the world have discussed various 'spatial effects' of such transnational economies through agglomeration within neighbouring areas. The research by Duranton and Kerr (2015) shows that 'agglomeration is a very complex process that involves trade-offs and equilibrium outcomes, and the best empirical progress in this field comes when researchers identify a razor-sharp way to cut through this complexity and identify causal relationships'. So, some spatial agglomeration even across borders may be gainful at the backdrop of sound conceptual and empirical research. Another recent study by M. J. Smit on the landscape of Europe shows that such interactions are typically weaker across the country borders than within countries, due to institutional, infrastructural or cultural factors. As 'border effects' with multiple countries generally remain strong in any spatial economic analysis through quantification, therefore, State policies aiming to maximize the intra-country effect need to create sound cross-border policies to promote various gainful interactions at the transnational level (Smit 2017). Diego Puga (2008), the pioneering scholar on agglomeration economies, also points out that cross-border infrastructure and agglomeration without policy safeguards are likely to increase regional inequalities. According to him, traditionally, spatial differences in production are natural due to differences in natural and other factor endowments such as capital accumulation, skills acquired by the workforce and differences in the technology available at different locations (2008). But sometimes it can also be beneficial, as shown by the World Bank Report, which highlights that if a firm's location is not constrained by physical geography and natural endowments unlike traditional theories based on comparative advantage, it has an important role in facilitating increased efficiency and growth, partly as a result of spatial concentration and wider gains from trade. Cross-border projects can have large effects that extend well beyond the boundaries of the national or local and regional administration. Thus, improving cross-border infrastructure projects and connecting 'lagging regions' with their existing key markets make it easier for firms in 'lagging regions' to reach new consumers. If agglomerated regions can withstand fiercer competition from firms in more developed areas, then these connecting regions are not likely to face the challenge of regional inequalities (2009). It is also therefore important for various developmental States to create a 'like-minded' (Carkoglu et al. 2005) space across the border through sustained regional cooperation and policy democratization and then engage with agglomeration economies in some specific sectors, especially where there are endogenous skills and strengths. This with adequate safeguards may become a gainful bottom-up approach and can justify the logic of economy within that region by delinking the agenda of the developmental State and disassociating from the larger capitalist network.

To countervail India's neoliberal economic agenda in the North East and its neighbouring areas, the tea industry can be investigated for agglomeration, which can not only retain the 'historical, cultural and ecological uniqueness' of this whole region but can also play a crucial role in providing livelihood and entrepreneurship to local people, while contributing significantly in the global market. Though India is the largest producer and consumer of black tea in the world, where Assam is traditionally the most important contributing state, the other states of the North East also have entered into the tea map as non-traditional states in recent years including Arunachal Pradesh, Manipur, Meghalaya, Mizoram, Nagaland and Sikkim (GOI 2017–18). India currently shares about 23 per cent in world tea production. Assam still enjoys a competitive advantage in this sector as a major contributor, with about 77 per cent of share in India's total production and 309,080 hectares of land under tea production. The other states of the North East share 12,290 hectares, and the neighbouring North Bengal, Dooers and Darjeeling share 1,40,440 hectares of land for tea production, amounting to total 462.41 thousand hectare land constituting India's 82 per cent of tea land. Despite being a significant sector, tea in this region is constrained by several externalities for expansion. With various regulations and Constitutional safeguards like Article 371A and the Sixth Schedule, which were originally aimed to protect traditional practices on land and resources in the North East, the extension of areas for tea land in the North East was therefore largely restricted. Similarly, the Forest Conservation Act 1980 also restricts the utilization of 'waste lands' for any other commercial activities like the expansion of tea plantation areas. The licensing system to procure tea land is suspended in this space largely to restrain 'outsiders' and outside capital in the traditional tea-growing areas of the North East. While protecting land from primitive accumulation, the laws have also restricted the scope of economic activities and expansion, which is currently essential to meet the issues of employment and livelihood challenges within the space. Such regulatory regimes to a large extent became counter-productive to expanding tea-growing areas within the North East and creating opportunities for local economies. As a result, the tea industry suffered from the issues of small scale and size, where the North East is typically challenged with severe spatial externalities (Asopa 2009). The tea industry in Assam also was affected largely during the militancy period between the 1980s and 1990s, and it lost many large-scale investments (Bhattacharya 2011).

As the North East is being projected as a 'peaceful and stable region now with much of its law and order issues under control', the developmental State is now aiming to revive many of its local and traditional industries. The board under the Tea Act currently initiated the formulation and implementation of development schemes aimed at increasing tea production and the productivity of plantations through activities such uprooting and replanting/rejuvenation of old-aged tea bushes and the creation of irrigation facilities, modernization of tea processing, packaging and value addition facilities and encouraging cooperative efforts among small tea growers to overcome market barriers. With such policy support, cross-border agglomeration of the tea industry also can create a *niche* in this region, as the neighbouring areas of Assam such as the northeastern part of Bangladesh that is Sylhet, the Terai region of Nepal and North Bengal and the Darjeeling District of West Bengal are traditionally tea-growing areas but face similar challenges like the North East. As all non-traditional states of the North East are also now under the tea map, Assam and other such states along with Sylhet, the Siliguri sub-division of North Bengal, Dooars from Jalpaiguri to Sikkim and the Darjeeling sub-division along with Terai region across Nepal can be conceptualized as the 'tea regions' for agglomeration. This intra-regional and cross-border sub-Himalayan agglomerated tea industry potentially can spread over roughly 5.71 lakh hectares of land with 98,724.02 hectares in Sylhet and 9,775 hectares in Nepal and can create a large and integrated tea market for competitive advantages at the global level. This can be routed to Southeast Asia via Myanmar to compete with China, Vietnam and Indonesia. The trilateral highway for India, Myanmar and Thailand, which is expected to be completed by December 2019, can be a corridor for tea economy of this entire sub-region of Asia. This conceptual approach towards the cross-border agglomeration of tea economy can create a region-centric endogenous market to resist various powerful players from outside. This necessarily needs to be tested with rigorous empirical research and micro-level data to unleash the scope, implications and limitations of such agglomerations of local industrial structures at the cross-border level while measuring regional industrial specialization, economic diversity, the industrial competitive structure and most importantly border effects and political cooperation. The scope of this chapter does not provide any such empirical research, but if any rigorous research can provide significant results, this large contiguous space can unleash a new economic geography. This, as mentioned by Puga (2008) elsewhere, can typically generate aggregate gains in all the regions involved, even if within each region there are both winners and losers from this process. To formalize this larger agglomerated economy in this sub-region, a 'supranational structure' (Paul 2013) and sub-regional cooperation are important to create modalities at the political level for wider socio-economic formation, labour mobility, regional cooperation and investment optimization to benefit all partnering neighbours of the tea region. This 'supranational structure' is also important to replace the existing infrastructure designed with the national market in mind towards an integrated region (The World Bank 2009). Sometimes such integration and agglomeration in 'backward' regions help address the issue of poverty and other deprivations and marginalization effectively. The South Asian economy in post-colonial times hardly has any successful economic integration from *within*, as it has been a site of conflicts for a long period of time. As India is now moving towards transforming one such conflict-prone area and integrating with neighbouring nations, such sustainable bottom-up approaches and endogenous economic models can be investigated seriously, both at policy and at research levels, to prevent new threats of peripheralization and regional inequality.

CONCLUDING OBSERVATIONS

The 'effective use of geography' as an approach in the contemporary period will expectedly change the North East with the larger State agenda of increasing supply chain, the production network and transnational economism, all of which are part of India's larger goal of a free market economy and its dream of becoming a regional power. In this context, the North East as an economic geography probably for the first time is projected by the post-colonial developmental State as a region with variety of pursuits and potential, almost in an 'exceptional' frame. This will change the North East and its external orientations where multiple interactions of the State, politics, economy, resource and geography at various scales will reconstruct this borderland with new narratives such as 'connecting gateway' and 'economic hub' and 'economic corridor'. At this crossroads, it will be intriguing to observe how such changes will negotiate with local factors like creating opportunities, livelihood, sustainability and integrating North East economy for the good or bad. As India is a young nation with 60 per cent of its population below 35, the North East is no exception, and the aspirations of its youth therefore have to be mapped and met carefully with gainful education, skills, entrepreneurship and employability. These can create a level-playing field where the region and its people will partner in the economic space making in production network, logistical expansion and trading activities and then create indigenous capital and industry to prevent falling into a new margin.

On the other hand, such a structural shift of the idea of the North East towards a transnational space does not necessarily take away the geographical imperative, where proximity and commonness have equal probability to generate intimacy and hostility at any time. So any political change in the neighbourhood can make the North East vulnerable and the interface of geopolitics and geoeconomics will be at jeopardy. The last decade has been extremely crucial for the North East in rebuilding trust and goodwill with its neighbours. For academia the challenge is even more fundamental. There cannot be any straightforward formula to fit the region into any transnational affairs and economic gains. Developing an epistemic and theoretical frame at this hour is essential to conceptualize this contemporary region and relocate it in State affairs with a 'superior modality', interdisciplinary method and bottom-up approach, where people and ecology essentially are the referent objects. An 'internal consensus' is essential for a sustainable and inclusive frame which has neighbouring areas more as its natural allies rather than as strategic partners. So as the developmental State today is determined to attain its larger agenda of economic expansion, by 'internationalizing' this borderland at the cost of its local spaces, such as land accumulation, hydropower generation, dam construction and other mineral resource extraction activities and cronyism, before these can set another 'exception' in the policy trend for the North East, a bottom-up endogenous sustainable economy must be in place. Also a debate on people's choices, partnerships, capacities and rights must be ensured to prevent new anxieties and contestations. It will be intriguing to probe such emerging developmental trends in the North East which is moving towards being a 'geographical heartland' of the Indian economy.

NOTE

1. See www.nhidcl.com (accessed in 2014). National Highways and Infrastructure Development Corporation Ltd (NHIDC), Ministry of Road Transport and Highways, GOI.

REFERENCES

Aaltola, M., J. Käpylä, H. Mikkola, and T. Behr. 2014. *Towards the Geopolitics of Flows: Implications for Finland*. Helsinki: The Finnish Institute of International Affairs.

Ahluwalia, M. S. 2002. 'Economic Performance of States in Post-Reforms Period'. *Economic Political Weekly* 35(19): 1637–48.

Asopa, V. N. 2009. *India's Global Tea Trade Reducing Shares, Declining Competitiveness*. Ahmedabad: Centre for Management in Agriculture Indian Institute of Management.

Banerjee, P. 2012. *Women, Conflict and Governance in Nagaland, Policies and Practices*, 51. Mahanirban: Calcutta Research Group.

———. 2014. 'New Conundrums for Women in North East India: Nagaland and Tripura'. *Economic and Political Weekly* 49: 43–44.

Barua, A., and A. Sawhney. 2015. 'Development Policy Implications for Growth and Regional Inequality in a Small Open Economy: The Indian Case'. *Review of Development Economics* 19(3): 695–709.

Bhattacharya, R. 2007. 'Indian Divide on Economic Growth: Northeast India in the Perspective of Globalization.' In *Asia Annual 2006*. New Delhi: Standard Publishers.

———. 2011. *Development Disparities in Northeast India*. New Delhi: Cambridge University Press.

———. 2014. *North Eastern India and Its Neighbours: Negotiating Security and Development*. New Delhi: Routledge.

———. 2015. 'Look East to Act East Policy: Is It a Renewal of Hope for Northeast India?' *Eastern Quarterly* 11(I and II): 3–17.

———. 2017. 'Insider or an Outsider: Where Is the Northeast in India's Act East Policy?' In *Mainstreaming the Northeast in India's Look and Act East Policy*, edited by A. Sarma and S. Choudhusy. New Delhi: Springer.

———. 2018. 'The North-east Beyond AFSPA'. *The Statesman*, 29 April.

Brunner, H.-P. 2010. *North East India: Local Economic Development and Global Markets*. New Delhi: SAGE Publications.

Carkoglu, A., M. Eder, and K. Kirisci. 2005. *The Political Economy of Regional Cooperation in the Middle East*. London: Routledge.

Chako, P. 2015. 'The New Geo-economics of a "Rising" India: State Transformation and the Recasting of Foreign Policy'. *Journal of Contemporary Asia* 45(2): 326–44.

Chakravorty, S. 2000. 'How Does Structural Reforms Affect Regional Development? Resolving Contradictory Theory with Evidence from India'. *Economic Geography* 76(4): 367–94.

Chandrasekhar, C. P., and J. Ghosh. 2004. *The Market that Failed: Neoliberal Economic Reforms in India*. Delhi: Leftword.

MDoNER. 2008. *Vision Document 2020 for Northeastern Region*. New Delhi: MDoNER.

Duranton, G., and W. R. Kerr. 2015. *The Logic of Agglomeration*, Working Paper 16-037. Cambridge, MA: Harvard Business School.

FICCI. 2004. *Gateway to the ASEAN India's North East Frontier*. New Delhi: FICCI.

———. 2017. *Harnessing the Potential for Cross-border Trade between North East India and Its Neighbouring Countries*. New Delhi: FICCI.

Ghosh, B., S. Marjit, and G. S. Neogi. 1998. *Economic Growth and Regional Divergence in India: 1960 to 1995*. Calcutta: Mimeo, Centre for Study of Social Science.

Goswami, A. 1981. 'Assam's Industrial Development: Urgency of New Direction'. *Economic and Political Weekly* 16(21): 953–56.

Government of India (GOI). 2017–18. 'India's Trade Back on Track', Annual Report. Ministry of Commerce and Industry, GOI.

Gupta, K. S. 2018. 'Northeast at Heart of Act East Policy', 4 February.

Hari, K. S., and N. Hatti. 2015. 'Poverty and Inequality in India: An Exploratory Analysis'. *Social Science Spectrum* 1(4): 249–61.

Indian Chamber of Commerce. 2013. *India's North East Diversifying Growth Opportunities*. New Delhi: Indian Chamber of Commerce.

Jha, R. 2004. *The Political Economy of Recent Economic Growth in India Rag*, ASARC Working Paper 2004/12. Canberra: Australian National University.

Koijam, P., and J. Yumnam. 2015a. *Brief Assessment of Mapithel Dam Impacts*. Manipur: Centre for Research and Advocacy.

———. 2015b. *Climate Crisis and Indigenous Peoples Rights in Manipur*. Manipur: Centre for Research and Advocacy.

Krugman, P. 1991. 'Increasing Returns and Economic Geography'. *Journal of Political Economy* 99(3): 483–99.

Kundu, A., and K. Varghese. 2010. *Regional Inequality and 'Inclusive Growth' in India under Globalisation: Identification of Lagging States for Strategic Intervention*. Oxfam India Working Papers Series. Oxfam: OIWPS-VI.

Kurian, N. J. 2000. 'Widening Regional Inequalities in India: Some Indicators'. *Economic and Political Weekly* 35(7): 538–50.

Luttwak, E. N. 1990. 'From Geopolitics to Geo-economics: Logic of Conflict, Grammar of Commerce'. *The National Interest* 20: 17–23.

Mattlin, M., and W. Mikael. 2016. 'Geo-economics in the Context of Restive Regional Powers'. *Asia European Journal* 14(2): 125–34.

Misra, T. 1980. 'Assam a Colonial Hinterland'. *Economic and Political Weekly* 15(32): 1357–64.

Misra, B. S. 2015. 'India's Growth Performance 2000–2012: Region-Based Perspective'. In *Regional Development and Public Policy Challenges in India*, edited by R. Bhattacharya, 19–72. New Delhi: Springer.

Mukul, Pranav. 2018. 'Telecom Connectivity to Northeastern States: Boosting the Network'. *The Indian Express*, 24 January.

Nayank, P. 2009. *Growth and Human Development in North-East India*. New Delhi: Oxford University Press.

Nayar, G. 2008. 'Economic Growth and Regional Inequality in India'. *Economic and Political Weekly* 43(6): 58–67.

NITI Aayog. 2017. *Three Years Action Agenda: 2014–15 to 2019–20*. New Delhi: NITI Aayog, Government of India.

Ottaviano, G. I. P. 2010. '"New" New Economic Geography: Firm Heterogeneity and Agglomeration Economies'. *Journal of Economic Geography* 1–10.

Paul, R. 2013. 'Migration and Mobility in the European Union'. *Journal of Ethnic and Migration Studies* 39(6).

Piketty, T. 2013. *Capital in the Twenty-First Century*. Cambridge, MA: The Belknap Press of Harvard University Press.

Planning Commission. 1981. *Report on Development of North Eastern Region*. New Delhi: National Committee on the Development of Backward Areas, Planning Commission, Government of India.

———. 1997. *Transforming the Northeast: Tackling Backlogs in Basic Minimum Services and Infrastructural Needs*. New Delhi: Planning Commission.

———. 2006. *Report of the Task Force on Connectivity and Promotion of Trade and Investment in NE States*. Planning Commission, Government of India.

———. 2012. *On Improvement and Development of Transport Infrastructure in North East*. New Delhi: Planning Commission, Government of India.

Puga, D. 2008. 'Agglomeration and Cross-border Infrastructure', European Investment Bank Conference in Economics and Finance. Madrid: Madrid Institute for Advanced Studies (IMDEA) Social Sciences.

Rajeev, M., and A. Akhtar. 2015. 'Intra and Interstate Inequality in the Northeastern Region with Special Reference to Assam'. In *Regional Development and Public Policy Challenges in India,* edited by R. Bhattacharya, 195–236. New Delhi: Springer.

Report. 2016. *Delhi Dialogue VIII*. Ministry of External Affairs, Government of India. Retrieved from http://www.mea.gov.in/media-advisory.htm?dtl/26363/Delhi+Dialogue+VIII

Romer, P. 1986. 'Increasing Returns and Long Run Growth'. *Journal of Political Economy* 94: 1002–37.

———. 1990. 'Capital, Labour and Productivity'. Brookings Papers on Economic Activity.

Sachdeve, G. 2000. *Economy of the North-East: Policy, Present Conditions and Future Possibilities*. New Delhi: Centre for Policy Research.

Scholvin, S., and Malamud, A. 2014. 'Is There a Geoeconomic Node in South Africa? Geography, Politics and Brazils's Role in Regional Economic

Integration', ICS Working paper 2, Institute of Social Sciences, University of Lisbon.
Singh, T. B. 2007. 'India's Border Trade with Its Neighbouring Countries with Special Reference to Myanmar'. *Margin: The Journal of Applied Economic Research* 1(4): 359–82.
Singh, E. B. 2009. 'Understanding Economic Growth in the North Eastern Region of India'. *Dialogue* 10(3).
Smit, M. J. 2017. 'Cross-border Agglomeration Benefits'. *Letters in Spatial and Resource Sciences* 10: 375–83.
Sparke, M. 2007. 'Geopolitical Fears, Geo-economic Hopes, and the Responsibilities of Geography'. *Annals of the Association of American Geographers* 97(2): 338–49.
Strategy Report. 2007. *Development and Growth in Northeast India: The Natural Resources, Water, and Environment Nexus, South Asia Region Sustainable Development Department Environment & Water Resource Management Unit.* The World Bank.
Stulberg, A. N. 2005. 'Moving Beyond the Great Game: The Geo-economics of Russia's Influence in the Caspian Energy Bonanza'. *Geopolitics* 10(1): 1–25.
The Indian Express. 2016. 'Connecting with Neighbours: Cross-border Infra Development to Open New Avenues for India'. *The Indian Express*, 6 January.
———. 2018. 'Trilateral Highway to Be Operational by 2019'. *The Indian Express*, 24 January.
The World Bank. 2009. *Reshaping Economic Geography*. World Bank Report No. 43738. Washington, DC: The World Bank.
Wu, F., and D. W. Koh. 2014. 'From Financial Assets to Financial Statecraft: The Case of China and Emerging Economies of Africa and Latin America'. *Journal of Contemporary China* 23(89): 781–803.
Xaxa. 2014. *Report on the High Level Committee on Socio-Economic, Health, Educational Status of Tribal Communities in India*. New Delhi: Ministry of Tribal Affairs, Government of India.
Youngs, R. 2011. 'Geo-economic Futures'. In *Challenges for European Foreign Policy in 2012: What Kind of Geo-economic Europe?* edited by A. Martiningui and R. Youngs, 13–17. Madrid: FRIDE.

Chapter 7

The Politics of Corridors
'Seamless Connectivity', Trans-regional Engagements and Narratives of Development

Anita Sengupta

Seamless connectivity (which includes sustainable infrastructure, seamless logistics, regulatory excellence, digital connectivity and mobility) is the new buzzword whether one is talking about the Chinese-led One Belt One Road (OBOR) or the much less ambitious and sub-regional corridors like the Bangladesh-Bhutan-India-Nepal (BBIN) Initiative. It is generally agreed that land connectivity between contiguous neighbours, be it through road, railways or inland waterways, can facilitate enhanced trade, cross-border investment, more people-to-people exchanges and tourism and the overall development of neighbouring regions. Neighbours can also serve as transit countries for exchanges with third countries if some of this connectivity can be extended. Two aspects are considered to be relevant here—one is the establishment of suitable physical infrastructure to enable connectivity and the other is putting in place necessary legal, institutional and other mechanisms that may have to be concluded for the uninterrupted transit of goods and passengers across the border as well as for delivery of goods and services. Most studies on corridors therefore begin with the following question. How can these corridors be successful? In other words, how does one transform transport routes into trans-regional economic corridors? And there are generally standardized responses to this which are the following. First is the timely completion of all multi-modal connectivity projects. Second is the need to transform these connectivity corridors into development corridors with thriving trade, investment and other commercial activities for mutual benefits which would include supportive infrastructure for the supply of power, communication, IT links and the creation of capacities for skill development and training. Putting in place efficient border trade and transaction arrangements would also be very important along with banking facilities, easy payment modalities, quick food safety checks, efficient customs brokering systems, single-window clearances for transactions and bringing transactional costs to the minimum. Other recommendations include the development of integrated check-post items that would be allowed to be traded as border trade and strictly implemented with minimal or no duties.

What is interesting is that few of these 'developmental' schemes take note of the fact that the routes that these economic corridors traverse have been pathways of connectivity for people over generations and are an integral part of their everyday life. While there is attention on geo-political strategy, resource utilization and power lobbying in the states these corridors traverse, there remain regular non-elite movements for economic/social/cultural/religious exchanges that also negotiate State borders and move beyond 'regional' confines. The motivation for these mobilities and the corresponding flow of remittances and commodity trade are the flip sides of larger visions of logistic spaces and bring into focus debates on development. Such schemes also ignore the fact that the present system of informal cross-border trade in Asian regions has many participants—women traders, professional carriers, wholesalers, distributors, transporters, retailers and consumers. Along most of the borders, informal trade is significantly higher than formal trade and has the added advantage of not affecting local sensibilities and environments. Large-scale logistic visions for economic corridors tend to flatten the physical, political and cultural geography of the terrain the corridor negotiates, thereby ignoring the fact that just like each State where the border is different and has to be dealt with differently, each terrain is also different and the corridors have to be in sync with this diversity.

In regions like South Asia where borders are seen as frontiers rather than zones of contact, seamless connectivity comes into conflict with State perceptions of border areas as 'marginal' with limited requirements of development.

This chapter looks into attempts to connect India's North East to other regions of Asia, in the background of a network of proposed transport corridors across Asia. The assumption is that enhanced connectivity would induce greater development in the region. Here, a number of cross-cutting arguments assume significance. One argument is that lack of connectivity is the basic reason behind the underdevelopment of the region. This extends to three levels—between North East India and other regions of South and Southeast Asia, between North East India and mainland India and within North East India itself. The other argument is that connectivity-induced development would lead to a solution to those conflicts that were identified to be mostly driven by competition over scare resources. When geopolitical compulsions of developing connections with East and Southeast Asia became imperative, there was a third and added argument that it was the North East that would become the fulcrum of routes, connecting a network of maritime ports and inland waterways to the regions to north and northwest of India. All of these were built on logistics visions that envisaged the political, economic and social acceptance of seamless connectivity across Asian states. The chapter therefore begins with a critical examination of some of these larger visions for connectivity across Asia and the broader debate on transforming transport corridors into economic corridors before moving to a discussion on the politics of corridors in the context of North East India where a debate on development as a solution to issues of security still engages policymakers, academics and a range of civil society participants. These corridors also traverse regions where overlapping multilateral organizations with their own logistic visions and connectivity projects operate and with which India would need to engage in its attempt to link the North East to Southeast Asia. The chapter examines some of these before concluding by pointing to changed geopolitical realities that could become crucial in determining the direction that the development of these corridors could assume.

ASIAN CONNECTIVITY AND THE MATERIALITY OF INFRASTRUCTURE

Once the setting for the historic Silk Road and host to a multiplicity of mobilities, Asia has re-emerged as a useful case study for exploring the complex relationship between pursuing economic development through trans-state linkages and promoting political agendas through securitization. The renewed focus on Asia's connectivity infrastructure has its roots in the far older stories of travels—from those of Marco Polo to the Mongol Empire and the fabled Silk Road. Subsequent engineering advances and infrastructure have made possible what was only imagined in previous generations. Over a century ago, global navigation and trade were reshaped by the construction of the Suez and Panama Canals. Today, the dream of the Ottoman sultans to connect the European part with the Asian part of Istanbul has become a reality with the construction of the Marmaray Tunnel. In modern times efforts to shape infrastructure across Asia have been under way for more than a century in Russian railway systems. Similarly, the Asian Highway and Trans-Asian Railway initiatives have been in place for nearly half a century. The more recent and popularly named 'New Silk Road' initiatives also refer to a variety of visions for formalizing transit flows across the Asian space and provide the justification for such approaches. The term 'Silk Road' has been used by a number of intra- and extra-regional players for the expansion of mobilities which require states to act as 'bridgeheads of connection and development' (Diener 2015, 377).

Constructing mobility technologies is an inherently political act involving financial, regulatory and technical relations that bring together the interests of actors at various levels. The various 'New Silk Road' initiatives provide opportunities for exploring the multifaceted impact of trans-State corridors on human/resource and ideational transit and were contingent on the assumed acquiescence of the participating states to varied modes of overland traversal in the interests of collective gain. Within the metaphorical frame of New Silk Road, there were a number of strategies. The New Silk Road strategies planned by the USA and the European Union were premised on prospects for overland connections among China, India, the Middle East, Europe and Russia, resulting in revenue for Central Asian States and particularly sustainable development of Afghanistan after US withdrawal.[1] From the US perspective, a South Asia–Central Asia transit corridor had been foreshadowed by the Northern and Southern Distribution Networks for provision of supplies for Afghanistan's military operations and included a number of infrastructural projects to facilitate the transport of resources.

However, while global logistic visions that span regions and continents are one part of the contemporary logistic story, the other part of logistics is the multiple alternative corridors that span these same spaces. Too numerous to enumerate or categorize, they nonetheless influence the functioning of the larger networks and occasionally even dispute their logic. In fact, the significant geographical challenges to connectivity in the areas that are the operating environments for these infrastructural projects mean that these alternative logistic arrangements may provide viable arrangements where larger projects fail to materialize. In fact, large-scale infrastructural projects have been subject to scrutiny to increase the host country's debt burdens, the high maintenance cost of low-quality products and inadequate environmental sustainability which is difficult to predict and may have unintended consequences. The much advertised Sino-Afghan Special Railway Transportation (that connects China to Afghanistan and is part of the OBOR trade corridor that connects China to Afghanistan, Uzbekistan, Kazakhstan and Iran), for instance, ran into trouble when it arrived in Hairatan and had to return empty on its way back to China as Uzbek authorities forbade cargo from arriving into their country from Afghanistan citing security reasons. According to the report from Radio Free Afghanistan, Uzbekistan wants goods to leave the Afghan border, city Hairatan, on ships instead of rail and cross the Uzbek border via the Amu Darya where it can be screened by Uzbek security forces. Only then would the cargo be reloaded into the Sino-Afghan train. This circuitous route would create delays for Afghan trade with China had not been anticipated earlier.

Similarly, the China–Pakistan Economic Corridor (CPEC) which the media projects as a 'game changer' and which envisages linking China's trading hub of Kashgar to the Arabian Sea via a network of roads, railways, oil and gas pipelines and fibre optic cables has faced opposition from minorities in Baluchistan who have argued that the line will bring no benefit to the locals and will in fact eradicate their cultural identity. The Gwadar port that Pakistan has leased to China on a 43-year lease and which is the heart of the CPEC project is located in Baluchistan and as such the region holds the key to success of the project. Baluch leaders have argued that just like the railway lines, bridges, telegraph lines and strategic garrisons were built by the British to maximize exploitation and counter the Russian movement towards warm water ports and were constructed without the participatory process of the local population, and proved to be non-beneficial, the CPEC is also as exploitative. While Pakistan has agreed to beef up security for CPEC's infrastructure and workforce, this could well prove to be counter-productive and encourage more sub-nationalist reactions. Also, besides Chinese personnel, the CPEC project will attract a large number of workers from outside Baluchistan. A change in Baluchistan's ethnic demography, already a sore point with nationalists, is likely (Saeed 2017).

Therefore, while mobility technologies are promoted on the assumption that infrastructure provides a solution to the problems of social or economic integration, transportation infrastructures (pipelines/ roads/bridges/airports/communication linkages) may also become sites of disjunction. Inexorable increases in human mobility and the impact of geography on travel and transport lead to varied understandings of what logistic strategies entail. Here, the centrality of governance to geographies of transport is as significant as changing labour regimes and economic/environmental/social concerns evident at local, regional and international levels to come to an understanding on the possible future trajectories. In fact, as Parag Khanna argues, China's relentless pursuit of infrastructural alliances in terms of 'global good' has elevated infrastructure to the stature of 'security' or 'environmental protection' in a world where geopolitics is played out in the matrix of physical and digital infrastructure (Khanna 2016). Logistics therefore is as much about imagining routes as constructing institutional setups and the actual corridors through which it operates.

As Giorgio Grappi argues, all transportational corridors have two components; they are both a spatial description of something happening on the ground and the projection of something to be realized (Grappi 2018, 182). As such they tend to shape a new imagination that follows existing supply chains but also the possibility of development powered by logistic connectivity. In recent times, logistic strategies have sought to reorganize and consolidate politics/economics/cultures and everyday existence along the routes that they traverse. While the focus is on geopolitics and economy, especially their potential to develop business opportunities, there is also the realization that it is cultural interactions that these corridors will engender that will make them the gateway for mobility and interaction among people. This has been historically true as Buddhism was one of the most significant commodities to travel along the 'Silk Road', together with musical instruments and tea. Similarly, the Indian Look/Act East Policy is grounded on the rediscovery of traditional Indian connections in Southeast Asia where trade enhanced cultural influence. There is, however, not much consensus on what economic corridors mean though it is generally accepted that:

Economic corridors capitalize on efficient multimodal transport network within a geography with the help of quality infrastructure, logistics, distribution networks that link production centres, urban clusters, and international gateways. Equally important for transforming transport corridors into economic corridors is an enabling framework that eases doing business and non-tariff measures to facilitate trade. Economic corridors promote growth by removing infrastructure bottlenecks, improving access to markets, stimulating trade and investment and boosting productivity and efficiency through associated network externalities and agglomeration effects. They attract private investments in productive assets, which generate employment. Economic corridors also promote inclusive growth by expanding economic opportunities in backward regions and linking cities and towns with urban centres and industrial clusters (De and Iyenger 2014, v).

While a heterogeneous range of documents, guidelines, policy papers and master plans has been produced by nation-states, regional cooperation organizations and other international bodies worldwide on these economic corridors, these have primarily been related to transport scholarship. However, corridors entail a direct role for the authorities ruling in the spaces they cross, including city/village councils, regions and states and international organizations concerned with trade, development and cross-border activities, while at the same time producing new governing dynamics and management agencies, whose roles are growing as a consequence of the relevance assumed by transport connectivity and logistical infrastructure for global exchanges.

In Asia, various economic corridors have been initiated including the Greater Mekong Subregion (GMS), the South Asia Subregional Economic Cooperation and the Central Asia Regional Economic Cooperation projects which involve the development of six transcontinental transport corridors. OBOR includes within its initiative six corridors at various stages of planning and implementation: the China-Mongolia-Russia Corridor, the New Eurasian Land Bridge, the China-Central Asia-West Asia Corridor, the China Pakistan Economic Corridor the China-Indochina Peninsula Corridor and the Bangladesh–China–India–Myanmar (BCIM) Corridor. The BCIM economic corridor (BCIM-EC) would impact the broader Look/Act East Policy as the North East constitutes the physical interface of overland infrastructural connectivity with Southeast Asia. What follows is an analysis of the viability of the BCIM-EC as a cross-border initiative[2] and as an instrument of development.[3]

The BCIM Forum for regional economic cooperation earlier known as the Kunming Initiative was founded in 1999 with the objective of promoting trade and economic development in the sub-region, stretching from south west China to eastern India via Myanmar, India's North East and Bangladesh. It was proposed that the BCIM would connect India's North East with China's Kunming Province, initially through road and subsequently, through rail connectivity. The understanding was that in case this corridor became operational it would imply not only enhanced trade and connectivity but would also open the door for China to upgrade infrastructure in port facilities in Bangladesh and Myanmar, key hubs in a potential Maritime Silk Road (MSR). In other words, BCIM would supplement the MSR, enabling China an easier political opening in the Bay of Bengal. Patricia Uberoi reiterates this argument when she notes that it was generally accepted that the

BCIM had been devised to serve China's geostrategic and economic interests in the region and allow China access to the Bay of Bengal and acknowledge the role of Yunnan in sub-regional cooperation (Uberoi 2014). However, she goes on to argue, despite India's Look East Policy, no such parallel role was conceived for the northeastern states of India. The unequal enthusiasm with which the initiative was visualized meant that despite the euphoria of the initial years, the Forum suffered from a lack of commitment until a joint statement made on the occasion of the State visit of the Chinese premier in May 2013 referred to the possibility of 'closer economic trade and people to people linkages and initiating the development of a BCIM Economic Corridor' (Uberoi 2014, 3). In India, while the idea of industrial corridors (the Delhi–Mumbai Industrial Corridor Project) and smart cities to create industrial and manufacturing hubs was in vogue, the developmental strategy that would go into the making of an economic corridor was still under review. In the first meeting of the BCIM-EC Joint Study Group held in Kunming in December in 2013, the scope of the corridor was defined so as to indicate that this would move beyond a linear connection between geographic points.

The proposed corridor will run from Kunming (China) in the east to Kolkata (India) on the west, broadly spanning the region including Mandalay (Myanmar), Dhaka and Chittagong (Bangladesh) and other major cities and ports as key nodes. With the linkages of transport, energy and telecommunications networks, the corridor will form a thriving economic belt that will promote the common development of areas along the corridor (2013, cited from Uberoi 2014, 6).[4]

The successive BCIM statement documents have emphasized the need to harmonize the infrastructural needs of the region and various suggestions, including facilitation measures at border crossings to ensure seamless movement of vehicles, goods and people, opening up direct flights and increased exchange of personnel, a feasibility study for a multi-modal transport route and possible funding for it, aligning it with the Asian Highway and Trans-Asian Railway as part of the Asian Land Transport Infrastructure Development project and connecting the missing links on a priority basis, the possibility of creating joint working groups for further improvement and developing bilateral and multilateral aid sources and technical know-how.[5] Its achievements however have largely been restricted to a car rally and the setting up of a business council.

Since most of the transport and development corridors like the BCIM-EC are cross-border initiatives, proposed bodies like the business council, for instance, become the connecting entities between political forms and administrative assemblages that exist formally and historically as separate while performing similar functions in different states. These bodies constitute an intermediate body of stakeholders in global trade. Given the proliferation of corridor initiatives, these different groups—consisting of technicians, representatives of national governments and international institutions and leading companies in the field of infrastructure, transport and production—represent intermediate bodies of the global political economy of logistics. What the different models of corridor organizations attempt is to synchronize logistical connectivity and transnational supply chains to both the physical functioning of infrastructures and the administrative, legal and governance procedures existing in a given space. Since this involves multiple states and stakeholders, multilateral engagements assume significance. It is in this background that the chapter now moves on to examine how India's logistic visions in the North East are influenced by her own position in three multilateral organizations—Association of South East Asian Nations (ASEAN), a regional organization with a strong projection on connectivity, the Shanghai Cooperation Organization (SCO), where India's logistic vision for the Southeast intersects with her vision for the Northwest, and BRICS which forms a common engagement platform where competition over shared spaces has been articulated.

CORRIDORS, MULTILATERAL ALLIANCES AND THE NORTH EAST

The Look East Policy was visualized as a new vision for the North East so that it can emerge as a gateway for linking India with the Southeast Asian economies. The assumption was that with this connection the peripheral nature of the North East would be transformed and there would be overall development. Among the connectivity projects that were envisaged was the four-lane trilateral highway, linking India

(Moreh in Manipur) with Mea Sot (Thailand) via Myanmar, which would expand to Laos, Cambodia and Vietnam. This highway would be sustainable only through economic activity and transport of goods through both Myanmar and the development of networks of connectivity in the North East that would include not just roads and railways but also rivers. Its viability would also depend on the setting up of economic hubs like local markets and the development of the local economy, allowing India to export products along the route rather than simply becoming a recipient of Chinese goods. Given the troubled nature of Myanmar's border areas and the fact that the development of economic 'hubs' along the border remains restricted, the viability of corridor remains suspect. Similarly, maritime connectivity with ASEAN had been envisaged through the development of the multimodal Kaladan Project, which would link Kolkata to the Sittwe Port in Myanmar and then through Mizoram to the transport corridors in the north. Other connectivity projects include restoring rail connectivity with Bangladesh and Myanmar and developing port townships along the Brahmaputra and Barak Rivers. Since the transformation of the Look East into Act East Policy, there have been efforts to ensure that relationships with organizations such as the ASEAN, which would be critical for the operationalization of the project, would be result oriented.[6]

While the general assumption seems to be that the development of connectivity corridors would be definitive, Atul Sharma argues that it is also necessary to understand how market integration works for the relationship to be viable (Sharma 2018, 25–43). Sharma begins by noting that market integration could lead to the emergence of new trade and industry but competition from more efficient integrating countries could also lead to problems, and he specifically examines the case of Assam to argue his point. Traditionally, Assam had significant trade connections to the Southeast and also Southwest China as well as Bhutan, Nepal and Tibet through intermediaries. However, this suffered whenever the Chinese imposed their authority on the intermediaries and finally with the closing of Tibet. In the colonial period infrastructure was built for the transport of tea, coal, petroleum and plywood, but there was little benefit derived from this export-oriented economy. With Partition, the North East was left with long international borders and a 22-km stretch connecting it with India, and most of the trade became informal. The Look East Policy reinstated the importance of the North East for linkages with Southeast Asia and a number of bilateral and multilateral agreements, and initiatives were negotiated for sub-regional engagement including the Mekong–Ganga Cooperation, the Bay of Bengal Initiative for Multi-Sectoral Technical and Economic Cooperation (BIMSTEC), the Kunming Initiative and the BCIM Forum for Regional Cooperation. Along with this were initiatives like the reconstruction of the Stilwell Road and linkages through the Trans-Asian Railway and the Asian Highway projects. However, highways, railroads, electricity networks, bridges and pipelines are only the 'hardware' of these visions, whereas reducing barriers to trade, standardizing customs duties and reducing the time to cross borders are the 'software' on which these short-, medium- or long-term projects depend. Implementing these projects across borders is the challenge that these engagements and initiatives would face. The reduction of high transactional costs for doing business on the one hand and improved political environment on the other hand is crucial for the success of market integration. It is here that engagement with multilateral forums is a crucial determinant as these forums negotiate both geoeconomic as well as geopolitical realities. While India is now member of a number of overlapping organizations, this section looks into India's engagement with the ASEAN, SCO and BRICS as crucial in this context as these now engage with a neighbourhood that extends across the southwest, west and northwest of India.

Among organizations that are considered crucial for transforming Asia into a single market is ASEAN. ASEAN has attempted to move towards inclusive growth through the development of connectivity projects which would reduce disparities in basic infrastructure. In this connection the adoption of the Master Plan on ASEAN Connectivity (MPAC) in October 2010 is significant. MPAC focuses on both physical connectivity including the completion of the missing links in the ASEAN Highway Network, the Singapore-Kunming Rail Links, the ASEAN Broadband Corridor and the Melaka-Pekan Baru Interconnection and institutional connectivity to facilitate the movement of goods, the operationalization of a national single window, phased reduction and the elimination of investment restriction services and labour across borders and also increased people-to-people contacts with deeper social and cultural interactions, education and capacity-building programmes and tourism promotion with the relaxation of visa requirements (ASEAN Secretariat 2016). India's interest in enhancing economic relationships with the ASEAN brings into focus the role that the North East can play by becoming the bridgehead of the relationship but also the numerous bottlenecks that this effort could face. For instance, Myanmar is the land that connects South and Southeast Asia; however, connectivity and trade between the North East and Myanmar remains limited. There are three routes that are considered to be critical here, the Moreh-Tamu, Zolkawtar-Rhee and Nampong-Pangsu that is also known as the Stilwell Road. An alternative route with the development of the Kaladan Multi-Modal Transit Transport Project is yet to be complete. However, Piti Srisangnam and Anupama Devendrakumar argue that unlocking the potential of the North East and ASEAN would require attention to both political, economic but also socio-cultural diversities and people-to-people contacts that go beyond the construction of physical infrastructure or the institutionalization of the 'software' of connectivity (Srisangnam and Devendrakumar 2018, 127–28).

There is today an infrastructural logic to most global political events and the significance of the 'infrastructural alliance', where the strength of ties that is measured by connectivity and volumes of flows is significantly higher than the disputed strips of land and encounters over varying perceptions of political frontiers and frontiers of influence. The increasing US-India engagement and the strategic implications of the USA seeking Indian assistance for a reinvigorated effort to stabilize Afghanistan, for instance, have not been lost on China which views this as a concern as it does the deterioration of the US-Pakistan relations and the continued American presence in Afghanistan. Similarly, China has taken note of the growing alignments among India, the USA, Japan and Vietnam. However, there is recognition of the fact that antagonism with India hinders OBOR corridors and brings into question the working of the Asian Infrastructure Investment Bank (AIIB). AIIB supports China's logistic vision of OBOR with the aim of bringing South Asian economies closer to China, Central Asia and West Asia and eventually also Europe and Africa.

As an initiative, OBOR is projected as an instrument to create a continuous land and maritime zone where countries will pursue convergent economic policies, underpinned by physical infrastructure and supported by trade and financial flows. The OBOR policy document further states that the initiative is designed to uphold an 'open world economy and the spirit of open regionalism', an obvious onetime counter to the more exclusive and now defunct US proposed mega-economic blocks, the Trans-Pacific Partnership (TPP) and the Transatlantic Trade and Investment Partnership (TTIP). Deeper economic integration within Asia is embedded in the larger framework of China's attempt to build rail, road and port infrastructures across Central Asia, Afghanistan and Pakistan, thereby dramatically shortening cargo transport time between Asia and Europe/the Middle East and Africa. OBOR has transcontinental (Silk Road Economic Belt) and maritime (MSR) components. From the Chinese perspective, OBOR is projected to be a 'game changer' which will eventually transform the way in which global politics is shaped.

For China, the SCO as a geopolitical platform is no longer crucial as the question of disputed borders has either been resolved or is no longer significant—they have become shared special economic zones or can be easily navigated by Chinese trucks carrying products for Central Asian markets. It is the OBOR, an infrastructural project with its own funding agency, the AIIB, that has assumed importance and SCO meetings reiterate commitment to both as an integral part of the organization. And it is the need for combined material and political commitment in infrastructural development that seems to be the motivating factor for the acceptance of expanded membership among the states. Similarly, connectivity played a large part in India's decision to apply for membership, with the general agreement that for India joining the SCO, it was about 'raising its stakes in Central Asia', greater connectivity to a wider resource-rich region and an opportunity to work on common issues of concern. This in conjunction with Iran's membership would ensure that India would be able to move towards developing a platform for trade and transit through Bandar Abbas and Chabahar, eventually linking with the North–South Corridor. There also remains the possibility of the SCO acting as guarantor for projects such as TAPI (Turkemnistan, Afghanistan, Pakistan India) and the IPI

(Iran, Pakistan, India) which have been in the pipeline for a number of years. This would also provide a useful interface for interaction with Afghanistan and its neighbourhood. However, the counter-argument that SCO engagement need not be over-emphasized as bilateral engagement with the Central Asian States works just as well as illustrated by the uranium supply deal with Kazakhstan during Prime Minister Modi's visit.[7] The Indian alternative through 'Connect Central Asia' that was projected as the policy initiative on the west, that would complement its Look/Act East Policy with an emphasis on the four 'Cs', commerce, connectivity, consular and culture, however, could not match Chinese engagement either economically or in political terms.

In fact, China's growing engagement in the global economy, its import-export markets and investments that exceed those of both the USA and Japan means that its domestic decisions on fiscal, wage and monetary policies have global impact. And because of this role in the global economy, China is today a global 'neighbour'. For instance, as China's investment and trade along the new Silk Road continues to grow, other competitors will eventually be eliminated as few states would be able to match the benefits offered by the Chinese (Ooi and Trinkle 2015). And this would increasingly be true of other regions as China moves towards what it considers to be a 'reform' of the international monetary system and its agencies (IMF, ADB, WTO) and is able to include growing numbers of states within an alternative system which would include the AIIB, New Development Bank (NDB) and other 'Asian' developmental funds. Engagement with China through platforms like BRICS would then also become crucial.

BRICS emerged from a market-driven intellectual inspiration to bring together a group of states with diverse histories, sizes, economic profiles, political systems, national preferences and strategic cultures in what former Indian Prime Minister Manmohan Singh aspired would be a meeting of equitable partners for a just and fair management of the global community of nations. The anticipation of a 'just, fair and equitable order' still seems to be the abiding expectation from the group along with policy coordination that would restructure outmoded economic and political institutions and global governance structures in a world that seems to be rapidly moving towards de-globalization (particularly due to decisions from its most vocal proponents in the West). So while commitment to the enhancement of the voice and representation of BRICS economies in global economic governance, along with a call to implement the Paris Agreement on climate change and common positions on Syria, Afghanistan and North Korea, is duly articulated, the intensifying completion over common strategic spaces, the drifting apart of a long-term relationship and political and economic instability in two other states are realities in the background of which it functions.

The BRICS expectation was that since all member states were interested in a more equitable global economic order, they would be the harbinger of a new matrix of global governance in trade, energy and climate change. BRICS Action Agenda on Economic and Trade Cooperation, BRICS Action Plan on Innovation Cooperation, Strategic Framework of BRICS Customs Cooperation, an MoU between the BRICS Business Council and NDB on Strategic Cooperation (a multilateral development bank set up by BRICS) and the BRICS think tank are significant in this context. What also remains significant of course is the potential of the organization which now accounts for 20 per cent of the global GDP and 40 per cent of the world's population. However, despite their cumulative power there is today debate on sustainability of the organization, and while a number of scenarios have been envisioned that predict the possibility of the organization remaining a 'club', increase its ability of influencing global affairs by building a political alliance and attempt the creation of an economic union or political and cultural integration, each implies a set of political and economic initiatives that are yet to be implemented (Shapenko et al. 2018). Also, as the requirement for formulating a concerted strategy for negotiations with the 'industrialized' West is reduced due to deep contradictions within them, the rhetorical character of the grouping for member states, that now seem to be striking their own individual paths of development and negotiating their own 'crises', seems to be ascendant. It is in light of this articulation of new strategies that the concluding segment examines the possibilities for the emergence of alternative corridors that traverse the maritime space rather than connect through land corridors.

CONCLUSION: THE CHANGING RHETORIC AND FUTURE OF CORRIDORS

The twenty-first-century MSR was proposed by Chinese President Xi Jinping in October 2013 during a speech to the Indonesian Parliament. The route of this MSR is through the cities Guangzhou, Fuzhou, Guangzhou, Haikou, Beihai, Hanoi, Kuala Lumpur, Jakarta, Colombo, Kolkata, Nairobi, Athens and Venice. The maritime areas of this MSR include the East China Sea, the South China Sea, the Indian Ocean and the Mediterranean Sea. Indian strategic thinking identifies the MSR as a repackaging of the 'string of pearls' strategy, a position reflected in C. Raja Mohan's *Samudra Manthan, Sino-Indian Rivalry in the Indo-Pacific*, where he argues that that land competition between China and India will spill out to the ocean and the Indo-Pacific is the new geographical space for this contest (Raja Mohan 2012).

The Indian alternative has been to focus on the eastern and western reaches of the Indian Ocean and the sub-continental landmass south of Eurasia but linked to it. The development of a network of Indian Ocean ports to serve as regional shipping hubs for littoral states with connecting highways and rail routes would mean leveraging India's location in one of the most strategic stretches of ocean space. The launching of a Spice Route, Cotton Route and the Mausam Project, all of which are attempts to tie together countries around the Indian Ocean, assumes significant in this context. At the macro-level the aim of Project Mausam is to reconnect and re-establish communication between countries of the Indian Ocean, world which would lead to enhanced understanding of cultural values and concerns, while at the micro-level, the focus is on understanding national cultures in their regional maritime milieu. The aim is not just to examine connections that linked parts of the Indian Ocean littoral but also the connections of these coastal centres to their hinterlands. The 'Spice Project' aims to explore the multifaceted Indo-Pacific Ocean World, collating archaeological and historical research to document the diversity of cultural, commercial and religious interactions in the Indian Ocean—extending from East Africa, the Arabian Peninsula, the Indian sub-continent and Sri Lanka to the Southeast Asian Archipelago. The broader aim is to connect these with the 'information silk route' where telecom connectivity between the countries would be made possible. Partly propelled by the advancement in IT in India and partly by the fact that connectivity on the ground has been restricted by political connections, these strategies need to be visualized as integrated aspects of both domestic and foreign policy (Sengupta 2016).

The Indian rhetoric is based on the interconnectedness of the Indian and Pacific Oceans, the importance of oceans in security and commerce and India's role within the broader region. This was articulated by Prime Minister Narendra Modi during the Shangri-La Dialogue in Singapore, where he clarified that this was neither a strategy nor an exclusive club. He described it as a 'natural region' ranging 'from the shores of Africa to that of the Americas' and argued that it should be 'free, open, and inclusive', grounded in 'rules and norms … based on the consent of all, not on the power of the few' and characterized by respect for international law, including the freedom of navigation and over flight. He went on to stress that it was not in conflict with ASEAN unity and centrality (Modi, 2018). While the articulation of the Indo-Pacific as a strategy to balance Chinese influence over the oceans was implicit in this discourse, the downplaying of the concept by the Chinese is a clear indication that the openness of the policy is in contradiction to their policy in stretches like the South China Sea.

Samir Saran, however, argues that efforts to shift global centrality to the 'Indo-Pacific' remain an insufficient response to China's spectacular measures to connect Europe and Asia (Saran 2018). Reiterating Mackinder's position, he contends that Eurasia remains the 'supercontinent' and the new world order will be defined by who manages it and how it is managed. It is in this supercontinent that the future of democracy, free markets and global security arrangements will be decided. Having assessed that the divide between Europe and Asia is artificial, China has moved towards the creation of a network of connectivity projects that have diluted the significance of sub-regions and upset power arrangements. He argues that an open Indo-Pacific vision is an insufficient response to China's relentless pursuit of building infrastructure, facilitating trade and creating alternative global institutions across Eurasia. A rejuvenated China has negotiated what will probably be a decades-long process of constructing new lines of communication

210 | Anita Sengupta

to the sub-regions of Asia. For China, it is incidental that India lies on the crossroads of Chinese silk routes. For India, however, this dynamic holds the potential to reshape its entire periphery and impact India's own role in South Asia, calling for enhanced engagement and expanded presence (Sengupta 2018).

Given the global reality of a China-centred network of corridors engulfing both Asian overland and maritime routes on the one hand and possibilities of the emergence of a new set of rules and regulations governing global trade on the other, either the development of a logistic alternative or connecting with the existing frameworks would be an essential enabler for India's agenda of economic development for the North East. However, a great deal of uncertainty surrounds the future. Serious concerns on the ecological and social impacts of connectivity projects seem to be clouding the future of China-centred trade networks with states like Sri Lanka and Malaysia critiquing connectivity projects that traverse their territories. Similarly, India's Act East Policy in a newly created Indo-Pacific space is a work in progress that awaits conceptual clarity but also policy consensus among a large number of stakeholders, including sub-regions, cities, ports and civil society actors. A meticulous balancing act between these realities call for the recognition of India's pivotal geographic position and requires an integrated and coordinated approach which would make use of past linkages, present assets and also the possibilities of future development. While the translation of logistic visions into strategic logistical spaces cannot be taken for granted, taking note of changing global networks, linking with other Asian logistic frameworks and keeping in mind the 'slip roads' that local mobilities traverse are just some of the imperatives that India would have to consider as it negotiates its own development in a future that belongs to fluidity.

NOTES

1. The US Department of State in the section Diplomacy in Action underlines four key areas of support: (a) regional energy markets, which include support for CASA (Central Asia, South Asia)-1000, that is, regional electricity grids/support for energy transmission lines, hydropower plants and 1000 megawatts to Pakistan's power grid; (b) trade and transport which include 3000 km of

roads built or rehabilitated in Afghanistan/support for Kazakh and Afghan accession to the WTO/technical assistance to Afghanistan–Pakistan Transit Trade Agreement and Cross-border Transport Agreement among Kyrgyzstan, Tajikistan and Afghanistan; (c) customs and border operations which include increasing trade/reducing the cost of crossing regional borders and streamlining customs procedures at seven Afghan border crossing points; and (d) business and people-to-people connects which include funding university studies for Afghan students in Central Asia and sponsoring the Central Asia and Afghanistan Women's Economic Symposium and South Asia Women's Entrepreneurship Symposium/organized trade delegations. For details, see U.S. Department of State (20 January 2009–20 January 2017).
2. For a detailed discussion of BCIM-EC that follows, see Sengupta (2017).
3. *Ibid.*
4. Minutes, 'First Meeting of the Joint Study Group', 18–19 December 2013. Retrieved from http://www.indianembassy.org.on/newsDetails. aspx?Newsid=455. Cited from Uberoi 2014.
5. For details, see Table 5.1 in Xiaowen's (2017) article.
6. For details, see the article by Wadwa (2018).
7. See *Business Standard* (2015). Also, for the membership to be useful, India would have to take a constructive approach rather than pushing anti-terrorism as an agenda with the obvious intention of pointing towards Pakistan. There also remains the criticism that beyond meeting annually and the creation of Regional Anti-Terrorist Structure (RATS), nothing constructive has come out of the SCO. Of course SCO meetings could provide a neutral ground for bilateral engagement and participation with new levels of intelligence sharing and the development of counter-terrorism strategies. However, this itself could become problematic in certain situations where India could consider its security as compromised by other members of the SCO. The facts that the core of the SCO would remain Russia and China and the two official languages of the SCO remain Russian and Chinese, despite expansion, are also significant in terms of SCO members' attitudes towards expansion. See also Pantucci (2015)

REFERENCES

ASEAN Secretariat. 2016. *Master Plan on ASEAN Connectivity 2025*. Jakarta: ASEAN Secretariat. Retrieved from http://asean.org/storage/2016/09/Master-Plan-on-ASEAN-Connectivity-20251.pdf

Business Standard. 2015. 'Realism in Central Asia: Advantages and Disadvantages to SCO Membership'. *Business Standard Editorial Comment,* 13 July. Retrieved from https://www.business-standard.com/article/opinion/realism-in-central-asia-115071301225_1.html

De, P., and K. Iyenger. 2014. *Developing Economic Corridors in South Asia*. Mandaluyong City, Philippines: Asian Development Bank.

Diener, A. C. 2015. 'Parsing Mobilities in Central Eurasia: Border Management and New Silk Roads'. *Eurasian Geography and Economics* 56(4): 377.

Grappi, G. 2018. 'Asia's Era of Infrastructure and the Politics of Corridors: Decoding the Language of Logistical Governance'. In *Logistical Asia: The Labour of Making a World Region*, edited by B. Neilson, N. Rossiter and R. Samaddar, 182. Singapore: Palgrave Macmillan.

Khanna, P. 2016. *Connectography: Mapping the Future of Global Civilization*. New York: Random House. Kindle Version.

Modi, N. 2018. 'PM Modi's Keynote Address at the Shangri La Dialogue in Singapore'. Narendra Modi, 1 June. Retrieved from https://www.narendramodi.in/pm-%20modi-%20to%20-deliver%20-keynote-%20address%20-at%20-shangri-la-%20dialouge-%20in%20-singapore-540324

Ooi, S.-M., and K. Trinkle. 2015. 'China's New Silk Road and Its Impact on Xinjinag'. *The Diplomat*, 5 March. Retrieved from https://thediplomat.com/2015/03/chinas-new-silk-road-and-its-impact-on-xinjiang/

Pantucci, R. 2015. 'India and the SCO: The Real Benefit'. *Gateway House*, 9 July. Retrieved from http://www.gatewayhouse.in/india-and-sco-the-real-benefit/

Raja Mohan, C. 2012. *Samudra Manthan: Sino Indian Rivalry in the Indo Pacific*. Washington, DC: Carnegie Endowment for International Peace.

Saeed, S. 2017. 'China's Plan to Rule the Seas Hit Trouble in Pakistan'. *POLITICO*, 8 August. Retrieved from https://www.politico.eu/article/china-plans-to-rule-seas-hit-trouble-in-pakistan-balochistan/

Saran, S. 2018. 'Eurasia: Larger than Indo-Pacific—Liberal World Must Stand Up and Be Counted, or Step Aside and Watch PaxSinica Unfold'. *Times of India*, 4 June. Retrieved from https://blogs.timesofindia.indiatimes.com/toi-edit-page/eurasia-larger-than-indo-pacific-liberal-world-must-stand-up-and-be-counted-or-step-aside-and-watch-pax-sinica-unfold/

Sengupta, A. 2016. 'Logistical Spaces IV: The Asian Paradigm'. *Policies and Practices* 79: 1–25. Retrieved from http://www.mcrg.ac.in/PP79.pdf

———. 2017. 'Logistical Spaces VI: Logistics and the Reshaping of Global Governance'. *Policies and Practices* 85: 9–10. Retrieved from http://www.mcrg.ac.in/PP85.pdf

———. 2018. 'The Great Maritime Game'. *Asia in Global Affairs*, 10 June. Retrieved from http://www.asiainglobalaffairs.in/reflections/the-great-maritime-game/

Shapenko, A., B. Nureyev, V. Korovkin, and D. Ontoev. 2018. 'Imagine BRICS: Four Scenarios of the Future'. *BRICS Business Magazine*. Retrieved from https://bricsmagazine.com/en/articles/imagine-brics-four-scenarios-of-the-future

Sharma, A. 2018. 'Integrating Northeast with Southeast Asia: Great Expectations and Ground Realities'. In *Mainstreaming the Northeast and India's Look East Policy*, edited by A. Sharma and S. Choudhury, 25–43. Singapore: Palgrave Macmillan.

Srisangnam, P., and A. Devendrakumar. 2018. 'Unlocking the Northeast Region of India: An ASEAN Connectivity Perspective'. In *Mainstreaming the Northeast and India's Look East Policy,* edited by A. Sharma and S. Choudhury, 127–28. Singapore: Palgrave Macmillan.

U.S. Department of State. 2009, January 20–2017, January 20. *U.S. Support for the New Silk Road.* U.S. Department of State. Retrieved from https://2009-2017.state.gov/p/sca/ci/af/newsilkroad/index.htm

Uberoi, P. 2014. *The BCIM Economic Corridor: A Leap into the Unknown.* Institute of Chinese Studies, Delhi. Working Paper, 1–19. Retrieved from http://www.icsin.org/uploads/2015/05/15/89cb0691df2fa541b6972080968fd6ce.pdf

Xiaowen, H. 2017. 'BCIM and OBOR'. In *One Belt One Road, China's Global Outreach,* edited by S. Kondapalli and H. Xiaowen, 162–64. New Delhi: Pentagon Press.

Wadwa, A. 2018. 'The Northeast Is Key to India's Relations with ASEAN'. *LiveMint,* 9 March. Retrieved from https://www.livemint.com/Opinion/o4QSDxyenyvZ0QGwX5mwdL/The-North-East-is-key-for-Indias-ties-with-Asean.html

Chapter 8

Development of India's North East
Cross-border Market, Trade and Sub-regional Cooperation

Gurudas Das

The development of India's northeastern region (NER) has long been a major challenge to policymakers both at the state and the centre. Neither the State-led development model followed till 1990 nor the market-led development initiative followed since 1991 could bring any respite for this landlocked region. The peripheral geographical location of the region stood in the way of her progress. The high transportation costs did not allow the region to grow in line with her comparative advantage. Also, the development of the region had long been hostage to State-centric security perceptions as the borders were kept inaccessible and cross-border synergies were ignored (Das 2012).

With the collapse of the bipolar world and the subsequent embracing of globalization by the Indian State, the geoeconomic importance of borders has come into the fore, relegating geopolitical considerations to the back seat. Borders, which are not militarily active, are now increasingly being viewed as gateways to markets in the neighbouring countries rather than as passages for the invading external forces. Like countries across the world, India has also started promoting cross-border trade and economic cooperation. This change in the perspective has immense implications for the development of the NER as it shares 98 per cent of its international borders with the neighbouring countries and is connected with the mainland only through a narrow strip of land euphemistically called 'Chicken's Neck'. Being away from the mainland, the markets in the neighbouring countries, which are much closer, can act as the vent for surplus produced in the region as well as the impetus for the utilization of her vast natural resources. Thus, cross-border trade and cooperation might be used as a strategy for the economic development of the peripheral bordering states in the NER.

CROSS-BORDER TRADE AND DEVELOPMENT OF INDIA'S NORTH EAST

Could trade with neighbouring countries alone trigger development in the NER? Except China, in spite of having a long post-colonial history of cross-border trade with Bangladesh, Bhutan and Myanmar, why did NER fail to develop herself? To find out, let us have a look at the basic characteristics of NER's trade with the neighbouring countries.

Studies on cross-border trade (Das 2000, 2002, 2005a, 2005b, 2006, 2008) have already demonstrated that NER's trade with neighbouring countries essentially reduces to trade only with one country, that is, Bangladesh. In fact more than 90 per cent of NER's trade flows to Bangladesh while her formal trade with Bhutan and Myanmar is abysmally low (Table 8.1).

Table 8.1 Share of NER's Trade with the Neighbouring Countries (1998–1999 to 2012–2013)

Country	Percentage Share of NER's Trade
Bangladesh	90.8
Bhutan	6.0
Myanmar	3.2

Source: Author's calculation based on customs' data.

216 | Gurudas Das

The reason for the overwhelming predominance of NER's trade with Bangladesh lies in their complementary structure of endowments between the two regions. While the hills of NER are rich in minerals like coal and limestone; horticultural products such as vegetables, ginger and turmeric; forest products such as honey, broom grass, betel nuts and so on, the plains of Bangladesh lack them. As a result, there exists a strong basis for trade between them. A look into the commodity structure of NER's trade with the neighbouring countries confirms our narrative (Table 8.2).

Trade between NER and Bangladesh has led to the evolution of a pattern of interdependence in which NER's natural resources are swapped for Bangladeshi manufacturing goods. While limestones are being exported across the border of Meghalaya to cement factories in Bangladesh, manufactured cement is being imported through different land ports in Tripura. Similarly, while coal from Meghalaya is being sent to the brick cline factories in Bangladesh, bricks are being imported by Tripura. In the same manner, while fresh vegetables, ginger, turmeric and various fruits are being exported to Bangladesh, processed food products such as jam, jelly, squash, pickles and other dry food preparations are being imported in NER. Thus, NER is not adding any value before she exports her resources to Bangladesh; rather, business and industry in Bangladesh benefit through value addition.

Table 8.2 Commodity Structure of NER's Border Trade (1998–1999 to 2012–2013)

Commodity Group	NER's Export (% share in total)	NER's Import (% share in total)
Agro-horticultural and allied products	5.2	39.9
Manufactured goods	6.4	43.0
Ores and minerals	79.6	13.9
Others	8.8	3.7

Source: Author's calculation based on customs' data.

Although some sort of a triadic resource-industry-trade linkage has been established in the case of cement industry where limestones in Meghalaya are used to manufacture cement that is mainly sold to local markets, the same is yet to develop for markets across the border. As communication bottlenecks have resulted in segregated regional markets, and national markets are far away, firms do not find it viable to produce at a large scale. Hence, a dyadic resource–trade linkage has evolved across the border where firms locate themselves in Bangladesh plains and produce cement at a large scale to cater to the needs of larger markets there. Cheaper labour, plenty of water, easily available land, better infrastructure including roads, railways and ports and above all access to a larger market—all have made Bangladesh a better location for production operations compared to the hills of North East India where except raw limes other factors are either not cost effective or are not available.

Thus, even if the northeastern hills are rich in minerals and horticulture, no strong resource-industry linkages grew that could act as the lead sector and drive regional growth. High transportation costs prohibit firms from producing in the region and supplying to national markets. Hence, the key for the acceleration of economic growth lies in reducing the distance between the NER and mainland India which can only be done through sub-regional cooperation between India and Bangladesh. Before we delve into this issue, let us turn our attention to the nature of cross-border trade of the region with the neighbouring countries Bhutan and Myanmar.

INDIA'S BHUTAN TRADE: IMPLICATIONS FOR THE NORTHEASTERN REGION

The competitive resource structure between the NER on the one hand and Bhutan and Myanmar on the other does not provide any firm basis for trade. Whatever trade flows through the land ports of NER to these two countries is essentially transit trade. Manufactured goods produced outside the region are exported through the NER. In spite of the fact that Bhutan enjoys a free trade status vis-à-vis India and her external trade is essentially India centric as, in 2017, 77.57 per cent of her total exports went to India and 80.54 per cent of her total imports came from India (Royal Government of Bhutan [RGB] 2017), NER's trade with Bhutan was negligible. The primary reason for this lies in the fact that while the resource structures between India and Bhutan are complementary in nature, the same between Bhutan and NER are competitive. It is only evident from Bhutan's export and import baskets. While Bhutan's export basket is mainly composed of intermediary products and raw materials such as electricity, mineral products, products of chemical industries, base metals and products and wood and wood products, her imports from India mainly consist of machinery, mechanical appliances, base metals, electronic items, foodstuffs and other basic necessities and consumer items.

Hydro-power generation is the leading sector that drives the economic growth of Bhutan. In 2017, electricity alone constituted for about 32 per cent of total exports from that country (RGB 2017) and the entire export went to India. Besides hydro-power, energy-intensive manufacturing products such as cement, ferro-alloys and carbide have contributed to about 19 per cent of the total exports of Bhutan. Another almost 45 per cent of exports consist of minerals such as dolomite, calcium carbide, silicon, gypsum, coal, manganese, silicon carbide and so on.

Thus, in a way, Bhutan is competing with the NER for Indian markets as both regions have similar resource bases. Bhutan, located much nearer to mainland India, can cater to the needs of the Indian business, industry and consumers in a much more cost-effective manner than NER. In fact, while the location of Bhutan has made it a captive market for India, the same has made NER a captive market for Bangladesh.

Moreover, much of Bhutan's trade to India flows through the Phuentsholing–Jaigaon border point as it lies on the commercial lifeline Thimphu-Phuentsholing-Jaigaon-Hasimara-Kolkata/Haldia road corridor. In fact, Phuentsholing is the commercial hub of Bhutan and about more than 80 per cent of Bhutan's trade flows through it. Besides connecting Thimphu to Kolkata, two other road corridors connecting Thimphu to Mongla/Chittagong in Bangladesh and Thimphu to Kakarvita in Nepal pass through Phuentsholing. Thus, West Bengal acts as landlocked Bhutan's gateway to other South Asian countries. As a result, not much of trade flows through the NER in spite of the fact that three land custom stations, that is, Darranga, Hatisar and Ultapani, are located along the Assam-Bhutan border and one of the important road corridors Samdrup Jongkhar-Guwahati-Shillong-Sylhet-Dhaka-Kolkata passes through it. Besides the issue of being cost effective for Bhutan to trade with mainland India, Bangladesh and Nepal using the road networks in North Bengal (the northern region of West Bengal), road networks of NER are usually avoided due to security reasons as, on a couple of occasions, Bhutanese traders were kidnapped by North East insurgent groups for ransom (Basu Ray Chaudhury and Basu 2017).

Be that as it may, a US$2.2 billion (2016) size of Bhutan's economy with only about 0.8 million in terms of population is too small to generate any growth impulse in the economy of NER. Moreover, the average annual GDP growth at the rate of 8.61 per cent for the current decade (2007–17) has fuelled unequal regional growth in favour of the western region while her eastern region has remained largely underdeveloped. As the NER is contiguous to the underdeveloped eastern region of Bhutan, there is hardly any scope for using cross-border synergies as drivers for growth on either side.

INDIA'S MYANMAR TRADE: IMPLICATIONS FOR THE NORTHEASTERN REGION

Myanmar, India's gateway to Southeast Asia, has a population of about 54 million (2018) and an economy of US$67.40 billion (2016). With 0.44 per cent of world area, 0.71 per cent of global population and 0.11 per cent of global economy, it has remained one of the least developed countries in the world. Needless to mention, with 1,05,770 sq. km (2007) of arable land, 23,070 sq. km (2014) of surface water, 3,12,892 sq. km (2007) of forest area,[1] 2,832 km of coastline,[2] more than 100 GW of hydropower potential,[3] almost 140 million barrels of oil and 322 billion cubic meters of gas,[4] besides rich reserves of precious stones like jade and ruby and significant occurrences of copper, tin, silver, lead, zinc, tin, antimony, iron and so on (Allan and Einzenberger 2013), Myanmar, the storehouse of natural resources, presents huge potential for growth, development, trade and commerce, which had not been hitherto realized due to an incongruent political regime. About five decades of isolation (1962–2011) coupled with sanctions by the West did not allow the economy of Myanmar to integrate with the global economy and hence the country's foreign trade is largely limited in terms of trade with the neighbouring countries in Asia (Table 8.3).

TRENDS IN INDO-MYANMAR BILATERAL TRADE

Although India is the second-largest neighbour of Myanmar after China, the economic engagement, measured in terms of the volume of bilateral trade and investments, is not as robust as it should have been compared to China. In 2016, while 40.84 per cent of Myanmar's total exports went to China, the same for India was merely 8.89 per cent (Table 8.3). Thus, the size of Myanmar's export market in China was about 4.6 times larger than that of India. Similarly, Myanmar drew about 34.42 per cent of her total imports from China, while the same for India was only 6.97 per cent, making the Chinese market 4.94 times attractive compared to India (Table 8.3). What is noteworthy is

Table 8.3 Myanmar's Share of Exports to and Imports from the Neighbouring Countries (2016)

Country	Share of Exports (%)	Share of Imports (%)
China	40.84	34.42
Thailand	19.20	12.65
India	8.89	6.97
Singapore	7.63	14.45
Japan	5.68	7.99
Total: (Above5 countries)	**82.24**	**76.48**
Rest of the World	17.76	23.52
World Total	**100**	**100**

Source: WITS, https://goo.gl/XWZjVH

that Thailand has made substantial inroads in Myanmar from which the Thai economy is being immensely benefited.

Although India is the third-largest destination of Myanmar's exports and fifth-largest source of her imports, the extent of this gap compared to other two bordering countries (China and Thailand) is indeed a matter of concern for Indian businesses and policy circles. The reason for the low Indo-Myanmar bilateral trade volume lies in the fact that unlike China and Thailand, India is not in a position to import oil and gas—Myanmar's main exports—across the border using pipelines as her productive regions—the southwest and southeast coastal areas—are far off from the NER that borders with Myanmar. As the region itself has remained economically underdeveloped due to lack of access to national market centres, high transportation costs prohibit resource acquisition across the border.

TRADE BETWEEN INDIA'S NORTHEASTERN REGION AND MYANMAR

In fact, unlike China and Thailand, bilateral trade between India and Myanmar mainly flows through maritime routes. As a result, the share of India's land border trade with Myanmar is abysmally low compared to other neighbours—China and Thailand (Table 8.4). Researchers of border studies often lament on this issue and consider it to be one of the weaknesses in India's neighbourhood policy. However, it is often oversight that a low volume of border trade does not indicate a low

Table 8.4 *Myanmar's Trade with Its Bordering Countries (2016; US$ Million)*

Country	Total Trade	Land Border Trade	Border Trade as % of Total Trade
China	10,163.78	6,296.65	66.83
Thailand	4,227.4	1,381.56	32.68
India	2,132.82	88.21	4.14
Bangladesh	40.93	10.59	25.88

Source: http://www.commerce.gov.mm

volume of bilateral trade as India is the fourth-largest trading partner of Myanmar, after China, Thailand and Singapore. Even then, keeping this fact in mind, one might be curious to know why the volume of trade between India's NER and Myanmar is so low.

The answer lies in the fact that both regions have competitive resource bases and hence there is hardly any strong basis for trade between them. As a result, unlike trade between NER and Bangladesh, which is quite robust and growth generating as the resource bases between them are complementary, the trade between NER and Myanmar is basically transit trade where goods produced in the third country or region are being traded. While a strong resource–trade linkage generates employment and income of the resource owners in case of NER and Bangladesh land border trade, it is missing in case of the region's land border trade with Myanmar.

The challenge before NER and Myanmar trade lies in transforming it from transit to growth-generating trade through dyadic linkages between trade and local resource bases and then further to a triadic linkage among resource–industry–trade. Once these triadic linkages have evolved, economies across the border will exhibit mutual interdependence in the production space, leading to the emergence of cross-border value chains which will in turn sustain the future momentum of land border trade and investment.

SUB-REGIONAL COOPERATION AND CROSS-BORDER MARKET INTEGRATION

The account of the status of cross-border trade between India's North East and the neighbouring countries, Bangladesh, Bhutan and Myanmar, outlined in the foregoing sections leaves no ambiguity to the fact that trade alone can hardly play the role of an engine of growth in spite of the NER being resource rich. The segregated internal market, poor connectivity—both within and across—and the peripheral location far away from mainland market centres coupled with strong 'border effects' have robbed her comparative advantages and have made her an unattractive destination for private investment. Extremely weak spill-over effects, security vulnerability and negligible bargaining power of the political class vis-à-vis the Indian federal polity have choked large-scale public investment in productive sectors. Whatever little trade flows across the borders is insignificant to generate any growth impulse for the region. As resource extraction in this peripheral region is ordered by the needs of the national economy, their utilization calls for a rise in scarcity to such an extent that it can justify their use at higher prices due to exorbitantly higher transport costs. As a result, the establishment of cross-border connectivity through sub-regional cooperation with neighbouring countries, strengthening of cross-border sub-regional value chains and encouraging cross-border market integration appears to be the appropriate development strategies for the underdeveloped NER.

CONNECTIVITY, CROSS-BORDER RESOURCE-INDUSTRY LINKAGE AND INDIA-MYANMAR-THAILAND TRILATERAL HIGHWAY

One such sub-regional cooperation initiative having tremendous development implications for the NER is the India–Myanmar–Thailand (IMT) Trilateral Highway. As both Myanmar and NER are resource-rich underdeveloped regions, Thailand, being industrially advanced, will play the role of the engine in IMT cooperation. Technology, capital and expertise of Thailand when combined with the natural resources of the otherwise industrially underdeveloped Myanmar and NER will help in forging a strong resource–industry linkages in the IMT area which will propel the growth.

This trilateral cooperation will not only transform NER from a landlocked area to land-linked area, but the Continental Route will provide the much needed logistical space for which the region could not reap the benefits of India's Look East Policy and has remained a passive onlooker while the coastal regions flourished.

How can IMT cooperation set the ball rolling for NER? We shall cite examples of two cases: pineapple and ginger that grow in plenty in the hills and the plains of NER. While India produces 6.34 per cent of the global production of pineapples, she only shares 0.06 per cent of global exports (FAO 2013). Within India, NER contributes to 48.33 per cent of the total national production. Thailand produces 8.92 per cent of global production but shares 13.37 per cent of global exports. As Thailand is one of the leading food processors and world's largest exporter of pineapple juice (17.92% in global share), pineapples produced in NER if exported to Thailand will be beneficial for both as it has been facing severe crises of pineapples for almost three quarters in a year (Q1, Q2 and Q4). Thus, supplying pineapples to Thailand via the IMT highway will be a win-win situation for both the countries. This resource (in NER)-industry (in Thailand) linkage will ensure remunerative prices for the farmers as well as profit margins for the intermediaries, leading to a rise in the level of their income. Our estimation shows that traders might reap about 90 per cent of returns on their investment even after paying nearly double the farm gate price (Das and Das 2017).

Similarly, while India is the number one producer of ginger in the world—it alone produces 26.6 per cent of global production—it only shares 2.74 per cent of the total global exports of ginger (FAO 2013). In contrast, China produces 15.19 per cent of global production but shares 52.16 per cent of global exports. Within India, 56.52 per cent of national production comes from the states in the NER. Much of this ginger is sold raw at a lesser price without any processing and value addition. A significant part of this raw ginger is exported to Bangladesh across the border in south Assam (Das and Das 2017).

As Thailand is one of the net importers of ginger and offers much higher prices compared to Bangladesh, it will be beneficial for both ginger cultivators in NER and ginger merchants in Thailand to trade. Thailand will have access to raw materials and NER will have access to a lucrative market. The technology, processing efficiency and market penetration skills of Thai firms while combined with raw materials available in the NER will create a win-win situation for stakeholders in both countries. As Japan and Singapore are also net importers of ginger, the ginger traders in Thailand due to their close networks in those countries might reap additional benefits by importing the surplus available in NER (Das and Das 2017).

Thus, trilateral cooperation along the Continental Route is certain to strengthen the dyadic resource–trade (Das 2010) linkages as well as the triadic resource–industry–trade linkages if Thai entrepreneurship is combined with resource availability in Myanmar and NER.

INDO-BANGLADESH SUB-REGIONAL COOPERATION, TRANSIT CORRIDOR AND ECONOMIC WELL-BEING OF THE NORTHEASTERN REGION

Like the IMT Trilateral Highway, NER will immensely benefit if she is allowed to access mainland India through the neighbouring Bangladesh. As elaborated elsewhere (Das 2012), once a transit corridor through Bangladesh is used, the distance between Agartala and Kolkata is reduced by 73 per cent. The people of the state of Tripura will not only enjoy lesser transportation cost due to the shortening of distance but will also save about 80 per cent in travel time. Like Agartala, the whole of south Assam will also immensely benefit from the transit facility through Bangladesh in terms of both reduced distance and travel time. Similarly, both Manipur and Mizoram will also be able to reap large benefits once the Bangladesh corridor is made operational. For both Manipur and Mizoram, the distance between their respective state capitals to Kolkata will reduce by about 850 km and travel time will reduce by about 100 hours. For Meghalaya, a diversion of traffic from the Chicken's Neck route to Bangladesh (the Dawki-Tamabil route) reduces the distance by 461 km and saves travel time by 34 hours. Although marginal, it is beneficial for traffic to take the route via Bangladesh from Guwahati rather than along the Chicken's Neck route as it reduces the distance by 261 km and saves travel time by 25 hrs. As the traffic from Nagaland and Arunachal Pradesh also move via Guwahati, they can also avail this marginal benefit if they choose to travel via Bangladesh (Das 2012).

It may be noted that the transport cost is a function of the distance to be covered. The further the distance, the higher the transport cost and vice versa. Assuming that transport cost per ton/per km is the same along the Chicken's Neck route and the route through Bangladesh, a sum of ₹4,477.20 will be saved if a ton of goods is moved via Bangladesh from Agartala to Kolkata rather than via the Chicken's Neck route. If 50 per cent of this cost differential is attributed as the transit fee to be accrued to Bangladesh, then business in Agartala will save ₹2,238.6 for every ton of goods moved through Bangladesh instead of the Chicken's Neck route. This will in turn bring down the cost of living drastically which will promote economic well-being of the people living in the border state of Tripura. The per ton transport cost differentials reveal that if goods are moved through the transit route via Bangladesh, immense benefits will also accrue to the south Assam region, Manipur and Mizoram. As these benefits will also accrue to outbound traffic from the northeastern states to mainland India as well, goods produced within the region can attain a competitive edge which will then encourage businesses to grow according to the comparative advantages of the region (Das 2012).

From Bangladesh's point of view, as the territory of Bangladesh lies between the NER and mainland India, she can make commercial use of her unique location by providing transit services to India. This will be beneficial for Bangladesh at least in two ways. First, in terms of transit fee, which will no doubt be a substantial amount as all the states in NER heavily depend on the supply from the mainland, it is approximated (from records available with inter-state custom gates) that annually 15 million metric tons of goods move between the NER and mainland India. If this traffic is diverted through Bangladesh as there is strong economic reason to do so, then Bangladesh can earn a hefty amount of transit fee which will substantially neutralize the chronic deficit balance of trade that Bangladesh is experiencing in her merchandize trade with India. Besides this transit fee for the inter-state movement of goods between the Indian states through Bangladesh, the transit fee for international exports and the import of cargo in the states of NER would also accrue to Bangladesh once the Port of Chittagong is opened up for them. Moreover improvement in connectivity between NER and Bangladesh will also boost the volume of trade between these two regions (Das 2012).

SECURITY, BORDER MANAGEMENT AND CROSS-BORDER TRADE AND DEVELOPMENT COOPERATION

As the Indian State looked at her northeastern borders through the geo-political prism till the other day, the dividing function of the border got prominence over their connecting roles. Even in a globalized era, not much change has taken place in this border security perspective and hence geoeconomic interests often become hostages of geopolitical thinking.

While a centralized State like China has devolved sufficient power to her bordering provinces so that they can carry out business deals and take up projects that require cross-border cooperation with the neighbouring countries across the border, in spite of being a federal republic, all such prerogatives are centralized in India. As a result, using the strategy of sub-regional cooperation, while China could negotiate the marginality of her peripheral regions, India could not even reap the potential of cross-border trade for the development of her border states.

China has converted the landlocked Yunnan into a huge connectivity hub by way of making it a part of the Greater Mekong Sub-region (GMS) initiative—an Asian Development Bank (ADB)-led regional cooperation initiative comprising six countries, initiated in 1992, which include China, Cambodia, Laos, Myanmar, Thailand and Vietnam. Yunnan, sharing borders with Myanmar, Laos and Vietnam, has been developed as a transportation hub in the region by way of creation of multi-modal transportation logistics connecting neighbouring countries (Fan 2011). As the markets in the neighbouring countries are far nearer than the main national markets, the integration of Yunnan with the economies of neighbouring countries was thought to be the best way to develop this landlocked peripheral area. Yunnan was developed so it could play the role of a bridgehead for GMS. Another sub-regional cooperation initiative called the Quadrangle consisting of Yunnan Province of China, Laos, Thailand and Myanmar was formed in 1993 with the objective of formalizing and developing existing cross-border trade, tourism and transport links among these countries (Than 2007). Thus, while China, leveraging from the sub-regional cooperation perspective, has negotiated the marginality of her peripheral regions like Yunnan by way of strengthening geoeconomic relations with the neighbouring countries across the border, India's NER still suffers from geographical isolation, absence of connectivity and utter underdevelopment. Although trade flows through land ports of all the countries with which NER shares borders, except China, unlike Yunnan, efforts to convert the region into a multi-modal transportation hub are yet to yield results.

Both geoeconomic interests for promoting cross-border trade and development cooperation and geopolitical concerns for the management of Indian borders could be served by way of adopting the 'smart border' approach (Federation of Indian Chambers of Commerce [FICCI] 2015) as is being done in the US-Canada borders as well as the intra-EU national borders (European Commission [EC] 2014). The establishment of an effective entry/exit system (EES), a registered traveller programme (RTP), as well as a mechanism for border crossings for third country national (TCN) travellers using biometric characteristics such as fingerprints (FPs), facial images (FIs), iris and so on and the integration of the biometric system with the Visa Information System (VIS) would provide the architecture of smart border management. To make these smart borders secure, besides the introduction of a technologically empowered multi-layered surveillance and guarding system, as is being done in the areas of interest (AOIs) along the western borders (LOC) with the help of thermal imaging, drones, ground surveillance radars, communications interception, unattended ground sensors, video surveillance and so on, it is also extremely important to integrate the communities living in the borderland areas with the security and surveillance module in order to instil a feeling of ownership and eliminate hostility towards the so-called 'others' who are deployed to guard the borders. As, unlike Pakistan and China, neither Bangladesh nor Myanmar have any territorial interest in the borderland areas in India, besides converting the northeastern borders into smart borders, these could be made 'shared borders' by way of establishing strong and mutually beneficial cross-border cooperation (CBC) by of sharing immigration databases, using e-passports and e-gates, establishing joint border outposts (BOPs) and establishing joint cross-border patrols. Like the border policy of a country which varies depending upon the threat perception across the border and bilateral relations with foreign countries with whom the host country shares its borders, there needs to be a built-in mechanism within the Indian federal framework for the empowerment of the bordering provinces at varying degrees so that they can take a lead in designing a framework of economic engagement and cross-border cooperation with the neighbouring countries within the broad framework of bilateral relationship. This will integrate the interests of both the local and the central and make our safe borders the gateways for trade and commerce, benefiting the people living in our borderlands, which will in turn weaken the raison d'etre of ethnic militancy. Otherwise, the locals would feel that their borders are being guarded by 'others' and the centre would view them as fringes living in 'our' border and the conflict of interest between the 'homeland' and 'borderland' will make our border management weak and ineffective which in turn will defeat the goal of promotion of cross-border trade and development cooperation with our good neighbours as well.

NOTES

1. http://en.worldstat.info/Asia/Myanmar/Land
2. https://www.dica.gov.mm/en/why-invest-myanmar
3. https://www.hydropower.org/country-profiles/myanmar
4. https://www.irrawaddy.com/news/burma/burmas-frontier-appeal-lures-shadowy-oil-firms.html

REFERENCES

Allan, D., and R. Einzenberger. 2013. 'Myanmar's Natural Resources: Blessing or Curse?' Retrieved from https://www.boell.de/en/2013/12/11/myanmars-natural-resources-blessing-or-curse

Basu Ray Chaudhury, A., and P. Basu. 2017. *India's Connectivity with Its Himalayan Neighbours: Possibilities and Challenges, Part 3*. Kolkata: Observer Research Foundation.

Das, G. 2000. 'Trade between the North Eastern Region and Neighbouring Countries: Structures and Implications for Development'. In *Border Trade: North East & Neighbouring Countries*, edited by G. Das and R. K. Purkayastha, 23–52. New Delhi: Akansha Publishing House.

———. 2002. 'Geo-Economy of Arunachal Pradesh: The Cross-Border Trade Dimension'. In *Cross-Border Trade of North East India*, edited by S. Dutta. Gurgaon, Haryana: Hope India Publications.

———. 2005a. 'Economy of Myanmar: Trends, Structure and Implications for Border Trade with India's North East' (with C J Thomas). In *Indo-Myanmar Border Trade: Status, Problems and Potentials,* edited by G. Das, N. B. Singh, and C J. Thomas. New Delhi: Akansha Publishing House.

———. 2005b. 'Sino-Indian Border Trade for Frontier Development: The Case of India's Northeast and China's Southwest'. In *India and China in an Era of Globalization: Essays on Economic Cooperation*, edited by J. K. Ray and P. De. New Delhi: Bookwell.

———. 2006. 'Border Trade in India's North East: Theory and Practice'. In *Challenges of Development in North-East India*, edited by D. R. Syiemlieh, Anuradha Dutta and Srinath Baruah. New Delhi: Regency Publications.

Das, G. 2008. 'Indo-Bangladesh Relations: Issues in Trade, Transit and Security'. In *Indo-Bangladesh Border Trade: Benefiting from Neighbourhood*, edited by G. Das and C. J. Thomas. New Delhi: Akansha Publishing House.

———. 2010. 'Development of National Peripheries through Mobilizing Cross-Border Synergies: A Case for Sino-Indian Cooperation for the Development of India's Northeast and China's Southwest'. In *India-China: Trade and Strategy for Frontier Development*, edited by G. Das and C. J. Thomas. New Delhi: Bookwell.

———. 2012. *Security and Development in India's Northeast*. New Delhi: Oxford University Press.

Das, G., and M. Das. 2017. 'India-Myanmar-Thailand (IMT) Trilateral Highway and Its Likely Impact on the Economic Integration between NER and ASEAN'. In *ASEAN Calling: Development of India's North-East through Sub-regional Cooperation*, edited by U. K. Paul, G. Das and C. J. Thomas. New Delhi: Pentagon Press.

European Commission (EC). 2014. *Technical Study on Smart Borders Final Report*. European Union. Retrieved from https://goo.gl/X4JjVW

Fan, H. 2011. 'China-Myanmar Transport Corridor'. *Ritsumeikan International Affairs* 10: 43–66.

FAO Stat. 2013. 'Data Relating to 2013'. Retrieved from http://www.fao.org/faostat/en/#data/QC

Federation of Indian Chambers of Commerce (FICCI). 2015. *Smart Border Management: An Indian Perspective*. New Delhi: FICCI.

Royal Government of Bhutan (RGB). 2017. *Bhutan Trade Statistics*. Department of Revenue & Customs Ministry of Finance. Retrieved from http://www.mof.gov.bt/wp-content/uploads/2018/04/Final-BTS-Publication-2017.pdf

Than, M. 2007. 'China and CLMV Countries: Relations in the Context of the Mekong Sub-region'. In *ASEAN-China Economic Relations*, edited by S.-H. Saw. Singapore: Institute of Southeast Asian Studies.

Chapter 9

Development through Trade
Re-examining India's Act East Policy and the Northeastern Region

Thongkholal Haokip

The present-day 'northeastern region' has been a meeting ground, a transit point and a southern trial of old trade routes. It has been the meeting ground of different people who migrated to the region from Southeast Asia and China at various points of history. As such the 'northeastern corner of India' has become 'a museum of nationalities' (Fuller 1909, xiii). The region had been known for her natural resources and maintained active trans-border trade with its neighbours during the pre-Independence period (Pommaret 1999, 285–303). It has 'a pre-history of a rich connected past', in which these elements 'continued to survive into the colonial and post-colonial period as well' (Misra 2011, 3). 'For a long time the climate and the regional political strongholds were seen as insurmountable obstacles to conquest' (Cederlof 2014a, 29) for different invading forces to this strategically located, so-called frontier region. However, the rugged terrains and monsoonal climate did not stop the East India Company (EIC) from 'risk-taking as the way to make a fortune' and 'For the next half-century, many EIC officers were more successful as merchants than as civil administrators' (Cederlof 2014b, 3). During such times 'the economy of the Northeast, if one draws from the pre-colonial and colonial experiences, the region had been thriving on trade not only within the region but also different areas bordering the region' (Haokip 2015, 148).

Since colonial period, the 'northeast frontier' has been a resource production and extraction region. Tilotoma Misra aptly termed the region 'a colonial hinterland' and argues that 'there has been a systematic exploitation of the rich resources of Assam, before 1947 by the colonial rulers, and since then by the Indian State and Indian capitalists who have continued the colonial tradition' (Misra 1980, 1357). She even considered the 'Assamese people of being subjected to gross economic exploitation on a scale comparable to and sometimes even worse than in, the pre-independence days' (ibid.). In this approach to political economy, when political integration of the 'North East' into the Indian State was compounded by economic exploitation, the northeastern region was converted into India's 'internal colony'. This condition emerged with the spread of industrialization from the Indian mainland to the peripheries. Capitalist industrialism created a new economic dependence of the periphery on the core. Trade and commerce in the North East is monopolized by members of the core, and economic development in the region is designed to complement and promote economic development of the core (Haokip 2012, 85). There are a relative lack of services, lower standards of living and higher levels of frustration among the members of these peripheral groups. There is national discrimination on the basis of language, religion or other cultural forms. Thus, the aggregate economic differences between the core and periphery are causally linked to cultural differences (Hechter 1975, 33–34).

In order to reduce frustration and schizophrenic alienation several political measures were adopted in the 1960s and 1970s, with the creation of new states—Nagaland, Meghalaya, Arunachal Pradesh, Manipur and Tripura. Tribal rights of access to and ownership of land and forests were protected through the Sixth Schedule of the Constitution, and representation in politics was secured through the reservation of certain tribal-dominated constituencies. However, political autonomy and political representation alone did not solve the problem. In the 1980s several State-led developmental schemes were initiated. The need was felt to counter several problems of the region through economic development. It was during this time that the Government of India

(1981) identified the region as backward but rich in natural resources. With the opening of India's economy in tune with the globalization of world economy through liberalization, the propagation of a borderless world economic diplomacy became the goal of India to promote trade and revive its economy. To further the economic objectives of foreign policy, cultural diplomacy was reoriented to enhance economic cooperation through cultural connections. An emphasis was placed on immediate and close neighbours to especially bring about the 'development' of the northeastern region through trade in goods and services, using cultural connections to further such goals.

This chapter critically examines the concept of 'development through trade' in the northeastern region, which was pushed under the 'Look East Policy' initiated by the Government of India in the middle of the first decade of the third millennia. It argues that until the North East can produce tradable items with the neighbouring countries, the whole idea of 'development in the northeastern region' through trade will be a lopsided policy, in which the region will be a dumping ground for cheaper goods from its neighbours.

DEVELOPMENT THROUGH STATE INTERVENTION

For four decades since Independence, India was a mixed economy with largely State-led development. The Nehruvian path of development was largely inward looking and based on an import substitution economy with an emphasis on heavy industrialization. Dams were built and mineral and natural resources explored and exploited. This path of development of the core-periphery relations created the North East as an internal periphery. The northeastern region was converted from a frontier region during the British rule to an internal periphery in the post-Independence period (Haokip 2012, 84). The development in this region can be termed 'internal colonialism', as noted earlier. Since then most economic analyses of India's North East in relation to the 'mainland' have been done on the centre/core-periphery and development-underdevelopment paradigm.

It was during the 1980s when India realized that its 'anthropological approach' towards the northeastern region and the efforts of 'political representation' failed to reduce tensions. These produced a new policy in the 1980s, which is often termed 'development paradigm', with the hope that development will 'transform material well-being and accelerate economic growth thereby creating space and opportunities for people' (Bhattacharya 2011, 1).[1] This paradigm assumes that 'if institutions of development were created and money poured into this region, the problems of politics, of society, of ethnic strife, and of integration will be abated' (Ramesh 2005). Thus, the public financial institution namely the North Eastern Development Finance Corporation Ltd (NEDFi) was established in the 1995. It 'provides financial assistance to micro, small, medium and large enterprises for setting up industrial, infrastructure and agri-allied projects in the North Eastern Region of India and also Microfinance through MFI/NGOs'.[2]

The period since the 1980s has witnessed an increase in public expenditure in the region. Developmental packages were announced by prime ministers in each of their visits to the region. In 1996, the then Prime Minister of India H. D. Deve Gowda announced an economic package of ₹6,100 crore, following his visit to the region. His successor I. K. Gujral endorsed this package. To boost economic development in the region the National Democratic Alliance (NDA) government led by Prime Minister Atal Bihari Vajpayee also announced another package—₹10,217 crore—in 1998. In October 1996, under the 'New Initiatives for North Eastern Region', it was stipulated that at least 10 per cent of budgets of the central ministries/departments should be earmarked for the development of northeastern states. As the expenditures in the North East by some union ministries during 1997–1998 fell short of the stipulated 10 per cent target, the NDA government created the Non-lapsable Central Pool of Resources to support infrastructure development projects in the region. Between 1990–91 and 2002–03, the region received about ₹108,504 crores (Sachdeva 2000). In 2001, Ministry of Development of the North Eastern Region (MDoNER) was formed to plan, execute and monitor developmental schemes and projects of the northeastern region including those in the sectors of power, irrigation, roads and communications. The ministry also coordinates 'with various Ministries/Departments primarily concerned with development and welfare activities in North Eastern Region'.

To boost industrialization and investment in the North East, the central government launched the North East Industrial and Investment

Promotion Policy 2007, turning the entire region into a special economic zone. The policy includes tax exemption, duty exemption, capital subsidies of up to 30 per cent, interest rate caps on loans, insurance reimbursements and special incentives for services sector, biotechnology and power generation to provide major incentives (mostly over a 10-year period) for new investments and the expansion of existing investments. This tax exemption was extended for another 10 years—from 2017 to 2027 (*Business Line* 2017).

However, this State-led development through the pumping of money has unintended consequences in the region. The largely bureaucracy-managed 'developmentalism' with its inherent red tape led to stagnation of the economy. It has also created a nexus among politicians, contractors, bureaucrats and insurgent groups. To mine this plentiful developmental money from the centre, this nexus is being used, and thus perpetuate corruption and insurgency. The money did not help achieve its goals. Besides, following the report of the Central Electricity Authority in 2001, identifying the Brahmaputra river basin with the potential for hydroelectricity generation of more than 60,000 MW, the Government of India intends to construct 168 hydropower projects, which will be double the total amount of hydroelectricity generated in India since Independence. There are also plans to exploit other resources such as oil in the northeastern states of Tripura and Manipur, besides Assam and Nagaland, after oil deposits were found in recent surveys. Many 'criticize state-driven growth models that relied on large-scale technological solutions, destructive to nature and to the people who depended on such natures for their livelihood' (Cederlof 2014a, 29). Thus, State-led growth needs a new direction and purpose, by way of being consistent with the ways of life and traditional economic activities of the region.

DEVELOPMENT THROUGH TRADE AND SERVICES

Since the 'liberal economic reforms' in June 1991, India put 'economics' at the forefront of its foreign policy. As such, economic diplomacy has become the priority of India's foreign policy. In India's search for vibrant economic cooperation and partnership, it found in its own neighbourhood in the East. Thus the Look East Policy was launched to promote economic integration with Southeast Asian countries through the Association of South East Asian Nations (ASEAN). With emphasis on this, India gained several levels of partnership with ASEAN— initially a sectoral dialogue partnership in March 1993 in three areas, namely, trade, investment and tourism; a full dialogue partnership in 1995 with the members of the ASEAN Regional Forum (ARF); and finally a summit-level partnership in 2002. With this enhanced partnership, trade between India and ASEAN phenomenally increased. But it has been felt that this increased economic cooperation between India and the ASEAN countries has overlooked the North East, through which India is physically connected. Baruah (2004, 23–24) with dismay pointed out that India has pursued largely maritime cooperation with Southeast Asia. He suggested that: 'The eventual success of India's Look East policy will depend on India's ability to embrace both a maritime and a continental thrust in its Look East policy'.

The northeastern region of India is ideally sandwiched between the Indian sub-continent and the Southeast Asia massif. With the joining of Myanmar as one of the members of the ASEAN in July 1997, the North East became physically connected to ASEAN countries. The coming of globalization propagates deterritorialization and a borderless world which is often associated with economic integration. With 98 per cent of its borders with China, Myanmar, Bhutan, Bangladesh and Nepal, the North East has better scope for development in the era of globalization through trade. Thus, in this line of thinking that a new policy developed among policy makers that one way the northeastern region must be looking to as a new way of development lies with political integration with the rest of India and economic integration with the rest of Asia, with East and Southeast Asia in particular as the policy of economic integration with the rest of India did not yield much dividends. The launching of the second phase of India's Look East Policy in 2004 aimed at partnership with ASEAN countries integrally linked to the economic interests of the northeastern region (Government of India 2004). Thus, the Look East Policy identifies the North East as the economic bridgehead and gateway to East and Southeast Asia; this is a major initiative undertaken by the Government of India. The focus now is on developing more intensive economic contacts with an emphasis on expanding trade and mobilizing investments.

The North East is not only physically located in the periphery of India, it is also at the cultural margin, despite being rich in culture. It has more cultural affinity with several East and Southeast Asian countries. Taking into account its geographical proximity, its historical linkage and cultural linkage with Southeast Asia and China (Baruah 2004, 33), it is expected that vibrant commercial exchanges with Southeast Asia can galvanise growth and development in the North East.[3] Contrary to the traditional conception of the North East as a cul de sac and periphery, the new policy, that is, the Look East Policy, intends to deliver a new political imagination of this region, which Samir Kumar Das (2010, 343–58) calls 'extended Northeast', which spreads across the international borders to include front-line states such as Myanmar and Bangladesh.

With the development of this new policy, the Government of India directed its Look East Policy towards developing the northeastern region. This policy is reflected in *Year End Review 2004* of the Ministry of External Affairs, which states that:

> India's Look East Policy has now been given a new dimension by the UPA Government. India is now looking towards a partnership with the ASEAN countries, both within BIMSTEC and the India-ASEAN Summit dialogue as integrally linked to economic and security interests, particularly for India's East and North East region. (MEA 2004)

Recognizing the advent of globalization, regional economic cooperation, new policy approaches for development and the massive changes which took place in the domestic and external fronts, the then Minister of External Affairs Pranab Mukherjee expounded that the North East has enormous potential for exploitation by taking 'geography as opportunity' (Mukherjee 2007). He stated that 'with the paradigm shift from state centrism to interdependence and global and regional cooperation, India is aware of the geo-economic potential of the North-Eastern region as a gateway to East and South-East Asia'. The border areas of countries neighbouring the North East are rich in natural resources.

They are at different levels of economic and industrial development and have different levels of natural endowments. A study conducted by a New Delhi-based policy research institute—Research and Information System for Developing Countries—found that the complementarities between the North East and its neighbouring countries are substantial and suggested that the geographical contiguity can facilitate the exploitation of the potential of efficiency, seeking restructuring of the industry (RIS 2004, 2).

Preparing the North East

Even after India's Act East Policy recognized the importance of the northeastern region, it does not go beyond looking at the region merely as an 'economic bridgehead and gateway to East and Southeast Asia'. It does not recognise the region as a resource production and export centre of products and still has a myopic view of it as a mere transit corridor for goods produced somewhere else. If the redirection of the policy is really meant for the northeastern region, it has to 'act' by making the region an ideal launching pad for all commercial relations with ASEAN countries through Myanmar. For this to happen, there are two things that have to be prioritized: India's North East has to be prepared and there has to be more intervention by India in Myanmar.

Preparing the North East, first, involves overcoming two most important and enduring problems in the region. There is wide recognition that the main stumbling block for economic development in the northeastern region is the disadvantageous geographical location (Sachdeva 2000, 145), of being a periphery of the other parts of the country. This 'disadvantageous geographical location' is now being re-imagined and repositioned, with the onslaught of globalization and the propagation of a borderless world at the centre of a sub-region in Bangladesh-China-India-Myanmar (BCIM) Forum for regional economic cooperation. As much as the geographical location of the region is now taken as an opportunity in this policy, the geographical terrain is still an obstacle to the policy itself. To overcome 'geography' involves huge infrastructural investment on all-weather roads and railways. Such huge investments can only come from the central government. The commitment of the central government to this policy has to be judged on its sanctioning of funds liberally. Besides the connectivity through the Asian Highway and Trans-Asian Railways between the North East with other countries in the east, intra-regional connectivity within the North East is still very poor. While the Asian Highway and railway projects have steadily progressed, there is an urgent need to also look afresh into the issue of intra-regional connectivity in the vision for a vibrant North East. A vibrant economic society cannot be internally locked inside and connected with the outside. It has to internally communicate and prepare together for a successful commercial intercourse with people beyond the border.

Second, the government needs to create a safer environment conducive to trade, investment and entrepreneur growth. 'North Eastern Region Vision 2020', a policy document of the Ministry of Development of northeastern region in 2008, identifies 'underdevelopment' as the region's 'economic imprisonment' and calls for a 'paradigm shift in development strategy' to alleviate poverty in the region through 'people-centric programmes based on harnessing the natural resources of the region'. The Vision document assesses the region's potential for investments by emphasizing the proximity of the North East to Southeast Asia and East Asia, particularly China, and postulates that investments will create opportunities, opportunities will create jobs and jobs will cultivate a peaceful region. This 'vision' will largely be a wishful thinking until the law and order situation in the region improves.

Most of the law and order situations in the region are triggered and exacerbated by armed groups rebelling against the Indian State. Investment cannot come and entrepreneurial environment cannot emerge due to the prevalence of extortion rackets by these parallel governments. Besides, a huge slice of public spending by the government is shared by them through different means and every developmental project cannot meet the quality standards due to the siphoning of money. Since the late 1990s, the governments at both the centre and the states in the region have attempted to negotiate with armed groups to solve their grievances. As such a semblance of order is slowly becoming visible. But to bring lasting peace in the region, all insurgent armed groups must be brought back to the mainstream, and the government has to restore confidence in potential investors and partners and anyone involved in any economic activity with regard to the safety and security of their undertakings.

Along with improving the law and order situation, governance in most of the states in the region has to be improved. The prevalence of corruption and red tape in most public offices and the large-scale absence of accountability have thwarted all economic and developmental efforts. Most public offices are half functional in the region. For instance, the Saikul Sub Divisional Office in the Kangpokpi District of Manipur can be taken as a reference point. This sub-divisional headquarters is located just 34 km from the State's capital Imphal. It is connected with proper roads and all modern amenities are available. The sub-divisional officer (SDO) is not stationed in the sub-divisional headquarters for more than a decade now but the sub-divisional office is functional in Imphal. Civil society organizations and some individuals of this sub-division gave an all-out effort to bring back the SDO to its headquarters. Recently an agreement was made and the SDO agreed to attend his office in Saikul thrice a week (Imphal Free Press 2017). As the location of sub-divisional offices gets further from the centre of power, the more the presence of the State's activity gets visibly thinner. The sub-divisional offices of Henglep in Churachandpur District and Khengjoy in Chandel District are functional in their respective district headquarters.

Trade is based on the free movement of goods and people across borders, whether they are international or sub-national State borders. In this regard the continuation of certain colonial regulations such as the Inner Line Regulation Act in states such as Nagaland, Mizoram and Arunachal Pradesh in the post-Independence period, especially in the globalised new millennium, is a concern. Such Acts and regulations were designed to serve the administrative, economic and strategic interests of the colonial government and were not in the interests and needs of the local people during that time. In recent years there have been growing demands by different ethnic groups in the states of Meghalaya, Manipur and Tripura for the extension and implementation of the colonial law and the establishment of the Inner Line Permit System in their respective states so that their 'vulnerable community' is legally protected by this regulation from the influx of immigrants from neighbouring countries and other parts of India. However, this demand has degenerated into the 'politics of indigeneity' where one community 'spurns' its 'neighbour' to gain legitimacy of its demand.[4] This has only exacerbated the prevailing tensions in the region. Thus, the Inner Line Regulation Act can hinder the implementation of the goals of the Act East Policy. As such, the concerns of people in the region such as protecting their identity, culture and land can be undertaken in ways without restricting the movement of people across State borders (Haokip 2010, 97).

Borderland Services

Writing an introduction for a recent volume the economist-political scientist duo add:

> In order to intensify the pace of economic engagement with ASEAN, India needs to diligently work for the early execution of FTA in services and investments, which would provide a space for the Indian service industries, in which India has comparative advantage, to play a role in furthering Indian trading interest with ASEAN. (Das and Thomas 2016, 5)

India's advancement in medical sciences and its relatively cheaper and better medical services have not been taken into account in its 'Act East' foreign policy. The country is known for its affordable medical services and is much sought by people from Africa and different parts of Asia, particularly its neighbours. This sector can be advantageously exploited, particularly in its borderlands in the North East. World-class hospitals can be established in border towns, and medical tourism can be promoted accordingly. As a pilot project in this endeavour a world-class hospital can be established at the border town of Moreh in Manipur, which is the thriving border trade point in the region so far. This will not only serve the people of the town and adjacent Myanmarese nationals in Sagaing Division and Chin Hills, but it will also bring better medical services to the remote borderlands on the Indian side who are denied of such facilities. There are many, even after 70 years of Independence, on the Indian side of the border who have no access to medical services and have to depend on traditional medicines or move to the other side of the border to avail minimal health-care facilities.

Beside medical sciences, India's technical know-how and English education are much respected and sought after in Southeast Asia, particularly in Myanmar. Technical institutes and English language training centres can be established in borderlands to promote education even in the most remote corners. This will be a goodwill gesture not only to the relatively underdeveloped parts of neighbouring countries but also to a similar population of its own in the most remote border areas who are deprived of public educational services.

The policy of 'Look East' was renamed 'Act East Policy' by the Narendra Modi government in 2014, to show its keenness to 'act' rather than just 'look' into the East. Despite its renaming, the policy is yet to see any visible change so far, or in other words, the pace of implementation of the main goals of the policy in the last 5 years of Bharatiya Janata Party (BJP) government at the centre has not accelerated. Pursuing the Act East Policy fervently should involve the deepening of India's cooperation in trade and investment, technology, transport and communications, energy and tourism with its Eastern neighbours. Sanjib Baruah, a staunch proponent of a continental Look East Policy, advocated that, 'India should take more advantage of Northeast India's history and culture as a soft power resource' (Baruah 2004, 33). This involves reviving the shared historical and cultural ties between the people of the North East and Southeast Asia.

FROM CULTURAL DIPLOMACY TO CULTURAL ECONOMY

Every nation and ethnic community in the world have a unique culture of their own. They preserve and promote their cultural practices. In fact, culture has long been regarded as the third pillar of foreign policy.[5] India is rich in culture and has influenced different parts of the world with its cultural values. Since Independence it has been trying 'to establish, revive and strengthen cultural relations and mutual understanding' with other countries. To this end the Indian Council for Cultural Relations (ICCR) was founded in 1950 'to establish, revive and strengthen cultural relations and mutual understanding between India and other countries'.[6] Currently, the ICCR has 35 cultural centres around the world, and there are plans to establish new centres in Yangon, Hanoi, Lagos and Singapore, among others. Besides ICCR, the Indian Council for World Affairs (ICWA), which was established in 1943, aims to 'promote India's relations with other countries through study, research, discussions, lectures, exchange of ideas and information with other organizations within and outside India engaged in similar activities'.[7] Both ICCR and ICWA have played a vital role in India's cultural diplomacy.

The external cultural policy of India has been to promote and disseminate India's culture through international cultural exchanges. The 'new cultural policy' espoused in the new millennium, at its best, however, attempts to 'reconstruct India's healthy past' and stresses on 'eternal values that have helped the Indian civilization to stay afloat and make Indian arts more creative' (*Times of India* 2002). In this attempt, not only mainland India has civilizational linkages with Southeast Asia, which is often referred to as 'civilizational Asian neighbours' in official diplomatic circles, the ethnic communities in its northeastern region have roots and intimate cultural links with China and several Southeast Asian countries. As Mahapatra (2016) has pointed out:

> though soft power resources, including culture, are not new, the increasing awareness and activism of India's political class to use those resources to realize foreign policy goals is recent. The focus on soft power, particularly cultural diplomacy, and its use in foreign policy, has become increasingly visible in recent years.

He argues that 'the increasing acceptability of its culture and values opens up possibilities for India to realize foreign policy goals'. Nevertheless this will not be an easy task unless there is prioritization of goals with the inclusion of the North East's cultural linkages with Southeast Asia, in an attempt to achieve economic objectives through cultural diplomacy.

Culture and economy have been regarded as separate entities in the national as well as foreign policy of nation-states. The two were treated as separate spheres till the 1980s. Modern economics have been, to a great extent, hesitant to examine this question. The neglect of the economic potential of cultural resources was evident when cultural policies served social and political agendas rather than economic ones during the 1970s and 1980s. The primary goal of cultural policy was to enhance community building and economic reconstruction though cultural resources were not critically on the agenda. Cultural diplomacy basically was to promote and strengthen 'a nation's cultural influence by funding artists' tours or by promoting the study of the national language and culture in universities abroad' (Mitchell 1986). It was through the multilateral agency, the United Nations Educational, Scientific and Cultural Organisation (UNESCO), that nation-states promoted their cultural heritage. The State's cultural mission on the international scene no longer simply entails promoting an already existing culture abroad. It involves a more visibly active role in protecting and developing national culture.

It was only in recent years that economists started to think seriously again about how culture may help explain economic phenomena. The relations between culture and economy have been increasingly emphasised on in the past two decades. Economy is now even viewed as culture and the focus is on 'the practical ways in which 'economically relevant activity' is performed and enacted' (du Gay and Pryke 2002, 5). Cultural activities have now become increasingly significant in the economic rejuvenation policy in many parts of the world. However, most State cultural policies have been based on the concept of culture as a domain separate from the domain of economic activity (Shuker 1994, 54). Since the last two decades scholars increasingly acknowledge the role played by culture in economic development, and economy is now increasingly viewed as culture. Given the close cultural affinity and historical roots of communities of the northeastern region with Southwest China and Southeast Asian countries, promoting a 'cultural economy' between them will not only result in the economic development of the region but also will reduce schizophrenic alienation of the peoples present among three sub-continents—South, Southeast and East Asia.

GENERATING ECO-FRIENDLY GOODS AND SERVICES

Traditional societies of the North East were known for their eco-friendly practices. Their primordial religions were close to nature and ecology. The nature of their livelihoods including *jhum* or shifting cultivation was consistent with sustainable practices. It is only with the onset of the commercialization of such practices that the process of environmental and ecological degradation started, coupled with increasing pressure on the land with an increase in population. To simultaneously provide livelihood and an income to rural folks, a commercial cultivation promotion plan is needed. The government needs to identify certain exportable eco-friendly commercial plants so that they can be encouraged for plantation widely and accordingly establish processing centres in the region so as to produce them in the industrial level.

The North East has largely been a 'consumer' rather than a 'producer' of goods for the last several decades since Independence. Most of their financial resources come from the union government as all the states in the region are given 'special status'; thereby 90 per cent of the funds required by these states are given as grants by the central government and only 10 per cent has to be raised by them. This categorization is mainly due to: '(i) hilly and difficult terrain (ii) low population density and/or sizeable share of tribal population (iii) strategic location along borders with neighbouring countries (iv) economic and infrastructural backwardness and (v) non-viable nature of state finances'.[8] Coupled with these features are

> Centuries of economic deprivation and neglect coupled with isolation from the mainstream of Indian states had resulted in widespread poverty, unemployment and economic backwardness of the people living within their territories. They have in fact been victims of the combined burden of history, geography, economics and governance. Even the resources that nature has endowed them with could not be harnessed and utilised for their development due to the pathetic state of their infrastructure and its continued neglect over decades. (Bhattacharjee 2014, 48)

Thus, much of the efforts of the chief ministers of the region are not only to obtain funds on time but also to beg for more funds. In another study I showed that this dependency of funds from the centre made a State like Manipur conform with party ruling at the centre. In Manipur,

> the last forty-five years of state politics had been unduly affected by the political regime at the centre mainly due to its sheer financial dependence. This perpetual state of financial dependency has often caused configuration and reconfiguration of the ruling parties depending upon the political regime at the centre making the state government inherently unstable. (Haokip 2017, 468)

To be consistent with the Act East Policy, borderland States should have long-term policies to achieve sustainable development goals not only for the livelihood projects of individuals but also for the State as well explore areas where they have a comparative advantage. This will eventually reduce the dependency to the centre. For making the region a producer of tradable products, it has to first enter into successful local partnership. Being basically a hilly area the production of agro-based products should be identified. After identifying areas of comparative advantage, individuals should be encouraged to enter into mass cultivation with the assurance of the market. The government needs to collaborate with private corporate entities and enter into joint ventures for small-scale industries. This joint venture will not only ensure efficiency and accountability but also profitability.

CONCLUSION

India's North East has been dependent on imported goods, mainly finished products, from mainland India and also from the neighbouring countries. The stimulus for entrepreneurship was absent due to the prevalent law and order situation and lack of financing in the region. Since the late 1990s, the Government of India's efforts to provide solutions to various armed rebellions in the region by holding out olive branches to all insurgent groups have brought most of them to the negotiating table. This has slowly started to improve the commercial and entrepreneurship environment in the region. However, in order to see the much-needed take-off, a lot still needs to be done—starting with bringing all elements of 'resistance' and 'rebellions' from the negotiating table to a settlement and ending the 'still' prevailing environment of extortion and tax collections by these so-called 'parallel governments'. Bringing back a peaceful environment will not only restore trust between ethnic groups 'in conflict' in the region, such an environment itself is the first step to the path of development.

In the currently identified 62 tradable items for border trade with Myanmar, most of them come under the formalization of informal trade that occurred before the agreement was signed. The traded items are mostly 'third-party' products to the North East—the exported items are mainly brought from mainland India and traded through border trade points, and many of the imported items are Chinese and Thai products. In order that the region benefits from border trade, it must first produce tradable items with its neighbours after a comparative advantage study.

While the Government of India's efforts to improve connectivity infrastructure in the region are visible in the last two decades albeit in a slower pace in the form of transnational highways, the intra-regional road connectivity is yet to gain its due attention. There are chances that while the North East can be well connected with its neighbouring countries, the states in the region can be cut off especially during the monsoon season. Adequate emphasis needs to be given on intra-regional connectivity and border roads development, so that remote areas in the region are not left behind. The Northeastern region has mainly been a passive consumer of foreign goods and evidently the balance of trade between the Northeastern region and the neighbouring countries has been consistently negative, despite the identification by concerned Indian Ministry of the ample scope for expansion. The region should be prepared for supplying goods that it has comparative advantage in trade with its neighbouring countries, such as agro-farming activities. Such goods should be identified and the cultivation and production in a large scale should be encouraged. Once the momentum for large-scale farming sets in, the governments have to provide the needed governance and market to these start-up agro-entrepreneurships.

NOTES

1. Since Independence the Government of India has adopted several policies towards its northeastern region. For detailed analyses of the continuity and change in India's North East policy, see Haokip (2010).
2. NEDFi website accessed on 8 October 2018 at: http://www.nedfi.com
3. Prime Minister Atal Bihari Vajpayee inaugural speech at the Second North-East Business Summit IBEF, 20 January 2004.
4. To look into this politics of indigeneity, see Haokip (2016).
5. It was Willy Brandt, the then Foreign Minister of Germany, who in 1966 declared cultural relations as the 'third pillar of foreign policy'.
6. http://www.iccr.gov.in/content/iccrs-centres-abroad-1
7. ICWA Website: https://icwa.in/aims.html
8. This information was given by the Minister of State (Independent Charge) for Planning, Shri Rao Inderjit Singh, in a written reply in the Rajya Sabha on 14 December 2015, reported by Press Information Bureau Government of India (PIB 2015).

REFERENCES

Baruah, S. 2004. *Between South and Southeast Asia: Northeast India and the Look East Policy*. CENISEAS Paper No. 4. Guwahati: OKDISCD.

Bhattacharjee, G. 2014. 'The Reality of Special Category States'. *Economic and Political Weekly* XLIX(40): 48–56.

Bhattacharya, R. 2011. *Development Disparities in Northeast India*. New Delhi: Foundation Books.

Business Line. 2017. 'Govt Extends Tax Exemption for Industry in North East, Hilly States'. Retrieved from https://www.thehindubusinessline.com/economy/policy/govt-extends-tax-exemption-for-industry-in-north-east-hilly-states/article9819762.ece

Cederlof, G. 2014a. 'Monsoon Landscapes Spatial Politics and Mercantile Colonial Practice in India'. In *Asian Environments: Connections across Borders, Landscapes, and Times*, RCC Perspectives, No. 3, edited by U. Muünster, 29–36. Munich: RCC.

———— 2014b. *Founding an Empire on India's North-Eastern Frontiers 1790–1840: Climate, Commerce, Polity*. New Delhi: Oxford University Press.

Das, S. K. 2010. 'India's Look East Policy: Imagining a New Geography of India's Northeast'. *India Quarterly* 66(4): 343–58.

Das, G., and C. J. Thomas. 2016. 'Introduction'. In *Look East to Act East Policy: Implications for India's Northeast*, edited by G. Das and C. J. Thomas, 1–16. New Delhi: Routledge.

du Gay, P., and M. Pryke. 2002. 'Cultural Economy: An Introduction'. In *Cultural Economy: Cultural Analysis and Commercial Life*, edited by P. du Gay and M. Pryke, 1–19. London: SAGE Publications.

Fuller, J. B. 1909. *'Introduction', written for Alan Playfair*, xii–xvi. London: The Garos.

Government of India. 1981. *Report on Development of North Eastern Region*. New Delhi: Planning Commission of India.

———. 2004. *Year End Review 2004*. New Delhi: Ministry of External Affairs, Government of India.

Haokip, T. 2010. 'India's Northeast Policy: Continuity and Change'. *Man and Society* VII: 86–99.

———. 2012. 'Is There a Pan-North-East Identity and Solidarity?' *Economic and Political Weekly* XLVII(36): 84–85.

———. 2015. *India's Look East Policy and the Northeast*. New Delhi: SAGE Publications.

———. 2016. 'Spurn Thy Neighbour: The Politics of Indigeneity in Manipur'. *Studies in Indian Politics* 4(2): 178–90.

———. 2017. 'Dereliction of Duties or the Politics of Political Quadrangle'. *Indian Journal of Public Administration* 63(3): 456–74.

Hechter, M. 1975. *Internal Colonialism: The Celtic Fringe in British National Development*. London: Routledge and Kegan Paul.

Imphal Free Press. 2017. 'ADC Sadar Hills Reinstates SDO/BDO Saikul', 6 September. Retrieved from https://www.ifp.co.in/page/items/34172/adc-sadar-hills-reinstates-sdobdo-saikul/

Mahapatra, D. A. 2016. 'From a Latent to a 'Strong' Soft Power? The Evolution of India's Cultural Diplomacy'. *Palgrave Communications* 2: 16091. doi:10.1057/palcomms.2016.91.

MEA. 2004. 'Year End Review 2004', Ministry of External Affairs, Government of India, New Delhi.

Misra, T. 1980. 'Assam: A Colonial Hinterland'. *Economic and Political Weekly* 15(32): 1357–64.

Misra, S. 2011. *Becoming a Borderland: The Politics of Space and Identity in Colonial Northeastern India*. New Delhi: Routledge India.

Mitchell, J. M. 1986. *International Cultural Relations*. London: Allen & Unwin.

Mukherjee, P. 2007. 'Geography as Opportunity'. Speech at Seminar on 'Look East' Policy, 16 June, Shillong.

PIB. 2015. 'Identification of Special Category States', 14 December. Retrieved from http://pib.nic.in/newsite/PrintRelease.aspx?relid=133172

Pommaret, F. 1999. 'Ancient Trade Partners: Bhutan, Cooch Bihar and Assam (17th–19th Centuries)'. *Journal Asiatique* 287: 285–303. English translation available online at http://www.bhutanstudies.org.bt/journal/vol2no1/v2n/ancienttrade.pdf

Ramesh, J. 2005. 'Northeast India in New Asia'. *Seminar*, No. 550, June. Retrieved from http://www.india-seminar.com/2005/550/550%20jairam%20ramesh.htm

RIS Publication. 2004. *Future Directions of BIMSTEC: Towards a Bay of Bengal Economic Community*. New Delhi: Research and Information System.
Sachdeva, G. 2000. *Economy of the North-East: Policy, Present Conditions and Future Possibilities*. New Delhi: Konark Publishers.
Shuker, R. 1994. *Understanding Popular Music*. London and New York: Routledge.
Times of India. 2002. 'New Culture Policy to Focus on Eternal Values', 17 July. Retrieved from https://timesofindia.indiatimes.com/india/New-culture-policy-to-focus-on-eternal-values/articleshow/16203307.cms

PART IV

Alternative from Below

Chapter 10

Environmental Security and Human Rights
Foundations for Real Development?

Felix Padel

Plans for 'development' in India's North East offer remote areas and the region as a whole connectivity, through roads, rail and investment, that promises to end a long-running situation of neglect and marginalization from India as a whole (e.g., Jha 2018). But this connectivity is also aimed at exploiting the region's natural resources, which constitute sources of life for diverse communities. This is most obviously the case with numerous large dam projects. In this chapter we shall survey a few of these, as well as cases of extractive projects over carbon deposits and minerals.

The movements against these projects have faced draconian repression, yet analysis of the situation as a whole, in terms of the environmental, social, economic and political impacts of these projects, suggests they have numerous inherent flaws, as well as obvious iniquities in how they have been imposed. India has recently fallen by 36 places in the Global Environmental Performance Index and is now among the lowest five countries, with the highest level of environmental conflict of any country, and the Himalayas (including Arunachal Pradesh) is said to have the highest density of big dams anywhere (Bindra 2018).

On this vital issue of big dams, the North East has experienced polarization, with many movements and acrimonious debates, replicating what was experienced around many other dams in India, from the Sardar Sarovar on Narmada to Polavaram on Godavari, and in many other countries. A key driving force is the demand from the centre for the North East's 'surplus capacity' in hydroelectricity, including Planning Commission Directives during the 1990s which pushed for many new dams in the North East.

The problem is that big dams' devastating impacts on communities and ecosystems appear to carry little or no weight compared with the statistics of projected benefits, especially in power generation; and with benefits to construction and power companies and the political-administrative-business elites they work with. Well-documented problems surrounding big dams in India and elsewhere laid out, for example, in the World Bank-funded World Commission on Dams' *India Country Study* (Rangachari et al. 2000) have not been taken into account. The complex economics of big dams is little analysed or understood. Among many other issues, the scandal of 'Clean Development Mechanism' (CDM) grants ('carbon credits') has to be more widely exposed (Lohmann 2006): dams regularly get large sums which act as subsidies. Lepcha leaders in Sikkim, among many others, have pointed out the huge irony in dams getting financial incentives on the basis of being 'green', for producing electricity without burning coal, while rotting generation and turbines produce large greenhouse gas emissions, and the destruction of forests and entire riverine ecosystems is the antithesis of 'clean development' (Yumnam 2012). Also, the economics of dams built by private or public corporations involves large bank loans that enmesh the State government into increasingly crippling burdens of debt, curtailing policy choices, while the bribes that are widely understood act as an incentive for State officials when they sign MoUs (Memoranda of Understanding) with these corporations represent a black economy, unmeasurable by definition (Chakravartty 2015; Tiwari 2016).

In an election speech in February 2014, Narendra Modi acknowledged the strength of feeling against big dams in the region, saying at

Pasighat (Arunachal): 'I know citizens of the region are against large power projects.... I respect your sentiments. But hydropower can also be harnessed using smaller projects, while protecting the environment.' (Duarah 2014). A 2014 study ordered by the Supreme Court on the Uttarakhand floods in June 2013 concluded that big dams were almost certainly a probable causal factor, a judgement with potent implications for the new dams planned for the North East (Schneider 2015).

Stakes rose in July–August 2018 with excess water suddenly released by the North East Electric Power Corporation (NEEPCO) authorities in charge of the Doyang Dam, in the Wokha District of Nagaland; it flooded huge areas of Assam and Nagaland from 27 July into August. At least 100,000 people in five districts of Assam, especially 116 villages in Golaghat District, were marooned or otherwise negatively impacted, with 26,000 people taking refuge in 123 camps and immense destruction of agricultural land, homes, documents and so on (*Gulf Times* 2018). Water allegedly built up beyond capacity in the Doyang reservoir; though there are also allegations that the water was released to boost electricity. In the words of Someshwar Narah, Convenor of Jeepal Krishak Sramik Sangha (JKSS), a local organization for farmers:

> This was deliberately done for generation of excess power from the turbines in the Doyang project. We have got details from Central Electricity Authority which shows that NEEPCO generated three times more electricity during the extreme rainfall event by compromising on dam safety parameters... What we are witnessing is not just lack of coordination during floods caused by dams but also extension of submergence even after the dam is functional so that more electricity can be generated. (Chakravartty and Dutta 2018)

Danger from earthquakes represents another major risk from dam building; with evidence that the blasting and tunnelling of mountains for the Teesta dams were key factors in triggering the devastating earthquake that hit Sikkim on 24 September 2011 (Yumnam 2012) and that blasting for oil exploration may have been a factor for the large earthquake in Manipur on 4 January 2016 (see later).

Some of these dams pose an especially insidious threat for core areas of several remote and distinctive tribal groups, such as Tipaimukh for the Hmar and Zelinangrong Nagas; the Siang dams for the Adis (formerly known as Abor); Upper Dibang for the Idu Mishmis; and Mapithel (or Maphou in Kuki language) Dam for Tangkul Naga and Kuki villagers, among many others. All these and many others testify that they were not properly consulted or given their consent for dam projects affecting them. Given the sophistication of these groups' ways of life, in terms of orientation towards long-term sustainability, with economy based in community values and ecological principles, the damage posed by damming their core culture areas is very severe, in a world that increasingly 'criminalizes' indigenous ways of life and indigenous activism aimed at environmental protection (Cultural Survival 2018; Tauli-Corpuz 2018).

The value of tribal peoples' traditional cultures is not something amenable to quantification and therefore tends to get completely overlooked; this is also because indigenous values tend to contradict the value systems taken for granted by capitalism and economics. At the heart of these cultures is a land-based identity among communities who have managed their landscapes over many generations, without the kind of commodification that has been imposed in more accessible areas. In other words, each of the dramatic valleys that is slated for flooding by big dams in the North East represents a unique symbiosis between local social structures and ecosystems (Vagholikar and Das 2010). Reservoirs created by big dams spell death for many life forms and for communities that have cultivated land in these valleys since recorded history began.

SOME CONTROVERSIAL MEGA-DAMS

The Tipaimukh Dam was opposed by Bangladesh as well as by groups in Manipur, Mizoram and Assam; it is in Churachandpur District in the southwest corner of Manipur (Churachandpur District), where these three states meet; on the Barak River it is joined by Tuivai, on its way towards Bangladesh. The dam's ostensible purpose is flood control of the Barak River, in addition to generating 1,500 MW; building a

165-metre dam would flood about 300 km² of land where over 1,300 tribal families of the Hmar and Zeliangrong Naga communities live in 90 affected villages; they have been at the forefront of opposition; 27,000 hectares of forest, including over 7 million trees, in the area will be flooded.

Tipaimukh is likely to have particularly devastating impacts in Bangladesh, drying up rivers that tens of thousands of people depend on (Zakaria 2012). The movement against Tipaimukh is notable for Bangladeshi and Indian groups working together, bringing a wide range of arguments, from the cultural extinction it would cause to flooded indigenous communities and the destruction of livelihoods of Bangladeshi farmers who are devastated by the drying-up of the Kushiara, Surma and Meghna Rivers that support them. The Tipaimukh project suffers from an extraordinary lack of democratic consultation and human rights abuses (Arora and Kipgen 2012; Islam and Islam 2016).

Despite opposition to the dam from the chief minister and assembly of Manipur from 1995 to 1998, the project was officially approved by the central government, in an opaque manner, between 1999 and 2001, and was entrusted to NEEPCO. In 2003, when the Public Investments Board and Central Electricity Authority cleared the project, its estimated cost rose to ₹5,163.86 crore, while power load factors cast doubts on the dam's efficiency (Sethi 2015). Five public hearings took place between 2004 and 2008, and environmental clearance was granted in October 2008, though there were strongly stated objections from local communities. Prime Minister Manmohan Singh laid the foundation stone, yet construction repeatedly was stalled (*Sangai Express* 2018; South Asia Network on Dams, Rivers and People (SANDRP) 2016), with the Citizens' Concern for Dams and Development (CCDD, a Manipur-based civil society group) urging the Government of Manipur to revoke the joint venture agreement it signed with the National Hydroelectric Power Corporation (NHPC, which has a 69 per cent stake) and Shimla-based Satluj Jal Vidyut Nigam Ltd (SJVNL, with a 26 per cent stake, leaving the Manipur government with a 5 per cent stake) on 28 April 2010, reaffirmed on 22 October 2011. The Forest Advisory Committee (FAC) refused clearance for the project in July

2013 and again in March 2018 (*Sangai Express* 2018; Sinlung Indigenous Peoples Human Rights Organisation (SIPHRO) 2013), and the project has been the subject of frequent high-level negotiations between India and Bangladesh, through the Joint Rivers Commission (Rashid 2015). Arora and Kipgen note

> the adverse impact on the indigenous Hmar and Zeliangrong Naga who will be displaced and dispersed. On a deeper level, there is a clash of development visions on the Barak: its existence as a profitable natural resource for the government and project developers, on the one hand, and its persistence as a locus of Hmar history and culture, and a life-line, on the other. (2012, 110)

In the words of a local spokesman, echoing voices from indigenous communities worldwide, 'For the Hmar people, the land is part of us. We are sustained by what it provides. We can say that we are the land'. Laltutlung Hmar, a leader of the Hmar People's Convention-Democratic, has stated: 'Our rich culture, tradition, history, language and memory flow in these rivers. We cannot allow the rivers to be disturbed. We are obligated to see that no outsiders, their forces and might will dam, destroy or disturb the natural flow of the rivers of life' (2012, 113–14). For example, the dam site is just half a kilometre from the major river confluence, sacred in much local mythology. Nearby, the Thiledam river island is where Hmars conceive their soul flies to during death, while the Zeilad Lake and the Barak Falls that would be inundated are sacred to the Zeliangrong.

Mapithel Dam, on the Thoubal River in the Ukhrul District of Manipur, was constructed against much local opposition, and in March 2018, villagers staged a boycott of the dam's official inauguration; 2,000 hectares was already flooded, including the land or homes of 8,000 villagers, with many refusing compensation (Chandran 2018).

This dam is geared towards providing water for Imphal as well as generating 7.5 MW of power. Police repression has been used to force villagers off their land, following plans made back in 1980 and a long history of resistance. Large numbers of armed forces were stationed in and around the dam site and protesting villages, at times occupying school buildings, and over 40 tribal protesters met with violent repression from the Indian Reserve Battalion on 3 November 2008; this strongly condemned by James Anaya, the UN Rapporteur on indigenous peoples, as it was the suppression of democratic demands from affected communities. In 2007 the Manipur Forest Department demanded a halt to work on the dam, since no forest or environmental clearance was obtained. The first-stage clearance was given by the Ministry of Environment and Forest (MoEF) only in 2010, when construction was already under way, and the final stage (stage two) by the MoEF was granted on 31 December 2013, under Veerappa Moily as Environment Minister, overriding the recent (26 November) MoEF Directive to facilitate land rights under the Forest Rights Act, 2006 (FRA), with cooperation from the Ministry of Tribal Affairs (MoTA) to make Mapithel a 'rare and unique' exception to the Directive. There has clearly been no proper rehabilitation for the Kuki and Tangkhul Naga people who have lost their land and homes, nor relief for Meitei people downstream, who have lost their water supply (Longjam 2015; Yumnam 2015). The Chandol Village, predominantly Tangkul Naga, was one of the first to have (exceptionally fertile) land and homes submerged and be cut off by road (Kipgen 2015; Yumnam 2015). The Mapithel Dam Affected Villages Organisation (MDAVO), created in 1990, protested repeatedly about the lack of Free Prior Informed Consent (FPIC) and required Environmental and Social Impact Assessments (EIAs, SIAs). As MDAVO indicated in a statement on 15 March 2015,

> Mapithel Dam was constructed forcibly without taking prior consent of the affected communities. The state adopted forceful construction of Mapithel Dam with militarization of their land and resources and further adopted divide and rule tactics among the affected communities... Resorting to military deployment to aid construction of the dam is in derogation of all democratic principles and practices upheld nationally and internationally, and an absolute violation of the human rights of indigenous people of the state. (Kipgen 2015)

Violent displacement in Manipur occurred due to the Loktak Multipurpose Hydroelectric Project, near Imphal. This started with the Ithai barrage, commissioned in 1984, which displaced several thousand people, submerging 83,000 hectares of agricultural land and badly damaging the lake's unique ecosystem, exterminating several species of fish and plants. Many of the displaced built floating houses on Loktak Lake to carry on their traditional livelihood of fishing, but between 2011 and 2013 security forces burnt several hundred of these island homes (Yumnam 2014). Presently, the NHPC is promoting a new Loktak downstream dam project that threatens more harm for local people, funded by loans from the Japan International Cooperation Agency (JICA) (*Yumnam* 2018).

The organization CCDD, created in Manipur in 1999, has been at the forefront of research and activism on Loktak, Mapithel and Tipaimukh Dams (SANDRP 2016). Over a dozen new mega-dams are proposed in Manipur, out of 168 for the North East as a whole. The high prevalence of armed conflict in Manipur that has tended to serve as a cover for suppression of dissent by armed forces is particularly problematic, especially in light of over 1,500 'fake encounters' and impunity for crimes by men in uniform under the the Armed Forces Special Powers Act of 1958 (Begum 2010; Bhuyan 2018; Hoenig and Singh 2014). Aram Pamei, Co-Convener of CCDD, has widely criticized the Manipur Hydroelectric Power Policy of 2012, on which new projects are based, asking

> Is gifting away our land and resources to multinational corporations without our consent forms of development? Is bribing the community leaders to agree to oil exploration forms of development? Why indigenous people of Manipur should sacrifice their land, forest and other survival sources for such unsustainable projects? (SANDRP 2016)

The CCDD has been asking how recommendations of the World Commission on Dams (2000) and the UN Declaration of the Rights of Indigenous Peoples (2007) can be ignored, if these projects are claimed as 'development'?

By far the largest number of big dams under planning and construction are in Arunachal Pradesh, where Jairam Ramesh referred to an 'MoU virus' hitting the State. Agreements for 108 big dams, to generate 30 MW, were signed between 2005 and 2015 (Chakravartty 2015), threatening remote areas and peoples with inundation, partly motivated by high levels of corruption (Greener Pastures 2014; Mazoomdar 2013; Saikia 2016; SANDRP 2014; Vagholikar and Das 2010).

The Lower Demwe Dam Project on the Lohit River in India's easternmost district is another mega-project, planned with a height of 124 m and aimed at generating 1,750 MW, for which Athena Demwe Power Ltd formed a special purpose vehicle after signing an agreement with the Arunachal Pradesh government in 2007. The dam was cleared by Jayanthi Natarajan as Environment Minister in February 2012, against opposition from all eight independent members of the National Board for Wildlife (NBWL) (with the four other members refraining from commenting), due to negative impacts on Kamlang Sanctuary (Mazoomdar 2013). After this clearance was overturned by the Chennai branch of the National Green Tribunal (NGT) on 10 October 2013, a new team from the Standing Committee (SC) of the NBWL visited the area in February 2018, staying in a company guest house and failing to meet local people from affected communities, leading to allegations of a clear conflict of interest. The project poses a threat to many species, including river dolphins; its planned reservoir is just half a kilometre from Kamlang Sanctuary, and 1–2 km from Parshuram Kund, a Hindu pilgrimage site of great cultural and natural significance with hot springs (Khandekar 2018). The decision in September 2018 by the SC-NBWL to clear the dam enraged environmentalists, since the destruction posed will be very great, with dire impacts for Dibru Saikhowa National Park in Assam, where India's only population of wild horses live, as well as islands in the Lohit River vital for rare bird species, which will be submerged (Karmakar 2018).

Another extremely controversial project is Upper Dibang, which is to give 3,000 MW, making it one of India's biggest dams ever, submerging an estimated 5,000 hectares of forest. Manmohan Singh laid the foundation stone in January 2008, despite no statutory clearances having been granted (SANDRP 2015), and the police fired on protestors in 2011. The dam was refused forest clearance by the FAC several times, most recently on 28 August 2014, on the grounds that it would drown 45 sq. km of forest, including parts of Dibru Saikhang

National Park (Assam), and 'ecological and social costs of destroying a vast tract of forest land which is a major source of livelihood for the state's tribal population would far outweigh the benefit likely to accrue for the project'. But less than a week later, the Cabinet Committee on Investment got the Prime Minister's Office to order the MoEF to give clearance (3 September) on the condition of a 20-metre reduction in dam height. Obviously the large investment involved, estimated at ₹16 crores (US$2.6 million), swung the balance (Choudhury 2014). Members of the Krishak Mukti Sangram Samittee (KMSS), an organization of farmers at the forefront of the anti-dam movement in Assam and the North East, saw this as a betrayal of what Prime Minister Narendra Modi said at Pasighat.

Above all, the dam threatens to destroy the cohesion of the Idu Mishmi people (Duarah 2014; Lenin 2014). Raju Mimi, a member of this community, explained why Idu Mishmis, who number between 9,000 and 12,000, opposed this dam:

> The whole dam-building process has been going on without taking the people into confidence or their participation. Most of the local people are dependent on agriculture and are not ready for such big dam projects. They will be further marginalised culturally, economically and politically. (Rehman 2012)

Many voices have been raised:

Dr Mite Lingi, Chairman of the Idu Indigneous Peoples Council, says,

> The 'small displacement' argument to sell these projects as being benign needs to be confronted. The entire population of the Idu Mishmi tribe is around 9,500 and at least 17 large hydel projects have been planned in our home, the Dibang Valley in Arunachal. As per this faulty argument, little social impact will be indicated even if our entire population were supposedly displaced! (Greener Pastures 2014)

The Siang or Dihang River is the main branch of Brahmaputra that is called Tsangpo Yarlung in China; it traverses several hundred kilometres in Tibet before entering Arunachal Pradesh. A Memorandum of

Understanding (MoU) with China in 2013 on 'strengthening cooperation on trans-border rivers' failed to mention dams, even though another nine are planned on the Chinese stretch of the Tsangpo alone, and contrary to the impression created in the media (SANDRP 2013), when the Lower Siang Dam's planned capacity was raised to 2,700 MW, the CRPF used teargas on protesters, at Pongging, on 26 May 2010. The project was transferred from the Brahmaputra Board to the NHPC, which was then handed over to Jaypee Associates (Saikia 2016).

The Lower Siang Dam poses a momentous threat to the Adi tribe, who number about 150,000. In the words of Azing Pertin, from a Siang Valley Forum for Indigenous Peoples,

> Since our state is hilly, there is very little land where permanent cultivation is possible. Virtually all our available arable lands will be submerged by the Lower Siang project. (Greener Pastures 2014)

The Adi believe the river needs to 'flow of its free will'. After more protests in between 2011 and 2012 and postponing three public hearings postponed, with strong critiques of the project's EIA (Choudhury 2014), the project was put on hold (Rehman 2012).

In 2017, two dams on the Upper Siang joined into one mega-dam project, aimed at generating 10,000 MW, with NEEPCO in charge. This too has been strongly opposed. The Upper and Lower Siang projects together would dry up 270 km of the Dihang/Siang River, inundating 18,000 hectares of forest. Another 41 large dams are planned on the tributaries of the Siang, which is known as 'Brahmaputra' from the point where the Lohit and Dibang Rivers join it (Mazoomdar 2013; Saikia 2017).

The Lower Subansiri Dam, further west, on the Assam-Arunachal border, has been stalled since December 2011 by an NGT judgement, as well as strong protests on the ground, led by All Assam Students' Union (AASU) and the KMSS. Opposition to big dams in the North East generally has been aided by the 'Subansiri effect' (Dutta 2015). Work on this dam started in 2005 and it was built to a height of 138 m before being stalled in 2011. It is another of the biggest dams ever planned in India and aims to generate 2,000 MW from eight turbines.

Construction design went through several drastic revisions from 2005 to 2011, due to unexpected geology and landslides. The river was diverted by November 2007, but the movement against the dam gathered force. In August 2010 Jairam Ramesh refused to stop construction:

> The minister said that dams were critical not only from the point of view of creating clean electricity but also from the strategic point of view. "The dams are also of strategic importance. If we don't build dams on the Siang River (in Arunachal Pradesh), our claim from China will weaken," he said adding: "The dams in Bhutan are also of strategic importance so don't say anything against our dams in Bhutan." (*Sify News* 2010)

However, in December 2011, the NGT order halted construction. The reservoir would submerge about 40^2 km along 47 km of the river, including parts of the Tale Valley Wildlife Sanctuary. In October 2017, the NGT ordered a new expert panel assess the environmental impact (Baruah 2017). Unfortunately, the panel appointed consisted of 'known experts' who already demonstrated pro-project bias, and Tularam Gogoi, former Vice President of AASU, refused to meet the panel, alleging that these experts had a conflict of interest (Mazoomdar 2017).

In westernmost Arunachal, the Kameng Dam Project, planned for generating 600 MW of electricity, involves dams on Bichom and Tenga Rivers. Work started in 2005 and neared completion in 2016, when allegations of large-scale fraud and corruption surfaced involving government and NEEPCO officials (Tiwari 2016). Early in May 2018, when these dams, and a tunnel connecting them, were about to be inaugurated by Prime Minister Narendra Modi, dangerous cracks appeared, raising fundamental safety concerns. The inauguration was postponed, NEEPCO's general manager was arrested and the KMSS demanded these dams' decommissioning, along with the termination of the other 167 dams being planned in Arunachal Pradesh (*Pratidin Time* 2018; Saikia 2018).

In Bhutan, west of the Kameng District, 74 new large dams have been planned, with the Bhutan government already 50 per cent dependent on hydropower projects, for which huge investments have been coming in from India. These dams will generate 10,000 MW, and about 80 per cent of this electricity will be sold to India. Until recently, Bhutan had to buy electricity from India during summer (Walker 2015).

Bhutan's first large dams were Chukha (336 MW, commissioned in 1988), on Wangchu River, financed by 60 per cent of grants, a 40 per cent of loan from India, a major revenue earner for Bhutan, and it is operated by Druk Green Power Corporation (DGPC); Kurichhu (60 MW, commissioned between 2001 and 2002), on a tributary of the Manas, similarly financed and operated by DGPC; Basochhu (40 MW), 56 per cent financed by a loan from the Austrian government, whose engineers played a major role in the construction; Tala, the fourth and the biggest (1,020 MW, commissioned between 2006 and 2007), operated by Tata Power, again with a 60 per cent grant from the Indian government; and Dagachhu (126 MW, commissioned in 2015), a joint venture between DGPC and Tata Power (International Rivers 2015). The framework agreement on hydropower development and trade signed between Bhutan and India in July 2006 allowed dams to be cleared before environmental and social impacts were assessed. Environmental impacts are obvious. Chukha and Tala have dried up 35 km of the Wangchu River, for example. The prime minister of Bhutan has defended agreements on new dams on the rationale that most are 'run of the river' (as opposed to reservoir) projects and environmental costs will be offset by incomes (Walker 2016).

Several massive dams are presently under construction in Bhutan, financed far less advantageously: Punatsangchhu I and II have been financed more by loans than grants (a 60:40 and 70:30 ratio, respectively) and have already caused widespread environmental disruption to forests and river systems, destroying the habitat of species such as the endangered white bellied heron and golden mahseer, a rare Himalayan carp (Premkumar 2016; Walker 2016). The cost of Punatsangchhu I (1,200 MW), which is nearing completion, escalated from US$554 million (2006) to US$1.74 billion (2016). In 2013 the right bank of the dam gave way, due to geological instability, to a massive landslide. The foundation stone was laid jointly by Manmohan Singh and the prime minister of Bhutan in 2010. In February 2015 the left bank nearly gave way. The Mangdecchu Dam (720 MW, 56 m, whose construction started 2009) suffered a landslide that killed five workers in August 2015. In June 2014, Narendra Modi laid the foundation stone for the 600-MW Kholongchu Dam (95 m, financed on a 70:30 debt-to-equity ratio) which is to be built by SJVNL with DGPC, involving a 15-kim-long tunnel. The Wangchhu Dam, on which construction began recently, will have a 134-m dam, aimed at generating 570 MW. The biggest of the new dams under planning is the Sankosh Dam (215 metres high, 2,560 MW), which is to have a reservoir (as opposed to being 'run of the river'). Bhutan's green image is obviously being tarnished by these dams, and dissent seems even harder than in India (Walker 2015).

In Sikkim, the Teesta dams have already caused severe negative impacts on at least 7,000 Lepchas in the remote northern region of Dzongu, around Kanchenjunga, the world's third-highest mountain. The Dzongu Biosphere and National Park have come under ecological pressure from dam construction, starting with Teesta V, which was cleared in 1999; it created a 23-km-long reservoir. Several dams have now been built and are thought to likely be a cause of the devastating 2012 earthquake. Lamas of the Bhutia and Lepcha communities in north Sikkim challenged the construction of the Ranthongchu Dam between 1993 and 1997, on the grounds that it was defiling a sacred landscape (Arora 2006). Lepcha activists have continued this argument regarding Dzongu, fasting in relay to create awareness and get dam projects cancelled, since as many as 26 new dams have been proposed on the Teesta River and its tributaries (Arora 2008). In the words of Dawa Lepcha, 'The entire Teesta river is being tunnelled. The main river of Sikkim is disappearing. Is this development?' (Mitra 2006; Sharma 2003). Many of Sikkim's mega-dams are getting huge sums in carbon credits on the false basis of 'clean development' (Yumnam 2012).

Among the earliest and most destructive big dams in the North East is the Dumbur Dam in Tripura (the Gumti Hydel Project), completed in 1976. Officially it displaced 2,845 families in the south Tripura District, most of whom were from the Borok tribe. These figures represent the minority of oustees who had official land titles, and the real number displaced is estimated at about 20,000 people. Almost certainly, resentment at this displacement fuelled insurgency in

Tripura, compounding the massive displacement of tribal people due to settlements of Bengalis in the State (Bhaumik 2003, 2012; Hoenig and Singh 2014).

COSTS AND BENEFITS OF BIG DAMS

The above list includes only a small selection of the North East's big dams, albeit some of the most controversial. It should be apparent that dam building in the North East has followed a very particular history and that it involves a very complex power structure and investment pattern. The first dams built in Bhutan from the 1980s to the 1990s were provided with 70 per cent of grants from India and 30 per cent loans; by 2015, these figures were reversed, as we have seen. Between 2000 and 2016, the Arunachal government signed 153 MoUs for big dams, to generate over 40,000 MW; however, with six dams on the Lohit River, and a number of MoUs cancelled, it became clear that not all these projects could be realized, and construction work on most projects was slow to start (Rahman 2016). Against this is the pressure from the centre to build dams quickly, so that India will have an advantage over China in terms of the first use of river power (Gamble 2015). In 2016, it emerged that many private dam builders wished to partner with the NHPC, since projects were delayed by peoples' movements and regulatory hurdles (Rahman 2016).

Negative impacts of big dams not only involve the destruction of fragile ecosystems and sustainable communities, but significant risks that are very hard to gauge, including that of catastrophic floods and earthquakes. Before more dams are built in the North East, it should be obvious that impacts of previous big dams have to be properly assessed. Among the worst in terms of displacement are the Dumbur Dam in Tripura, the Loktak Hydel Project in Manipur (Yumnam 2014), Pagladia in Assam, Ranganadi in Arunachal and the Doyang Dam in Wokha District of Nagaland, which displaced an estimated 30,000 people without proper compensation (75 MW, a land compensation agreement signed 1992, *Morung Express* 2011); this caused devastating floods during July-August 2018 (see earlier), due to the sudden release of pent-up water.

On the CDM scam, a diplomatic cable on 16 July 2008 from the US consulate in Mumbai to the US State Department, released by Wikileaks, revealed that 'most of the CDM projects in India should not have been certified because they did not reduce emissions beyond those that would have been achieved without foreign investment'.

'What has leaked just confirms our view that in its present form the CDM is basically a farce', says Eva Filzmoser, Programme Director of CDM Watch, a Brussels-based watchdog organization. 'The revelations imply that millions of tonnes of claimed reductions in greenhouse-gas emissions are mere phantoms' (Schiermeier 2011).

In 2008, 346 Indian projects were registered for carbon credits. By 2011, the number had risen to more than 720, even though most of India's carbon-offset projects fail to meet the CDM requirements set by the UN Framework Convention on Climate Change. Obviously, the northeastern dams gain huge sums from such 'green' funding. For example, when the eligibility for CDM credits of the Rampur hydro-dam in Himachal Pradesh was challenged by International Rivers (based in Berkeley, California), it emerged that SJVNL (the developer) stood to gain approximately 15 million carbon credits from 2012 to 2022, amounting to an estimated US$150 million.

In other words, in effect, CDM credits are used to fund dams by offsetting the debts created by building them. Yumnam (2012) shows the economic and ecological madness involved in the case of the Myntdu Leshka Dam in Jaintia Hills, Meghalaya, at a trijunction of the Umshaking, Myntdu and Lamu Rivers, among many other cases analysed in detail.

Opinion is deeply polarized on the subject of big dams. During the 1990s, there was much debate on claims and counterclaims (e.g., Dhawan 1990; Saleth 1992; Singh 1997). D'Souza (2008) summarized previous research, showing how the benefit cost ratio of dams discounted environmental and social costs, and we can see how the economic benefits of dams are distorted through corruption and CDMs. Where is the holistic cost benefit analysis that gives proportional weight to economic, ecological and social criertia? (Dandekar and Unni 2013, 47–68; Padel 2016) Updated information on northeastern dams is often hard to find, but a lot of material is summarized in a report by Laishram and Yumnam (2016).

The biggest 'benefit' is clearly electricity, with flood control highly questionable, irrigation usually much less than cultivated areas that are inundated and employment and boost for the economy again highly questionable, with local labourers and contractors repeatedly invading remote areas, undermining local livelihoods.

> India's Central Electricity Authority has promoted the Northeast dams on the rationale that they are a 'future powerhouse', that will solve India's need for electricity; with a projected installed capacity from 168 new dams estimated at over 63,000MW. Most of the electricity generated is therefore to be sold outside the Northeast. (SANDRP 2016)

As discussed, Bhutan earns a large part of its revenue by selling electricity to India. But is the investment that big dams, extractive industries, road and rail construction bring to governments in the North East automatically a benefit for citizens on the ground? For some millions of village people displaced by big dams in India alone, dam projects represent the opposite of 'development'. To call these people's situation one of 'Development-Induced Displacement' is therefore a misuse of language. The process should be termed 'Investment-Forced Displacement' (Padel 2016).

Another benefit of building big dams quickly on the rivers coming from China is 'strategic', establishing first use of hydropower (Gamble 2015).

Probably the biggest benefits are actually financial, however, for the construction and power companies and government officials involved. As in India and other countries, dam construction has enmeshed countless governments and countries in unrepayable burdens of debt. The 'MoU virus' in Arunachal Pradesh seems to be based on 'speculative investment and political brokering' (Mazoomdar 2013).

The destruction of ecosystems and communities is impossible to quantify. Planners who do not know impacted landscapes perceive the projects statistically and financially, while for locals the loss is beyond calculation. Movements against the dams gathered pace in 2005 with stands taken by AASU, KMSS and many other organizations against Lower Subansiri Dam (Dutta 2015). Most conspicuously in Manipur, but throughout the North East, opposition to dam construction has often met severe repression. While the Congress-led government started the 'MoU virus' around 2005, the BJP-led government since has continued the trend, and it is noteworthy to understand how many northeastern dams have had their foundation stones laid by prime ministers from both parties.

EXTRACTIVE INDUSTRIES AND INFRASTRUCTURE

The industrialization in Meghalaya, the huge extent of coal mining, limestone quarrying and cement plants there and the complex challenges and environmental impacts of these industries have been written about (e.g., Kharkongor and Dutta 2014; Schneider 2014). Similarly with attempts to exploit Meghalaya's uranium deposits, at least plans for exploration in the Balpakram National Park, in the Garo Hills, have been laid aside (Juneja 2015).

The issue of oil exploration in Nagaland and Manipur is less well known. ONGC (Oil & Natural Gas Corporation, GOI) started oil exploration back in 1973 and started extraction around the villages of Champong and old Tssori in the Wokha District of Nagaland, near the border with Assam, in 1984. These efforts disregarded local land rights and devastated land in the area by the time production stopped in 1994, with over a million tonnes of oil extracted. In that year, with threats from a militant group, ONGC left the area without properly decommissioning the wells, which contaminated large areas. After 20 years, in 2014, Metropolitan Oil and Gas Company Private Ltd (Delhi) restarted exploration in Wokha. Tribal student protestors were beaten up by police, and Section 144 was imposed (Chakravarty 2018).

In Manipur, the main companies involved are the Jubilant Oil and Gas Company/Jubilant Energy, a Dutch company, and its Noida-based subsidiary. Villages in the Tamenglong, Churachandpur and Jiribam (Imphal East) Districts have experienced blasting and drilling before receiving any information; it started in 2011, with Jubilant hiring Asian Oilfields for exploration and Alpha Geo for aerial surveys using drones (Chaoba 2012; Thangjam 2017; Yumnam 2012, September 2). The Manipuri government signed a deal with Jubilant in November 2010 for exploration of nearly 4,000^2 km, with no publicity. When villagers made their opposition clear at public hearings in 2012, exploration apparently ended, though Jubilant Energy's Annual Report for 2014 announced that the exploration in these three districts was complete. There was evidence of attempts to bribe villagers to obtain no objection certificates (NOCs). Initial surveys suggest that Manipur has nearly 5 trillion cubic feet of oil deposits, in two main blocks.

In January 2017, a similar chain of events took place with exploration for Oil India Limited by Asian Oilfields, in Tamenglong, Jiribam and Imphal West districts. Blasting started without warning near Khaidem Village (Imphal) in May 2017, again, with no prior announcement. Khaidem Village passed a resolution refusing an NOC for exploration, with other villages following suit (Thangjam 2017); after this many organizations met to pass a resolution against oil exploration in Manipur, and widespread opposition has continued (E-Pao 2017; Bhattacharyya 2018). The Jiribam-Imphal Highway (NH-37) was financed by Asian Ddevelopment Bank, evidently with a view of facilitating oil companies. It is evident that recent policy documents and legislation, such as the 'North East Hydrocarbon Vision, 2030' (2016) and the Open Acreage Licensing Policy (OALP) 2017 contain no recognition of community rights and no role in local decision-making regarding oil exploration, nor does it contain recognition of the possible role that blasting may play in triggering an earthquake, in light of the huge one, measuring over 6 on the Richter scale, that hit Manipur on 4 January 2015, with its epicentre in Tamanglong. The OALP allows oil companies to explore and even extend exploration without prior bidding and identification of oil blocks, with no accountability to the people. In December 2016, a 22,000-crore package was allotted from the centre for roads in Manipur, with 'special status' for the State, ostensibly to create 'standard' quality roads, replacing 'substandard' ones, which were too small and narrow to transport the large drilling equipment needed for oil exploration. Just before, Jubilant had threatened to withdraw due to substandard roads (Sharma 2018).

While road and rail projects have been welcomed as obvious benefits by large sections of the North East's population, they transform and often cause great damage to ecosystems, and many movements have organized resistance. For example, in February 2018, Marangching Village in Tamenglong District of Manipur demonstrated against the new rail project in Imphal (*The People's Chronicle* 2018). As roads have penetrated remote areas, the relations between the people and environment have changed enormously. Reports suggest that even previously inaccessible areas have suffered extensive deforestation from various causes, including the timber mafia (Roychoudhury 1992), and hunting has made previously common and unique species very rare. Many of the traditional cultures in the North East have strong traditions of protecting forests, however, such as the Angami Naga (e.g., Souza 2001).

People's decisions against oil exploration in Manipur and Nagaland have come about after the extensive damage in the Wokha District caused by the ONGC. The Agartala Declaration of 15 February 2013 asserted 'that land, forests, rivers and all natural resources in North East India belong to the indigenous people of the region.... Our land and all the natural resources are inherent sources for our Life, Culture, Identity, Survival and future of our present and coming generations.' The main focus was against big dams, including misuse of the CDM, carbon trading credits (Lohmann 2006) and extractive industries (*Hueiyen News Service* 2013; International Work Group on Indigenous Affairs (IWGIA) 2013).

The Agartala Declaration was followed by a similar Dimapur Declaration in May 2013, following the North East Peoples' Convention on Water Sources (*Imphal Free Press* 2013). Both events emphasized the principle of FPIC, which so far has not been adhered to in decisions about giving clearances to big dams. Both these declarations follow from the Cochabamba Declaration that was made in Bolivia in April 2014, asserting the rights of nature or Mother Earth, in a formulation inspired by indigenous peoples (World People's Conference on Climate Change and the Rights of Mother Earth 2010; *Economic and Political Weekly* 2012).

CONCLUSION

What therefore constitutes real development for people in the region we know as the 'North East'? Connectivity by transport and investment is much needed, but how conscious are decision-makers about the human and environmental costs of new roads and railways? Even financial investment can be a 'poisoned chalice' when projects paid for involve large-scale corruption and obliterate ancient landscapes full of biodiversity and ancient communities who developed sustainable lifestyles generations back. Many smaller-scale alternatives exist, more adapted to local conditions and far less destructive. Shouldn't any large-scale changes to the landscape follow local people's wishes? Can overriding basic human rights, and the vital principle of FPIC, bring real development at all?

Dams are still often promoted as symbols of development, because of the technical achievement they represent and the electricity they provide, even though their negative impacts on people's lives and the destruction of ecosystems seem to far outweigh any benefits. Hydropower as well as oil offers state governments huge possibilities of investment, revenue and 'development'. Yet a more reliable indicator of development is surely people's security of life, which means security of food, water and livelihoods and above all, respect for human rights and the security of healthy ecosystems to pass on to future generations.

REFERENCES

Arora, V. 2006. 'Roots and the Route of Secularism in Sikkim'. *Economic and Political Weekly* 41(38): 4063–70.

———. 2008. 'Gandhigiri in Sikkim'. *Economic and Political Weekly* 43(38): 27–28.

Arora, V., and N. Kipgen. 2012. '"We Can Live Without Power, but We Can't Live Without Our Land": Indigenous Hmar Oppose the Tipaimukh Dam in Manipur'. *Sociological Bulletin* 61(1): 109–28.

Baruah, P. 2017. 'NGT Orders Formation of Expert Panel on Subansiri Dam'. *Times of India*, 17 October. Retrieved from https://timesofindia.indiatimes.com/city/guwahati/ngt-orders-formation-of-expert-panel-to-review-subansiri-dam/articleshow/61110673.cms

Begum, A. A. 2010. 'AFSPA and Unsolved Massacres in Manipur'. *Two Circles*. Retrieved from http://twocircles.net/2010nov03/afspa_and_unsolved_massacres_manipur.html#.Visk53gxHEY

Bhattacharyya, R. 2018. 'Oil India Reacts Cautiously as Seismic Survey Hits Roadblock in Manipur after Rebel Group Abducts Sub-contractors'. *First Post,* 20 April. Retrieved from https://www.firstpost.com/india/oil-india-reacts-cautiously-as-seismic-survey-hits-roadblock-in-manipur-after-rebel-group-abducts-sub-contractors-4430261.html

Bhaumik, S. 2003. 'Tripura's Gumti Dam Must Go'. *Ecologist Asia* 11(1): 84–86.

———. 2012. *Tripura: Ethnic Conflict, Militancy and Counterinsurgency*. Policy and Practice 52. Kolkata: Mahanirban Calcutta Research Group. Retrieved from http://www.mcrg.ac.in/PP52.pdf

Bhuyan, A. 2018. 'Fifteen Murderers Are Roaming Around in Manipur: Supreme Court Judge to CBI'. *The Wire,* 31 July. Retrieved from https://thewire.in/law/manipur-fake-encounter-case-supreme-court-cbi

Bindra, P. S. 2018. 'India Dealing with Environmental Crisis but Government in Denial, Says Lawyer Ritwick Dutta'. *First Post,* 2 February. Retrieved from https://www.firstpost.com/india/india-dealing-with-environmental-crisis-but-govt-in-denial-says-lawyer-ritwick-dutta-4356487.html

Chakravartty, A. 2015. '"MoU Virus" Hits Arunachal Pradesh'. *Down to Earth,* 4 July. Retrieved from https://www.downtoearth.org.in/news/mou-virus-hits-arunachal-pradesh-33962

Chakravartty, A., and D. J. Dutta. 2018. 'How the Doyang Hydroelectric Project Flooded Assam and Nagaland'. *The Wire,* 22 August. Retrieved from https://thewire.in/environment/how-the-doyang-hydroelectric-project-flooded-assam-and-nagaland

Chakravarty, I. 2018. 'Bone of the Land: The Search for Oil Shapes Politics in this Corner of Nagaland'. *Scroll India,* 20 February. Retrieved from https://scroll.in/article/869167/bone-of-the-land-the-search-for-oil-shapes-politics-in-this-corner-of-nagaland

Chandran, R. 2018. 'Protests Planned Against Opening of Mega Dam in Northeastern India'. *Reuters,* 2 March. Retrieved from https://www.reuters.com/article/us-india-landrights-protests/protests-planned-against-opening-of-mega-dam-in-northeastern-india-idUSKCN1GE0X5

Chaoba, P. 2012. '30 Oil Wells Detected in Manipur'. *Kangla Online,* 15 July. Retrieved from http://kanglaonline.com/2012/07/30-oil-wells-detected-in-manipur/

Choudhury, A. 2014. 'Comments on the EIA of the Dibang Multipurpose Project'. Retrieved from http://www.ercindia.org/files/eiadocuments/eiareports/Comments%20on%20Dibang%20EIA%20-%20Anwaruddin%20Choudhury.pdf

Cultural Survival, USA. 2018. 'UN Special Rapporteur Releases Report on the Criminalization of Indigenous Peoples'. 24 September. Retrieved from https://www.culturalsurvival.org/news/un-special-rapporteur-releases-report-criminalization-indigenous-peoples

D'Souza, R. 2008. 'Framing India's Hydraulic Crises: The Politics of the Large Modern Dam'. *Monthly Review* 60(3): 112–24.

Dandekar, A. and J. Unni. 2013. *Ecology, Economy: Quest for a Socially Informed Connection*. Delhi: Orient Black Swan.

Dhawan, B. D. ed. 1990. *The Big Dams: Claims and Counterclaims*. Delhi: Commonwealth Publishers.
Duarah, C. K. 2014. 'India Gives Green Light to Build Country's Largest Dam'. *The Third Pole*, 29 September. Retrieved from http://viewsweek.com/economy/water-security/india-gives-green-light-build-countrys-largest-dam/
Dutta, A. P. 2015. 'Assam's Dam Crisis'. *Down to Earth*, 17 September. Retrieved from https://www.downtoearth.org.in/news/assams-dam-crisis-1978
E-Pao. 2017. 'Public Meet Resolves No Oil Exploration in Manipur by Asian Oil Limited'. 24 May. Retrieved from http://www.e-pao.net/epSubPageExtractor.asp?src=news_section.Press_Release.Press_Release_2017.Public_Meet_resolves_No_Oil_Exploration_in_Manipur_by_Oil_India_Limited_20170525
Economic and Political Weekly. 2012. 'If Mountains and Rivers Could Speak'. *Economic and Political Weekly* 47(2): 9.
Gamble, R. 2015. 'China and India's Border Dispute Is a Slow-Moving Environmental Disaster'. *The Conversation*, 25 June. Retrieved from https://www.hongkongfp.com/2018/06/25/china-indias-border-dispute-slow-moving-environmental-disaster/
Greener Pastures. 2014. 'Dams Versus Northeast India: Celebrating Indigenous Cultures'. *North East India Travel Blog*, 9 August. Retrieved from https://thenortheasttravelblog.com/2014/08/09/dams-versus-northeast-india-celebrating-indigenous-peoples/
Gulf Times. 2018. 'Water Released from Dam Floods Villages'. 6 August. Retrieved from https://www.gulf-times.com/story/601976/Water-released-from-dam-floods-villages
Hoenig, P., and N. Singh. 2014. *Landscapes of Fear: Understanding Impunity in India*. Delhi: Zubaan.
Hueiyen News Service. 2013. 'Agartala Declaration Says No to Dams'. 11 February. Retrieved from http://e-pao.net/GP.asp?src=28..120213.feb13
Imphal Free Press. 2013. 'Dimapur Declaration Sets Tone for People's Rights to Natural Resources'. 18 May. Retrieved from http://kanglaonline.com/2013/05/dimapur-declaration-sets-tone-for-peoples-right-to-natural-resources/
International Rivers. 2015. 'Status of Hydropower Dams in Bhutan'. 14 April. Retrieved from https://www.internationalrivers.org/resources/8703
International Work Group on Indigenous Affairs (IWGIA). 2013. *Agartala Declaration of Indigenous Peoples' Consultation on Dams and Natural Resources Protection in India's North East, 10-11 February*. Agartala, Tripura, Denmark: IWGIA. Retrieved from http://www.iwgia.org/iwgia_files_news_files/0745_AGARTALA_DECLARATION_OF_INDIGENOUS_PEOPLES.pdf
Islam, M. S., and M. N. Islam. 2016. '"Environmentalism of the Poor": The Tipaimukh Dam, Ecological Disasters and Environmental Resistance Beyond Borders'. *Bandung: Journal of the Global South* 3(27). doi: 10.1186/s40728-016-0030-5
Jha, D. K. 2018. 'NE Put on Right Track'. *The Pioneer*, 20 May. Retrieved from https://www.dailypioneer.com/2018/sunday-edition/ne-put-on-right-track.html

Juneja, S. 2015. 'Garo Hills Spared of Uranium Exploration'. *Down to Earth*, 4 July. Retrieved from https://www.downtoearth.org.in/news/garo-hills-spared-of-uranium-exploration-648

Karmakar, R. 2018. 'Arunachal Mega Dam Near Pilgrimage Cleared, Environmentalists See Red'. *The Hindu*, 29 September. Retrieved from https://www.thehindu.com/news/national/other-states/arunachal-mega-dam-near-pilgrimage-cleared-environmentalists-see-red/article25066578.ece

Khandekar, N. 2018. 'Many Questions as Government Team Visits Lohit Hydro Project'. *Thirdpole*, 27 February. Retrieved from https://www.thethirdpole.net/en/2018/02/27/many-questions-as-government-team-revisits-lohit-hydro-project/

Kharkongor, G. L., and R. Dutta. 2014. *Status of Adivasis/Indigenous Peoples Mining Series-4. Meghalaya*. Delhi: Aakar.

Kipgen, N. 2015. 'Dissenting Voices from the Margins: Mapithel Dam in Manipur'. *Economic and Political Weekly* 50(39). Retrieved from https://www.epw.in/journal/2015/39/reports-states-web-exclusives/dissenting-voices-margins.html

Laishram, S., and J. Yumnam. 2016. *State of India's Rivers: North East, for India Rivers Week*. Delhi: SANDRP. https://sandrp.files.wordpress.com/2017/03/north-east-report.pdf

Lenin, J. 2014. 'India's Largest Dam Given Clearance but Still Faces a Flood of Opposition'. *The Guardian*, UK, 22 October.

Lohmann, L. ed. 2006. *Carbong Trading: A Critical Conversation on Climate Change*. Uppsala, Sweden: Dag Hammarskjold Centre. Retrieved from http://www.thecornerhouse.org.uk//resource/carbon-trading-0

Longjam, M. 2015. 'Mapithel Dam and Its Impact on Chadong'. *E-Pao*, 5 August. Retrieved from http://e-pao.net/epSubPageExtractor.asp?src=news_section.opinions.Opinion_on_Building_of_Tipaimukh_Dam.Mapithel_Dam_and_its_impact_on_Chadong_By_Meena_Longjam

Mazoomdar, J. 2013. 'Another Disaster in the Making'. *Tehelka*, 13 July, 28(10). Retrieved from http://old.tehelka.com/another-disaster-in-the-making/

———. 2017. 'Hydel Project: NGT Wants Neutral Panel, Centre Picks "Known" Experts'. *Indian Express*, 29 December. Retrieved from https://indianexpress.com/article/india/hydel-project-ngt-wants-neutral-panel-centre-picks-known-experts-5003166/

Mitra, M. N. 2006. 'Dam on Teesta Spells Doom'. *Down to Earth*, 30 November. Retrieved from http://www.downtoearth.org.in/node/8713

Morung Express. 2011. 'ZSUM [Zeiliangrong Students' Union of Manipur] Wants Benefits in Exchange for Dam Programme'. 11 June. Retrieved from http://morungexpress.com/zsum-want-benefits-in-exchange-for-dam-project/

Padel, F. 2016. 'India's Grassroots Movements Against Investment-Forced Displacement'. In *Global Implications of Development, Disasters and Climate Change: Responses to Displacement from Asia Pacific*, edited by S. Price and J. Singer, 115–25. London and New York: Earthscan, Routledge.

Pratidin Time. 2018. 'Huge Cracks Detected in a Tunnel of Kameng Hydro Electric Project'. 10 May. Retrieved from https://www.pratidintime.com/huge-cracks-detected-at-a-tunnel-of-kameng-hydro-electric-project-hep/

Premkumar, L. 2016. *A Study of the India-Bhutan Energy Cooperation Agreements and the Implementation of Hydropower Projects in Bhutan*. Delhi: Vasudha Foundation. http://www.vasudha-foundation.org/wp-content/uploads/Final-Bhutan-Report_30th-Mar-2016.pdf

Rahman, A. P. 2016. 'Private Dam Builders Back Out of Brahmaputra Dams'. *Third Pole*, 25 February. Retrieved from https://www.thethirdpole.net/en/2016/02/25/private-dam-builders-back-out-of-brahmaputra-dams/

Rangachari, R., P. Banerji, R. R. Iyer, N. Sengupta, and S. Singh. 2000. *World Commission on Dams: India Country Study*. Cape Town: WCD.

Rashid, H. 2015. 'Tipaimukh Dam: What Is the Current Position?' 1 February. Retrieved from http://www.hidropolitikakademi.org/en/tipaimukh-dam-what-is-the-current-position.html

Rehman, T. 2012. 'Brahmaputra: Towards Unity'. thethirdpole.net. Retrieved from https://s3.amazonaws.com/cd.live/uploads/content/file_en/6797/brahmaputra-v13.pdf

Roychoudhury, A. 1992. 'Chopping Down the Future'. *Down to Earth*, 31 May. Retrieved from http://www.downtoearth.org.in/coverage/chopping-down-the-future-29723

Saikia, A. 2016. 'Arunachal's Great Hydro Game'. *Fountain Ink*, 6 February. Retrieved from https://fountainink.in/reportage/arunachal039s-great-hydro-game

———. 2017. 'The Centre's Proposal to Build a Mega Dam in Arunachal Pradesh Makes Even Hydropower Companies Wary'. *Scroll India*, 18 October. Retrieved from https://scroll.in/article/853655/the-centres-proposal-to-build-a-mega-dam-in-arunachal-pradesh-makes-even-hydropower-companies-wary

Saikia, K. 2018. 'KMSS Demands Termination of Kameng Dam Construction'. *Northeast Now*, 6 May. Retrieved from https://nenow.in/north-east-news/kmss-demands-termination-kameng-dam-construction.html

Saleth, R. M. 1992. 'Big Dams Controversy: Economics, Ecology, Equity'. Economic and Political Weekly 27(30): 1607–09.

Sangai Express. 2018. '*Tipaimukh Project Runs into Forest Clearance Wall*', 20 March. *Retrieved from http://e-pao.net/GP.asp?src=13*

Schiermeier, Q. 2011. 'Clean-energy Credits Tarnished: Wikileaks Reveals that Most Indian Claims Are Ineligible'. *Nature*, 27 September. Retrieved from https://www.nature.com/news/2011/110927/full/477517a.html

Schneider, K. 2014. 'India's Treacherous Coal Mines in Meghalaya'. *Circle of Blue*, 15 May. Retrieved from https://www.circleofblue.org/2014/world/meghalayas-treacherous-coal-mines/

———. 2015. 'Arunachal's Unfinished Lower Subansiri Dam Could Be Tomb for India's Giant Hydropower Projects: Lower Subansiri River Construction Site Was Shut in 2011 and Never Restarted'. *Scoll India*, 12 June. Retrieved from http://scroll.in/article/718809/uttarakhands-unfinished-lower-subansiri-dam-could-be-tomb-for-indias-giant-hydropower-projects

Sethi, N. 2015. 'Tipaimukh in Manipur Driving a Wedge'. *Down to Earth*, 7 June. Retrieved from https://www.downtoearth.org.in/coverage/tipaimukh-dam-in-manipur-driving-a-wedge-8478

Sharma, A. 2003. 'Teesta Dams: A Recipe for Disaster?' *Down to Earth* 11(15). Retrieved from http://www.indiaenvironmentportal.org.in/node/34607

Sharma, G. A. 2018. 'Roads after the Companies'. *Imphal Free Press*, 1 April. Retrieved from https://www.ifp.co.in/page/items/47914/roads-after-the-companies/

Sify News. 2010. 'Assam Dam Project May Continue: Jairam Ramesh'. 12 August. Retrieved from http://www.sify.com/news/assam-dam-project-may-continue-jairam-ramesh-news-national-kimpEcidiaa.html

Singh, S. 1997. *Taming the Waters: The Political Economy of Large Dams in India*. Delhi: Oxford University Press.

Sinlung Indigenous Peoples Human Rights Organisation (SIPHRO). 2013. 'FAC Decision on Tipaimukh Dam a Just Decision: SIPHRO'. 29 July. Retrieved from http://e-pao.net/epSubPageExtractor.asp?src=news_section.Press_Release.Press_Release_2013.FAC_decision_on_Tipaimukh_Dam_a_just_decision_SIPHR_20130730

South Asia Network on Dams, Rivers and People (SANDRP). 2013. 'Media Hype Vs Reality: India-China Water Sharing Information MoU of October 2013'. 24 October. Retrieved from https://sandrp.in/2013/10/24/media-hype-vs-reality-india-china-water-information-sharing-mou-of-oct-2013/

——— 2014. 'Review of Water Sector in Northeast India in 2013: Increasing Threats to Rivers, People and Environment'. 14 January. Retrieved from https://sandrp.in/tag/northeast-india/

———. 2015. 'India's Free Flowing Frontier Part I: Dibang at Nizamghat'. 29 December. Retrieved from https://sandrp.in/2015/12/29/indias-free-flowing-frontier-part-i-dibang-at-nizamghat/

———. 2016. '"Citizens" Concern for Dams and Development'. 2 December. Retrieved from https://sandrp.in/2016/12/02/citizens-concern-for-dams-and-development-the-voice-of-vulnerable-honored-with-bhagirath-prayas-samman-at-india-rivers-week-2016/

Souza, A. D. 2001. *Traditional Systems of Forest Conservation in North East India: The Angami Tribe of Nagaland*. Guwahati: North-Eastern Social Research Centre.

Tauli-Corpuz, V. 2018. 'Special Rapporteur to the UN on the Rights of Indigenous Peoples'. *Attacks Against and Criminalization of Indigenous Peoples Defending their Rights*, Report to Human Rights Council. United Nations. Retrieved from http://unsr.vtaulicorpuz.org/site/index.php?option=com_content&view=article&id=251:report-hrc2018&catid=11:annual-reports&Itemid=40&lang=en

Thangjam, H. 2017. *Search for Black Gold in Sanaleibak Manipur*. Manipur: Centre for Research and Advocacy. Retrieved from https://cramanipur.wordpress.com/page/3/

The People's Chronicle. 2018. 'Villagers' Opposition Derailing Rail Project Works'. 19 February. Retrieved from https://cramanipur.wordpress.com/page/3/

Tiwari, D. 2016. 'Vigilance Probe Red-Flags Fraud and Corruption in Arunachal Hydro Project'. *Indian Express,* 13 December. Retrieved from https://indianexpress.com/article/india/vigilance-probe-red-flags-fraud-and-corruption-in-arunachal-hydro-project-kiren-rijiju-4424240/

Vagholikar, N., and J. P. Das. 2010. *Damming North-East India.* Pune/Guwahati/New Delhi: Kalpavriksha, Aranyak and Action–India.

Walker, B. 2015. 'Will Mega Dams Turn Bhutan's Happiness Sour?' *The Guardian,* UK, 20 May. Retrieved from https://www.theguardian.com/sustainable-business/2015/may/20/will-mega-dams-turn-bhutans-happiness-sour

———. 2016. 'Bhutan's PM Defends Hydropower Dams Against Blistering Report'. *Third Pole,* 4 October. Retrieved from https://www.thethirdpole.net/en/2016/10/04/bhutans-pm-defends-hydropower-dams-against-blistering-report/

World People's Conference on Climate Change and the Rights of Mother Earth. 2010. 'People's Agreement of Cochabamba 24 April 2010: Building the People's World Movement for Mother Earth'. Retrieved from https://pwccc.wordpress.com/2010/04/24/peoples-agreement/

Yumnam, J., and Citizens' Concern for Dams and Development. 2012. *An Assessment of Dams in India's North East Seeking Carbon Credits from Clean Development Mechanism of the United Nations Framework Convention on Climate Change.* International Rivers Network. Retrieved from https://www.internationalrivers.org/sites/default/files/attached-files/damsandcdm_ne_india_april__2012.pdf

———. 2012, September 2. 'Oil Exploration: Boon or Bane for Manipur?' *E-Pao.* Retrieved from http://e-pao.net/epSubPageExtractor.asp?src=education.Science_and_Technology.Oil_Exploration_Boon_or_Bane_for_Manipur

———. 2014. *Loktak Wetlands Eviction: A Case of Development Crisis in Manipur.* Imphal: Centre for Research and Advocacy. Retrieved from https://static1.squarespace.com/static/50ec44f5e4b050fcaabb6e6f/t/54946df1e4b041d6f14eefc3/1419013617006/LOKTAK+WETLANDS+AND+EVICTION+CRAM+2014.pdf

———. 2015. 'Mapithel Dam Submerges Chadong Village in Manipur'. *Seven Sisters Project,* 8 June. Retrieved from http://sevensistersproject.com/mapithel-dam-submerges-chadong-village-in-manipur/

———. 2018. '66 MW Loktak Downstream Project, JICA Financing Plans and Concerns', Imphal Free Press. 24 March. Retrieved fromhttps://www.ifp.co.in/page/items/47684/66-mw-loktak-downstream-project-jica-financing-plan-concerns/

Zakaria. 2012. 'Tipaimukh Dam Dispute and Bangladesh-India Relations'. 26 June. Retrieved from http://zakaria062.blogspot.in/2012/06/tipaimukh-dam-dispute-and-bangladesh.html

Chapter 11

Conservation versus Peoples' Entitlements
Contestations in Kaziranga National Park

Akhil Ranjan Dutta

Kaziranga National Park (KNP) in Assam, located in India's North East is one of the incredible success stories of preserving one-horned rhinos. The park hosts almost two-thirds of the entire global population of one-horned rhinos. Kaziranga is also a national pride for Assam and it echoes in the rhythms of the nationalist imagination of its people. A UNESCO World Heritage Centre, KNP hosts, apart from the one-horned ungulate, a huge variety of 'globally threatened species including tiger, Asian elephant, wild water buffalo, gaur, eastern swamp deer, Sambar deer, hog deer, capped langur, hoolock gibbon and sloth bear' (UNESCO). The park has the highest density of tigers in India and has been declared a tiger reserve since 2007 (UNESCO). The ecology of the park is very complex, and it is composed of wetlands, foothills and floodplains, and it witnesses regularly the succession between grasslands and woodlands. The park has undergone changes in its form, substance and size since the beginning of the twentieth century. The colonial imagination of the park was associated with the political economy of tea plantations that required secure landscapes that used to be the habitat of a variety of wild animals. Kaziranga, therefore, is also testimony to the fragmentation of the landscape of Brahmaputra Valley in Assam under the necessity of the colonial plantation economy (Saikia 2011). Declared as a forest reserve in 1908, Kaziranga was re-designated as a game sanctuary in 1916. It was declared as a wildlife sanctuary in 1950. In 1974, Government of India accorded the official status of a national park to Kaziranga after the Government of Assam had enacted the National Park Act in 1968 and declared Kaziranga as a designated national park. In 1985, the UNSECO accorded the World Heritage Centre status to Kaziranga. As the protection of wildlife and conservation of forests have emerged as new milestones for national imagination, Kaziranga continues to expand by adding the neighbouring human habitations to the park, which, in turn, provoke conflict between the park and its neighbourhood.

In recent times, the park has become an epitome of controversies that mark a conflict between the State-driven discourse of conservation and that of communities living in its vicinity. The expansion of the park, by attaching six adjacent areas (officially called additions), which was done through bureaucratic exercises without taking the communities into confidence, has provoked conflict and tension in neighbouring human habitations. The verdict of Gauhati High Court (19 October 2015) that resulted in ruthless eviction drives in September 2016 and the documentary prepared by British Broadcasting Corporation (BBC) titled 'Our World: Killing for Conservation' (February 2017) generated intense debate in India and abroad on the conversation model and the brutality in the name of conservation in Kaziranga. The origin of the conflict may be traced back to the enactment of the Wildlife Protection Act of 1972 and the Forest Conservation Act of 1980. These Acts fused the initiatives of wildlife protection and forest conservation with the nationalist sentiment of the State. Such conservation nationalism, which is mostly elitist in nature, fails to recognize the interrelationships between the forest and its animal habitats with that of the surrounding human habitations. The mainstream discourse of conservation manufactures animosity between the forests and the communities in their vicinity. This conflict has immense significance in understanding the limits of the development paradigm and the conservationist models in India in general and the North East in particular.

THREE CULTURES: GROWING ANTAGONISM

At the heart of the intense global debate surrounding the development discourse is whether it only involves two 'cultures'—developmentalism and environmentalism—or whether there are more, which may also include the culture of peoples' entitlements that confront both. This is a pertinent and politically provoking question that encounters the State- and corporate-driven development and conservationist agenda in India in general and the North East in particular. Jairam Ramesh, former Environment and Forest Minister of India, under the United Progressive Alliance (UPA) government, argues that there are two mutually antagonistic approaches to development, which he termed 'two different cultures'. Referring to the British physicist-author C. P. Snow, who spoke of 'breakdown of communications between the "two cultures" of modern society- the culture of science and that of humanities', Mr Ramesh explores 'a later-day facet of the "two cultures" syndrome' (Ramesh 2010, 13). Here, he outlines the mutually incompatible approaches of faster economic growth and the protection of the environment. Ramesh argues that

> on the face of it, there should be no gap at all—who can argue against faster economic growth since that alone will generate more jobs and at the same time who can argue against the preservation of our rivers, lakes, mountains and wonderful biodiversity in its myriad forms since that alone will make sustainable development. (Ramesh 2010, 13)

Ramesh, however, laments that both these approaches stick to their exclusive concerns and look at each other, rather than explore the possibility of convergence and dialogue. Ramesh also points out that both the approaches talk of a balance but with contrary articulations. The proponents of growth talk of a 'fetish which is being made of the environment' and the environmentalists talk of the fetish which is 'being made of economic growth'. Ramesh's primary concern, as a Minister of Environment and Forests, was to explore a possibility of bringing these two contrary approaches to dialogue. In his judgement, there are three approaches to development or for that matter, faster economic growth. They are 'yes', 'yes, but' and 'no'. While the growth constituency primarily stands for 'yes' it concedes to 'yes, but' and cries foul with 'no'. The environmentalists believe in the reverse sequence: 'no', 'yes, but' and they denounce 'yes'. Ramesh's mission was to enhance and expand the category of 'yes, but'. He himself found lot of shortcomings in understanding growth itself and therefore reiterated a lot of new innovations undertaken by different thinkers and agencies. He mentions the transition of GDP from Gross Domestic Product to Green Domestic Product and GNP from Gross National Product to Green Nature Product. Ramesh argues that such new innovations will adequately and properly reflect 'the consumption of precious depletable natural resources in the process of generating national income' (p. 14). He also argues that environmental concerns cannot be reduced to elitist concerns for clean air and protection of tigers alone. It should be able to address the larger public health issues arising out of faster economic growth. Finally, Ramesh looks for a solution and argues:

> Having said this, I want to return to the very formulation of this modern-day 'two cultures'. Is the debate really environment *versus* development or is it one of adhering to rules, regulations and laws versus taking the rules, regulations and laws for granted? I think the latter is a more accurate representation and a better way to formulate the choice. (Ramesh 2010, 15)

Ramesh thinks that the Indian Parliament has enacted several progressive laws to address the concerns of these two cultures. Important among them are The Wildlife (Protection) Act of 1972, the Water Act of 1974, the Forest (Conservation) Act of 1980, the Air Act of 1981, the Environment (Protection) Act of 1986 and the most recent, the Forest Rights Act of 2006. For Ramesh,

> The question before the country is very, very simple: are these laws to be enforced or are they to just adorn the statute books, honoured more in their breach than in their observance. This is the intellectually honest way of formulating C P Snow's dialectic in the Indian context today. (Ramesh 2010, 15)

While appreciating environmental concerns, Ramesh would also make a difference within the environmentalist approach: 'Livelihood environmentalism as I would term it as opposed to lifestyle environmentalism of the privileged sections' (p. 16). In other words, environmentalism is also a class question, which invites serious attention. This empirical study of KNP seeks to analyse the issue, which has emerged as a centre stage of debate in recent years due to the growing conflicts between the State-driven conservationist model and the communities living in its vicinity.

In a rejoinder to Jairam Ramesh, Hiren Gohain, an eminent intellectual and activist on issues around peoples' entitlements of Assam, argues that there are indeed three cultures, not two, in Ramesh's formulations. And they are in 'opposition to each other: the corporate-driven campaign for economic development at any cost, the elitist concerns articulated by non-governmental organisations, and the desperate struggle of indigenous people who are under the threat of extinction' (Gohain 2010, 79). Gohain points out that Ramesh, through his proposition of a dialogue between two antagonistic cultures, introduces and legitimizes the hegemonic logic of development. Gohain also finds it problematic to accept Ramesh's proposition of equating development-generated employment with that of livelihood. Livelihood is a larger issue and it encompasses concerns beyond employment. Under the present hegemonic order, the balance that Ramesh proposed is bound to break down, Gohain argues. With empirical evidences from the North East, particularly with reference to the on-going struggles of the indigenous people in the region against the hydropower projects, Gohain suggests that policy structures and priorities of the Government of India (GoI) themselves are anti-people, and therefore, the balance explored by Ramesh is unachievable and unsustainable.

This debate provokes us to investigate the political economy of both paradigms, namely, developmentalism and environmentalism, to explore and expose the vested interests within them. The following section is a brief reflection on it.

DEVELOPMENTALISM AND ENVIRONMENTALISM

Developmentalism in the post-colonial context is an outcome of the State's obsession with a growth model aimed at overcoming the development deficits caused by colonial exploitation and appropriation. It was also necessitated by the new comparative parameters of political studies promoted mostly by American scholars who pushed categories such as political culture, political socialization and political development and so on. These categories equate the mobility of political culture, like democracy, to a higher level with that of the European-American experience of industrialization and technological innovations. A homogenous notion of development, devoid of the political economy of colonial exploitation and appropriation, emerged as the global consensus. The post-colonial states, particularly its intellectuals and policymakers, were trapped in this discourse. During anti-colonial movements, as was the case with India, a development model different from the colonial patriarchs was perceived, debated and planned, taking into account the concerns of the larger needs of the new nation. Under constraints of resources on the one hand, and growing expectations of the masses on the other, the state emerged as the real driving force of development. There were constitutional requirements to be fulfilled, as mandated by Directive Principles of State Policies in India, which emphasized on welfare of the masses based on the larger values of equality and social justice. This required the State to undertake important missions like land reforms and distribution of various resources and services to fulfil those larger values. Ceiling Acts, for example, emerged as a legal instrument in this regard. However, the issues of development with distribution are embedded into the larger question of class and ideology. The political economy trapped into the interests of the feudal oligarchies and that of self-seeking national bourgeoisie does not allow a development model which pursues the issues of equity and social justice requiring the distribution of resources. In such a situation development gradually gets eroded into obsession with 'growth' devoid of social distribution. In the case of India, the State confronted with vested class interests spread over political elites, feudal landlords, bureaucracy and judiciary while undertaking the mission of social distribution. As a result, the larger politics of social distribution gradually became diluted. The State's endeavours of land reforms, bank nationalization, the abolition of privy councils and bringing the insurance sector under the public domain were not at all easy processes. Those were strongly and consistently resisted by the forces from within the State system and by the conservative and feudal forces from outside. Atul Kohli (1987) provides a detail account of the State's predicaments which emanated both from ideology and institutional vested interests in pursuing land reforms in India. The State's own obsession with development in such a context degrades to a level of 'developmentalism', a regimented development obsession. It gets trapped into the aggregated parameters of growth measured through GDP, GNP and so on. In the process it costs people basic freedoms and entitlements such as livelihoods, basic health requirements, and nutrition and so on. The larger political economy of these crises is embedded into the issue of ecology. How the State plans to appropriate and utilize the resources around land, water, forest, mines, oil, natural gas and so on finally determines the plight of the common masses under State-driven developmentalism. On the State's part, there are other compulsions too, the issues of territorial security, which, in turn, are linked to the concerns of national security. In such a context developmentalism also gets trapped into national security. Global imperial designs make it more challenging and problematic. The State, in such a situation, steps in the ruthless pursuit of development, which causes further harms to the greater ecology, rivers, forests, biodiversity and so on bringing to the forefront the issues of global warming, erosion, unpredictable weather fluctuations and so on. In other words, developmentalism pushes one to a state of anxiety and uncertainty regarding the sustainability of the greater ecology. How do we come out of it? The most appropriate approach would be to dismantle the growth obsessive model and transform development into a process of peoples' entitlement. This requires linking peoples' livelihoods, basic health and nutrition issues to issues of ecological conservation. It would have facilitated an organic link between ecology and the larger human as well as non-human animal communities. But such an approach is possible only in an environment of social equality, an environment of a greater share of resources by the larger population who live in the margins. A growth model, steered by the State, which has already created enormous inequality, and wherein the State itself is trapped in the vested interests of the forces who appropriate profits over inequality, feudal lords, national bourgeoisies, political elites and the bureaucracy, will not allow the sharing of resources by the larger majority. In the macro-global political economy, all these forces are integrated to global monopoly capital and its institutional pillars such as the World Bank,

International Monetary Fund and other international financial and commercial institutions. How does such a growth and inequality obsessive national and global political economy perceive, plan and execute the model of conservation of environment and ecology? One has to be very clear that the basic objective of such a model of preservation is not to upset the existing pattern of resource distribution. Under such a model, therefore, 'environmentalism' also emerges as an obsession which will be devoid of concerns for the communities in the margin. Rather, in the long run, it emerges as a regimented model of preserving forests and wildlife, even at the cost of human habitations, livelihoods and their access to basic services of health and nutrition. Such a model of 'environmentalism' does not have the scope of questioning the very vested interests who are responsible for ruining the ecology. Therefore, the 'environmentalism' of this kind is a necessary product of developmentalism and not an alternative to it. Enactment of the Wildlife Protection Act, 1972, and the Forest Conservation Act, 1980, despite having valued stated objectives, cannot be an alternative to State-driven developmentalism. The growing conflict between environmentalism and that of the concerns of human habitations in and around the forest and sanctuaries and so on is a product of the fundamental follies in this larger political economy. The Forest Rights Act, 2006, was an attempt to resolve this conflict. However, the developmentalist State that seeks to pursue environmentalism in a ruthless manner refuses to accept this Act as the instrument of dialogue and reconciliation between the conservation of wildlife and the forest and that of human habitations and their concerns of livelihoods living in the vicinity of the forests and the sanctuaries. The on-going conflicts in Kazringa are testimony of the unresolved anxiety between the regime of conservation and that of human habitations.

The following sections are devoted to understanding this anxiety by examining two significant issues through which Kaziranga became an epicentre of intense debate on conservation. The first one is the Gauhati High Court verdict on KNP in October 2015 (Gauhati High Court 2015) and the subsequent eviction drives undertaken by the Government of Assam in September 2016. The eviction led to the direct confrontation between the State police and that of the local habitants, resulting in the killing of two persons in police firing. It also surfaced an intense debate around the national identity of the people in the vicinity of the park. The conflict and the confrontations unfolded larger issues concerning the faultiness in the political economy of con servation in Kaziranga.

The second one is the BBC documentary on Kaziranga titled 'Our World: Killing for Conservation' which was telecast on 11 February 2017. The documentary heightened the debate on the conservation model in the national park. The basic argument of the documentary is that in KNP, the forest guards have been granted extrajudicial power with immunity and the guards have indulged in killing suspected poachers to protect one-horned rhinos. It argues that the number of people killed in the park is higher than the number of rhinos being killed. The documentary provoked widespread controversies, forcing the BBC to stop the circulation of the documentary. Subsequently, the broadcasting company came under severe scrutiny and faced a 5-year ban on documenting/filming tiger reserves in the country. Ironically, both the government and conservationists objected to misrepresentation of the facts on Kaziranga in the documentary, but the local communities came out in support of this bold documentation. While the BBC refrained from broadcasting the documentary again, however, the report prepared by Justin Rowlatt, its South Asia correspondent, titled 'Kaziranga: The park that shoots people to protect rhinos', which first appeared on the BBC news website on 10 February 2017, is still available to read. It was also Justin Rowlatt who prepared the controversial documentary.

KAZIRANGA VERDICT AND THE BRITISH BROADCASTING CORPORATION DOCUMENTARY: CONSERVATIONISM VERSUS HUMAN ENTITLEMENTS

Regarding the Gauhati High Court verdict on KNP and the evictions, Fanari and Doley (2018) observe:

> The question that arises is, whether the warped issue of eviction is actually linked to the danger of poaching, or is it related to an ever-expanding lexicon of neo-conservation policies that always find a reason to dispossess the most marginalised? The policies of Kaziranga National

Park, that plans to double its own territory in the name of additions and corridors, continuously feed the need of displacement, exacerbating into an environment of conflict.

The Gauhati High Court delivered a combined judgement and an order on 9 October 2015 in two public interest litigations (PILs) and two writ petitions on KNP. Whereas the PILs were concerned with the illegal poaching of rhinoceros and killings of wild animals in the park that required evictions of human habitations in and around the park, the two writ petitions were concerned with restraining evictions. The illegal poaching of rhinos in the park has been in the media for quite a long time, and it has been a widely contested political issue in the State as well. In 2014, on the eve of general elections, the issue of poaching the rhinoceros became a contention among competitive political forces. BJP's Prime Ministerial candidate Narendra Modi alleged the Congress of indulging in the killing of rhinos with the objective of clearing jungles and resettling illegal Bangladeshis there. The Congress regime in Assam became a target from different quarters for its inability to stop the killings of the rhinos in Kaziranga. The park emerged as a determining political dynamic both in the 2014 general elections and in the 2016 State assembly elections.

The Gauhati High Court *suo moto* registered a PIL (66/2012) 'to inquire into the news report regarding illegal poaching and killing of wild animals in the KNP' (Gauhati High Court 2015, 6). The *suo moto* registration was provoked by reports of killings of rhinos and wild animals in three leading news dailies, *The Telegraph*, *The Indian Express* and *The Hindu* in September 2012 (Gauhati High Court 2015, 6). Along with the *suo moto* registration, the High Court also admitted another PIL (67/2012) filed by Mrinal Saikia, currently the BJP MLA of the Khumtai constituency, which, apart from petitioning to enquire into the killings of rhinos and wild animals, sought 'an additional relief of removal of human habitation and encroachment in the animal corridors in and around the KNP' (Gauhati High Court 2015, 6). The writ petitions [WP(C) 648/2013 and 4860/2013] were concerned with protecting human habitations and ensuring measures against any drive of evictions without compliance to the provisions of Forest Rights Act of 2006, as well as past decisions of successive governments in settling the habitations with relevant procedures and sanctions. The writ petitions also offered certain models of co-habitation between human and wildlife, which, however, did not draw attention in the final judgement. There were two intervening applications (IAs) (IA 1261/2015 and 1262/2015) filed by the applicants to be impleaded in PIL 66/2012. The IAs asserted that the contested habitations are indeed revenue villages with habitants holding *pattas* and therefore cannot be evicted. The verdict delivered on 9 October 2015 rejected in entirety both the writ petitions and the IAs with the following understanding on part of the court:

> The individual claims for a handful of persons are in conflict with the public and national interest. There have been persistent and repeated reports of poaching of rhinoceros, elephants and other wild animals. It is irresistible inference that the habitants in KKP area would fall in suspect group and they would be well-acquainted with the areas and animal movements, therefore they would alone be in a position to do poaching successfully or abet poaching by others. The concept of national park in the Wildlife Act contemplates that there should be no human habitation. (Gauhati High Court 2015, 34)

In its judgement and the order, the court invoked the Directive Principles of State Policy (Article 48A) and the Fundamental Duties of Citizens [Article 51A(g)] enumerated in the Constitution of India, concerning the responsibility of the State towards protecting the environment and wildlife and the responsibility of the citizens in this regard (Gauhati High Court 2015, 34–35).

The court, from the very beginning of the hearing, was seriously concerned about illegal poaching and kept directing the appropriate authority from time to time to stop the killings of rhinos at any cost. In its order dated 4 March 2014, the court, while directing the director of Kaziranga National Park 'to submit the detail report on or before the next date of hearing suggesting therein the effective and remedial steps for implementation to curb poaching of "rhinos" in the Kaziranga National Park', said:

> We express our serious concern about the incidences of poaching in Kaziranga National Park which have recently taken place and are

taking place from time to time, we view it seriously. At any cost, in our view, the same must be stopped at the earliest to save the nature's most priceless and precious endangered species 'Rhino'. Indeed, it is our duty to preserve this God's gift to this world at any cost. (Gauhati High Court 2015, 8)

A critical reading of the judgement and the order reveals that the court got trapped into one dimensionality due to its overriding concern over the illegal poaching of rhinos in KNP. The genuine concern of the court is evident from the fact that the court *suo moto* registered the PIL. However, this one dimensionality of the concern, as evident from the judgement and the order, forced the court to prioritize the Acts concerning the protection of wildlife and the conservation of forests over the Forest Rights Act that provides the entitlements of the forest dwellers. The possibility of co-habitation of the wildlife and the human being was completely ruled out in the process. The legal technicalities received more priority over substantive issues. As a result, the court legitimized the State's language regarding the protection of wildlife and the conversation of forests. The court had the opportunity of balancing between wildlife protection and the protection of human habitation, as the Forest Rights Act, 2006, was already available for them to lean on. When we argue that the court indeed validated the State's language, we draw the evidence from the fact that the court relied on the reports of State officials alone—either the director of the Kaziranga or the high-powered committee—in arriving at the conclusions over its (court's) concerns.

A chronological reading of the judgement, which passed through a series of hearings and orders, will be relevant in understanding the one dimensionality in the judgement and the order.

In one of its orders dated 4 March 2014, granting 2 months of time, the chief justice of Gauhati High Court issued directions to the director of KNP 'to submit a detailed report about the geographical features, the flora and fauna, the animal life, the contributory reasons, which is aiding the poaching and illegal activities and also to give long-term solutions to remedy the ills affecting the Park' (Gauhati High Court 2015, 7). The director in a 402-page-long report documented the multidimensional issues associated with the killing of rhinoceros in the KNP. He stated:

The factors identified as threat to the survival of the rhinos, other than poaching, are loss and fragmentation of habitat, lack to technology and strategic advantage over poachers, certain lacuna in policy and law and their implementation, challenges of growth and development on the fringes of the park and possible impacts of climate change and climate variations. The approach to mitigate the threats and ensure long term survival of Kaziranga is multi pronged and multi disciplinary with a series of immediate, short term, medium term and long term measures to be undertaken. Some of the suggested measures include erosion control, habitat improvement, extension of habitat, corridors retrofitting, upscalling of anti poaching infrastructure, security and surveillance in and around the Park, adopting a landscape based approach and constitution of a landscape authority for conservation and development of the areas, adopting a green growth approach for development in th landscape, adopting better management strategies such as organizational restructuring, increased staff strength, staff welfare and creating some key and necessary infrastructure, adopting better policies and strengthening further the legal provisions, and above all creating several secure habitats outside Kaziranga for the rhinos. (Gauhati High Court 2015, 9)

The director further noted:

The actual implementation of the recommendations would require a series of ground surveys, in depth study, execution of Proof of Concepts, preparation of DPRs and Technical Feasibility Reports. The implementation would largely depend upon how strong is the institutional framework, availability of funds, support of the stakeholders, especially the local stakeholders, and the monitoring and feedback mechanisms put in place. (Gauhati High Court 2015, 9)

As is evident from the director's report, the issue of poaching cannot be reduced to one or another factor. It also cannot be reduced to a nexus of the local people with the poachers. There are larger issues, which as the director suggested in his report require ground surveys and validation and the execution of existing concepts and impression surrounding illegal poaching in KNP.

In the court's final judgement and order dated 9 October 2015, all these issues did not figure at all. It was reduced to invasion by the encroachers, and the local inhabitants were put into the shadow of suspected facilitators of poaching of rhinos in KNP.

A high-powered committee was constituted by the court, and the Committee was

> told to do the counting of residences in the Kaziranga National Park area, which would include the first Addition to sixth Addition, and also to survey the population in the residential buildings, huts, etc. The committee shall also take biometrics of the people residing in the area and submit the report by 26th June, 2015. (Gauhati High Court 2015, 11)

This high-powered Committee constituted by the court was not an independent committee. It was composed of the commissioner (Home), Government of Assam; revenue secretary, Government of Assam; inspector-general of Police (border), Assam; director (NE-II), ministry of Home Affairs; and inspector-general (Forest), National Tiger Conservation Authority regional office (Gauhati High Court 2015, 10). The court, which heard *suo moto* the PIL, and the two writ petitions that contested the concerns of the court PIL, could have appointed a committee that had an independent standing.

This committee visited the additions to KNP, the core national park areas and the vicinity and interacted with the people. The committee primarily investigated the nature of habitation, probable duration of stay, the pattern of houses, land entitlements and so on and directed the deputy commissioners of the three districts that KNP falls in and other appropriate authorities to document 'encroachers/settlers on the government land in the vicinity of Kaziranga National Park'. There is a fundamental difference between the report submitted by the director, KNP, and the approach adopted by the high-powered committee. While the Director approached the problem from a wide range of issues, including lacunae in the existing laws and lapses in security and so on, the committee was asked only to document encroachment and illegal settlement near the national park. The committee, while doing so, gave its abstract observations without a comprehensive enquiry. In case of the second addition to the KNP, the committee report suggests:

The Committee observed that the general impression after the field visit, in the 2nd Addition areas, was that most of the constructions were new dating back from last one to ten years and temporary and semi permanent in nature, which has been erected with an apparent intention of bargaining for land elsewhere. (Gauhati High Court 2015, 12)

In case of the sixth addition, the Committee observes:

In the 6th Addition, the sami-permanent, make-shift bamboo structures called *khutis* were observed to have been put up recently. It could be sensed on talking to the encroachers that many of them had mischievously been planted by some vested interests. (Gauhati High Court 2015, 13)

Are not these very casual statements? Have the entitlement documents been examined carefully to arrive at such conclusions? In case of Banderdubi and Deuchur, the two most contentious habitations in Kaziranga, the Committee informed that 'a detailed in-depth survey of individuals/families occupying Government land along with land status report is to be prepared by the concerned DC/SDO (Civil) and it should be provided to police within one month for taking further action' (Gauhati High Court 2015, 12).

Banderdubi Village and Deuchur Chang Village, which are outside the additions to the KNP, have become key battlegrounds of contestations after the High Court verdict. The counsel for the *suo moto* PIL asserted that in the Banderdubi Village, 183 families lived encroachers, and in Deuchur Chang Village, 122 families lived as encroachers; thus, 305 families lived as encroachers. Curiously though, the said families had received building materials under Indira Awas Yojana, a government scheme for building houses. It was also said that LP schools, *madrassas, Iddgah* and *masjids* were constructed in the villages. Arguments were also made that the government encouraged encroachments and facilitated their permanent settlement. Many residents of these villages, as reported by independent reporters, settled much before Kaziranga was declared a national park. The residents of the villagers are also not illegal migrants or 'Bangladeshis'. The villages have a composite demographic character, and they are not only East Bengal-origin Muslims but also of different indigenous communities of Assam. Indeed, many Muslim families settled in those villages much before the indigenous Assamese people settled there. Banderdubi is a very old village. The government constructed a *pucca* masjid and a *Naamghar* in 1951. The first primary school was established in 1960, which was provincialized in 1966. There are 1,735 *bighas* of government land in the village, and after a survey, in 1963, Banderdubi was recognized as a village in 1963 by the revenue department of the Government of Assam (Dutta 2016, 61). However, these issues were not comprehensively surveyed by the authorities appointed by the court. These villagers were simply dubbed as encroachers, and in its order dated 15 July 2015, the court directed: 'In so far as the Bandarubi and Deuchur Chang villages are concerned, the Deputy Commissioner, Nagaon shall evict the encroachment of Government land from the said two villages on or before 12-08-2015, if necessary with effective police assistance'. (Gauhati High Court 2015, 14)

The verdict cited government data, information and the report to substantiate its concerns over the illegal poaching of rhinoceros and killings of wild animals in Kaziranga. The counsel on behalf of the PIL, the *suo moto* one, also argued elaborately on the provisions of the Wildlife (Protection) Act, 1972, and the Forest Conservation Act, 1980, as well as referred to relevant verdicts by the Supreme Court that substantiate the concerns of the *suo moto* PIL. The Forest Rights Act, 2006, did not figure much. The dominant popular perception that poaching is an act of illegal migrants and that the communities living around the park are illegal encroachers almost was validated through the verdict. One can reasonably argue that the case was fought between two unequal parties. On the one hand there were the court, which registered the *suo moto* PIL, and the government officials to invoke the court's concerns on encroachments and, on the other hand, there were the alleged 'encroachers', who were already under the imminent threat of eviction.

The writ petitioners came up with internationally recognized models of co-existence between animal and human habitations. The court could have examined these models through an independent committee. It could have also directed a body to experiment the models for a certain period before ordering for eviction. The court, however, did not consider these steps to be appropriate and relevant and ordered for eviction. Therefore, the verdict, rather than bringing a resolution, legitimized the State's coercion. Not only that, the verdict also helped the dominant forces to play the communal card.

It is pertinent to ask an important question here: who came first, the proposal for expansion of KNP through new additions to the park or the habitations in the contested additions? It is in this context that a report published in *The Wire* titled 'As Kaziranga Expands, the Fate of Grazing Communities Hangs in the Balance' (Fanari and Doley 2018) is worth mentioning. Fanari and Doley traced the history of habitation in the addition to understanding the conflict between wildlife in Kaziranga and the local community. The contested territories were used by cattle-rearing families prior to Independence. The government accorded permission for that. The conflict became visible in the mid-1980s and since, 'when Kaziranga decided to expand its boundaries to the northern bank of the Brahmaputra river' (Fanari and Doley 2018). But the local people reported that there were rumours of expansion of Kaziranga since the early 1970s, just after the enactment of the Wildlife Protection Act, 1972.

> The notification to include the north bank of Brahmaputra under the KNP came out only in 1986, and it comprised the sand bar islands (*chapori*) and the banks, the mobile stretch of land that gets repeatedly reshaped by the endless movement of the river. These fertile green areas represent an integral part of the rural economy for grazers, farmers and fishing communities, and are considered vital for the survival of more than 10,000 families. (Fanari and Doley 2018)

The local communities filed a petition in Gauhati High Court and challenged the decision of inclusion of the areas into the KNP in 1994. The court took more than a decade to decide the fate of the petition. After examining the claims and counterclaims on the issue, the court finally announced its verdict on 22 November 2001 and advised a state of hold with the direction to 'determine the rights of occupants (petitioners) in the notified area and till such determination is made the authorities were directed not to disturb the possession of such lands'

(Fanari and Doley 2018). When the matter was in court, the government issued a notification in 1999 and declared an area of 37,600 hectares under the sixth addition. After that, violence and harassment escalated, and the grazers filed another petition in Gauhati High Court in 2006. The court gave its verdict in 2013 and declared that 'no illegality has been committed in proposing to evict the encroachers of forest land' (Fanari and Doley 2018).

Amid these developments, in 2012, the Gauhati High Court registered the *suo moto* PIL on the issue of the poaching of one-horned rhinos and killings of wild animals in Kaziranga. The verdict delivered on 9 October 2015 categorically stated the following:

> Keeping in view the larger interests of the public and the Constitution mandates, the claim of the petitioners in WP(C) 4860/2013 is held to be untenable and accordingly the writ petition is dismissed. Similarly the claim of the applicants in IA 1261/2015 and 1262/2015 for the reasons stated above is dismissed. The claim of the petitioners in WP(C) 648/2013 is rejected. The Deputy Commissioners of Golaghat, Sonitpur and Nagaon are directed to take expeditious steps to evict the inhabitants in the second, third, fifth and as well the six additions of the Kaziranga National Park, including Deurchur Chang, Banderdubi and Palkhowa, within one month. (Gauhati High Court 2015, 36–37)

The High Court verdict drew national attention when the eviction drive was undertaken by the Government of Assam in September 2016 as per court order; it received strong resistance from local inhabitants. It is important to point out that the eviction was selective, it did not cover the habitations in the second, third, fifth and sixth additions of KNP but the villages of Deurchur Chang, Banderdubi and Palkhowa. Banderdubi was the high spot in the eviction drive (Dutta 2016, 62). The confrontation led to police firing against a peaceful demonstration under the banner of Krishak Mukti Sangram Samiti (KMSS), Assam, and killed two persons on 19 September 2016. The opinion of the state was also polarized, with the elite sections in the greater society dubbing the protestors as illegal migrants. The polarization was so high that there was not enough scope to know the identity of the protestors. The government was praised for its bold decision, and the government justified the eviction drive by referring to the court order.

The firing on 19 September 2016 brought several other issues into focus. First of all, it only exposed the hollowness of elitist conservationism. However, it cannot entirely be rejected as elitist conservationism, because the whole issue of poaching of rhinos provoked huge condemnation too. Here lies the question of media trial as well. The local media reported that there have been encroachments in and around Kaziranga and that the encroachers are illegal migrants, mostly Bangladeshis. Therefore, along with the conservationists, nationalist organizations, such as All Assam Students Union (AASU), not only supported the eviction drive but also 'voted for the BJP on the plank of eviction of Bangladeshi settlers' (Kashyap 2016). Using all coercive means, including heavy equipment like bulldozers, the eviction team removed 331 houses and cleared over 2,400 *bighas* of land. There was resistance against the move in Banderdubi Village on 19 September 2016 under the banner KMSS. The police fired on the protestors which led to the killing of two persons.

There are a number of controversies on the identity of the villagers and their rights over the settlements.

> Some groups have debated claims that the encroachers had rights over the land. The court order, however, states that Deuchur-chung was notified as a reserved forest in 1916, Banderdubi is not only social forestry land but also a tiger resort and animal corridor, and Palkhowa too is forest land. (Kashyap 2016)

But there are counter-narratives to it. Fanari and Doley argue,

> The violation perpetuated in the name of these additions, today considered under Kaziranga by the official documents, is questionable. First, its own notification, as observed above, has ignored the important judgment of 2002 and indiscriminately encroached upon the revenue land of people. Second, after Kaziranga was declared a Tiger Reserve in 2007, the sixth addition was categorised under the buffer area, a land territory 'which aims at promoting co-existence between wildlife and human activity with due recognition of the livelihood, developmental, social and cultural rights of the local people'. Moreover, according to the Forest Rights Act, 2006, land tenure and customary rights should

be recognised to all the Scheduled tribes and forest dwellers traditionally inhabiting these lands. (2018)

The question finally raised by Fanari and Doley is the following.

The question that arises is, whether the warped issue of eviction is actually linked to the danger of poaching, or is it related to an ever-expanding lexicon of neo-conservation policies that always find a reason to dispossess the most marginalised? The policies of Kaziranga National Park, that plans to double its own territory in the name of additions and corridors, continuously feed the need of displacement, exacerbating into an environment of conflict. (2018)

BRITISH BROADCASTING CORPORATION DOCUMENTARY ON KAZIRANGA: THE CONTESTATIONS

Before the controversy around evictions in the vicinity of KNP in September 2016 faded away, the BBC created a storm by telecasting a documentary on KNP on 11 February 2017 titled *Our World: Killing for Conservation*. Prepared by BBC South Asia correspondent Justin Rowlatt, the BBC also published a detailed account on Kaziranga prepared by the same correspondent in its website just one day ahead of broadcasting the documentary, that is, on 10 February 2017, titled 'Kaziranga: The park that shoots people to protect rhinos'. While the documentary has now been banned, the original article as well as the radio version of the documentary is still available (Mazoomdaar 2017). The documentary is alleged to have done 'irreparable damage ... to India's reputation', and therefore, the BBC has been banned for 5 years in terms of filming national parks and sanctuaries in India (Mazoomdaar 2017). Just after the broadcasting of the documentary, the National Tiger Conservation Authority (NCTA) issued a show cause notice to BBC for grossly erroneous reporting and recommended 'the black-listing of the BBC's South Asia correspondent Justin Rowlatt for a documentary that highlighted the government's 'ruthless anti-poaching strategy' for Kaziranga tigerreserve in Assam' (Mazoomdaar 2017). The NTCA, in its memorandum dated 27 February, directed the chief wildlife wardens of all tiger range states and the field directors of tiger reserves not to grant permission for filming to the BBC for 5 years. The MoEF extended the ban to all national parks and sanctuaries through its order dated 10 April 2017 (Mazoomdaar 2017). It was alleged that the documentary deviated from the original script submitted to the MoEF, GOI, and the NTCA, and 'projected a negative, malicious and sensational portrayal of India's conservation success story at Kaziranga Tiger Reserve' (Mazoomdaar 2017).

The controversy related to the BBC documentary lies on the contention that forest guards have been given almost impunity for shooting a suspected poacher by the Government of Assam under Section 197(2) of Code of Criminal Procedure (CrPC), 1973, which reads,

> Only if it is held by an Executive Magistrate through an enquiry that use of firearms have been unnecessary, unwarranted and excessive and such a report has been examined and accepted by the Government, then alone any proceeding including institution of a criminal case of any nature or affecting an arrest can be initiated by police. (Mazoomdaar 2017)

The BBC documentary reveals that in 11 years, before this immunity was provided to the forest guards, that is, from 2000 to 2011, 17 poachers were shot dead inside Kaziranga, while 68 rhinos were killed. However, after impunity was provided to the forest guards, between 2011 and 2016 alone, 59 poachers were killed while 103 rhinos were poached.

The documentary and the detailed reporting by Justin Rowlatt reveal the coercive approach of conservation that creates a sort of violent relationship between the park and its neighbourhood. The State's regimented approach to conservation is revealed through this relationship, which was also evident in the Gauhati High Court verdict of September 2015.

Justin Rowlatt explores and exposes certain kinds of narratives and relationships in the conservation discourse and culture of India. One dominant narrative is nationalism. Conservation is also about how we perceive nationalism, where tigers and wild animals are projected as the pride of the nation and where the communities near conservation centres become perpetrators/infiltrators/encroachers and so on. In the Assamese nationalist discourse, Kaziranga has appeared as one of the reference points.

The public discourse, directed by the sense and sensibilities of Assamese nationalists, has over the years pushed the KNP into a space whose management is beyond public criticism. The desire to preserve the KNP, well pronounced in Assamese public life, is not essentially driven by a sense of the recovery of a natural space but more specifically its embodied cultural value. This cultural value is further reinforced by the fact that, unlike in the nineteenth century, the Brahmaputra Valley has lost its importance as an undisturbed natural space. It is because of both these reasons that the protection of prized species became an important agenda in Assamese public imagination (Saikia 2011, 13).

The second dominant narrative is tourism, particularly foreign tourists. Kaziranga hosts around 170,000 tourists annually. Conservation centres are also the showcases of the nation to outsiders. People living in the vicinity, who are poor, malnourished, illiterate and not so sophisticated, may put the nation in a bad light to outsiders. With such strong perceptions in the conservation culture, the nation builders create an unbreakable boundary between the conservation centres and the communities around them. The expansion of the conservation centres becomes important and necessary, even at the cost of neighbouring communities. Such a culture gives the State and other authorities much impunity, including impunity for shooting under suspicion. In other words, the impunity granted under Armed Forces (Special Powers) Act, 1958, for the protection of the nation from insurgency is expanded in kind to conservation authorities. In an interview with Justin Rowlatt, a forest guard said, 'The instruction is whenever you see the poachers or hunters, we should start our guns and hunt them.... Fully ordered to shoot them. Whenever you see the poachers or any people during night-time we are ordered to shoot them'. They have no fear of consequences. Using the language of the critics, Justin Rowlatt calls it 'extrajudicial executions'. The impunity granted to forest guards under the CrPC cannot theoretically be blanket impunity because, if proved guilty of using firearms without them being necessary, one can be booked for criminal offences. However, proving such an offence is very difficult, because it can be proved only if a magisterial enquiry takes place and if the enquiry comes up with a report stating 'firearms have been unnecessary, unwarranted and excessive and such a report has been examined and accepted by the Government.' Therefore, Survival International, a London-based charity, has argued that 'the park is being run with utmost brutality ... there's no jury, there's no judge, there's no questioning. And the terrifying thing is that there are plans to roll (out) the shoot at sight policy across [the] whole India' (Rowlatt 2017).

The bigger issue that has emerged from the Kaziranga episode is that brutality operates in an environment of interdependent relationships between the park and the communities around. Where is the boundary and how is that boundary drawn and maintained in KNP? Is that boundary settled? Rowlatt mentions that 'There are no fences or signs marking the edge of the park, it just merges seamlessly into the surrounding countryside and fields'. Rowlatt documented the stories of a disabled boy Gaonburah and the school-going boy Akash Orang, who survived the firing by the forest guards and now live miserable lives. The incidents of this kind only expose the brutalities committed by the forest guards in the undemarcated boundaries of the park.

Human rights activists argue that this brutality will be of no help. Justin Rowlatt quotes Pranab Doley, a tribal rights campaigner, who asserts that 'the park is in collision with the local people'. And he firmly believes: 'Without the people taking care of the forest, no forest department will be able to protect Kaziranga. It's the human shield which is protecting Kaziranga' (Rowlatt 2017). Arupjyoti Saikia, a researcher on the forest and ecological history of Assam, argues that fault lines lie in the conservation discourse and its implications for KNP.

A conservation discourse which identifies people as the powerful enemy of nature is bound to invited unwelcome repercussion. Without taking the neighbourhood social milieu into account, conservation has a long way to go before it can achieve its goal—that the rural non-industrial world in Assam create mechanisms to ensure its means of livelihood, that is, the ecological landscape, is recognized. This will not only ensure adequate community participation but will also integrate local ecological understanding with macro-conservation science and hopefully hold a better future for the KNP and other protected areas of the valley (Saikia 2011, 13).

The Gauhati High Court verdict of 2015 could not appreciate these wider dimensionalities of challenges to the KNP and therefore the crisis in the park was reduced to a mere matter of illegal poaching. It also did not consider the challenges posed by polluting industries, such as stone quarries, oil refineries and parasitic rubber plantations in the Kaziranga-Karbi Anglong landscape (Gogoi 2015). Therefore, the verdict failed to bring any new insight to the on-going conflict between the State-driven culture of conservation and peoples' entitlements for life and livelihood.

REFERENCES

Chaubey, K. N. 2017. 'Turning the Tide in Forest Rights?' *Economic and Political Weekly* 52(1). Retrieved from https://www.epw.in/journal/2017/1/commentary/turning-tide-forest-rights.html

Dutta, T. N. 2016. 'Kajirangar Tinikhon Ucchedit Gaon [The Three Evicted Villages of Kaziranga]'. *Natun Padatik* (October), 60–63.

Fanari, E., and P. Doley. 2018. 'Kaziranga Expands, the Fate of Grazing Communities Hangs in the Balance'. *The Wire*, 26 February. Retrieved from https://thewire.in/environment/contested-boundaries-eviction-in-the-sixth-addition-of-kaziranga-national-park

Gauhati High Court. 2015. PIL (suo motu) 66/2012, 67/2012, and WP(C) 648/2013 and 4860/2013. Retrieved from http://ghconline.gov.in/Judgment/PIL662012.pdf

Gogoi, M. 2015. 'Kaziranga under Threat: Biodiversity Loss and Encroachment of Forest Land'. *Economic and Political Weekly* 50(28). Retrieved from https://www.epw.in/journal/2015/28/reports-states-web-exclusives/kaziranga-under-threat.html

Gohain, H. 2010. 'Livelihood Losses and National Gains'. *Economic and Political Weekly* 45(51). Retrieved from https://www.epw.in/journal/2010/51/discussion/livelihood-losses-and-national-gains.html

Kashyap, S. G. 2016. 'The Politics of Cleaning Up Kaziranga'. *The Indian Express*, September 27. Retrieved from https://indianexpress.com/article/india/india-news-india/kaziranga-eviction-drive-assam-elections-bjp-sonowal-government-politics-dead-3051774/

Kohli, A. 1987. *The State and Poverty in India: The Politics of Land Reforms*. Cambridge: Cambridge University Press.

Mazoomdaar, J. 2017. 'Kaziranga Film: BBC Banned for 5 Years from All National Parks, Sanctuaries'. *The Indian Express,* 15 April. Retrieved from https://indianexpress.com/article/india/kaziranga-film-bbc-banned-for-5-years-from-all-national-parks-sanctuaries-4613758/

Ramesh, J. 2010. 'The Two Cultures Revisited: The Environment-Development Debate in India'. *Economic and Political Weekly* 45(42). Retrieved from https://www.epw.in/journal/2010/42/commentary/two-cultures-revisited-environment-development-debate-india.html

Rowlatt, J. 2017. 'Kaziranga: The Park that Shoots People to Protect Rhinos'. *BBC News,* 10 February. Retrieved from https://www.bbc.com/news/world-south-asia-38909512

Saikia, A. 2011. 'Kaziranga National Park: History, Landscape and Conservation Practices'. *Economic and Political Weekly* 46(32). Retrieved from https://www.epw.in/journal/2011/32/states-columns/kaziranga-national-park-history-landscape-and-conservation-practices

UNESCO. 'Kaziranga National Park'. Retrieved from https://whc.unesco.org/en/list/337

Chapter 12

International Financial Institutions in India's North East
Pattern and Impact on People and Environment

Jiten Yumnam

The increased financing of various international financial institutions (IFIs) and development financial institutions in the recent past, such as the World Bank, the Asian Development Bank (ADB), Japan International Cooperation Agency (JICA), German Development Bank (DEG)/KfW of Germany in shaping the development discourse, have become a dominant feature across India's northeastern states. This discourse has intensified ever since India adopted a neoliberal development model and lately the aggressive pursuance of its Act East Policy, erstwhile christened the Look East Policy, to consolidate and expand its economic and political influence with Southeast Asian countries and beyond. The North East is at the crossroads of India's Act East Policy, China's One Belt One Road (OBOR) and Japan's Free and Open Asia-Pacific Strategy that also overlaps with other Asia-Pacific strategies of the USA, European Union, Russia and so on. India and Japan especially with US support have increasingly been synergizing their strategies to counter China's OBOR, which aims to control land, resources and strategic locations with economic and political domination in Asia.

The ADB, European Investment Bank (EIB), International Finance Corporation (IFC), Islamic Development Bank (IDB) and so on are some of the multilateral IFIs across India's northeastern states, comprising seven states with Sikkim (Organisation for Economic Co-operation and Development [OECD] 'Development Finance Institutions...'). Bilateral IFIs such as Agence Francais De Development (AFD) of France, the DEG/KfW of Germany, JICA and so on are extensively involved in India's North East, financing a range of development projects. These institutions mostly finance projects, primarily in infrastructure and connectivity, with a strong emphasis on the role of the private sector in financing and implement development projects mainly through equity investments, long-term loans and so on.

India's liberalization programme since the 1990s has led to significant investment from IFIs due to the structural reform agendas directed by IFIs as part of balance of payments to the economic crisis that afflicted India in 1991. In June 1991, India launched a comprehensive economic reform programme, with the World Bank financing of US$500 million under its structural adjustment programme (SAPs), and India vigorously pursued the privatization process and opened up its economy to international finance. Similarly, the ADB also initiated similar focus with a US$300 million Financial Sector Program Loan to India in 1992, infusing finance to the crippled banking sector while also financing significant wide-ranging reforms (Asian Development Bank 'ADB's Work in India'). The introduction of a new economic policy in 1991 also led to privatization and the opening up of international trade (*Quartz India* 2016). After becoming a member of the World Trade Organization (WTO) in 1995, India initiated rapid privatization in almost all sectors (Purohit 2017). The reforms introduced by the World Bank and ADB in the early 1990s paved the way for massive infusion of foreign capital, liberalization, deregulation and the extensive opening up of the economy to foreign capital, including from IFIs. The liberalization process encouraged foreign direct investment (FDI) by increasing the maximum limit on the share of foreign capital into joint ventures—from 40 to 51 per cent with 100 per cent foreign equity in priority sectors (Sharma 2017). Before 1991, foreign investment was negligible. However, by 31 March 2016, India received a total FDI of US$371 billion (Rao and Kadam 2016). India remains one of the largest recipients of loans from the World Bank and as of 31 December 2015, India's loans stand at US$104 billion (Mallapur 2016).

Since 1991, the regulatory environment for foreign investment has consistently been eased to make it investor friendly (Invest India 'Foreign Direct Investment'). The reform process is ongoing and IFIs continues to finance projects with in-built policy suggestions for reforms, such as in the power sector and urban governance and so on, including in NEI. The FDI policy of 28 August 2017 further relaxed FDI norms, allowing 100 per cent foreign investment including in sectors such as mining and exploration of petroleum and natural gas; this will lead to an increase in extractive industries across the North East.

Policies on the privatization of services and the changing of existing laws to foster greater privatization of services, such as the enactment of Public Private Partnership (PPP), are being pursued. India developed the PPP policy in 2011. A key intention of the introduction of Finance Act, 2017, is to curb the powers of the National Green Tribunal, established to monitor the violation of 'forest clearance' and 'environment clearances' in development projects (*The Live Mint* 2017). There is a process to weaken the Forest Rights Act (FRA) of 2006 and the Land Acquisition Act of 2013 (Mahaprashasta 2016).

INDIAN STATE AND INTERNATIONAL FINANCING INSTITUTIONS ACROSS THE NORTHEASTERN REGION

India's adoption of the Look East Policy and later the Act East policy with a focus on India's North East to connect India's neighbours and beyond in Asia is indeed part of the implementation of the India's neoliberal policies. The Government of India, while signing the Free Trade Agreement (FTA) with ASEAN countries at Ventianne in Laos in November 2004, and in subsequent agreements, referred to India's Northeast region as the gateway to Southeast Asia for trade and investment. The overt focus on regional connectivity, cross-border trade and commerce and to unlock the North East as defined in India's Act

East Policy requires setting up massive infrastructure, roads, railways, waterways, high-voltage transmission lines, the exploration of oil and gas, oil pipelines and so on; these require significant financing across the northeastern region. In line with India's extensive borrowings from IFIs for its major infrastructure projects across India, this financing gap will to be filled up with IFI financings, primarily as loans.

An agreement was indeed signed between the Governments of Japan and India to support India's Act East Policy during the 12th Indo-Japan annual summit on 3 August 2017 when Japanese Prime Minister Shinzo Abe visited India, which culminated in the formulation of the India-Japan Act East Forum. An agreement was also additionally signed at the bilateral summit to combine the aims of Japan's Free and Open Asia-Pacific Strategy and India's Act East Policy (Cyrill 2017). The India-Japan Coordination Forum for Development of the North East was also established in 2017 to execute infrastructure-building projects.

The Government of India is actively pursuing seeking financing from ADB and the World Bank to implement its key flagship projects such as smart cities. The Ministry of Urban Development, Government of India, even issued a guidance note to enable smart cities to borrow from multilateral development banks such as the ADB and World Bank for project execution in August 2016 (*The Hindu* 2016). Most of the new road infrastructures in the North East as part of fostering connectivity projects under India's Act East policy are under direct financing from the World Bank, ADB and JICA.

IFIs also framed their strategic plans to further facilitate India's pursuance of neoliberal policies. In the Country Partnership Strategy, 2013–2017, the ADB included special emphasis on the northeastern region as a strategic location to promote cross-border regional cooperation and as a gateway to Southeast Asia for trade and investment, which adheres to goals of India's Act East Policy. The ADB's Country Partnership Strategy (CPS), 2018–22, for India aims to support the government's goal of faster, inclusive and sustainable growth accompanied by rapid economic transformation and job creation. ADB's annual lending to India is proposed to be raised to a maximum of US$4 billion (Asian Development Bank 'India and ADB'). Earlier, the ADB's 2003

Country Strategic Plan for India accorded special emphasis on India's North East, and the plan outlined that the region will offer a strategic location to promote cross-border regional cooperation with neighbouring countries. ADB is also directly involved in preparing Vision 2020 for the northeastern region. The implementation of India's Look East and now Act East is associated with increased financing of large-scale projects in myriad sectors across the North East, which commenced with development of technical assistances (TAs). And indeed, India has been ADB's largest borrower for energy projects from 2007 to 2015, accounting for 25 per cent of ADB's total investments in energy projects in the Asia-Pacific region (Asian Development Bank 'India and ADB').

These IFI financings are also part of unlocking the region, implying that the region was kept locked for long by the government. The unlocking would mean not only opening up its borders but land and natural resources for exploitation and investment. The ADB indeed maintained that the northeastern region has unexploited natural resources and has stressed that the creation of its action plan would enhance the conditions for private sector-led growth and increase participation in global and regional markets (Asian Development Bank 2004). ADB is focusing on financing infrastructure and connectivity projects across the North East, focusing on roads, water and sanitation, agri-business, power sector reform and so on. The technical assistances (TA) of IFIs in sectoral financings and so on uniformly uphold the neoliberal framework of development propagated by the WTO. The ADB's TA for the North East power development project, prepared in 2004, outlined the development of locally available resources, including hydropower, natural gas and renewable energy sources. The TA also aimed to assist in institutional strengthening in the power sector to prioritize and create a favourable environment for private sector investments and participation (ADB Report 2004). And indeed, the creation of massive infrastructure is also associated with the simultaneous push for building more than 200 dams, extensive oil exploration and mining projects and plantations across northeastern region, with subsequent of relevant policies for such plans, such as the Manipur Hydro Policy 2012, the North East Hydrocarbon Vision, 2030 and so on. The formulation of the Northeast Hydrocarbon Vision 2030 in

January 2016 emphasized the creation of massive infrastructure for the exploration and marketing of oil and gas from the northeastern region. This reveals the correlation of infrastructure push and exploitative industries in the region.

ADB has agreed to fund a US$425-million multi-tranche SASEC Road Connectivity Investment Programme approved in 2014; it envisages to build extensive network of roads across India's North East to connect to border trading areas in the neighbouring countries (*The Telegraph* 2015). From 2007 to 2017, JICA provided India with soft loans worth US$23.36 billion for infrastructure projects. The World Bank focused on infrastructure projects across the North East, primarily on roads and high-voltage transmission and distribution (T&D) lines across the region. The World Bank Board on 24 June 2016 approved a US$470 million loan to support six states in the northeastern region to augment their transmission and distribution (T&D) networks (World Bank Press Release 2016). The World Bank on 12 June 2014 approved a US$107 million credit for Mizoram State Roads II—Regional Transport Connectivity Project to improve transport connectivity for the landlocked State of Mizoram and enhance Mizoram and other northeastern states' links with Bangladesh, as well as with Nepal, Bhutan and Myanmar (World Bank Press Release 2014). IFC, the investment arm of the World Bank Group, is planning to invest about US$6 billion through 2022 in several sustainable and renewable energy programmes in India (Foreign Direct Investment (FDI) Report 2018). During 2017–18, India received FDI from the USA to the tune of US$2.10 billion and US$1.61 billion from Japan, in addition to receiving aid from other countries such as Singapore, Mauritius and so on (*The Financial Express* 2015).

Japan is extensively involved in financing a range of development projects in the region but it is focused on infrastructure projects, primarily roads. From 2007 to 2017, JICA provided India with soft loans worth US$23.36 billion for infrastructure projects in transport, water, energy, agriculture and the forestry sectors, among others. In April 2017, the JICA signed an agreement with the union government in New Delhi to provide over 67 billion yen (US$610 million) for Phase I of the North East Road Network Connectivity Project. Phase 1 will see the enhancement of National Highway (NH-) 54 and NH-51 in Mizoram and Meghalaya. The improvement of NH-54 will enhance the connectivity of the Kaladan Multi-Modal Transport Corridor, which seeks to link India's northeastern states with the rest of India via Myanmar, by roads, inland water transport and so on (JICA Press Release 2018, April 2).

Transnational corporations, both foreign and India based, are the biggest beneficiaries of the aggressive introduction of neoliberal projects and FDIs in the North East. The massive financing of infrastructure projects by IFIs and the conditionalities imposed on such financings have enormously benefited corporate bodies, such as consultancy firms, suppliers and manufacturing companies from the countries of origin of support. And as such, there are concerns that much of the financing returns back to donors for consultancy services and procurement works, such as in the case of the French- and Japanese-funded Imphal water supply projects and the Manipur sericulture projects. Japanese consultancy firms benefited from the projects funded by JICA and the French company, Degremont, benefited from supply works in the case of the Imphal sewerage project, even if the project was a failure. The French mining giant, Lafarge, benefited from financing by the ADB and IFC together in the case of the Lafarge mining project in Meghalaya.

THE SITUATION OF INTERNATIONAL FINANCIAL INSTITUTION-FINANCED PROJECTS AND IMPACTS ACROSS THE NORTH EAST

Road Infrastructure Projects

A primary infrastructure project supported by development finance institutions (DFIs) is road projects as part of the South Asia Subregional Economic Cooperation to link countries in South and Southeast Asia. The World Bank, ADB and JICA complemented each other's initiatives in financing road projects implemented by multinational road-building companies and this involved the privatization of access to roads, such as Guwahati–Shillong road. The World Bank is directly involved in financing road projects in Mizoram while the ADB and JICA financed road projects all across northeastern states.

The World Bank on 12 June 2014 approved a US$107 million credit for the Mizoram State Roads II—Regional Transport Connectivity Project to improve transport connectivity for the landlocked State of Mizoram and enhance Mizoram and other northeastern states' road links with Bangladesh, as well as Nepal, Bhutan and Myanmar (World Bank Press Release 2014). The Mizoram state road project earlier financed by the World Bank from 2002 to 2009 and implemented by RBM Tantia (part of the RBM Road Builders of Malaysia), Baghareetha Private Ltd, CCAP Ltd and Termat Engineering and Infrastructure Private Ltd has also been met with controversy. Issues have included project delays, problems with compensation and the rehabilitation of affected communities (Yumnam and Wangkheirakpam 2006). The implementation of the road project is also marred with substantial delays and poor contract management and the failure to pay compensation to families of two employees who died in an accident in April 2016 (Goswami 2017).

Loan agreements between the Government of India and ADB were also signed for the Northeastern States Road Investment Program in July 2012 (tranche I) and in February 2014 for tranche II at a total cost of US$200 million (Loan Agreement 2014). The implementation of tranche II is in progress in the North East, while the roads projects from Tupul to Bishnupur and from Thoubal to Kasom Khullen in Manipur have been taken up (Loan Agreement 2014). On 31 March 2017, JICA signed an agreement with Government of India to provide 67,170 million yen (approximately ₹4,000 crores) ODA for the North East Road Network Connectivity Project (Phase I) (JICA Press Release 2017). JICA further signed an agreement with the Government of India in April 2018 to provide ODA loans of 38,666 million yen (approximately ₹2,500 crore) for the North East Road Network Connectivity Project (Phase 2) (JICA Press Release 2018, April 4).

Several communities affected by the ADB-financed Imphal ring road project in Manipur expressed objections to the road widening plan, given its multifaceted impacts and the lack of holistic impact assessments and consultations and consent of affected communities by the project proponents. The residents of Kongba Makha Nandeibam Leikai in Manipur in a meeting on the proposed eviction plan on

21 September 2014 resolved to oppose the project as the project implementation and land acquisition process failed to take their consent (Yumnam 2014). Villagers affected by the ADB-financed Imphal Moreh Road demand information provision and rehabilitation and resettlement acceptable to them.

IFI financing for infrastructure, primarily road projects in India's North East, evokes another dimension of conflict. The potential for intense conflict in the North East is visible when the Japanese efforts to fund infrastructure projects, primarily road projects in Arunachal Pradesh, are met with stern objections from China, which claims that Arunachal Pradesh is part of South Tibet. India and China has been in conflict over the control of Arunachal Pradesh, one of the states in India's North East. Indeed, a war between India and China broke out in 1962, over China's claim to Arunachal Pradesh (*North East Today* 2015). China also denunciated the joint statement issued between Japan and India in September 2017 to cooperate on infrastructure projects such as road connectivity and electricity in India's northeastern states (Apurva 2017).

IFIs Co-financing Lafarge Mining in Meghalaya

The ADB, EIB, IFC, the DEG and several other bilateral DFIs have co-financed the limestone mining operation in Meghalaya with the Lafarge Group of France and Cementos Molins of Spain. The Lafarge Surma Cement (LSC) Project, run by the French multinational company Lafarge, received a loan of US$45 million from the IFC in 2003. The violation of India's forest laws, the Forest Conservation Act, 1980, and the FRA, 2006, is evident in the case. In 2008, a confidential report by an ADB mission highlighted the lack of transparency in the purchase or lease of land which belonged to indigenous peoples (Bouissou 2010). In January 2014, the Khasi people affected by the IFC- and the ADB-funded limestone mining filed a complaint with the compliance advisor ombudsman (CAO), the IFC's accountability mechanism, saying that Lafarge has illegally infringed on their land without consent. They also complained that they have been denied justice and invited the CAO to investigate the violations by IFC. The

CAO found the complaint eligible for assessment and has initiated the investigation process (Bretton Woods Project 2014).

Water, Sanitation and Privatization

The water supply and sewerage projects are mostly financed by the DFIs; mostly JICA and AFD along with ADB in India's North East insisted on the privatization of services and increase in tied aid. JICA funded the Imphal Water Supply Augmentation Project (IWSP) in support of the Mapithel Dam. JICA's pre-feasibility study for IWSP suggested a policy change in the Manipur Water Supply Act, 1992 (Manipur Act No. 1 of 1993), that would privatize water supply services. This Act requires that the State Government of Manipur adopt a flat rate for their water supply service. This project financing will lead to the privatization of water supply and legitimize the violations and deprivation of people's livelihoods, due to submergence of their land by the Mapithel Dam.

In the water supply project for Guwahati in Assam funded by JICA, the Louis Burger International Inc, a US-based consultancy firm, was found to have bribed officials of the Assam government in order to win contracts. Directed by the Guwahati High Court, the Central Bureau of Investigation (CBI) of the Government of India is investigating the Louis Berger corruption case and is filing an FIR against unknown officials of the company. The technical support for the French-funded Imphal sewerage project in Manipur, under construction, was undertaken by a French company, Degremont a subsidiary of Suez (*The Sangai Express* 2015). This was due to the requirements of French aid, which ties the provision of ODA to the procurement of services by French technical and consultancy firms. The project also envisaged privatization of its service.

Energy Projects

The financing of Energy projects and related infrastructures is also one of the major focus points of the DFIs. The World Bank is currently financing high-voltage transmission and distribution lines across northeastern states. The JICA and KFW are funding the Tuirial

Hydroelectric Project in Mizoram and the Pare Hydroelectric Project in Arunachal Pradesh, respectively. The JICA had also financed the renovation of Umiam Stage IV in Meghalaya. The ADB is extensively engaged in the power sector reform, mainly towards privatization of energy provisions. In the experience of projects financed by JICA in India's North East, the 60-MW Tuirial Hydroelectric Project financed by JICA in Mizoram landed in wide controversy due to inadequate rehabilitation and resettlement. Project work stopped in 2004 with regard to problems with rehabilitation and resettlement. The Tuirial Crop Compensation Claimant Association complained of failure to provide compensation for crop loss in the land forcibly acquired. The project was also marred with inordinate delays and cost overruns, leading to high costs of power per unit. The financing of the 400-KV high-voltage T&D lines by the World Bank all across the northeastern states and the continued approval of the World Bank to finance these T&D networks will further facilitate the construction of more than 200 mega-dams by corporate bodies across the region with wide social and environmental implications. The Government of India sought financial assistance from the JICA in early 2018 to fund the 66-MW Loktak Downstream Hydroelectric Project, that envisaged utilizing waters discharged from the controversial hydropower project, the 105-MW Loktak Multipurpose Hydroelectric Project in Manipur. The Loktak Downstream Project will worsen communities' livelihood impact and unaccountability of the project proponents (Yumnam 2017).

ISSUES WITH INTERNATIONAL FINANCING INSTITUTIONS ACROSS INDIA'S NORTH EAST

1. *The non-recognition of indigenous peoples' rights:* A significant challenge in road projects financed by the ADB and JICA has been the lack of recognition of indigenous peoples' pattern of land ownership. There has been a failure to conduct detailed impact assessments with rightful participation of these communities. These assessments are extremely important as they help to determine the best possible measures for affected indigenous peoples' rehabilitation and resettlement. A clear illustration of these issues are seen in both the Heirok-Khudengthabi road project and the Imphal-to-Moreh Road, financed by the ADB. In both cases, the impact on the

livelihoods of indigenous communities due to road cutting in hills and forest areas, the failure to rightfully involve the affected communities in conducting impact assessments and failure to adopt a clear rehabilitation and resettlement policy acceptable to them are significant problems of these projects.

2. *Failure to implement the free, prior and informed consent:* The pursuance of infrastructure, extractive and energy projects financed by IFIs, such as the Lafarge Limestone mining in Meghalaya, the Pare Hydroelectric Project in Arunachal Pradesh, the Imphal Ring Road the Imphal Water Supply Project, etc., to be financed by the ADB, IFC, KFW JICA, etc., have severe limitations in rightful involving affecting communities, especially in taking their free, prior and informed consent of communities affected by these projects. The ongoing oil and gas exploration and drilling by Jubilant Energy Private Limited and Oil India Limited have failed to take the consent of communities in Manipur. Residents of the Kambiron, Sibilong and Oinamlong Villages as well as others from the Tamenglong District rejected the efforts of Asian Oilfield Services to seek No Objection Certificates for surveys without providing information. On 17 May 2017, villagers of Khaidem stopped the company, Asian Oilfield, from conducting surveys in their village due to lack of information and consultation.

3. *Roads and natural resource extraction by corporate bodies:* The extensive financing of roads by bilateral and multilateral DFIs is clearly to pursue corporate interests towards expropriating the land and natural resources of indigenous peoples. Most of the roads financed by ADB, JICA and the World Bank are rich in natural resources or are geographical strategic areas for promoting trade and commerce for the private sector, as also propounded by ADB, JICA and so on. The Pare Hydroelectric Project with KfW financing in Arunachal Pradesh and the proposed 66-MW Loktak downstream envisaged for JICA financing in Manipur have already been met with wide opposition. ADB makes an explicit reference in its TAs for promoting infrastructure projects to enhance the private sector's role in tapping the unexplored natural resources from across India's North East. Oil companies such as the Jubilant Energy, Canoro, Oil India Limited, Asian Oilfields and so on are involved in both exploration and drilling.

4. *Environmental impacts:* Environmental impacts are a significant and growing concerns. Limestone mining by Lafarge in Meghalaya with ADB and IFC financing is afflicted with forest rights violations and the matter even reached the Supreme Court of India. One of the main complaints is the use of heavy explosive materials in blasting the hills for limestone. Due to blasting, cracks have appeared on the Earth, causing drinking water sources, spring water, to run dry in the Shella region of Meghalaya (Wahlang 2006). Private companies involved in the railway works in Tamenglong District have blatantly disregarded the devastating impact the project inflicted on the environment. These impacts have included the destruction of forest areas and the discharge of contaminated and chemical-laden liquid wastes in Ejei, Barak and Irang Rivers in Manipur. The railway works also violate the FRA, 2006.
5. *Impacts of privatization:* IFIs have been forcibly endorsing the privatization of services. The privatization of water in India often is afflicted with problems of increased water tariffs. The privatization of drinking water services in Nagpur in a PPP project financed by the World Bank is an example of a failed model. The tariff of water increased four times. Earlier, the Nagpur Municipal Council (NMC) signed a concession agreement with the Orange City Water Private Ltd (OCWL), a joint venture of Vishwaraj Environment Pvt Ltd and Veolia Water (India) Pvt Ltd. The privatization process neither brings water leakages down nor ensures the sufficient supply of water to the residents. There was a 328 per cent increase for domestic consumers after privatization—from ₹1.37 per unit in 2002 to ₹5.87 per unit in 2013. The privatization and corporatization of the power sector across the North East since financing by the ADB was met with wide objections. In Assam, the Assam State Power Workers Union, the Biswanath Chariali Division, staged a protest against the Assam government's move to privatize APDCL's 33/11-kV stations across the State on Friday. Earlier, the government invited tender for privatization of 47 such power stations. The Assam State Electricity Board (ASEB) Pensioners' Association also joined the protest (Islam and Biswanath 2018).
6. *Corruption:* Corruption is another major concern, primarily because of some of the controversial processes found in development projects implemented by the private sector. The JICA-financed

Guwahati city water supply project is marred with case of bribing officials of the Assam government by the Louis Burger International to win contracts, a company based in the USA. An investigation is still under way by the CBI, Government of India. The World Bank-funded road project in Mizoram was marred with corruption and favouritism to politicians of Mizoram when the contract for road building was awarded to Sunshine Overseas (Rajshekar 2015).

7. *Public private partnerships, the privatization agenda and concerns:* IFIs and private companies involved in road building, railway works and oil exploration and so on have failed to assume any responsibility for the violations of community rights, for not recognizing their rights over their land and resources, for failing to take their free, prior and informed consent and for violation of the existing social, environmental and human rights legislations. Mechanisms and policies to ensure the accountability of corporate bodies are still absent. These companies have also failed to assess, address and resolve social, environment and other impacts. The cumulative implementation of the policy prescription of IFIs and the increased role of the private sector in all the sectoral financings of the IFIs have led to increased privatization of services, such as water and power supply, which will inflict multifaceted impacts. Most PPPs that were financed, such as the build operate transfer projects and road projects with toll roads along Guwahati and Shillong, led to much inconvenience on people as they had to incur additional expenses to travel on the road. There is a limited regulatory framework to ensure that PPP operations focus on high-profit sectors such as roads, railways, ports and power services and so on. Charging user fees is more feasible in such projects.

The extensive sand and stone mining from the Ejei River by the ABCI company, involved in the construction of the ADB-financed road project from Bishenpur to Tupul, has led to massive soil erosion, receding water levels and the loss of fish habitat. The companies have failed to take responsibility for the destruction of the environment and the social impacts inflicted by these projects on indigenous peoples. Indeed, communities are compelled to resort to court of law and approach the ADB to address these violations. Communities affected by the ADB-financed road project

in Kasom Khullen in Ukhrul District, Manipur, challenged ADB's violations and impacts in the Manipur High Court, seeking redressal and justice for violations but to no avail (*The Sangai Express* 2014).
8. *Undermining international financing institutions' safeguards:* The non-application or the violation of safeguards of DFIs is also a major concern. Lafarge has failed to adhere to the ADB's policies on indigenous peoples, rehabilitation and resettlement and so on. Similarly, there are concerns with the non-application of ADB's safeguard policies, primarily on indigenous peoples and involuntary resettlement such as projects like the Imphal to Moreh road and the Wangjing to Khudengthabi road financed by ADB in Manipur. Policies to promote human rights to development are missing in most DFIs in their development project financings.
9. *Problems with implementation:* The JICA-financed Tuirial Hydroelectric Project in Mizoram is afflicted with undue delays, leading to cost overrun and the high cost of power units. Similarly, the World Bank-financed road project in Mizoram again is also afflicted with significant delays. The French-supported Imphal sewerage project is also delayed even after 15 years of project commencement, and the Government of Manipur has yet again set December 2018 as the timeline for the completion of the project. French companies, such as Degremont, received contracts to supply essential parts for this project even though it has remained a non-starter. The project is almost considered a failed one.

IFI FINANCING AND INTENSIFICATION OF CONFLICT SITUATION IN THE NORTH EAST

The increased infusion of financial capital has additionally complicated the armed conflict situations pervading across the Northeastern region with regard to the movement for self-determination with myriad and contesting demands. The advancement of the corporatization process in negating communities' rights and unaccountable forms of development processes have led to much resentment from the communities. The Indian State recourse is often militaristic in nature. The Government of India's militarization through the enactment of special legislations, such as Armed Forces Special Powers Act (AFSPA), 1958, introduced to counter the self-determination movement, is primarily considered central to ensure India's control and provision of security for key infrastructures that are essential for advancing India's commercial and political interest in the North East.

The militarization processes are further exacerbated by the aggressive push for large infrastructure projects and extractive industries, that is, mining, oil exploration and so on under India's Act East Policy. The Indian armed forces deployed for counter-insurgency operations in the North East to subdue myriad self-determination movement are also involved in protecting key infrastructures such as hydroelectric projects, mining sites and road projects financed by the ADB, World Bank, JICA and so on. More than 1,500 security forces from different paramilitary units are deployed for the protection of the Trans-Asian Railway works that are under construction in Manipur (*The Financial Express* 2018). The efforts for economic cooperation at the regional level also emphasized the suppression of voices of resistance in the pretext of counter-terrorism. For instance, the India and ASEAN Free Trade Agreement included explicit reference and focus to jointly fighting terrorism.

The militarization has led to extrajudicial executions, arbitrary killings, enforced disappearances, sexual harassment and so on with complete impunity conferred to Indian Army officials perpetuating such violations under the AFSPA, 1958. The APFSA, 1958, derogates fundamental rights, that is, right to life, right to justice remedy and so on, and has legitimized intense militarization of the Indian armed forces in Manipur and across the northeastern region. The Supreme Court of India continues to hear a Public Interest Litigation (PIL) seeking probe in the 1,528 cases of extrajudicial executions from 2000 to 2012 committed by the Indian security forces and Manipur police (*Times of India* 2017). The aggressive push for unsustainable development processes facilitated by the militarization process will intensify the pattern of conflict and human rights violations.

Community leaders striving for the defence of land and natural resource and rejecting the current unsustainable development models, such as dam building, oil exploration, mining and so on, are often branded as anti-development, anti-national, insurgents and so on, being subjected to human rights violations. Many are killed, jailed and tortured. Communities resisting oil exploration in Manipur are subjected to threats.

India's development cooperation with developed countries and the choice of financing of IFIs also involve efforts to serve its strategic, economic and political interests. India is increasingly aligned with Japan and the US and seeks investment from IFIs dominated or influenced by them, such as World Bank and the ADB, to counter China's effort for dominance in South and Southeast Asia. There is also increased military cooperation with countries such as Japan, the USA and Australia. India and Japan agreed to step up their defence cooperation in the Annual India-Japan Ministerial Defense Dialogue in September 2017, including on anti-submarine exercises and counter-terrorism measures (*Deccan Herald News Service* 2017). The USA, India and Japan conducted joint naval exercises in July 2017 to increase defence cooperation in the Indo-Pacific region as part of the trination Malabar exercises in the Bay of Bengal (George and Wu 2017).

RESPONSE TO THE INTERNATIONAL FINANCIAL INSTITUTIONS' INVOLVEMENT ACROSS INDIA'S NORTH EAST

The increased IFI investment and the focus on large-scale infrastructure projects for cross-border regional connectivity projects and in the process to expropriate land and natural resources across the region have been met with much resistance. The massive environment damages caused by unsustainable development projects financed by IFIs have led to protests by communities affected by such projects. There has been a series of protests by the Khasi people affected by the ADB- and the IFC-financed limestone mining project and they have even challenged the multiple violations by French mining giant Lafarge in the Supreme Court of India. The exclusion and arbitrary nature in decision-making processes and the potential for wide implications on agricultural land, forests, inhabited areas and other survival sources have compelled communities to reject the ADB-financed Imphal ring road project. The rejection of polices towards corporatization and the increased financialization of development are other major forms of resistance. The massive environment and social impacts unleashed by the ADB financed

Trans-Asian Highway led to protests and expressions of concern in Manipur. Communities in Mizoram protested land rights violations and the failure to adopt comprehensive rehabilitation and resettlement plans in the case of the JICA-financed Tuirial Dam Project and the World Bank-funded Road Project in the State. The proposed JICA financing plan for 66 MW of the Loktak Downstream Project and also the Imphal water supply project to draw water from Mapithel Dam in Manipur was also resented by communities who would have been affected by such projects. In Meghalaya, the state electricity board (MeSEB) employees' staff union raised their concerns with the initiatives to privatize this board (MSEB). In a memorandum submitted to the chairman by the MSEB for reviewing the 2003 Electricity Act, the union stated that previous experiences of dismantling state electricity boards in Assam, Orissa and Delhi and the privatization of electricity supply proved to be a total failure for both power distribution and revenue collection. The new Land Use Policy introduced in Manipur in 2014 had to be withdrawn due to strong community objection because of the policy's over-reliance on the commercialization of agriculture practices and undermining traditional agriculture. The neoliberal development model introduced by the Indian State along with its allies has increasingly been challenged both at the ideological level and at its implementation stage in projects across the region. Efforts to understand and reflect the implications on the social, environmental, economical, political and cultural aspects of the region have been explored and are captured in the increased resistance to the aggressive unsustainable development order across the region.

CONCLUSION

The involvement of IFIs in India's North East is severely challenged with failure to respect indigenous peoples' rights over their land and resources and their rightful participation in decision-making, affecting their land, lives and future. The increased opposition to dam building in Manipur, to oil exploration and mining and so on in Manipur and Meghalaya are simply testament of the failure to respect the rights of communities in Manipur and across the North East.

IFIs' overt focus on infrastructure and connectivity projects and overwhelming emphasis on corporate roles and the privatization of the development process in India's Act East Policy, complemented by IFIs' financing, will only lead to the plunder of natural resources, the privatization of services and subsequent impoverishment of communities. Such a focus leads to an uncontrolled plunder of natural resources in the region and the privatization of services, adversely affecting the physical and spiritual survival of indigenous peoples. Rather than freeing up resources for social sector spending, governments entering into IFI-designed public–private partnerships confront mounting debt across the North East.

The failure to involve indigenous peoples affected by the dominant development model introduced in the North East and the militaristic approach adopted in pursuing such a development model by states, corporate bodies and IFIs and the exclusion and non-recognition of community rights will only fuel multilayered conflict. The State's policies of subjugation, the militarization of communities and suppression of resistance while facilitating the corporate plunder of resources will strengthen their resistance. The undemocratic and exclusionary development-making process, the reliance on security forces for the protection of infrastructure of corporate bodies and other financiers coupled with State restriction and surveillance on the functioning of civil societies have posed many challenges. There is increased targeting of community leaders and the conscription of the civil societies, while fostering an enabling environment for IFIs' investments and corporate body roles in unsustainable development practices.

There are clear challenges in seeking justice as regards IFI-financed projects affecting indigenous communities. Indigenous peoples affected by Lafarge mining in Meghalaya complained to the CAO of IFC. However, the IFC failed to take appropriate steps and recommendations for compliance to ensure the human rights compliance of the corporate bodies. The government simply does not have clear and strong accountability mechanisms for communities challenged and affected by large-scale development processes with IFI financing in their endeavor to seek redress for violations of their rights. All corporations involved in developing countries should carry out fair, inclusive and transparent environmental and social impact assessment, and the definition of feasible alternatives before introducing projects based on people's intrinsic relationships with the land and survival as well as the promotion of ecological integrity should be made clear. Bilateral IFIs should frame policies so as to promote indigenous peoples' rights as per the United Nations Declaration on Indigenous Peoples, 2007.

The government should issue enforceable human rights and environmental guidelines for IFIs and corporations. The decision-making processes and priority settings by donors have to involve civil societies and communities to ensure sensitivity to the way of life and intrinsic survival dependence of communities to their land and resources. The militaristic development model introduced, without caring for peoples' rights and strongly relying reliance on the State's apparatus without a clear accountability mechanism, and the reinforcement of the interests of developed and emerging countries in the North East will further complicate the patterns, manifestations and impacts of conflict. The government should stop all forms of militarization and human rights violations unleashed on indigenous communities in the pretext of its Act East Policy. IFIs and corporate bodies should desist from colluding with governments to commit human rights violations, such as forced evictions or forced labour. IFIs should formulate appropriate and accessible complaint mechanisms in accordance with the prevailing best development standards and ensure the compliance of social, environmental and human rights safeguards in all involvements in development financing. Any development policies formulated across the North East should be compatible to developmental wishes, aspirations and self-determined rights of the indigenous peoples of the region.

REFERENCES

ADB Report. 2004. *TA to India for Preparing the Northeast Power Development Project*. TAR: IND 38312, December. Manila: ADB.

Apurva. 2017. 'No Third-Party Meddling in North East: China on Japan FDI Plan'. *Indian Express*, 16 September. Retrieved from https://indianexpress.com/article/world/no-third-party-in-india-north-east-states-n-e-china-on-japan-fdi-plan-shinzo-abe-narendra-modi-4845773/

Asian Development Bank. 2017. 'Together We Deliver: 50 Stories of ADB's Partnerships in Asia and the Pacific'. Retrieved from https://www.adb.org/publications/together-we-deliver-50-stories

———. 'India and ADB'. Retrieved from https://www.adb.org/countries/india/main

———. 2004. *Technical Assistance to India for Preparing North Eastern States Trade and Investment Creation Initiative.* TAR: IND 37407, October.

Bouissou, J. 2010. 'Lafarge's India-Bangladesh Cement Project Remains Frozen'. *The Guardian*, 20 August. Retrieved from https://www.theguardian.com/world/2010/aug/13/india-bangladesh

Bretton Woods Project. 2014. 'Complaint Filed Against IFC Funded Lafarge Mining Operation'. 26 February. Retrieved from http://www.brettonwoodsproject.org/2014/02/complaint-filed-ifc-funded-lafarge-mining-operation/

Cyrill, M. 2017. 'Japan's Investments in India Unveil Growing Economic Partnership'. *India Briefing*, 19 September.

Deccan Herald News Service. 2017. 'India, Japan to Step Up Defense Cooperation'. 6 September. Retrieved from https://www.deccanherald.com/content/631725/india-japan-step-up-defence.html

Foreign Direct Investment (FDI) Report. 2018. 'India Brand Equity Foundation'. July. Retrieved from https://www.ibef.org/economy/foreign-direct-investment.aspx

George, S., and H. Wu. 2017. 'US, India and Japan Begin Naval Exercises, as China Looks on'. *CNN*, 12 July.

Goswami, R. 2017. 'Bank Warns Mizoram on Trady Project Pace'. *The Telegraph*, 25 February. Retrieved from https://www.telegraphindia.com/1170225/jsp/northeast/story_137587.jsp

Invest India. 2017. 'Foreign Direct Investment in India'. Annual Issue. Department of Promotion of Industry and Internal Trade, Government of India. Retrieved from https://dipp.gov.in/sia-newsletter/foreign-direct-investment-india-annual-issue-2017

Islam, K. J., and Biswanath. 2018. 'Assam State Power Workers Union Protest Against Privatization of Power Stations'. *North East News, North East Now*, Assam, 4 May. Retrieved from https://nenow.in/north-east-news/assam/assam-state-power-workers-union-stages-protest-against-privatization-of-power-stations.html

JICA Press Release. 2017. *JICA Extends ODA Loan of Approximately INR 4,000 Crores for the North-East Road Network Connectivity Improvement Project (Phase I).* 31 March.

———. 2018, April 2. 'JICA to Invest in Improving Transitability by Extending ODA Loan of Approximately INR 2,500 Crore for the North East Road Connectivity Project-Transforming Infrastructure in North East India'. Retrieved from https://www.jica.go.jp/india/english/office/topics/press170331_01.html

———. 2018, April 4. 'JICA Signs ₹2,500-cr Loan Pact for NE Road Projects'. *The Shillong Times*. Retrieved from http://www.theshillongtimes. com/2018/04/04/jica-signs-rs-2500-cr-loan-pact-for-ne-road-projects/

Loan Agreement. 2014. 'Loan 3073-IND: North Eastern State Roads Investment Program'. Loan Number 3073-IND, Project Agreement (North Eastern State Roads Investment Program–Project 2) between ADB and Government of Manipur with MDONER, 17 February.

Mahaprashasta, A. A. 2016. 'PMO Wants to Sidestep Gram Sabha's Consent for Underground Mining'. *The Wire*, 4 May. Retrieved from https:// thewire.in/33774/pmo-wants-to-exempt-gram-sabhas-consent-for-underground-mining/

Mallapur, C. 2016. 'India Largest Recipient of Loans from World Bank for 70 Years'. *First Post*, 13 January. Retrieved from https://www.firstpost.com/world/india-largest-recipient-of-loans-from-world-bank-for-70-years-says-lending-report-2581900.html

North East Today. 2015. 'Japan Agency to Finance Projects in Arunachal'. 8 June. Retrieved from https://www.northeasttoday.in/japan-agency-to-finance-projects-in-arunachal/

Organisation for Economic Co-operation and Development (OECD). 2018. 'Multilateral Development Finance: Towards a New Pact on Multilateralism'. Retrieved from http://www.oecd.org/dac/multilateral-development-finance-9789264308831-en.htm

Purohit, M. 2017. 'Water Privatization Has a History of Failure in India. Let's Free Our Waters'. *Your Story*, 23 February. Retrieved from https://yourstory.com/2017/02/water-privatisation/

Quartz India. 2016. 'After 25 Years of Liberalization, India's Rich Are Growing Richer and the Poor Poorer'. 21 July. Retrieved from https://qz.com/737196/after-25-years-of-liberalisation-indias-rich-are-growing-richer-and-the-poor-poorer/

Rajshekar, M. 2015. 'Scroll Investigation: Mizoram CM Gave Road Contracts to Firm in Which His Brother Held Shares'. *The Scroll*, 29 June. Retrieved from https://scroll.in/article/736549/scroll-investigation-mizoram-cm-gave-road-contracts-to-firm-in-which-his-brother-held-shares

Rao, A., and K. Kadam. 2016. '25 Years of Liberalization: A Glimpse of India's Growth in 14 Charts'. *The First Post*, 7 July. Retrieved from https://www.firstpost.com/business/25-years-of-liberalisation-a-glimpse-of-indias-growth-in-14-charts-2877654.html

Sharma, Y. P. 2017. *Daily Excelsior*, 3 March. Retrieved from http://www.daily-excelsior.com/economic-liberalization-india/

The Financial Express. 2015. 'FDI Inflows: Who Is Investing in India and in What Sectors?' 12 January. Retrieved from https://www.financialexpress.com/opinion/fdi-inflows-who-is-investing-in-india-and-in-what-sectors/28737/

———. 2018. 'Jiribam-Tupul-Imphal Rail Link: How Indian Railways Is Working on Big Manipur Project Amid Militant Threats'. PTI, 11 May. Retrieved from https://www.financialexpress.com/infrastructure/railways/jiribam-tupul-imphal-rail-link-how-indian-railways-is-working-on-big-manipur-project-amid-militant-threats/1163847/

The Hindu. 2016. 'Urban Development Ministry Outlines Roadmap for SPVs'. 9 August. Retrieved from https://www.thehindubusinessline.com/news/real-estate/govt-to-handhold-smart-cities-in-borrowing-from-adb-world-bank/article8964073.ece

The Live Mint. 2017. 'Green Activists Oppose Finance Act 2017, Say It Curtails NGT's Independence'. 5 July. Retrieved from http://www.livemint.com/Politics/X4R0eZMQ5R6i5SlW0oGjoL/Green-activists-oppose-Finance-Act-2017-say-it-curtails-NGT.html

The Sangai Express. 2014. 'Construction of Thoubal-Kasom Khullen Road: Asian Development Bank Served Notice'. 18 August. Retrieved from http://www.thesangaiexpress.com/construction-of-thoubal-kasom-khullen-road-asian-development-bank-served-notice/

———. 2015. 'Sloppy Sewerage Project Gets Final Thrust'. 28 May. Retrieved from http://www.thesangaiexpress.com/page/items/39181/sloppy-sewerage-project-gets-final-thrust

The Telegraph. 2015. 'Manipur to Benefit from ADB Loan—Ring Road Part of Project'. The Telegraph, 27 March. Retrieved from http://www.telegraphindia.com/1150327/jsp/northeast/story_11074.jsp#.VxjhRHonI2w

Times of India. 2017. 'Supreme Court Orders CBI Probe into Extra-judicial Killings in Manipur'. PTI, 14 July. Retrieved from https://timesofindia.indiatimes.com/india/supreme-court-orders-cbi-probe-into-extra-judicial-killings-in-manipur/articleshow/59591193.cms

Wahlang, D. P. 2006. 'Proceedings of the Environmental Public Hearing in Respect of the Proposed Mining of Shale and Siltstone of M/S Lafarge Umiam Mining Pvt. Ltd', held at Shella, East Khasi Hills District on 18 January 2006, East Khasi Hills District: Meghalaya.

World Bank Press Release. 2014. '$107 Million World Bank Project to Connect Mizoram with Bangladesh and Myanmar via Roads'. 12 June. Retrieved from http://www.worldbank.org/en/news/press-release/2014/06/12/107-million-world-bank-project-to-connect-mizoram-with-bangladesh-and-myanmar-via-roads

———. 2016. 'World Bank Approves US$470 Million to Improve Electricity Supply in the North Eastern Region, India'. 24 June. Retrieved from http://www.worldbank.org/en/news/press-release/2016/06/24/world-bank-approves-usd470million-improve-electricity-supply-the-north-eastern-region-india

Yumnam, J. 2014. 'ADB's Imphal Ring Road Controversies'. Imphal Free Press, 21 November.

———. 2017. 'NHPC's Untimely Push for 66 MW Loktak Downstream Project'. Imphal Free Press, 19 December.

Yumnam, J., and R. Wangkheirakpam. 2006. 'Insidious Financial Institutions in India's North East'. ICR & FIPA, April 2006.

About the Editor and Contributors

EDITOR

Rakhee Bhattacharya is Associate Professor and teaches Development Economics at the Special Centre for the Study of North East India, Jawaharlal Nehru University (JNU), New Delhi. Some of her earlier professional associations were with Rajiv Gandhi Institute for Contemporary Studies, Rajiv Gandhi Foundation, New Delhi, Maulana Abul Kalam Azad Institute of Asian Studies, Kolkata, and National Council for Applied Economic Research, New Delhi. She has worked on several national and international research projects, including with United Nations Development Programme (UNDP). She has done both policy and academic research in various issues of political economy, development economics and security studies. She was an Endeavour Post-Doctoral Fellow at the School of International Studies, University of South Australia, Adelaide. Her areas of research interests are political economy, development economics, regional economy, transnational economy and geoeconomics, poverty and inequality, geopolitics and security, India's North East and its neighbourhood. She has a number of publications to her credit in both national and international journals. She is also a regular columnist in the *Statesman*. Some of her edited and co-edited books are *Regional Development and Public Policy Challenges in India* (2015), *A Journey through the Stilwell Road* (2011, with B. K Mishra), *Perilous Journey: Debates on Security and Development in Assam* (2011, with S. Pulipaka), *Tradition and Modernity in Arunachal Pradesh* (2012, with S. Pulipaka and Sarit Chaudhuri) and *Sikkim's Tryst with Nathu La: What Awaits India's East and Northeast?* (2009, with J. K. Ray and K. Bandyopadhyay). She has authored *Development Disparities in Northeast India* (2011) and *Northeastern India and its Neighbours: Negotiating Security and Development* (2014).

CONTRIBUTORS

Gurudas Das is Professor at the Department of Humanities and Social Sciences, National Institute of Technology, Silchar, Assam. Earlier he was associated with the Centre for Himalayan Studies, North Bengal University, Siliguri, St Anthony's College, Shillong, OKD Institute of Social Change and Development, Guwahati, and North Eastern Hill University, Shillong. His areas of research interests include security and development, cross-border trade and development cooperation and geoeconomics and geopolitics of regional growth and development. Besides contributing to many edited books, he is also widely published in many acclaimed national and international journals. He has authored *Security and Development in India's North East* (2012), co-authored and co-edited *Look East to Act East Policy: Implications for India's Northeast* (2015) and *BCIM Economic Cooperation: Interplay of Geoeconomics and Geo-politics* (2018).

Samir K. Das is Professor of Political Science at the University of Calcutta, Kolkata. He is former Vice Chancellor of the University of North Bengal. He was the Post-Doctoral Fellow of the Social Science Research Council (South Asia Program), Visiting Fellow at the European Academy, Bolzano, Italy, Adjunct Professor of Government at the Edmund A. Walsh School of Foreign Service, Georgetown University, and Visiting Professor of the North East India Studies Programme at JNU and at the University of 13 Sorbonne-Paris-Cite. His areas of research interests are ethnicity, identity, security, migration, rights and justice. He has contributed over 190 research papers to both national and international journals and edited many books. Some of his authored books include *Migrations, Identities and Democratic Practices* (2018), *Governing India's Northeast: Essays on Insurgency, Development and the Culture of Peace* (2013) and *Conflict and Peace in India's Northeast: The Role of Civil Society* (2006).

Akhil Ranjan Dutta is Professor in the Department of Political Science at Gauhati University, Guwahati. He is an academic activist and engaged with both academic research and socio-political activities concerning human rights and dignity in the region of the North East. He was a Rotary World Peace Fellow in 2009 at the International Centre for Peace and Conflict Studies at Chulalongkorn University, Bangkok. His areas of research interests include citizenship, human rights and security and development studies. He has compiled and edited *The Conscientious Statesman: Gaurisankar Bhattacharyya in Assam Legislative Assembly* (2015) and *Human Security in North East India: Issues & Policies* (2009) apart from contributing research articles in *Economic and Political Weekly*, *Social Change* (SAGE Publications), *Studies in Indian Politics* (SAGE Publications) and so on. He is also a regular columnist in Assamese dailies.

Walter Fernandes is a Senior Fellow at the North Eastern Social Research Centre (NESRC), Guwahati, Assam. He was Director of Research at Animation and Research Centre, Yangon, Myanmar (2013–15), and Founder-Director of NESRC (2000–11). Before moving to the North East, he was Director, Director of Research and of Tribal Studies at Indian Social Institute, New Delhi (1977–99), and Editor of the journal *Social Action* (1985–93). He has also been on several Government of India committees. His areas of research interests include tribal issues, gender issues, development-induced displacement, conflicts and peace. He has more than 40 books and around 200 professional articles on these issues to his credit. Some of his authored and co-authored books are *The Challenges of Development: Displacement in Nagaland, 1947–2010*; *Progress: At What Costs? Development induced Displacement in West Bengal, 1947–2000*; and *The Development Dilemma: Displacement in Meghalaya, 1947–2010*.

Thongkholal Haokip is Assistant Professor at Centre for the Study of Law and Governance, JNU. He was formerly with the Department of Political Science, Presidency University, Kolkata. His areas of research interests include governance, ethnicity and ethnic relations, borderland studies, India's Look East Policy and North East India studies. He has authored *India's Look East Policy and the Northeast* (2015), edited *The Kukis of Northeast India: Politics and Culture* (2013) and jointly edited *The Anglo-Kuki War 1917–1919: A Frontier Uprising against Imperialism* *during the First World War* (2019). He is the editor of *Journal of North East India Studies* and executive editor of *Asian Ethnicity*.

Deepak K. Mishra is Professor of Economics at the Centre for the Study of Regional Development, School of Social Sciences, JNU. His research interests include the political economy of agrarian change, rural livelihoods and agrarian institutions, migration, gender and human development. He has a large number of publications to his credit. He has co-authored *The Unfolding Crisis in Assam's Tea Plantations: Employment and Occupational Mobility* (2012), has jointly edited *Rethinking Economic Development in Northeast India: The Emerging Dynamics* (2017) and has edited *Internal Migration in Contemporary India* (SAGE Publications, 2016). He has contributed to the first *Human Development Report of Arunachal Pradesh* (2005) and the *Arunachal Pradesh Development Report* (2009).

Tiplut Nongbri is Dr Saifuddin Kitchlew Chair Professor, Centre for North East Studies and Policy Research, Jamia Milia Islamia, New Delhi. She was Professor of Sociology at the Centre for the Study of Social Systems, JNU. She was the founding Director of the North East India Studies Programme at JNU. Her areas of research interest include sociology of kinship, gender studies, environmental sociology, ethnicity and identity issues, sociology of tribes and marginal groups. She has a number of publications to her credit, and she has authored *Gender, Matrilini and Entrepreneurship: The Khasis of North-East India*; *Tribal Demography and Development in North-East India* (with A. Bose and N. Kumar); *Development, Ethnicity and Gender*; and *Migration, Identity and Conflict: Lived Experiences of Northeasterners in Delhi* (with Shimreiwung).

Felix Padel is research associate at the Department of Anthropology at Oxford and at the Centre for World Environment History at Oxford. He has been professor and has held visiting positions at various institutes of higher education in India including the North East India Studies Programme at JNU. Being an anthropologist, his areas of research interests include indigenous and tribal people, environmental and human rights issues. He has written extensively on these issues. He has authored and co-authored *The Sacrifice of Human Being: British Rule and the Konds of Orissa* (1995, new edition 2010 as *Sacrificing People: Invasions of a Tribal Landscape*); *Out of this Earth: East India Adivasis and the Aluminium Cartel* (2010, with Samarendra Das); and *Ecology, Economy: Quest for a Socially Informed Connection* (2013, with Ajay Dandekar and Jeemol Unni).

Anita Sengupta is Director of Calcutta Research Group, Kolkata. She was a Fellow at Maulana Abul Kalam Azad Institute of Asian Studies, Kolkata. She is an area studies specialist and engages with issues of identity politics, migration, gender, borders, critical geopolitics and logistics. She is a regular commentator on debates on Asian affairs and is part of Asia in Global Affairs, an independent research forum that looks at a wide range of global issues from an Asian perspective. She has authored *Symbols and the Image of the State in Eurasia* (2016); *Myth and Rhetoric of the Turkish Model: Exploring Developmental Alternatives* (2014); *Heartlands of Eurasia: The Geopolitics of Political Space* (2009); *The Formation of the Uzbek Nation-State: A Study in Transition* (2003); and *Frontiers into Borders: The Transformation of Identities in Central Asia* (2002).

Archana Sharma is Professor of Economics at Gauhati University, Guwahati. She was the Director of Women's Studies Research Centre, Gauhati University, for more than 16 years and established the Centre as a full-fledged department. Her areas of research interests include woman studies, labour market, poverty, inequality and income distribution in India with special emphasis on the North East. She has a number of publications to her credit. She has contributed immensely in designing and structuring various important curricula and courses at both university and college levels. She has co-authored many textbooks on economics and has written in popular journals.

Jiten Yumnam is a human rights activist and holds the position of Secretary at the Centre for Research and Advocacy, Manipur, an indigenous peoples' human rights organization based in Manipur in the North East. He is the former Co-Chair of the post-2015 Working Group of CSO Partnerships for Development Effectiveness (CPDE). He currently is an advisor of the Asia Pacific Indigenous Youth

Network. His areas of interests include indigenous people, ethnic community, human rights issues and environment. He writes regularly with media units in the North East, such as *Imphal Free Press*, *Sangai Express* and so on. He is also a filmmaker and produces documentary films on indigenous peoples' rights and issues in Manipur.

Index

Act East Policy, 174
Ahom period, 53
Armed Forces Special Power Act, 175
ASEAN Regional Forum (ARF), 236
Asian Development Bank (ADB), 227
Assam
   B. C. Allen notes, 46–7
   coarse cotton cloth, 51
   history, 46
   integrated economic system, 48
   manufacture, 51
   shifting cultivation, 51
Association of Southeast Asian Nations (ASEAN)
   maritime connectivity, 202

Bandardubi and Deuchur Chang villages, 294–5
Bangladesh Bhutan India Nepal Initiative (BBIN), 192
Bangladesh China India Myanmar Corridor (BCIM), 199, 238
Bangladesh-China-India-Myanmar Forum for Regional Cooperation, 203
Bay of Bengal Initiative for Multi Sectoral Technical and Economic Cooperation (BIMSTEC), 203
Brahmaputra Valley, 47, 49
British Broadcasting Corporation (BBC)
   documentary on Kaziranga contestations, 299–303
   verdict, conservationism vs. human entitlements, 288–99

China Pakistan Economic Corridor (CPEC), 196–7
colonial period
   northeast frontier, 232
community property resources (CPR), 95
constructing mobility technologies, 195
controversial mega-dams in North East, 256–67
   Bhutan's dams, 265–6
   costs and benefits, 267–70
   Dumbur, 266
   Kameng, 264
   Lower Demwe, 261
   Lower Siang, 263
   Lower Subansiri, 263
   Mapithel, 258–61
   Sikkim's dams, 266
   Tipaimukh, 256–8
   Upper Dibang, 261
   Upper Siang, 263
culturalist paradigm, 72
cultures
   growing antagonism, 282–4

Development Induced Displacement and Deprivation (DID), 91
   impoverishment, 108–10
   land alienation, 108
development-induced DP-PAPs, 106–8

Index | 335

indication of a large number, 107
rehabilitation, 107
development
   paradigm, 97
   state intervention, 233–4
   trade and services, 235–42
developmentalism
   environmentalism, 284–8

ease of doing business, 71
economic corridors
   Asia, 199
   BCIM, 199
   importance, 198
Entry/Exit System (EES), 228
environmental security and human rights in North East, 256–67
   controversial mega-dams, 256–67
ethnically configured market, 75
   ethnic exclusion, 77–80
   ethnic monopoly, 76–7

Ganga-Mekong Cooperation, 203
Greater Mekong Sub-region (GMS), 227

High-Powered Committee, 293
hydro-power generation, 218

India-Myanmar Bilateral Trade
   share of exports to and imports, 1, 230
   trends, 220–1
India-Myanmar-Thailand Trilateral (IMT)
   connectivity, cross-border resource-industry linkage, 223–5
Indian alternative
   reaches of the Indian Ocean, 208
Indian Council for Cultural Relations (ICCR), 150, 243
Indian Council for World Affairs (ICWA), 243
Indian Council of Social Science Research (ICSSR), 150
Indian economy
   structural shift, 170
Indian mainland, 72
Indian rhetoric, 209
India's economic liberalisation, 169
India's North East, 45, 117, 246
   analysis and discussion, 54–9
   Asian connectivity and materiality of infrastructure, 195–6
   borderland services, 241–2
   connecting with Asia regions, 194
   consequences of developmentalism, 121
   corridors, multilateral alliances, 201–7
   cross-border trade and development, 215–7
   culture and economy, 244
   developmentalism, new capital and social mapping, 175–81
   displacement, 102–12
   distribution of internal migrants, 1
   eco-friendly goods and services, 245–6
   environmental security and human rights, 253–6
   extractive industries and infrastructure, 270–2
   geography and transnational market, 181–6
   historical backdrop, 47–8
   IFIs financing, 305–7
      conflict situation, intensification, 319–21
      issues, 315 9
      state and across, 307–11
   key elements of developmentalism, 118–21
   labour migration and citizenship, 128–40
   livelihood strategies and practice, 48–54

neoliberal developmentalism, state strategy, 169
new cultural policy, 243
number of out-migrant, 1
outmigration and discrimination, 140–1
postcolonial market, 67–70
preparing, 238–41
response to IFIs involvement, 321–2
roots of underdevelopment, 59–61
rural and urban, usual status unemployment, 147
situation of IFIs financed projects and impacts across, 311–5
specificities, 118
state developmentalism, 172
studies, 57
sub-regional cooperation and cross-border market integration, 223
traditional economy, resilience and challenges, 61–2
types of DID, 95–7
usual status unemployment, 122
Indo-Bangladesh sub-regional cooperation
transit corridor and economic well being of NER, 225–6
infrastructure
land loss in India's North East, 109–10
road projects, 311–3
internally displaced persons (IDPs), 102–6
disaster and conflict induced, 105
natural disasters, 103
rise in level of Brahmaputra, 104
International Financial Institutions (IFIs), 305
financing and intensification of conflict situation, 319–21
financing in India's North East, 305–7

issues with financing, 315–9
response to involvement, 321–2
situation of financed projects and impacts, 311–5
state and across northeastern region, 307–11

jhum, 50

Kaziranga National Park (KNP), 280–1
Khasi and Jaintia Hills, 53
Kunming Initiative, 199, 203

labour migration and citizenship, 128
demand, 138
internal, 130
political economy framework, 129
primitive accumulation, 130
land alienation, 108
liberal economic reforms, 235
Look East Policy (LEP), 173, 236

Maritime Silk Road (MSR), 208
market society, 70, 74, 75
Master Plan on ASEAN Connectivity (MPAC), 203
micro, small and medium-sized (MSM) industries, 71
migration
cause, 128
political economy framework, 129
mode of production debate, 80
moral economy, 80
Myanmar and NER
trade, 221–2
Myanmar's trade with bordering countries, 1

National Highway and Infrastructure Development Corporation (NHIDC), 176
National Sample Survey Office (NSSO), 151

national to transnational
    India's North East, state strategy, 172–5
neo liberal market reforms, 70
New Silk Road, 195–6
North-East Frontier Agency (NEFA), 150
northeastern region (NER), 214
    commodity structure, 1, 230
    India's Bhutan trade, 217–9
    India's Myanmar trade, 219
    share with neighbouring countries, 1, 230

One Belt One Road (OBOR), 204
'Our World: Killing for Conservation', 288

pattern of development, 92
    development paradigm and displacement, 98–102
    five-year plans, 95
    land and legal system in North East, 94
    law and land loss, 97–8
    paradigm and laws, 93–4
    persons displaced (DP), 92
    policy reforms, 71, 72
    project affected persons (PAP), 92

seamless connectivity, 192
sectoral distribution
    men and women
        analysis of data, 156
        low-paid jobs, 157
        sex ratio, 154–6
Silk Road, 195
state developmentalism
    changing strategy, 172
    structural reforms, 173

trade, 240
Tripura Land Revenue and Land Reforms Act 1960 (TRLR&R), 97

weaving, 52
women labour market
    in India's north east, development
        agriculture sector, 149
        Boserup's (1970) study, 149
        growth rate, 148
        Indian Council of Social Science Research (ICSSR), 150
        National Sample Survey Office (NSSO), 151
        North-East Frontier Agency (NEFA), 150
        post-liberalization period, 152
        poverty, problem of, 149
        region-specific studies, 150
        technology-driven, 149
        urban household industry, 151
        urban industrial sector, 149
        women's work participation rates (WPRs), 150–1
work participation rates
    men and women
        highest sex ratio, 163
        manifestation of commonalities, 152
        NSSO data, 152–3
        rural males and females, 160
        sectoral distribution, 162–3
        sex and sex ratios, 157–2
        types of work, 153–4
        urban females, 161
        urban Nagaland, 164